ATHENS AND JERUSALEM:
GEORGE GRANT'S THEOLOGY, PHILOSOPHY, AND
POLITICS

EDITED BY IAN ANGUS, RON DART, AND
RANDY PEG PETERS

Athens and Jerusalem:
George Grant's Theology,
Philosophy, and Politics

UNIVERSITY OF TORONTO PRESS
Toronto Buffalo London

ISBN-13: 978-0-8020-9176-5
ISBN-10: 0-8020-9176-8

Printed on acid-free paper

Library and Archives Canada Cataloguing in Publication

Athens and Jerusalem : George Grant's theology, philosophy and
politics / edited by Ian Angus, Ron Dart, and Randy Peg Peters.

ISBN-13: 978-0-8020-9176-5
ISBN-10: 0-8020-9176-8

1. Grant, George, 1918–1988.   I. Angus, Ian H. (Ian Henderson), 1949–
II. Dart, Ron Samuel (Ronald Samuel)   III. Peters, Randy Peg

B995.G74A84 2006   191   C2006-903710-8

Publication of this book was made possible by grants from University College
of the Fraser Valley, Trinity Western University, and Simon Fraser University.

University of Toronto Press acknowledges the financial assistance to its
publishing program of the Canada Council for the Arts and the Ontario Arts
Council.

University of Toronto Press acknowledges the financial support for its
publishing activities of the Government of Canada through the Book
Publishing Industry Development Program (BPIDP).

Contents

Preface

Tertullian (c. 160–c. AD 220) is well known for the rhetorical question 'What has Athens to do with Jerusalem? What has the Academy to do with the Church?' The question reveals the fact that there is a tension between Athens and Jerusalem. For George Grant, this tension is good and necessary but ultimately Athens and Jerusalem, philosophy and theology, require one another. Grant rejected emphatically the view of 'a certain kind of Protestant church-goer' that religion could do without philosophy, arguing instead that 'a moral code, the authority for which is based solely on faith and that makes no attempt to define itself rigorously, is a dying code, a closed morality, a morality that does not care about its own communication.'[1] But he also remained firmly committed to his early affirmation to the Massey Commission that 'philosophy is the analysis of the traditions of our society and the judgment of those traditions against our varying intuitions of the Perfection of God.'[2] Grant was convinced, on grounds of both faith and reason, that Christianity and philosophy not only were ultimately compatible but also required each other for completion. The relation between Christian faith and philosophical questioning was a constant issue in Grant's work and even can be seen as the grounding question that drove his work forward. He strove to articulate a conception of Christianity compatible with philosophy and also a Platonic conception of philosophy compatible with a certain understanding of Christianity. While his position can be summarily labelled Christian Platonism, that term is more a heading for a catalogue of questions than a finished position. The present collection of essays investigates and seeks to clarify this catalogue.

There has been considerable discussion of George Grant's political writings. However, less attention has been paid to the theological and philosophical underpinnings of the political writings, even though their relevance has been noted. This collection of essays is primarily an elaboration and critique of the theological and philosophical basis of Grant's work. To be sure, it addresses the more familiar themes of nationalism, Canada and the United States, modernity, technology, and liberalism, but it does so with an orientation towards the basic theological and philosophical questions that stand behind such themes. One of the foremost reasons why Grant's work has become significant for several generations of Canadian thinkers is that it connects practical and political issues of our common life to the deeper questions of Western civilization, ontology, and religion. Grant drew upon the biblical and Greek philosophical roots of Western civilization to diagnose its present condition, to criticize current deficiencies, and to suggest alternative sources of illumination.

We are lucky to be able to print for the first time in this collection four of Grant's notes for lectures in which he addresses the relation between Athens and Jerusalem directly.[3] The sixteen original essays have been grouped into thematically organized sections which ascend from the concrete issues of Canadian politics (Part One) to the situation of modernity in North America (Part Two) and finally to Christian theological commitments (Part Three) and philosophical questions (Part Four). The intention is to show that the theological and philosophical issues are not abstracted from practical action but rather inhere in it.

Part One, 'Canadian Toryism,' begins by formulating these issues in the context of Canadian political culture and with close attention to the historical record as well as Grant's texts themselves. It begins by noting the affinity of his thought with that of Stephen Leacock in the Canadian Tory tradition (Dart), and it continues by explaining the Grantian case that can be made for Quebec's national claims (Caldwell) and by examining Grant's substantive political commitments (Christian and Davis).

Part Two, 'Modernity in North America,' begins with Grant's 'Lecture on Technology and the Tradition,' in which the influence of Leo Strauss on his reading of the history of political philosophy is evident. The next essay addresses Hegelianism in Canada, following Grant's argument that Hegelian modernism must lead to the disappearance of Canada (Sibley). Two essays consider the nature of the influence of Leo Strauss (Havers) and its implications for understanding modernity (Duff). One examines James Doull's critique of Grant's argument concerning modernity and North America (Robertson) and another criticizes his understanding of the United States (Von Heyking and

Cooper). The final essay reflects on the applicability of Grant's thinking to contemporary Quebec (Roy).

Part Three, 'Christian Commitments and Theological Questions,' begins with Grant's illuminating 'Five Lectures on Christianity.' It addresses the theological commitments on which Grant's critique of modernity was based – the Platonic influence of the Eastern Orthodox Church (Peters), the example of Simone Weil (McCarroll), and the central Christian symbol of the cross that allows an appropriation of philosophy (Athanasiadis).

The concluding Part Four, 'The Tension between Athens and Jerusalem,' begins with notes for two lectures in which Grant explained the core of Platonic philosophy as he understood it. These lectures show how and why Grant thought that Christian Platonism provided the best philosophical and theological ground for an appreciation of being as good. It is this ground upon which the critique of technology ultimately rests. The succeeding essays consider the nature of Grant's Christian Platonism. Each argues a different position: with Grant, that its dual sources can be synthesized (Heaven), that they can and should be kept apart (Nicholson), and that there is really no synthesis at all but rather a Christian appropriation of philosophy that occludes what is properly philosophical (Angus).

Short introductions to these four sections have been provided in order to aid the reader in placing the essays in relation to the whole that the entire collection represents. The editors would like to thank Shiela Grant and Art Davis – editor of Grant's *Collected Works* for the University of Toronto Press – for kindly allowing prior publication of the Grant lectures pertinent to the topic of this book. We would consider the purpose of the collection to be well served if the debate between philosophy and theology in the context of contemporary practical issues were to be clarified, and if Grant scholarship were to explicate these commitments and their implications within the more dominant accounts of Grant as a political thinker and critic of technology.

NOTES

1 George Grant, *Philosophy in the Mass Age,* ed. William Christian (Toronto: University of Toronto Press, 1995), 94.

2 George Grant, 'Philosophy,' *Royal Commission on National Development in the Arts, Letters and Sciences* (Ottawa: Queen's Printer, 1951), 119.

3 Grant's notebooks are in the possession of his wife, Sheila, in Halifax, Nova
   Scotia. In this book, all lectures have been reproduced in their original form,
   apart from minor changes made in the interests of editorial consistency and
   greater readability.

PART ONE

Canadian Toryism

GEORGE GRANT was a Canadian who lived, wrote, and thought in the latter half of the twentieth century. Athens and Jerusalem still had their hold on him as sources ultimate of meaning, but Grant constantly asked himself what these might signify in his time and place. What were the substantive political questions for Canadians in the twentieth century? We could take Tertullian's rhetorical question and reframe and rephrase it this way: What has Washington to do with Ottawa? What has the older Anglo-Canadian High Tory tradition to do with modern Anglo-American and Anglo-Canadian liberalism?

Part One explores the tradition of Canadian Toryism that was the basis of Grant's political engagements. Such a Toryism was not a mere conservatism in the sense of conserving the early-modern liberal political roots of capitalism but was rested on a Burkean suspicion of the French revolution itself – extended also to the similar eighteenth-century Enlightenment origins of the American revolution. Toryism rejects the notion that society is a contract of self-interested individuals and trusts tradition more than the truncated instrumental reason of the Enlightenment. 'Stephen Leacock and George Grant: Tory Affinities,' by Ron Dart, sketches this tradition through a comparison of Leacock and Grant. 'Grant and Quebec,' by Gary Caldwell, argues that Grant's political thinking has relevance for Quebec as it faces the challenge of becoming both more liberal and more American. William Christian's 'Was George Grant Red Tory?' addresses the meaning of the term Red Tory and the question of whether Grant can be considered one. 'Did George Grant Change His Politics?' by Arthur Davis tracks Grant's reflections on the larger question of freedom and grace in the context of his political engagements.

1

Stephen Leacock and George Grant: Tory Affinities

RON DART

Leacock was a friend of the [Grant] family who had also taught Maude [Grant's mother] and later George's sister Margaret at McGill. Leacock was in and out of the house a lot when George was young. George recalled that his father used to try to provoke Leacock into swearing to annoy Maude. Later, when Maude was working at McGill after William's death, Leacock helped to sort out difficulties concerning her pension. George recalled him as 'a sweet man' and very loyal to his friends.[1]

William Christian, George Grant

A JOURNEY

I have, over the years, been interested in the Tory affinities between Stephen Leacock (1869–1944) and George Grant (1918–1988). Many is the Leacock scholar and fan who devotes much time to the life and writings of Leacock. Many is the Grant scholar and fan who commits much time and energy to unpacking and unravelling Grant's thought and life. But rare indeed is the article or book that draws together the Tory affinities of both Leacock and Grant. This is rather surprising given that Leacock was closely connected to the Grant family and that Grant's mother and sister studied with Leacock at McGill. Leacock taught at Upper Canada College (UCC) in the 1890s, and Grant's grandfather (George Parkin) was principal of the school in Leacock's final years there. It was probably Parkin who encouraged Leacock to go to the University of Chicago to do his PhD, and Parkin's involvement in the Imperial Federation League would have done much to faster Leacock's budding nationalism. Leacock's son, Stevie Leacock, was at UCC when George Grant was a student there, and both George Grant and Stevie Leacock belonged to the same 'religious discussion group'.[1] It is these educational, political, familial, and religious connections that open up the possibility of a study on the Tory affinities of Leacock and Grant.

The publication of Charles Taylor's *Radical Tories: The Conservative Tradition in Canada* (1982) did much for me to bring into focus, in an elementary sort of way, the affinities between Leacock and Grant. Taylor, in *Radical Tories*, has separate chapters on Leacock and Grant, and he places them within a tradition of Canadian Toryism that cannot be equated with the 'Blue' Tories in the modern-day Conservative Party. Taylor's chapters, 'A Special Destiny: Leacock, Sandwell and Deacon,' and 'Threnody: George Grant,' clearly demonstrate there is more to Canadian Toryism than we might think, and that both Leacock and Grant belong to an old tradition of conservative thought. The rest of this study will thread together the Tory affinities of Leacock and Grant and, by doing so, highlight a Canadian political tradition that is in danger of being written out of our communal memory.

Most of us who grew up in Ontario a few decades back took in Leacock's many books of humour with our mother's milk. Laughter did, indeed, hold both its sides when Leacock was read, and Leacock was seen (both within and outside Canada) as our national court jester. The publication of *Literary Lapses* in 1910 launched a literary career that ended, thirty-five books later, with *Last Leaves*, which appeared after Leacock's death in 1944. But there was more to Leacock than his stellar and sterling career as a writer of humour, a literary critic, and a biographer of such humorists as Dickens and Twain. In fact, Leacock published, in total, sixty-one books in such fields as literature (thirty-five), literary criticism (five), political science (six), economics (two), history (nine), biography (three), and education (one). He also published eighty-eight articles, which spanned a variety of disciples, and he published both in serious academic journals and in a more popular and accessible ones. As an academic, he began teaching in the political science department at McGill in 1900, and, with the defence of his PhD thesis, 'The Doctrine of Laissez Faire' in 1903, he was promoted to a full-time position at McGill; he retired from the political science department (amidst some protest) in 1936. But there is even more to Leacock than the political theorist and humorist. Leacock was also an Anglican, and many scholars have tended to ignore this aspect of his story. It is impossible to understand Leacock the High Tory without seeing the world through his Anglican soul and eyes.

George Grant, like Leacock, cannot be reduced to a specialist in one academic discipline. Grant was interested in theology, philosophy, literature, politics, education, and law and he too was an Anglican. He did his PhD in theology – his dissertation was entitled 'The Concept of Nature and Supernature in the Theology of John Oman' (1950) – he did much work for the Canadian Association for Adult Education (1943–5), and he appeared regularly on the CBC. Grant's primary interests were theology and philosophy, unlike Leacock's, which were more in the areas of political economy, political science, and literature, but both men crossed disciplinary boundaries with much ease and brought forth many insights as a result of their interdisciplinary approach. Grant had an interest in law, education, politics, and 'hot-button' social issues such as abortion and euthanasia, and in each of these areas he made probing, illuminating contributions.

We cannot, in short, reduce either Leacock or Grant to one area of interest or thought. Both men emerged from an older humanist tradition, a tradition rooted and grounded in the classics, with an abiding concern for both the meaning of citizenship and how such a notion could be thought through and lived out in an age of scientific dominance, technology, and the emergence of corporate power. Indeed, both Leacock and Grant were cut from an older cloth. Both were grounded and rooted in the fullness of the Western tradition, and both sought to make sense of such a tradition in a world and ethos that was becoming more liberal, progressive, modern, and, ironically, reductionistic all the time.

The tory affinities between Leacock and Grant have not been noted before, and, for the remainder of this chapter, I will touch on three themes: 1) public education: *paideia* or 'techne' (*knowing* in the service of *making*, a defining characteristic of the techological age)? 2) Tory politics: right or left?; and 3) religion: spirituality or church? Each of these themes will highlight important points of convergence between Leacock and Grant, and, equally so, clarify the place of historic Toryism in their thought.

PUBLIC EDUCATION: PAIDEIA 'TECHNE'?

What the teacher 'teaches' is by no means chiefly in the words he speaks. It is at least in part in what he is, in what he does, in what he seems to wish to be. The secret curriculum is the teacher's own lived values and convictions, in the lineaments of his expressions and in the biography of passion or self-exile which is written in his eyes.

Jonathan Kozol *The Night Is Dark and I Am Far from Home*

It is a rather simple and obvious truism, for those who have spent many years in university life, that the humanities have been under siege for a long time. The excessive fascination with an empirical methodology, a form of knowing that sets the other as an object over against the detached observer, and a squirrel-like attention to the gathering of ever more facts, have taken their toll. The tendency to measure students' skills by focusing exclusively on their ability to gather and spit forth facts for exams, combined with the inclination of university authorities to go on bended knee before corporations, has had its impact on the meaning and significance of the academic curriculum and life. Leacock and Grant, in their different ways, saw the writing on the wall, protested against it, and offered up an older notion of education. Both men raised strong objections to an educational culture that genuflected to 'techne' as a way of knowing and a way of being. Both men realized this approach would never slake the human thirst for meaning even though such an approach might produce a well-trained hive of bees or well-disciplined worker ants. How, though, did such men protest against the imperial and colonizing nature of 'techne,' and how could paideia – the older tradition of humanist education – be the counter-cultural force they turned to in their fight to displace the merchants of knowledge from their central place in the academy?

An intense battle had been waged in the nineteenth century at the university and in the broader culture. Science, with its empirical methodology, had ascended the throne and the humanities were under siege. Knowledge that could not be taken captive, controlled, mastered, verified, and falsified by a certain type of science was seen as suspect. Matthew Arnold's *Culture and Anarchy* and the equally important *Idea of the University* by John Henry Newman spoke to the dilemma of Victorian culture and offered a more balanced way. Stephen Leacock was well aware of the shift, at universities, from the humanities to the social sciences and the hard sciences. The turn, of course, had a purpose, or telos. The institution of education was now meant, above all else, to train students for jobs, for the workforce. And who were the mandarins of this new reality? They were the chief executive officers of corporations. And so, if the task of universities was to train incoming students for jobs, university authorities had to work hand in hand with the corporate sector and the university curriculum had to be tailored accordingly. The close connection and cooperation between business and the universities was not totally wrong, but the increasing dominance of this model did not bode well for the future of the humanities. Leacock saw this, as did Grant. Of course, Leacock perceived the trend much earlier, and he wrote with much concern about it.

Leacock's first foray into this area can be found in his novel *Arcadian Adventures with the Idle Rich* (1914). Most Canadians know Leacock through his earlier novel, *Sunshine Sketches of a Little Town* (1912), but *Sunshine Sketches* and *Arcadian Adventures* need to be read together; they very much complement one another. Leacock makes it unmistakably clear in *Arcadian Adventures* what he sees as the central problem of education. The move from the small-town Ontario of Mariposa in *Sunshine Sketches* to the big city of *Arcadian Adventures* transfers the discussion, for Leacock, to the world of wealth and poverty, big business and education. The link between *Sunshine Sketches* and *Arcadian Adventures* is the Mausoleum Club (the name speaks much). Mariposa is held up as an imperfect yet desirable ideal in *Sunshine Sketches* (even Dean Drone of the Anglican parish turns again and again to the Greek classics). The bridge between these two novels, though, is the final chapter in *Sunshine Sketches of a Little Town*. The chapter is called 'L'Envoi: The Train to Mariposa,' and it is there that two worlds are brought into interaction. The city and the country 'meet and greet,' and those who have been a success in the city ponder what they have lost in the process.

In *Arcadian Adventures*, the town of Plutoria, and more particularly the university of the same name, is seen as the death knell to the human spirit and life. It is from Plutoria that the president of the university, Dr Boomer, broadcasts his ambitious aims for the university. The university will be a thriving business in which all subjects can and will be taught, and the university, in doing such a thing, will be like any other marketplace. Those who can advertise and sell their products the best will thrive and prosper, while those who cannot compete in the marketplace of ideas will wither on the vine. The aim, or telos, of all this is wealth, and the university exists to prepare people to make such wealth. Relationships rise or fall on who has wealth, who might have it, and who is losing it. Plutoria University, Leacock argued in this novel, had very much lost its educational way. In short, as a traditional Tory, Leacock knew in his bones that learning had something to do with wisdom, character formation, and hearing and heeding the wisdom of the past, but what was happening at Dr Boomer's Plutoria University had nothing to do with such ideals.

Leacock begins and ends *Arcadian Adventures* with a long, hard look at slum dwellers, servants of the 'Idle Rich,' and the working poor. This is a Tory with a conscience, and his conscience would not be muted or cauterized. Leacock, in *Arcadian Adventures*, tends to juxtapose two approaches to learning. There was the crude, money-making, business approach of Dr Boomer, then there was the quieter and more seasoned way of learning of Concordia College. Leacock sought, as a true classicist and Tory, to hold together both wisdom and justice, and he did not think Plutoria University was heeding either tradition from the past. Instead, he held up, in *Arcadian Adventures*, an alternate view of reality that contests and opposes the idle rich, Plutoria, Plutoria University, and the Mausoleum Club. It is to this alternate view of the Duke, the Little Girl in the Green, the Tomlinsons, Concordia College, and the deeper core of religion as expressed in the life and teachings of the Reverend McTeague – that Leacock and the older Tory tradition turn for educational insight.

Arcadian Adventures was not the only book of Leacock's that fixed and focused on the drift and direction of public education. *Essays and Literary Studies* (1916) addresses the same topic. Three articles in *Essays* particularly stand out in this regard. 'The Apology of a Professor,' 'The Devil and the Deep Sea,' and 'The Lot of the Schoolmaster' pull no punches and, without flinching, raise some of the hard questions about the role of education, the meaning of teaching, and the deterioration of ethics in an age when foundation stones were being dismantled. Leacock, in these probing essays, saw a close connection between the captains of industry redefining the curriculum, the loss and eclipse of the humanities, and the erosion of ethical discourse. For much of his life, Leacock attempted to achieve, through public education, what Gerald Lynch has called 'a kind of memory-mining for the true gold of human community.'[2] It is not that Leacock saw no good in technical training and, in a limited aspect, the desire to know and master things. But there was a worm in the apple, a serpent in the tree. Leacock saw technical training as a lower good, and the humanities as offering a higher, more human and humane, good. The technical approach to knowing had two aspects: a way of knowing that was reductionistic and that which was produced from such a way of knowing.

Leacock's final book of short stories, *Last Leaves* (1944), clings to many of the same concerns that animated *Arcadian Adventures* and *Essays and Literary Studies*. Articles such as 'What Can Izaak Walton Teach Us?,' 'The School Is the Lever,' 'Rebuilding the Cities,' 'Common-sense and the Universe,' 'A Lecture on Walking,' and 'Good-Bye, Motor Car' take us into a contemplative and moral way of seeing the universe and being educated that forms a link between the early and the later

Leacock. It is this more contemplative approach, this slower-paced and listening attitude, this inner receptivity that needed to be recalled and retrieved. Leacock had seen all of this his early academic career, and his essays in *Last Leaves* point in the same direction. At the same time, though, Leacock argued that the humanities had played a significant role in bringing about their own demise. For if, in the area of theology, philosophy, ethics, political theory, and economics, the centre and ground could not hold, and all was a matter of subjectivism and relativism, then it made some sense that those in search of certainty and order would turn to the hard sciences and the assured results of what 'techne' could offer. In other words, if the humanities could do nothing but waffle on important ethical and social questions, the vacuum could and would be filled by those who did not forever vacillate and offer nothing but cynicism and scepticism by day's end. Leacock sought to find a middle way between a form of cynicism that led to paralysis and a form of certainty that tended to distort the deeper and fuller mystery of life. It was this *via media* that tended to shape Leacock's approach to public education. But much deeper than the middle way between absolutism and scepticism is Leacock's notion of human nature, and the purpose and end (*telos*) of such a nature. It is one thing to protest the dominance of 'techne' as a way of knowing and being and to use the educational language of *paideia* as the alternate way. It is quite another to define and decide what is meant by paideia. If the purpose of learning is to speak to the human condition, what is the human condition and human nature that such learning must speak to?

Is the turn to the classical tradition merely meant as a means to compare and contrast alternate ways of being and seeing, or is it a turn to the truth of being itself? It is these sorts of questions that, when answered, separate and differentiate the Tory approach to, *paideia* from the more liberal approach. Leacock and Grant tended to stand within the more classical and Tory tradition of *paideia*, and it is this approach that distinguishes, for example, the Leacock/Grant/Bloom turn to the 'Great Tradition' from the dialectical approach of the 'Great Books Series' of Mortimer Adler (for whom Grant worked between 1959 and 1961).

George Grant, like Leacock, had a distrust of education as 'techne'. *The George Grant Reader* (1998) threaded together some of Grant's best insights on education and the relationship between a contemplative way of knowing and a more technical way of knowing. The essays 'Philosophy and the Perfection of God' (1951), 'The Role of Education' (1955), 'Resignation from York' (1960), 'The Multiversity' (1975), and

'Research and Resignation' (1980) speak volumes about Grant's attitude and approach to public education. In 'Philosophy and the Perfection of God,' Grant offended the philosophic Sanhedrin in Canada by
daring to argue that philosophy was about the quest for meaning, for
wisdom, for justice, rather than dissecting the meaning of words and
following the scientific path down the road of logical positivism and
linguistic analysis. Grant took the position that philosophy was about
openness to the perfection and goodness of God, and, as such, this contemplative way of knowing came as a criticism of the one-dimensional
and single-vision approach of science. The tension between the two
goes back to the differences between Plato and Aristotle as well as the
medieval clash between the monastic and scholastic way of knowing so
well articulated by J. Leclercq in his classic work, *The Love of Learning
and the Desire for God* (1957). The rationalist-romantic debate and dialogue of the Enlightenment, the two cultures of C.P. Snow, and Hans-
Georg Gadamer's grappling with the dominance of the scholastic-ratio-
nalist method in *Truth and Method* speak to this dilemma. These different ways of knowing have a long tradition and pedigree, and there are
serious consequences to face for saluting the one and either subordinating or banishing the other. Both traditions tend to yield different
results, and the wise recognize the strengths of each. The dilemma, for
those like Leacock and Grant, was this: the empirical, scholastic, rationalist, scientific, mastering way had come to dominate the world of
thought and university life to such an extent that the contemplative,
meditative, receptive, listening, romantic, and attentive way of knowing had been exiled or reduced to the private and subjective. This, of
course, has serious implications for religion, ethics, culture, and politics. And it is why Grant, again and again, returned to the issue of the
telos of human nature and public education. Grant, in this debate
between different ways of knowing, traced the problem back to Plato
and Aristotle. Here he was indebted to Erich Frank's article, 'The Fundamental Opposition between Plato and Aristotle.'[3] In Grant's mind, it
was the fundamental clash, built into the beginnings of Western intellectual life, between Plato and Aristotle, that prepared the stage for the
modern dominance of the Aristotelian way of knowing and being.

  If the purpose of public education, in the classical sense, was to open
the mind and imagination to the overtures of the divine, but modern
education had turned against anything that could not be mastered and
controlled, then was it possible for public education to truly educate
anymore? If the ethos of public education banished any thought of God

to the private sphere of arbitrary subjectivity, or reduced the study of religion to an object of university study like any other, the real life and fire of authentic religion would be put out. Grant saw the modern approach to knowing as the death knell to a serious and substantive approach to education. In this sense, Grant stands very much in the line and lineage of an older notion of the purpose of education. That intellectual tradition led him to do battle in 1960 with York University, and, when he left McMaster University in 1980, he fleshed out his arguments in the article 'Research and Resignation.'

As I have mentioned above, the debate about the hegemony of 'techne' as a way of knowing and being, and the countering of such a way of knowing and being with *paideia*, raises substantive questions. What do we mean by *paideia*. Is there a nature and telos towards which humans can and should be formed, informed, and shaped or is human nature an open-ended project? The turn to the 'Great Books' traditions raised questions for Grant. How were the 'Great Books' to be studied, and who defined what books were to be canonized? Grant, as I have said, had been involved with Mortimer Adler and the 'Great Books' series between 1959 and 1961, and when he was a student at Queen's, he wrote a review of Robert Maynard Hutchins's work, *The Higher Learning in America*. Grant found himself a dissident within the liberal ranks of the 'Great Books' clan. Adler tended to see a study of the 'Great Books' as a way of opening up a student to a vast array of choices. Exposure to the classics was a way into a wider and fuller horizon, but Adler (being the good Aristotelian he was) was rather shy about suggesting that studying the classics led to a knowing of the truth. Adler's article 'Great Books, Democracy and Truth,'[4] in *Freedom in the Modern World: Jacques Maritain, Yves R. Simon, Mortimer Adler* (1989), clarifies his difference with Allan Bloom in this regard, and Grant was closer to Bloom than Adler. Adler argued that a 'dialectical' approach rather than a 'dogmatic' one was the best way to study the 'Great Books.' It does not take too much reflection to realize what is at stake in this debate. Is there such a thing as truth? Can it be known or are we just left with a pondering of ponderous insights, perspectives, and positions from the past? The answer to these sorts of questions shapes, therefore, how the turn to *paideia* will be taken as a corrective to the dominance of 'techne.'

Grant, like Leacock, tried to find a middle way between intellectual cynicism/scepticism and a simplistic certainty/absolutism. Both men attached a high value to the contemplative and meditative way of knowing, a way of knowing that personally connects the reading of classical texts with inner formation and transformation of the inner-outer life in opposition to a way of knowing that was merely for technical information or the reduction of learning to the status of a 'museum culture.' They both thought there was such a thing as an innate human nature that, through education, could be drawn forth, and, in the drawing forth, the wisdom and presence of the past could still teach much. Each had emerged from the same culture. Both were Tories of an older ilk, and, as such, both viewed the role of public education in a more human and humane way than many of their contemporaries did. They knew they were battling against a methodological liberalism that genuflected, on substantive issues, to the empirical way of knowing and corporate power alike. In contrast, they adhered to a contemplative way of knowing, one marked by an openness to the wisdom of the humanities and a desire to see the public institution of education as a means to raise the more important questions of wisdom, justice, citizenship, and the longing for God.

It is this older Tory attitude about education that very much informed and shaped the educational vision of Leacock and Grant, and its loss has been well traced by Philip Massolin in his informative book, *Canadian Intellectuals, The Tory Tradition, and the Challenge of Modernity, 1939–1970* (2001). Although *Canadian Intellectuals* tends to confuse, at some important points, the classical Tory and liberal approach to education (hence the meaning of *paideia*), there is much in this book that highlights the intellectual and institutional problems that Leacock and Grant faced as they engaged the direction of public education.

TORY POLITICS: RIGHT OR LEFT?

We have seen in Canada, in the last few decades, the language of conservatism take on a different meaning than it once had. The more Canada has veered away from its English moorings and come within the gravitational pull of the United States, the more our understanding of conservatism has come to echo and ape the American republican way of interpreting conservatism. The American republican tradition seeks to conserve the first generation of liberal political thought. This is the world of Locke, Smith, Hobbes, and Hume. It is also the ethos of Burke, who accepted the fiscal and economic liberalism of Locke and Smith while resisting and opposing their middle-class liberalism on social issues. C.B. Macpherson, in both *The Political Theory of Possessive Individualism: Hobbes to Locke* and *Burke*, has highlighted the possessive individualism that gives the liberal tradition 'underlying unity.' Similarly, Grant calls many of the liberal political theorists listed above 'philosophers of greed.' In fact, Grant, like Macpherson, tends to place Burke in the same family and tribe as Locke, Hobbes, Smith, Kant, and Hume. In *English-Speaking Justice*, he makes this point poignantly and succinctly:

In that bourgeois dominance the notes of comfort, utility and mastery could alone ring fully in the public realm. Among those who wrote political philosophy since Hobbes and Locke, there has been little more than the working out in detail of variations on utilitarianism and contractualism, their possible conflicts and their possible internal unclarities. What do Bentham or J.S. Mill or Russell add to Locke at the level of fundamental political theory? Indeed it is better to put the question: what has been lost in them of his comprehensiveness, subtlety and depth? The confidence of that Whig dominance is illustrated by the way that Burke has been interpreted since his day. He has been taken as our chief 'conservative' in contradistinction of our 'liberals.' In fact he was in practice a Rockingham Whig, and did not depart from Locke in fundamental matters, except to surround liberalism with a touch of romanticism. That touch of the historic sense makes him in fact more modern than the pure milk of bourgeois liberalism. Such figures as Swift and Johnson and Coleridge, who attempted (in descending order of power) to think of politics outside the contractarian or utilitarian contexts, were simply taken as oddities dominated by nostalgia for a dying Anglicanism, and having no significance for the practical world.[5]

Grant makes it clear in this passage that, in the area of political philosophy, there is a distinct Liberal and Tory family tree and lineage. Grant agrees with Macpherson that Burke is very much a liberal, and must be seen as such. He and Macpherson (who was identified with the political left in Canada) also agree on the deeper underlying unity of liberalism, but Grant turns to an older Toryism that is rooted in the Anglican ethos and is embodied in Swift, Johnson, and Coleridge. It is this tradition that Grant holds high, at the level of philosophic principle, and that he uses to questions and interrogate the hegemony of liberalism in the modern world.

Classic liberalism tends to be somewhat suspicious of the state (except for support of the military and police), wary of increased taxation for state activities in distributing wealth and social welfare, and, of course, keen on the market economy and free trade. The elevation of the Protestant work ethic, the responsibilities of the individual, the equality of each and all, and the ideal of liberty dominate this brand of liberalism, which is the type that American republicans seek to conserve. Such underlying principles as liberty, individualism, equality, and the will to power (progress and technology) serve, therefore, to define and shape views of religion, economics, education, culture, and politics within the American republican tradition.

But is this notion of conservatism true and faithful to the Anglo-Canadian tradition of conservatism? Has the 'Tory touch' within Canada nudged us to understand conservatism in a different way and manner? The Canadian tradition has tended, at its best, to hold in tension the commonweal and the individual, order and liberty, the good and power, reason and will, and an organic nature of society (with obvious differences and gifts) with equality. We have had a higher respect for Swift, Johnson, and Coleridge in Canada than is the case in the United States. Conservatism in Canada has never been as opposed to the use of the federal state to create and bring into being the common good as has American conservatism. If, as I have mentioned above, Canadian Toryism is, in some ways, the polar opposite of American conservatism, do Leacock and Grant reflect this tendency? Just as we saw that Leacock and Grant had many of the same concerns about the drift and direction of education (hence their Tory affinities), so we will see that, in the area of politics, both Leacock and Grant shared many of the older Tory notions of the commonweal, and it was such notions that also gave them a certain affinity with the political left. Let us briefly see how this was the case.

Leacock, in the preface to *Sunshine Sketches of a Little Town*, said that 'in Canada, I belong to the Conservative party.'[6] His understanding of what such a statement meant is in stark contrast to the view that tends to define conservatism today. Leacock completed his PhD on 'The Doctrine of Laissez Faire' at the University of Chicago. The thesis was hardly an unqualified defence of laissez-faire in the marketplace. Leacock, in his thesis, tracked and traced, in a historic way, the doctrine of laissez-faire and raised some telling questions about it. Such a stance would hardly endear Leacock to contemporary conservatives. Later, Leacock's *Greater Canada: An Appeal*, published in 1907, called for a form of Canadian nationalism that would and could not be taken captive by American or English imperialism. Again, this sort of position would hardly earn Leacock the blessings of our modern conservatives. The subsequent publication in 1914 of *Arcadian Adventures with the Idle Rich* and in 1920 of *The Unsolved Riddle of Social Justice* made it clear that Leacock sought to find a middle road between socialism and capitalism. Leacock, unlike modern-day conservatives, was as critical of the excesses and abuses of capitalism as he was of socialism. His nimble and subtle economic and political mind refused to succumb to the ideologues of the right and left.

As I mentioned above, Leacock began teaching at McGill as a sessional in 1900 and by 1903 had been hired on a permanent basis. Soon he was made chair of the department of political economy/science and he retained that post until his retirement in 1936. It is important to note that McGill was a hotbed of leftist thought and radicalism at the time, and many of the students and staff who were front and centre in this regard were either Leacock's students, former students, staff he hired, or staff he defended when pressure came from the board and president to encourage them to go to other places. It was Leacock who suggested to Frank Scott, Leon Edel, and A.J.M. Smith that a new magazine was needed at McGill to ask some of the hard questions that beset Canada in the first two decades of the twentieth century. Scott, Edel, and Smith founded the *McGill Fortnightly Review* (1925–7), and Leacock helped fund the magazine and contributed to it. Leacock hired the controversial Eugene Forsey as a sessional lecturer in 1929, and when King Gordon and Eugene Forsey dared to defend some of the more positive aspects of the Soviet experiment, many at McGill suggested to Leacock that he should let Forsey go. But Leacock refused to bend to corporate pressure, and he kept Forsey on staff. Another Leacock protégé was Leonard Marsh, who was hired in the economics department in 1930 and the following year, at Leacock's suggestion, was given a tenured post. Marsh served as the national president of the League for Social Reconstruction from 1937 to 1939, and in this capacity he wrote a report that called on Canada to bring into being a solid and sound social policy. In sum, Leonard Marsh, Eugene Forsey, King Gordon, Frank Scott, and David Lewis, to name but a few, were all thinkers in the 1920s and 1930s, and Leacock did not turn against them as many did. In fact, he often came to their aid and assistance. This is hardly the type of conservatism that dominates the stage today.

When Leacock died in 1944, he had four manuscripts ready to go to press. Two of these, *While There Is Time: The Case against Social Catastrophe* and *Last Leaves*, highlight Leacock's abiding passion for the commonweal, the role of the state and society in bringing about such a good, and the need for Canada to take a leadership role in the acena of political thought and action. Leacock wrote a telling introduction to Prime Minister R.B. Bennett's *The Premier Speaks to the People* (1935), and both Leacock's introduction and Bennett's five addresses argue, quite clearly, that the state must be more interventionist on a variety of social and economic issues. Leacock had, also, done a tour of western Canada in the mid-1930s, which left him alarmed by the strength of the Social Credit Party in Alberta. His book *My Discovery of the West: A Discussion of East and West in Canada* (1937) makes plain what he thinks of Social Credit and, more to the point, the economic philosophy that undergirded and justified it. Leacock's understanding of conservatism was grounded and rooted in a much older notion of conservatism, and it was this older approach – with its concern for the common good and the role of both the state and society in bringing about such a good – that gave Leacock some affinities with the political left.

Long after Leacock's death, an important music festival (which drew many of the protest activists of the counter-culture) was lunched. Called the Mariposa Festival, it was first held in Orillia in 1961, but because of opposition from some people in the town, it was later moved to Centre Island in Toronto. Mariposa, of course, was the name of Leacock's town in *Sunshine Sketches of a Little Town*. Nicholas Jennings, in *Before the Gold Rush: Flashbacks to the Dawn of the Canadian Sound* (1997), has written: 'The founding manifesto [of the Mariposa Festival] stated that an annual festival could help folk singers make a career in Canada instead of having first to be recognized in the States. The mission statement added earnestly: We also want to make the people of Canada familiar with their own folk songs. All that was left was to select a name. They chose Stephen Leacock's fictional name for Orillia – Mariposa.'[7] Clearly, Leacock's brand of conservatism had lived on into the 1960s as the activists of that decade noticed an affinity between what Leacock said and did in his time and what they were attempting to do in theirs. In short, conservatism and the left are not necessarily opposed in the Canadian conservative and Tory tradition.

George Grant, like Leacock, did not see a stark and unbridgeable opposition between conservatism and the political left. In fact, Grant, like Leacock, realized that there was much in common between these two traditions. His 1945 book *The Empire: Yes or No?* (1945) echoes much of what is found in Leacock's *Greater Canada: An Appeal* and *Last Leaves*. Similarly, Grant's CBC lectures in the late 1950s that were to become *Philosophy in the Mass Age* highlight, all so clearly, his suspicion of individualistic liberalism and his openness to some aspects of Marxism. Marxism, unlike some variants of liberalism, recognizes the value of community, the fact we are social beings, and the need for the state to protect the collectivity against the corrosive impact and influence of technology and the will to power of powerful individuals who have no sense of restraint, limitation, or the common good.

The publication of 'An Ethic of Community' in *Social Purpose for Canada* (1961) clearly aligned Grant with the political left and the emerging vision of the New Democratic Party (NDP), although Grant did have serious philosophic concerns about some of the deeper principles of the 'New Left.' When the NDP and the Liberals voted to bring down the government of John Diefenbaker in 1963, Grant was appalled. He saw in Diefenbaker, flawed and fallen though he was, a man who would be willing to stand against the wealthy elite and the military industrial complex of the United States, and who would be prepared to stand or fall on that position. For Grant, there was something heroic about Diefenbaker and, perhaps even more so, his defence minister, Howard Green, and this conviction led to *Lament for a Nation* (1965), a political and philosophic tract for the times that praised an older conservative vision which was, even in those years, being eroded in Canada by Goldwater-type republicanism. *Lament for a Nation* stirred and awoke a new generation of leftist political activists. Gad Horowitz called Grant a 'Red Tory' and others saw him as a member of the protest left of the 1960s. Many of Grant's students and friends, such as Dennis Lee, Matt Cohen, James Laxer, Bob and Art Davis, and Gad Horowitz were involved with many of the celebrated causes of the day. Lee and Cohen were active in the controversial Rochdale College (as were some of Grant's children) and Laxer and Horowitz were keenly committed to the NDP. Laxer was at the forefront of the 'Waffle' movement in the NDP in the late 1960s and early 1970s, a movement that attempted to unseat the party's Lewis dynasty and move it in a more decidedly leftist and nationalist direction. Grant wrote a generous foreword to Laxer's *The Liberal Idea of Canada: Pierre Trudeau and the Question of Canada's Survival* (1977). Coincidentally, just as Leacock, in his final days, left manuscripts ready to go to the press that articulated his brand of compassionate Toryism, so Grant made it clear in his final days in 1988 that he stood by the side of John Turner against Brian Mulroney in the forthcoming federal election. Turner was against free trade with the United States and more in touch with a Canadian nationalistic perspective, while Mulroney not only supported free trade but was a committed fan of Ronald Reagan. Grant's High Tory nationalism was not, in short, bound to any party. Turner, in the 1988 election, stood closer to historic Tory thought, and Mulroney was much more the dutiful liberal.

This blend of Diefenbaker-type conservatism and leftist thought was central to Grant's brand of Toryism. The fact that students in the 1960s asked Grant to speak at 'teach-ins' spoke much about his affinity with the left. But Grant, like Leacock, although an admirer of the left, did have his questions. 'A Critique of the New Left' (1966) and 'The Value of Protest' reveal Grant's ability to see not only the good in the left but also the movement's Achilles heel. *Lament for a Nation* very much emerges, politically and philosophically, from a classical perspective, a perspective that is grounded in the Western intellectual and political journey but that is also applied to the twentieth-century Canadian and American context.

Grant's brand of Canadian conservatism, with its concern for justice, the common good, the proper and due end and purpose of human existence, and the disturbing fact that all this was being forgotten, erased and eclipsed by modernity and liberalism, meant that a voice had to be raised in protest. Grant did turn to the classical tradition of Plato (as interpreted by Simone Weil and Iris Murdoch), to the English High Tory tradition of Hooker, Swift, Coleridge, and to the Canadian Tory tradition of John A. Macdonald, R.B. Bennett, and John Diefenbaker. It was this older tradition, as applied, interpreted, and made sense of in Canadian history, that drew and held Grant, just as it did Leacock. In his mind, one of the most important figures in that tradition – one that linked Canada to Britain – was Benjamin Disraeli. In Grant's 1982 review of a biography of Disraeli, he emphatically states the connection between the vision of Disraeli and that of Macdonald. 'To take a small influence: one cannot understand the conservatism of Canada (Macdonald, Whitney, Borden, Ferguson, Bennett, Diefenbaker) without thinking of Disraeli'.[8] The literary and political conservatism of Disraeli, as Grant was obviously aware, involved a concern for the poor and marginalized and the use of the state and society to minimize glaring social injustices. That form of conservatism, which antedated Disraeli, of course, was rear and dear to Grant, as it was to Leacock, and it had little in common with the 'Blue Tory' tradition of the modern-day Conservative Party of Canada. The conservatism of both Grant and Leacock, in short, was of the classical variety that had some affinities with the political left rather than the political right and that set the Canadian tradition apart from the American.

I think it can be argued that, just as Leacock and Grant, in the area of public education, sought to find a middle way between *paideia* and 'techne' (while elevating the former and subordinating the latter, in opposition to the trends of the time), so in the area of politics both Leacock and Grant sought to find a middle way between capitalism and socialism, hence their High Toryism. Both were committed to the older classical form of education, and this that, in the area of public education, wisdom took precedence over knowledge, and, in the area of public politics, justice and idealism took precedence over realism and pragmatism.

RELIGION: SPIRITUALITY OR THE CHURCH?

Charles Taylor's recently published work, *Varieties of Religion Today: William James Revisited* (2002), reveals much about the contemporary quest for spiritual meaning. Taylor points out here that William James, in his *Varieties of Religious Experience*, was a bridge between the romantic perspective of the eighteenth and nineteenth centuries and postmodern spirituality. The Jamesian form of spirituality pits experience against tradition, individualism against community, feelings against dogma, and contemplation against the institutions that bear and carry the tradition and doctrines of the historic community. Experience, individualism, feelings, and contemplation are idealized, whereas tradition, community, dogma, and institutions are seen as forces that inhibit and repress an authentic and genuine quest for Leacock and Grant, as Tories grounded in an ancient way, would find this stark contrast between spirituality and religion (the former idealized, the latter subordinated or demonized) both shortsighted and, sadly and tragically so, reductionistic and reactionary. Taylor, of course, sees James's perspective simplistic and silly, but he does note that the romantic-Jamesian-postmodern approach to spirituality has won the day for many.

Stephen Leacock, like George Grant, was committed to both spirituality and religion, experience and the institutions that carry the truths of the past from one generation to the next. Their organic view of religion and society, also, recognized the close relationship between faith and justice, spirituality and the politics of the commonweal. The connection between spirituality and dogma, the church and public/political life, was part and parcel of the way Leacock and Grant understood their faith journey. Leacock, like Grant, was a member of the Anglican Church of Canada, but not uncritically so. Just as Erasmus in his *Colloquies* and *The Praise of Folly* could lampoon much of the theology and religious practices of his day and yet remain a faithful Roman Catholic, and just as Chaucer could do the same in *Canterbury Tales*, so Leacock and Grant could and would criticize the Anglican tradition but still remain faithful to its inner core and essence. Many have assumed that Leacock was a sceptic who had no real interest in religion other than as an organization and way of life to make sport of, but there was more to Leacock than that. It is true, of course, that Leacock takes to task the follies and aberrations of religion in *Sunshine Sketches of a Little Town* and *Arcadian Adventures with the Idle Rich*, but in the same works he also demonstrates a certain fondness for those who live their lives with integrity. Dean Drone does have his appeal, as does the Reverend McTeague. Carl Spadoni, in his annotated edition of *Sunshine Sketches of a Little Town*, correctly notes Leacock's nuanced understanding of the role of religion and the Anglican tradition. In Leacock's final book, *While There Is Time*, he praised comments by the archbishop of Canterbury on the beatitudes, and when he died in the spring of 1944, the archbishop of Canada, Derwyn Owen (a friend of Leacock), travelled north to Sibbald Point to lead the funeral service at St George's parish. In short, the High Toryism of Leacock was quick to point out folly and foolishness, but, when day was done, Leacock knew what he valued and why. He was aware of the danger of being too certain on religious matters, but, as his essay 'A Rehabilitation of Charles II' makes plain, he was also alert to the danger of excessive scepticism. It is within the classical Anglican middle way (or *via media*) between scepticism and certainty, socialism and capitalism, knowing and not knowing, wisdom and knowledge, spirituality and religion, that Leacock can be placed. By positioning him there, we can see his Toryism in the best possible perspective. In fact, the place where Leacock is buried is also the resting place of many of the finest Anglican Tories of the nineteenth and twentieth centuries. Susan Sibbald (a good friend of Bishop John Strachan) is buried at St George's, as are Mazo de la Roche and Caroline Clement. In short, although Leacock did not write a great deal about theology and philosophy, there is little doubt that his faith was a central part of his being and was deeply rooted and grounded in the Anglican way and tradition.

Leacock tended to be more interested in examining the sociological and political aspects of religion than in probing religion's philosophical and theological core. George Grant was the opposite. The fact that Leacock's doctoral dissertation was in the area of political economy and Grant's was in the area of philosophical theology speaks much about their different leanings and tendencies. Yet, even so, both men had an abiding concern for the larger questions of faith and religion.

George Grant, unlike Leacock, was not a cradle Anglican. He was a

Presbyterian by birth, and his wife, Sheila, was raised a Roman Catholic but she had left that church by the time she met Grant. The genius of the Church of England has been the way it is catholic but not Roman Catholic and reformed but not schismatic. It is this middle way between Roman Catholicism and Protestantism that defines the Church of England and the Anglican way and ethos. It is a tradition always on the alert for the best in various perspectives but quite clear-eyed about the dangers of excesses and extremes. George and Sheila Grant became Anglicans in 1956 while George was teaching philosophy at Dalhousie University, and although Grant, like Leacock, could never be seen as an orthodox churchman, both men lived their faith from an Anglican genetic code. Grant read, with great interest and sympathy, Hooker, the Caroline Divines, Swift, and the English High Romantics, and he and Sheila participated in C.S. Lewis's Socratic Club while they were at Oxford. Grant had an abiding respect for Lewis, and at Oxford he was quite taken, too, by Austin Farrar. When the Grants were in Halifax, they had a close connection with the University of King's College (the oldest university in Canada and a bastion of High Church Anglicanism). Grant, in 1955, published 'Adult Education in an Expanding Economy' in the *Anglican Outlook.*

After the Grant family moved to the Hamilton area, Grant was involved in a variety of issues in his diocese. He and Sheila were active in nominating and supporting a conservative bishop (Joe Fricker), and both opposed the new Sunday School curriculum and jointly wrote an alternative one for their parish. George and Sheila, by the mid-1970s, saw the direction the Anglican Church of Canada was going on the issues of abortion and euthanasia, and they wrote copiously on these subjects. The article 'Abortion and Rights: The Value of Political Freedom,' in *The Right to Birth: Some Christian Views on Abortion* (1976), stated their views clearly. (Significantly, this book was published by the Anglican Book Centre and edited by the well-known Anglo-Catholic Anglican, and professor at Trinity College, Eugene Fairweather.) By the late 1970s, Grant had become increasingly disgruntled with the liberal drift of the Anglican Church of Canada. He would often speak at Low Church parishes – the Low Church wing had a perspective more in keeping with his own – and when he was given an honorary doctorate at Thornloe University in 1979, he gave a stirring, powerful, and never to be forgotten homily at Church of the Epiphany on justice and righteousness.[9]

It is essential that Grant's understanding of the Good and God be seen together, and that his interpretation of the Good/God not be distorted by the culture wars of either his ethos or ours. Grant spoke against ills and evils of abortion, euthanasia, and the breakdown of the family, and for the importance of historic and institutional religion (which seemed to put him on the political right), but, at the same time, his commitment to the commonweal, his pacifism, his opposition to the Vietnam War, his stinging criticisms of the American imperial way, his hostility to corporate wealth, and his support of the Canadian state as a means of bringing into being the common good seemed to place him on the political left. Grant, in short, deftly eludes the ethical tribalism that so dominates the landscape of the political right and left and points to a third way that cannot be easily appropriated by political ideologues.

To those who turned against the more formal, institutional side of religion, Grant would often ask this simple question: Have you worn the robes? People who have not taken the time to wear such robes (in thought, word, and deed), he said, often caricature and dismiss that which they know little about. It is in the willingness (never easy) to wear such robes that Leacock and Grant part company with those who would, in glib and reactionary ways, sever spirituality from the church. When this is done, spirituality becomes thinned out, reductionistic, and somewhat narcissistic. It seems to me that the prophetic nature of Leacock and Grant is best understood in the way they lived from within their tradition yet were critical of it. In short, Grant was never reluctant to raise all the hard questions about the Anglican Church of Canada – he was no churchman in the classical sense of the term – but in entering this fray and fighting the good fight, he did so as a loyal (if troubled) Anglican. An interesting sidebar here is that, although Leacock and Grant played substantive and public roles in Canada, and did so as Anglicans, most histories of Anglicanism in Canada have ignored them. This omission is remarkable, given that Leacock and Grant were probably the finest Anglicans at work in the areas of political economy, literature, culture, public education, theology, and philosophy in twentieth-century Canada.

Grant was also a theologian and philosopher of some note, and this needs to be unpacked in more detail by way of conclusion. Grant's thinking always turned to the mystery at the heart of things, the God of Love whom we could sense but never fully know. It was this blending of the *via positiva* (cataphatic) and the *via negativa* (apophatic) that attracted Grant to the riches and bounty of the Orthodox tradition near the end of his life. Since there has been much interaction between Orthodoxy and Anglicanism, the transition was not hard for Grant. Grant's reading of

Phillip Sherrard's *The Greek East and Latin West* confirmed for him, as did his reading of the Christian Platonist Simone Weil, that unless the intellect (*nous*) was illuminated by the mystery of love, much would remain hidden and obscure. The Greek Orthodox tradition views God's essence as being beyond any categories, although his energies can be known by analogies. It is this essence-energy distinction in the area of both theology and philosophy that drew Grant in his latter years. Grant also wanted to make it quite clear that talk of God had to be equated with the classical notion of the Good. George and Sheila spent time with Iris Murdoch and her husband, John Bayley, while at Oxford, and Murdoch always emphasized that God and the Good were one and the same. This is, I might add, Simone Weil's position also. Weil connected faith and charity and faith and justice in a way that turned the tables on the usual discussion of faith and metaphysics. Much of theology at the time was more concerned, in the area of apologetics, with the relationship of faith and what the mind and imagination could and could not know. It was this way of doing theology and philosophy that Grant had problems with. The connection and unity between faith, God, and the Good (hence the Platonic concern for justice) separate Grant/Murdoch/Weil from Martin Heidegger. Murdoch, like Grant, had strong Church of England connections, and her affinities were with the High Church party.

It seems to me that, if we are ever going to understand Grant as a theologian, we need to hold, in tension, three areas of his thought. There was, as I have said, his interest in the Orthodox way. The Orthodox tradition stresses the sheer mystery and unknowability of God. Hence, the human journey is one of ever greater openness to the divine love that can be received only as a mystery and gift. Second, there was Grant's commitment to seeing God and the Good as one and the same. Grant would and could not sever and separate the God of mystery, love, and the Good. This meant, therefore, that the mystery of God's love was not so unknowable that silence about the ultimate was the final position. Because God was, is, and always will be the God of goodness and justice, ethical and political decisions can be made, theologically, about injustice in the world. And, third, there was the theology of the cross. Grant sought to make sense of Luther's theology of the cross and theology of glory in a way that led him straight into the mystery and redemptive nature of the cross and suffering.

Plato's notion of the Good identified God as sheer goodness, but this was a mystery that we could know only through a glass darkly. The journey to the Good is fraught with many perils, and those who elevate the triumphalistic theology of glory while sidestepping the theology of the cross misunderstand the nature of the Good. Christ, on the cross, illuminates for us the divine nature of the Good. God becomes the servant, and dies for us, so that we may live the divine life. God, as the embodiment of the Good and love comes not as victorious warlord and conqueror but as a suffering servant, embracing the sadness and tragedy of the human condition. The cross, in this sense, demonstrates the real nature of God, the Good, and divine love. The Good is incarnated in time and history, and on the cross we come to see the real nature of the Good as suffering love, a letting go. This dying God, in Christ, demonstrates and illuminates for us that divine love and goodness are one and the same. It is in seeing the theology of the cross as the door into the resurrection and the theology of glory that we come to see that divine love and goodness are about suffering with others so each and all might live the abundant life. The true divine mystery is that goodness is about a God who seeks, through suffering alongside us, to draw each and all back into the unity of love. The longings and hunger of Plato find their embodied fulfillment in the Christ of the cross. Plato, Orthodoxy, and the Roman Catholic-Protestant traditions (Paul-Augustine-Luther-Calvin) are brought together. Grant drew from these various and varied wells, and the bucket he returned with carried waters from many places. Indeed, in many ways, Grant was one of the most articulate and probing theologians Canada has produced, and as more of his manuscripts are published, we will come to see why. I think that Grant, as an Anglican, has a theological vision with all sorts of ecumenical possibilities. He goes further than most in synthesizing the best of the Protestant, Roman Catholic, and Orthodox traditions, and, in this sense, he is very Anglican. True, Grant is not systematic in his thinking, but there is a reason for this. The danger of 'techne,' of mastering, of controlling, of demanding of the other its reasons (in thought and deed), is the great temptation of the West. Grant points, probes, tosses out flares, and, in doing so, like Simone Weil, he begs us to be attentive and alert to what might speak to us if we have contemplative and meditative ears to hear. Those who use the Baconian and Cartesian mind might see some things, but the deeper illumination of divine love is missed. Grant directs us to what we miss in our modern approach to knowing and being, and he asks of us that we heed such 'intimations of deprival.'

Grant spent half of his academic life (the initial and latter half) in Halifax, and while at Dalhousie, as pointed out earlier, he was closely involved with the University of King's College. At the heart of King's is the commitment to carry forth the classical Anglo-Catholic tradition of faith and the classics. King's stands as a academic bulwark against the corrosive nature of modernity and liberalism. Although Grant would not have been drawn to the High Church liturgical tradition of King's, he certainly shared its passion for the ancient way in opposition to the modern one. Much more work needs to be done on Grant and the High Church King's College tradition to get a firmer feel for Grant's deeper Anglican way and how it informed many of the issues he engaged in. Near the end of his life, for example, he published 'Nietzsche and the Ancients: Philosophy and Scholarship' in *Dionysius* and 'Abortion and Rights: The Value of Political Freedom' in *Holy Living: Christian Morality Today*. Both *Dionysius* and *Holy Living* are journals closely connected to the High Church Anglican tradition of King's College. It is also significant that Grant's tombstone has the following inscription: 'Out of the Shadows and Imaginings into the Truth.' These words have been attributed to J.H. Newman, and the sentiment they express accords with the Platonic Anglicanism that Grant welcomed and sought to understand and live out in his life. It is only when we come to a full appreciation of this that we will understand Grant's opposition to Hegel, as well as to the theological and philosophical vision of James Doull (who dominated much of educational life at Dalhousie-King's for many decades). A book is yet to be written on the Grant-Doull debate and its significance for both Anglican and Canadian theological, philosophical, and political thought and action.

CONCLUSION

I began this chapter with the argument that nothing of a comparative nature has been done on Stephen Leacock and George Grant. This is a rather disturbing fact given that both men have important Tory affinities. Their affinities can be best seen in their approach to public education, political theory and the relationship between spirituality and the church. Both men, in a critical, ongoing, and active way, were committed to calling the public institutions of their time (education, political parties, and the Anglican Church of Canada) back to their founding visions. In this sense, both men were reformers and prophets. The Tory affinities that they shared is a subject deserving of much more research, and, in this regard, my effort is little more than a dipping of the toes into the water. The longer swim and deep dive to find the pearls remains to be done.

NOTES

1 William Christian, *George Grant: A Biography* (Toronto: University of Toronto Press, 1993), 30.
2 Gerald Lynch, 'Afterword,' in *Arcadian Adventures with the Idle Rich* (Toronto: McClelland and Stewart, 1989), 211.
3 Erich Frank, 'The Fundamental Opposition between Plato and Aristotle,' *American Journal of Philology* 61, no. 1 (1940): 34–53.
4 Mortimer Adler, 'Great Books, Democracy, and Truth,' in *Freedom in the Modern World: Jacques Maritain, Yves R. Simon, Mortimer Adler*, ed. Michael Torre (Mishawaka, IN: University of Notre Dame Press, 1989), 33–45.
5 George Grant, *English-Speaking Justice* (Sackville, NB: Mount Allison University, 1974), 49–50.
6 Stephen Leacock, *Sunshine Sketches of a Little Town* (Toronto: McClelland and Stewart, 1947), viii.
7 Nicholas Jennings, *Before the Gold Rush: Flashbacks to the Dawn of the Canadian Sound* (Toronto: Viking, 1997), 33.
8 George Grant, 'British Conservatism: Benjamin Disraeli,' in *The George Grant Reader*, ed. William Christian and Sheila Grant (Toronto: University of Toronto Press, 1998), 138–41.
9 Phone Conversation with Ted Heaven, 3 June 2003.

2

Grant and Quebec

GARY G. CALDWELL

When George Grant wrote *Lament for a Nation* in 1964, he dealt extensively with the 'Quebec question' since French Canada was itself, in his mind, the keystone of Canada. In this chapter I attempt to set out the essence of Grant's thought on Quebec. I then proceed to consider how his diagnostic of 1964 compares with subsequent events in Quebec. And, finally, I offer an interpretation of the contemporary political scene in Quebec as seen through the prism of Grant's Red Toryism.

The major thesis of Grantian political thought was that modern liberalism, the handmaiden of technology, was moving us inexorably towards a homogeneous, universal – hence centralized – order that would make all local cultures anachronistic, and that this state of affairs would lead to a tyranny that would crush the human spirit. For those of us old enough to remember a time when shopping involved real human contact with sales staff, it is jarring to be confronted now with a sales clerk who, because he or she does not know you and knows little about the products or services you are purchasing, is literally plugged into a computer, eyes fixed on the screen. But this reality, the dehumanization occasioned by the new world order being ushered in by bureaucratic state capitalism, was the cornerstone of Grant's political thought.

Writing in the 1960s, 1970s, and early 1980s, Grant was convinced that the geopolitical instrument of this process was the American empire, and the local indigenous cultures with which he was most concerned were, of course, those of his own Canadian society, constituted mainly of British and French cultural traditions. Although he saw no way for the demise of local indigenous cultures to be avoided, he very much admired those who resisted. He lamented that the indigenous local culture he identified with – that of the British tradition in Canada – had effectively ceased resisting. However, part of Canada – French-speaking Canada – was continuing to resist. For this he was both grateful and full of admiration – thankful because his own ancestors (the Larkin and Grant families) had contributed to the construction of Canada as a conservative society standing apart from the Great Republic[1] and admiring because he was convinced that Canada could survive – as it was created – only on the basis of a continuing alliance of the two founding European cultures.

For Grant, one of the great tragedies of Canadian history was that English Canadians, notably John Diefenbaker (one of the principal protagonists of *Lament for a Nation*), had, in the twentieth century, failed to realize that their own fate as an independent country was entirely dependent on such an alliance. 'The keystone of a Canadian nation is the French fact,' 'English-speaking Canadians who desire the survival of their nation have to co-operate with those who seek the continuance of French-American civilization.'[2] Grant would have liked that Diefenbaker had allied himself with the likes of Paul Sauvé, a respected Quebec conservative leader from Trois-Rivières. As a young man, Grant had become acquainted with members of the French-Canadian elite. Their assumption of personal responsibility for the well-being and fate of their society, the depth of their historical consciousness, and the shared sympathy with their compatriots that he witnessed in practice left a lasting impression on him. (He actually was present at one of Henri Bourassa's public speeches in the Eastern Townships.) Indeed, Grant was very much an admirer of the conservative French-Canadian society of his time, with its articulation and defence of a common good, its Christianity, its civility, and its loyalty to the institutions that made all the above possible, notably the Catholic church and the classical colleges. Grant perceived that in French Canada there was a virtuous and noble tradition that was being actively and courageously perpetuated.

His admiration was such that he was prepared to accept Quebec's prerogative to strike out on its own if necessary.[3] This prerogative could mean, he was well aware, political separation, to avoid being dragged into the Great Republic by an English Canada that had lost any real sense of cultural distintiveness. Quebec's possible recourse to separate political nationhood was, in Grant's mind, justified both by the need to continue its resistance, be it alone, and by English Canada's having abandoned the original joint Canadian political project. For Grant, the imposed 1982 constitution was unjustified and the consequence of

English Canada's having abandoned the Canada of the British North America Act of 1867.

Yet admiring French-Canadian civilization was one thing and believing in its capacity to resist the excesses of modernization was another. The question had to be asked: Would Quebec be able to resist, alone, unhampered by the dead weight of an English Canada already integrated into the empire of the Great Republic? Grant did not, ultimately, believe so. He was so overwhelmed by the corrosive power of modern liberalism – the ideology according to which human beings could, via technology, free themselves from the limitations of nature – that he believed Quebec would also, like the rest of Canada, succumb. There would be resistance, but 'when the dam breaks the flood will be furious.'[4]

The dam would break because, although French Canada enjoyed a rooted culture already three hundred years old, a vision of the eternal carried forward by the Catholic church, a conception of virtue, and an educated political elite, it would be no match for the chimera of personal liberation as driven by an all-pervasive American culture with its enormous technological means, notably television after 1952. Although Catholic societies were harder to modernize than Protestant ones – there would be an active and conscious resistance – it was to no avail. Collapse could come within a single generation because the members of the body politic were not personally immunized against modernization (Catholic virtue being in large part a collective virtue, not as internalized and personal as Protestant virtue).

And the dam did indeed burst. It happened soon after Grant predicted it would, in the late 1960s. A torrential flood of change continued unabated for the next forty years: first, the so-called Quiet Revolution of the 1960s, then an unrelenting pursuit of modernism. Quebec's quest to become modern began with a honeymoon of consumer materialism and was followed by an embrace of technology in all its forms, from industrial agriculture to scientific pedagogy; indulgence in personal liberation, particularly the rejection of the then prevailing sexual mores; and a fanatical intellectual secularism so pervasive that even the Quebec Catholic episcopate withdrew from the public stage.

These changes are the backdrop of Denys Arcand's three-film series: Le déclin de l'empire américain (1986), 'Jésus de Montréal (1989), and Les invasions barbares (2003). The first film epitomizes the rot in the head of the body politic; in the second, the body resists, unsuccessfully, the infection; and in the third, the body of the pre-modern society has given up the ghost and a new world, peopled by individuals for whom the old world is completely foreign, is in place. The films were produced well after Grant had offered his own prediction about the future of French Canada.

Grant's insights about the fate of societies undergoing what is now termed 'late accelerated modernization' – Quebec, Ireland, Spain, Italy, and Poland all come to mind – were indeed remarkable, pointing to realities that sociologists recognized only after the fact. Quebecers did indeed being their journey towards modernism by indulging in a honeymoon of consumerism: the locally made pine kitchen furniture was quickly consigned to the woodshed,[5] to be replaced by a linoleum-covered and chrome-bordered 'modern' kitchen table, basking in the illumination of a new fluorescent light. Thereafter Quebecers embarked on kitchen 'modernization' every ten years or so. Nor did the makeover stop with the kitchen. In rural Quebec, houses that have had their wooden exterior modernized several times, from paper 'insul-brick' to aluminium 'siding' to masonite 'board' to plastic 'vinyl siding' to the contemporary composite (pressed sawdust) 'simul'(ated) wood siding, are legion, although some may have skipped over one, even two, of these five distinct fashions.[6] Vermonters, who, by contrast, have stuck with real wood siding, are distinctly old-fashioned.

As for the embrace of technology in industry and public administration, Quebec was exemplary, particularly in the public and para-public sector. Hydro-Quebec became a leader in Canada in electrical production and transmission, as did the Caisse Populaire movement in the application of information technology to banking. The Quebec government was quick to introduce information technology in the education, health, transport, and taxation sectors. Centralized college-student admissions and medical-care cards were up and running by the early 1970s. By the 1980s, every road culvert in Quebec had its individual identification, stored in a computer in Quebec City. All of these technologies and many others were, of course, accompanied by an inescapable bureaucratization and centralization which had as an offshoot the need for a whole new class of technicians and managers. The private sector, financed in part by public loans or guarantees, also became committed to the potential of the new technologies. For instance, both public and private managers were confident that they were ready to conquer markets in the United States, which many companies did in fact do. It was this confidence that was at the origin of the Quebec's support for free trade agreement with the United States. When, after the agreement came into effect, American companies began conquering markets in Quebec, in financial services, for instance,[7] the same managers were dismayed, revealing their naivety about the new order.

With respect to the third facet of the modernization process, liberalization from traditional institutional and moral constraints, the elite of the 1950s who owed their social status to their education in the province's classical colleges set their minds to dismantling – in the name of technology and equality – the very same institutions, and by the late 1960s they had succeeded. A quarter of a century later, the same elite had succeeded in liberating Quebecers from the constraints of marriage, denominational education, and responsibility for the educational and health needs of their children, as well as the 'duty' of even having children.[8] Quebec was, few realize, the first Canadian province to legislate away the traditional definition of marriage (a man and a woman): the vote took place in the National Assembly in the summer of 2002, and it was unanimous![9] Apart from a brief sent to the parliamentary commission whose deliberations proceeded the vote, the Catholic Church did not take issue. The brief was never distributed to Quebec parishes and the media totally ignored it.

Although Grant was fully cognizant that social-democratic regimes – he perceived Quebec to be such – were not exempt from the appeal of technology, and that the forces to be resisted were corporate business and bureaucratic centralized government, he did not apprehend that the transformation of Quebec into a fully modern society would be accomplished not so much by corporate capitalist business as by social-democratic government. Indeed, the Quebec cultural and political elite that came of age in the immediate post-war period, by exploiting brilliantly the corporate levers at their disposal – notably those of the provincial state and the para-public sector, as opposed to those of the economy, gave rise to a technocracy more pervasive than that which exists elsewhere in Canada. I suspect that he did not fully appreciate that the institutional model of the Catholic Church, a monopolistic centralized model, would be so persistent, despite being emptied of its 'Catholic' content, thus facilitating the work of the new technocracy. In other words, the immensity of the transition from conservative, nationalist, even romantic leaders such as Jean Allaire to liberal, technocratic, professional politicians such as Mario Dumont,[10] was probably more than Grant envisaged. No de Gaulle, as in France, emerged capable of carrying forward the resistance.[11] The Parti Québécois (PQ) leaders who succeeded René Lévesque were, republicans at heart and liberals in spirit.[12]

What are now, in terms of a Grantian perspective on Quebec, the prospects for the pursuit of a Franco-American civilization (as he rightly called it) in Quebec? Must we also 'lament' the defeat of this nation?

In the mid-1990s there took place in Quebec a change in the educational system that reflects both the degree of penetration of liberal-technocratic culture in Quebec society and how difficult it will be to salvage Franco-American civilization. Previous to this, bright, educated, and passionate young Quebecers could become, if they decided they had such a vocation, primary or secondary school teachers by taking, after graduating from university, a one-year diploma course in a faculty of education, followed by a two-year probationary period of full-time teaching. However, it was decided by the educational establishment – there was no public or legislative debate about this change – that future teachers would no longer require an extended disciplinary preparation in a given subject matter. Even an undergraduate degree would not be needed. Future teachers would rather undertake a four-year 'education' BA. During these four years they would be prepared, by taking two or three courses per subject matter, to teach two, even three, subjects. Most of the four years would be devoted to pedagogical training and practice teaching on a part-time basis.

The graduates of this program who are just now coming 'on stream' do not have the equivalent of a specialized degree in a subject matter; and they will have been subjected to a four-year socialization in an education faculty without prior study in a discipline; nor will they require the approbation of teachers in a school before receiving life-long teaching certification. No others will be allowed to teach in Quebec.

The technocrats of the science of education prevailed (one could hardly say triumphed, because there was no struggle). This change constitutes the victory of technique over substance and virtue. No longer will the bright, inspired, and passionate who, having acquired a competence in a discipline, be able to become teachers. Teaching in Quebec is now a career one enters by going directly (after junior college, the CEGEPs) into a four-year program in an education faculty,[13] staffed by professors who have little contact either with an academic discipline or, for that matter, with schools.

Although it went largely unnoticed, this change is, arguably, the point of downward inflection of what Grant called Franco-American civilization, just as, I would argue, the emergence of the classical college system in mid-nineteenth century was the point of upward inflection. What is even more revealing is the fact that the cultural and political elite acquiesced, with barely a squeak, in this change. There was little resistance.[14] Only now, as we have realized that our more gifted and spirited university-educated sons and daughters have been excluded from teaching in our schools, are we faced with the enormity of what happened. What is more humbling is that it is these same sons and daughters who are drawing it to our attention. They, in fact, hold us responsible for not having resisted.

Although only one change among many, what has happened in teacher certification offers a powerful caricature of the technocratization of Quebec society.[15] In the context of the present discussion, the pertinent question is whether resistence can change this, and what form that resistence should take; the same question applies to Quebec's schools, hospitals, credit and savings cooperatives, child- and seniors-care facilities, and municipal organizations. How can control over all these institutions be transferred from the technocratic elite to civil society, where they originated and flourished before the technocracy appropriated them.

The answer, in terms of the Grantian discourse, is, I suspect, that it would not be possible to shake loose, from within, the grip of the technocracy on these institutions, just as Grant himself never succeeded, in his lifetime, in making a serious dent on the Canadian university establishment. Not only would such thinking be incomprehensible to the modern liberal corporate minds of those actually running the system, their vested material interest is now too great.

What, then, are the other eventualities that could lead to a rolling back of the immense Quebec technocracy? One is a collapse of the system itself, a collapse brought on by unbearable costs and inadequate performance. The possibility of such a collapse should not be dismissed: it is already under way in the health-care system. Another possibility is desertion. In a liberal market society, consumers can simply desert the state-mandated technocratic institutions if they are willing to pay twice. This is happening in education by recourse to private schools and home schooling. A third possibility, in domains where there is not a non-state alternative, is political activism. The struggle over local municipal institutions is an instance of this.

Municipalities in Canada are creatures of the provincial state and an individual is not free to live outside a state-consecrated municipality, with the exception of 'unorganized' territories in remote or sparsely populated areas. One may move from a municipality but only to another governed by the same state. For the last quarter century, there has been a concerted effort by the Quebec state technocracy to close down municipalities by merging them into larger units.[16] The history, rationale, means, and success of this program cannot be discussed here. What is pertinent is the resistance that has surfaced in the last decade. For instance, in the most recent phase of the 'consolidation' program – in the second half of the 1990s – of the three hundred municipalities that were enjoined, under the threat of being cut off from much of future municipal funding, to begin a merger process by initiating feasibility studies, a full half simply turned a deaf ear to the state. They flatly refused even to envisage the possibility of liquidating themselves.

Faced with the dissolution of their municipal institutions, often the work of over a century of community effort and public service, communities began to resist something they did not do when their schools, hospitals, and credit and savings cooperatives were appropriated. This resistance became widespread in the 1990s and led to considerable political activism. Indeed, the 2003 Liberal Party victory over the incumbent PQ government can be attributed in part to Jean Charest's election-campaign promise to allow for 'de-mergers' in cases where municipalities were forcibly merged. And, despite the universal condemnation of de-mergers by the media and the intellectual and cultural elite, de-mergers did take place.

Such resistance to the suppression of municipalities has not, to my knowledge, occurred in other Canadian provinces. Do we have here the first manifestation of a conservative resistance in Quebec? Is it conceivable that, in the age of the globalization of modern liberalism and technology via American media dominance, a new awareness of the importance of local cultures and the role of civil-society institutions – such as local municipalities – in maintaining these same cultures will open the door to a successful resistance? Despite the Charest government's watering down of its promise – the conditions under which de-mergers could take place were made onerous, and de-merged municipalities never regained all their former powers – roughly half of merged municipalities did indeed de-merge!

Public discussion of de-mergers was revealing. The entire media and cultural elite was against de-mergers. Indeed, to follow the media coverage and listen to commentators and experts, one would have imagined that de-mergers would lead to chaos and municipal breakdown. In these circumstances, the fact that so many former municipalities voted, nonetheless, to de-merge is extraordinary.

Still, little will change in contemporary Quebec until there is a fundamental cultural shift: from the prevailing liberal-technocratic modernism rhetoric propagated by the current cultural and political elite to a more populist traditionalism. Whether this has begun to take place or not is an intriguing question. Two current issues that will bear watching in this regard are the debate over whether the 'notwithstanding' should be invoked again to permit the continuation of religious classes in schools for those who wish them (it was most recently invoked in 2005); and the continuing controversy in English Canada over definition of marriage issue, which is supposedly a non-issue in Quebec.

Quebec, via its cultural and political elite, presents Quebec as being in favour of same-sex marriage. The rub is that the population was never asked for its opinion; it was rather imposed upon, if not intimidated. If and when the population gets an opportunity to say what it thinks, the results may be surprising for the Quebec liberal technocracy: a populist moral force may manifest its resistance to the expropriation of one of its cherished institutions, marriage and the family, as it has existed throughout the course of French Canadian history.

And the unpredictable vicissitudes of our democratic political process may have presented just such an opportunity for the population of Quebec to express itself on this issue. The Conservative Party of Canada incorporated the maintenance of the traditional definition of marriage into its electoral platform at its founding convention in Montreal in March 2005, and the same party not only emerged victorious in the 2006 federal election but made an unexpectedly strong showing in Quebec.

All of us who recognized in Grant's writings a true diagnostic of our times and fate, and who still hold out hope for a salvation of the original Canadian political project, have, I submit, an interest in the success of de-mergers and the affirmation of the traditional definition of marriage in Quebec. It could be the beginning of a successful resistance which could conceivably – given the right configuration of social and political events – lead to a rehabilitation of Franco-American civilization and, subsequently, new hope for the Canadian political project as construed by Grant. Failing such a successful resistance, what is to be done? At the very least, we can do our best to see that future generations of Canadian students read *Lament for a Nation*. After all, it took a quarter of a century before it became available in French![17]

NOTES

1 George Grant, 'Canadian Fate and Imperialism,' in *Technology and Empire* (Toronto: House of Anansi, 1969), 68.

2 George Grant, *Lament for a Nation* (1965; repr.: Montreal and Kingston: McGill-Queen's University Press, 2000), 38.
3 Ibid., 40. See also the many references to Quebec's dilemma in this regard in William Christian, *George Grant: A Biography* (Toronto: University of Toronto Press, 1993), and William Christian and Sheila Grant, eds., *The George Grant Reader* (Toronto: University of Toronto Press, 1998).
4 Ibid., 91.
5 Interestingly enough, although much of this furniture was salvaged during the 1980s by the urban middle class, it was subsequently ushered out again a decade or so later, after it ceased to be fashionable. Undoubtedly, the 1980s fashion was an ephemeral response to the continental 'colonial furniture' vogue, whereas its subsequent disfavour is a reflection of how thoroughly modernized Quebec has become.
6 Incidentally, the 'asbestos-shingles' siding of the 1940s and 1950s, made from Quebec asbestos, was not popular in the province.
7 In the last few years, American interests have become active in the field of property evaluation for municipal tax purposes.
8 Tubal ligation was so common in the 1980s that women made their personal reproductive status a matter of public knowledge.
9 Since marriage is a federal jurisdiction, this language change in the context of a provincial law on 'civil unions' had no legal significance.
10 I mention these two as they are co-founders of the new Action Démocratique political party.
11 Grant was an admirer of de Gaulle for this very reason.
12 Jacques Parizeau, Lucien Bouchard, and Bernard Landry. Such was not Lévesque's case.
13 Of which there were, in the 1990s, thirteen in Quebec!
14 Claude Lessard, himself professor of education at the Université de Montréal, was one of the few.
15 Marc Chevrier, a contemporary Quebec social critic, sees this change as the consecration of the very demise of Quebec society.
16 As has been the case elsewhere in Canada.
17 It was Jacques-Yvan Morin who was responsible for having it translated. It is also noteworthy that Fernand Dumont and George Grant, contemporaries and comparable figures in their respective philosophical and national settings, never, to my knowledge, actually met. A French version of this article was published in *Egards* 4 (Summer 2004).

3

Was George Grant a Red Tory?

WILLIAM CHRISTIAN

I don't like the term Red Tory ... very much; but, you know, if one goes into the public world, anybody can call you anything, and I think quite rightly. I'm not trying to stop them.

George Grant in Conservation

Canada has not contributed too many terms to political discourse, but 'Red Tory' is one of the most distinctive. Over time, its meaning has changed. Some former members of the Progressive Conservative Party have claimed it to differentiate themselves from the Canadian Alliance supporters with whom they merged to form the modern Conservative Party. Prior to that, it had been a term used mostly by journalists to distinguish certain members of the Progressive Conservative Party who favoured fiscal restraint but who were also sympathetic to the welfare state and progressive social policies. Although they constituted a minority within the party, former leaders Robert Stanfield and Joe Clark were considered Red Tories.

The origin of the term was quite different. In 1966 Gad Horowitz published one of the most influential articles ever to appear in the *Canadian Journal of Political Science*, 'Conservatism, Liberalism and Socialism in Canada: An Interpretation.' Horowitz's article attempted to address the reasons for the different ideological structures in the United States and Canada. The United States was almost a purely liberal society. The differences arose, in part, he suggested, because Canada possessed a 'tory touch' that it inherited from the United Kingdom. Toryism, as an ideology, contained an element of collectivism, as did socialism. There was a point of contact between the collectivist Tory and the collectivist socialist.

Horowitz, somewhat unhelpfully, offers different definitions of the term 'Red Tory.' At the simplest level, he says, a Red Tory is a Conservative who prefers the New Democratic Party (NDP) – or its precursor, the Cooperative Commonwealth Federation (CCF) – to the Liberals, or a socialist who prefers the Conservatives to the Liberals, without really knowing why. There are certainly people like this, but I don't think that they are of much interest in this context. People vote tactically, as, we will see, Grant himself did in the 1963 federal general election. At other times, voters use political parties to make general protests against the system in general and the ruling party in particular. That was the case for many who voted NDP but switched to the Reform Party after the NDP appeared to join the political establishment when it supported the Charlottetown Accord of 1992.

Next, Horowitz points to three individuals whom he describes as Red Tories. The first is a conscious ideological Conservative with some 'odd' socialist notions, the historian W.L. Morton; the second is a conscious ideological socialist with some 'odd' Tory notions, the constitutional scholar and labour historian Eugene Forsey;[1] and the third is the philosopher George Grant,[2] with whom he had been fairly intensely, but briefly, involved in a television series shortly before writing his article.

This chapter will address two questions. The first question is less important, but it is still interesting and has never been explored in detail. Just what were George Grant's politics and did he, as Horowitz says a Red Tory should do, move from the CCF/NDP to the Conservatives or vice versa out of a basic dislike for Liberal individualism? The second and more important question is Horowitz's suggestion that Grant's Red Toryism was a unique synthesis of socialism and Toryism so thorough that it constituted a singular, and probably uniquely Canadian, philosophic vision. 'Such a red tory is George Grant, who has associations with both the Conservative party and the NDP and who has published a book which defends Diefenbaker, laments the death of "true" British conservatism in Canada, attacks the Liberals as individualists and Americanizers and defines socialism as a variant of conservatism (each "protects the public good against private freedom").'[3]

I will argue that Grant's political preferences were so heterogeneous that he certainly does not qualify as a Red Tory in the first sense and that Horowitz is basically wrong to say that *Lament for a Nation* defends Diefenbaker. In terms of Horowitz's characterization of Grant's political position, I will suggest that he, like most others, completely misunderstands Grant. First, for Grant, the heavenly, not the earthly city, is primary: politics takes place within the context of eternity. Secondly, human life is sacred: pacifism is required in the face of war. Abortion is also an unacceptable evil. Thirdly, human souls are equal before God. Some inequality is inevitable in all societies, but extremes of wealth are unacceptable, as are extremes of power. Concentrations of power such as big business and the Roman Catholic Church need to be opposed.

Was Horowitz correct to describe Grant as a Red Tory during the period he knew him? Is this term accurate in describing the trajectory of Grant's political life from his teenage years to his death in 1988? I will argue that George Grant was not a Red Tory, in either of the senses that Horowitz uses the word.

CHILDHOOD

George Grant came from a political family. Both his grandfathers were active in the imperial federation movement; indeed, his maternal grandfather, George Parkin (knighted in 1920, towards the end of his life) was one of its leading spokesmen. They wanted the British Empire to remain a strong and cohesive military and economic unit and they believed that British values represented a high achievement in the history of civilization that Canada should strive to preserve and advance. They could both be described as tories. Both were educators as well. G.M. Grant was the great principal of Queen's University. George Parkin was principal of Upper Canada College (UCC), a private boys' school in Toronto, and later founding secretary of the Rhodes scholarships. William Grant, George's father, was also principal of UCC.

Politically, Grant was a precocious child and he showed evidence of a social conscience at quite an early age.[4] William Grant was wounded in the Great War, and George believed that the spiritual damage was greater than the physical. When one of UCC's Old Boys donated twenty-five copies of Beverley Nichol's pacifist tract *Cry Havoc* (1933) to the school, Grant was deeply moved. It changed his life. He participated in anti-war protests in Toronto with some of his UCC schoolmates. After this, pacifism increasingly became central to his political vision. In an undated poem (but written about this time) he connected it with his religious thought.

Peace

Its echoing and far echoing sounds
Reach over earth to where on heaven's throne
Almighty God sits in his pomp alone

And when he sees he smiles
And when on his smile comes life
Which is our hope and our salvation.[5]

Although trust in the eternal was the essence of Grant's thought, there were many tactical twists and turns along the way. Politically, at sixteen, Grant was a Liberal, indeed head of the Liberal Committee at UCC for the 1935 election. He came by this political heritage honestly. Although Grant's father was not involved in partisan politics (Grant later speculated that he sympathized with the CCF), his uncle, Vincent Massey, certainly was: in 1930 he became president of the Liberal Party to help it rebuild following its defeat at the hands of R.B. Bennett's Conservatives in the federal election of that year. When Massey and Liberal leader Mackenzie King had to meet in Toronto, they often did so at William Grant's residence at UCC. It was not unusual for George Grant to bump into the former (and future) prime minister in his living room. With these connections, it is not surprising that he backed the Liberals. He even chided his mother for her lack of partisan enthusiasm in the 1935 general election. 'I am ashamed that you have not stayed in Canada to cast a vote for freedom and good government.'[6]

One of the principles that runs through Grant's whole life was a distaste for big business and a fear of its malign influence in social and political affairs. Where it came from is impossible to say. It is possible that he absorbed it from his father over the dinner table, since it was present even in his youthful comments. 'The Conservatives will get in at School,' he wrote in a 1935 letter, 'because most of the boys' fathers are small industrialists.'[7] It surfaced again during his student years at Queen's. When Sir Edward Beatty, head of the Canadian Pacific Railway, came to receive an honorary degree, Grant was outraged. 'The unity of Big Business certainly degraded Grant Hall as it has never been degraded before. It was abysmal. Cleverly covered up[,] the subject, really, was "We have the money and if you university professors don't do and say what we want, out you get."'[8]

His general sympathies could, at this time, be described as left-leaning. He despised Quebec's Union Nationale leader, Maurice Duplessis, and supported his Liberal rival, J.-A. Godbout.[9] Internationally, he supported the Republicans (he called them 'the socialists') in the Spanish Civil War.[10] The pope's role in the war, which Grant saw as lending support to Mussolini and Franco, encouraged his growing anti-Catholic feelings. 'Franco keeps on advancing with the Catholic Church right behind him.'[11] While at Queen's, Grant paid relatively little attention to domestic Canadian politics. He was active in the International Relations Club, and foreign affairs attracted most of his attention. The possible link between his hostility to big business and the Roman Catholic Church is that they both represented oppressive concentrations of power that threatened the basic equality of human beings.

By now, however, the determining element of his political thinking was, and would remain, except for a brief period in the later 1940s and very early 1950s, his religious pacifism. Early in 1939, he came to the conclusion that the sincere Christian could not fight in a war. Christ, he wrote to his mother, had possessed the temporal power to dominate Jerusalem. He chose not to use it, because such a victory would be only temporary. A spiritual change was necessary, what Grant called 'the permanent protest of non-resistance.' Therefore, he concluded, if 'one is a Christian, one cannot fight.' In the secular world, matters were different. States would continue to behave as states and most individuals would support them. 'Of course, again if you say that Christ was not divine, then the whole argument is broken through.'[12]

THE SECOND WORLD WAR

After considerable soul-searching, Grant decided to take up his Rhodes scholarship and study in Oxford, in spite of the war. He watched the war spread to Norway and Denmark, and then to Finland. When the Germans crushed the Netherlands, he observed that England was 'no longer fighting for liberty, but for her life.'[13] He admired the Dunkirk retreat as the kind of physical bravery he most admired, quiet defeat,[14] but when France fell he was devastated. It was, he wrote, 'hate's most gruesome orgy.'[15]

In the middle of July 1940, his attention was drawn to the United States and Franklin Roosevelt's bid for re-election. Oddly, perhaps, his interest was not primarily in America's foreign policy, as one might have expected under the circumstances. He was most concerned with the impact that a victory by Roosevelt's Republican opponent might have on the accomplishments of the New Deal. Wendell Wilkie, he worried, was likely to limit the Tennessee Valley Authority, reduce the influence of the Securities Exchange Commission, and curtail the Wagner Act, which provided limited regulation to labour relations. 'It seems obvious that Big Business will put all their weight behind their last throw, but I feel the States have enough sense to re-elect Roosevelt.'[16] He greeted Roosevelt's victory with great enthusiasm. 'Yes my darling Roosevelt's was a great victory. Yes all the powers of undemocratic background – economic mainly – were arrayed against him, but he won.'[17] However, Grant objected to the United States selling arms to Britain, and he hoped that it would stay out of the war. He was worried that Anglo-American capitalism was driving the movement for American involvement.[18]

The German invasion of Russia changed the balance of power, not just in military terms but also in intellectual ones. 'One thing that the Russians seem to have placed clearly before the world is the fact that our standards have little validity for them. I guess if we had read Tolstoy and Dostoevsky more carefully, we wouldn't have been so at sea. Their success will give them power at the conference table & their heroism is giving them a real hold over the public opinion of this country.'[19] However, the attack on Pearl Harbor and the subsequent U.S. entry into the war sent Grant into almost suicidal despair. More than 130 million Americans had been taken further from the face of God. In secular terms, though, the likelihood of an Anglo-Saxon world civilization had drawn closer.[20] The future of the world lay in the cooperative governance of the United States and Great Britain. The League of Nations had failed; the Germans were attempting to impose their vision of a new world order. 'Anyway, I prefer to have England and the USA govern the world than Germany, as long as they do it passably, do not ask too high a price, and do not ask me to govern or help enforce that government when the war is over.'[21]

Early in 1942 Grant returned to Canada. His experience of the war ended with a bout of tuberculosis, and for the next year he was assiduously tended by his mother. While lying in bed, he had plenty of time to reflect on the world's future. England, he decided, would become more collectivist, though the United States and Canada would incline towards a more free-enterprise economy. It was nonetheless in Canada's interest to maintain a close relationship with the United Kingdom because of the 'the very practical, if intangible advantages of a North American country freely keeping in close cooperation & friendship with a country on another continent.'[22] What could be expected of Mackenzie King's regime? It was, Grant thought, a government 'mightily attacked at the time of its being' but one of great prudence, not the ideally best but the best possible.[23] In general, though, he found the Liberals dull, and M.J. Coldwell, the CCF leader, the best of the parliamentarians.[24] He regretted that David Lewis, a labour lawyer and CCF organizer, was defeated in a by-election in Montreal. 'CCF in Ontario particularly good for it came from (1) middle class urban (2) mining – definitely not from the farms. I am sick of grass roots glory.'[25]

For the last year and a half of the war, Grant's political involvement largely took the form of social activism. He was national secretary of the Citizens Forum. The Forum was an attempt, through radio, to persuade Canadians to think about the post-war needs of the country. Grant was also a tangential member of the Canadian Civil Liberties Union and an active participant in the social and architectural experiment led by a friend of his mother, Humphrey Carver, an architect. The outcome was the Regent Park housing development, an early attempt to provide affordable housing for Toronto's poor.

After the war, Grant returned to Oxford. He switched his field of study from law to theology, but the change did not prevent him from continuing a keen interest in politics. He was distressed by the harsh attitude that the United States was taking towards Germany after its defeat. President Harry Truman had fallen into 'the hands of the worst type of capitalist.' Great Britain was better; he liked the new labour government. '[Stafford] Cripps [president of the Board of Trade] is great,' he wrote to his friend, social worker Alice Boissoneau, 'and [Ernest] Bevin [foreign secretary] goes on from strength to strength.'[26]

The next year, as Churchill toured the United Nations and gave his celebrated 'Iron Curtain' speech, Grant became more and more worried. The British Conservatives, he thought, seemed determined to turn the country into a satellite of the United States, while in the United States itself he feared that American capitalism was forging an alliance with the 'sinister real politik of the Vatican against totalitarian USSR.' If it ever came to a conflict, the choice would be hard, 'but on the whole the USSR.'[27] Grant thought British foreign policy should attempt a rapprochement between Russia and the United Kingdom, though Russian diplomatic tactics seemed to be driving the United Kingdom into the arms of the United States.[28]

Grant was worried that war would erupt between the two Cold War superpowers, but he knew what he had to do. Pursue peace as the primary goal, but if peace were not possible, Grant's choice was clear. Pacifism trumped all other alternatives for him. 'I know categorically that, in any war between the USA and Russia, the Christian must just not take part. The revoltingness of the Roman Church in the USA putting Jesus on their banner against Communism, without attempting to understand the no doubt wrong, but great hope of communism. Jesus didn't try and misunderstand people who disagreed with them, but understand. This sounds rather sloppy liberalism but I mean it at the depth of love. The people who try and condemn the USSR without attempting to see its qualities and its grave failings are so cruel.'[29]

GRANT'S AUGUSTINIANISM

Grant's position is more or less consistent, if you take the heart of it to be the goals of preventing war and limiting the power of concentrations of power, indifferently seen as American capitalism, Soviet communism, or Roman Catholicism. At a higher level, tying together Grant's position was the influence of St Augustine, whose thought he understood through the filter of Charles Cochrane's masterpiece, *Christianity and Classical Culture* (1940), which he described as 'the most pertinent writing on the modern world I have ever read.'[30] Cochrane understood Augustine as a foundational figure of Western civilization. One of his key images was the contrast between the city of God and the city of man. Human beings were born into secular political units, and force was a primary determinant of relations within states and, even more, in conflicts between states. However, the Christian had a choice. He or she could decide to become a citizen of the city of God. This city had no terrestrial existence, but it was nonetheless real. Ultimately, if there were a serious clash between moral and political claims, the Christian had to follow Christ. Each world was driven by its own imperatives: the one by force, the other by love. 'I am not a Tory, but I see less & less logic in any position that is not either Tory or Christian pacifist. It is the liberal progressives & general puttlers in between that give one the cramp.'[31] Tories accepted the world of force without regret and happily lived in the city of man. Christian pacifists chose the heavenly city as their habitation. Liberal progressives did not understand that salvation was not possible in this world, but they tried to achieve it anyway, often with disastrous consequences.

The contrast between these two worlds was clear in Grant's reaction to Gandhi's assassination. He saw Gandhi as a spiritual figure, whose political disobedience spoke to the reality of human existence. Politicians like Nehru were mistaken, Grant believed, to regard it merely as a political tool, a successful instance of the use of power. He applied the same insight to Canada. The CCF, especially its pacifist leader J.S. Woodsworth, lived the moral life they preached and were inspired by the hope of secular redemption. The Conservatives, from this Augustinian view, were equally admirable. They were 'always fair straight and honest that civilization was only maintained by the bayonet and rightly.' It was the Liberals, like Mackenzie King, he now believed, who were tragically confused. They had once believed in the possibility of isolationist humanitarian nationalism but their belief that this way of life was possible was foolish and misguided. Now they were forced by their American alliance to 'prepare for atom warfare to spread the civilization of Hollywood.'[32]

Grant approved of Truman's victory in the 1948 election because, on the whole, 'farmers, labour and housewives seem to me better people than the American business community.'[33] He even found himself 'strangely attracted' to Mackenzie King's successor, Louis St Laurent. He was somewhat amused that he would come close to what he called 'Gritdom,' but he also hoped that the Conservatives would do well in the 1949 election, since an uncle, Jim Macdonnell, was prominent in the party.

In 1950 Grant returned to England to complete his doctorate. In the British general election, he declared himself '100% for Labour.' The upper-middle class, which had been such a driving force over the past fifty years, had shown themselves unfit. 'The new up and coming lower middle class seem to have so much more vigour than the old soft one. But it's mainly the sheer crudity of the Tory appeal, promises they can't possibly expect to keep, makes me such a rip-roaring Labourite, far, far more than I would be CCF in Canada.'[34]

When the Korean War broke out in 1950, Grant had decided that he could not participate in any way, whatever the personal consequences. The best hope for peace was that, after he took office in 1953, President Dwight Eisenhower and his secretary of state, John Foster Dulles, would put their country above their party. 'We can know nothing of what is happening and just must trust that the American government is seeing us through.' This was a time for Canada to stand side by side with the United States. 'I can't make out at all what a fellow like Pearson is doing – but I presume that the Grit party having spent two generations to tie us up to the USA is not backing out just at the moment when we should be close to the USA.'[35] Even a denizen of the heavenly city found himself constantly drawn to the events of the earthly one.

When the American presidential election arrived in 1952, Grant temporarily gave up on the Democrats because, in his view, Truman had sold out to the unions in the steel strike. Grant had, he said, become a fervid Republican.[36] He wanted Eisenhower to win because it was time for a change and, if the Republicans didn't gain power with someone who was fundamentally decent like Eisenhower, they might get someone beholden to the 'money bags' instead.[37] However, by 1956, Grant had changed his mind about Eisenhower, who had sold himself to 'the public relations boys and the general platitude gang.' Grant hoped against hope that Adlai Stevenson would defeat him.[38]

JOHN DIEFENBAKER AND LAMENT FOR A NATION

The Canadian general election of 1957, which brought the Conservatives to power after a twenty-two year absence, filled Grant, he said, with joy. We have to be careful here, though, since there is no indication that Grant was a Diefenbaker partisan before that election. He had a couple of good reasons for welcoming the victory. In the first place, he had watched the decline of Great Britain, often at first hand, and the assumption of leadership of the English-speaking peoples by the Americans. Except for the immediate post-war period, he thought the American empire, on balance, superior to the Russian, but the British had, in its day, been better than both. However, he knew that British world leadership was now gone, and the Liberals, led to a great extent by Lester Pearson as secretary of state for external affairs, had drawn Canada step by step closer to the United States in policy and, more seriously, in spirit as well. Grant did not like what he described as the Liberal attitude: 'the desire to be left alone to make money combined with general piety is not very impressive.'[39]

Grant also had personal reasons for welcoming Diefenbaker's victory. His uncle, Jim Macdonnell, had devoted more than twenty years of his life to the Conservative Party, in some people's view saving it from extinction in the early 1940s. Although Grant had had his differences with his uncle when he was younger over what Grant considered Macdonnell's closeness to business, he was happy that the old man finally got a place at the cabinet table. Ironically, Diefenbaker, who also thought Macdonnell represented central Canadian business interests, appointed him only with reservations and got rid of him as quickly as possible.[40]

Another connection was more important. Derek Bedson served briefly as what would now be called Diefenbaker's chief of staff (private secretary was the contemporary title). Grant and Bedson had become very close friends at Oxford. He admired Bedson's intelligence, but, perhaps more so, he deeply respected Bedson's Christian view of politics. As he wrote just after the Diefenbaker landslide of 1958:

'If ever there was a need of spiritual conservatism (I do not mean economic) it is now and you have it. I thought of what Milton wrote about Abdiel who was not moved by Satan:

'Among the innumerable false, unmoved.
Unshaken, unseduced, unterrified.'

The people of character count so much in times of success. I am therefore so glad you are there.[41]

So it is essential to remember two points. The first is that Grant's attitude to the Diefenbaker government was, from the beginning, coloured by the fact that a relative and a close friend were part of the new administration. Secondly, Grant expressed his admiration, not for Diefenbaker or his policies, but for what he called Bedson's spiritual conservatism, a quality that he never imagined Diefenbaker to possess. When Bedson left in 1958 to work with Duff Roblin, the Conservative premier of Manitoba, this emotional connection with the federal Conservative government was broken.

In the 1958 Diefenbaker landslide, the CCF was almost eliminated from parliament. It then took the difficult decision to disband and refashion itself as a new progressive party with greater trade-union support, a goal that was achieved with the formation of the NDP in 1961. In 1960 Grant was part of group of intellectuals invited to contribute essays to *Social Purpose for Canada*, a work that was meant to serve for the new party what *Social Planning for Canada* had done for the CCF – give it a solid intellectual foundation. Grant's contribution concerned itself with the issue of equality,[42] and his Augustinianism permeated its principal conclusion. The only equality that really mattered was the equality of souls before God and political, social, or economic equality had to be built on that foundation. The basis of equality is 'essentially religious.' 'Such a foundation will seem to the unbeliever too limited a basis for social principle. It must be insisted, however, that the idea of equality arose in the West within a particular set of religious and philosophical ideas. I cannot see why men should go on believing in the principle without some sharing of those ideas.'[43] The new party, by contrast, was secular. Grant knew this and criticized it. Though many men and woman have believed in equality outside the religious tradition, Grant thought they were wrong. 'The question is rather whether they have been thinking clearly when they so believed. This religious basis for equality seems to me the only adequate one, because I cannot see why one should embark on the immensely difficult social practice of treating each person as important unless there is something intrinsically valuable about each personality. And what is intrinsically valuable about all persons except their freedom as moral agents?'[44] Still, there was a congruence between the new party's political aims and Grant's spiritual ones. Grant did not know how long this relationship would last, but he knew that it was unlikely to prove enduring. He had little reason to suspect how short his connection would be, but he was genuinely happy when his Aunt Louise went to the founding convention of the New Democratic Party in 1961 and he regretted that he was not able to accompany her.

When Diefenbaker called an election for 1962, Grant hoped that the NDP would have a solid representation. If so, it could act as 'a solid restraint on capitalism.' Though he was invited to stand as a candidate, he easily turned the offer down 'for it seemed as my job is to be a theologian.'[45] In both his vision of society and his understanding of his personal role, faith was primary. Yet, even if he was not a candidate, he did undertake the 'pitiable and boring' task of serving as a constituency agent.

If hostility to capitalism was one aspect of Grant's politics, fear of Canada's absorption by the United States ran a close second. He worried in a letter to Bedson that the Liberals thought they had a divine right to run Canada. 'If they get in they plan to sell us to the USA lock stock and barrel.'[46] Both he and Eugene Forsey feared the consequences of a Liberal victory, but they had little enthusiasm for the Conservative alternative. 'You would have been amused to hear Forsey and I talking the other day. Two socialists whose main political interest was that the Conservatives hold off the Liberal threat. As I know you know, I wish the Conservatives (federally) were wiser in their relations with the academic community.'[47]

In late 1962 and early 1963 the Diefenbaker government faced a defence crisis that soon destroyed the government. Two issues were salient. During the Cuban Missile Crisis, the Kennedy administration considered it possible that the Soviet Union would launch a manned bomber strike against the United States. They put their own air force on a high level of readiness and asked Canada to do the same. Diefenbaker resisted, in part out of anger that President Kennedy had not consulted him more fully and earlier about American intentions towards Cuba. But, without Diefenbaker's knowledge, his defence minister, Douglas Harkness, did what the Americans had required.

The second issue was more complicated. Diefenbaker's government had agreed to allow Bomarc missiles on Canada soil. These missiles were meant to intercept and neutralize Soviet nuclear bombers as they were passing Canadian airspace en route to attack the United States. In order to be effective, the weapons required nuclear warheads. Canada had the missiles, but they were useless without the payload. The Americans were becoming more insistent that the Canadian government live up to its agreement, and many of Diefenbaker's cabinet colleagues agreed with them. If the United States could not get its way with the Conservative government, it was prepared to assist a 'regime change' to bring in the more accommodating Liberals.

The Conservative government disintegrated as the opposition parties acted in concert to defeat the minority government on a vote of confidence. Grant telephoned NDP leader T.C. Douglas to persuade him not to defeat the government, but failed. Grant thought the NDP's behaviour reprehensible and immediately thought of resigning from the party. There were two separate issues involved. The first was Canadian independence. 'Whatever Dief's failings, he has in the clinch spoken for Canada.' Canadian independence, though, was not the primary issue and Diefenbaker certainly was not the main hero. Nuclear weapons reinforced Grant's long-standing pacifism; such instruments were 'intrinsically wicked for the Christian.' In his mind, Howard Green, the secretary of state for external affairs, was the real hero of the crisis. He not only understood what was at stake but was prepared to take on Grant's consistent enemy, big business. 'Green has deeply cared for the most important political cause of all – disarmament – and has been willing to risk the wrath of big business on this issue.'[48]

An old friend of Grant's, the novelist Hugh MacLennan, commented to Grant that the first chapter of Lament for a Nation appeared to champion Dief 'in the eyes of people who don't read carefully.' Diefenbaker was, MacLennan agreed with Grant, 'a fraud and a paranoic.'[49] Grant made a similar point on a CBC radio program. After blaming C.D. Howe for undermining the basis of Canadian nationhood, he turned to Diefenbaker. 'My book is not a defence of Mr Diefenbaker. There is a whole chapter saying that he had no constructive nationalist legislation when he was in ... Before the Defence Crisis I saw nothing in his favour, just nothing. I thought he had a very poor regime. If that wasn't implied in the book, then I must write very unclearly. Over the Defence Crisis, I see the hero of this book as Mr Green, not as Mr Diefenbaker.'[50]

However, for all his failings, Diefenbaker was the only game in town. Grant now absolutely rejected the NDP, regretted that he had ever written anything in support of it, and declared himself 'an unequivocal anti-progressive.' Although he intended to vote Progressive Conservative even after Diefenbaker's departure, he would not do so with much enthusiasm. For him, Canadian politics came down to one thing only – nationalism,[51] and nationalism meant opposition to big business. 'No small country can depend for it existence on the loyalty of its capitalists. International interests may require the sacrifice of the lesser loyalty of patriotism. Only in dominant nations is the loyalty of capitalists ensured.'[52]

When Diefenbaker died in 1979, Grant wrote an assessment of his career for the *Globe and Mail*.[53] This article probably confirmed most reader's belief in Grant's Diefophilia. He criticized Diefenbaker's antediluvian rhetoric, the egocentricity that transcended his principles, and his messianism without content, and he also noted that Diefenbaker's choice of French Canadian colleagues was so appalling that he seemed ignorant of what Grant called the first principle of Canadian politics, that no party can rule Canada for long without solid support in Quebec. On the positive side, he praised the populism that allowed Diefenbaker to have meaningful contact with the common people, his love of the British tradition of the primacy and nobility of law, and, most important, his rooted nationalism, which assumed that Canada was our country in a way that the United States was not. For Grant, though, these qualities, however noble in the city of man, would not suffice for the city of God. 'The virtues necessary for political life are not altogether the same as those necessary for the contemplative life. The latter require that one be open to everything, and this includes putting everything in question ... Diefenbaker's strength was that his fundamental principles were loyalties which he did not put in question ... People therefore knew where they stood with him and loved him for it.' But Diefenbaker's strength was the mirror of his weakness. He lived his principles but did not think them. He lived, though not completely, within 'that oblivion of eternity which now defines the West.'

So Grant had no high expectation of Diefenbaker when he came into office and he was not surprised when the government collapsed. His concerns with the Liberals were that they were too close to big business and his worry was that big business was selling the country to bigger

American business. With the nuclear crisis, his pacifism trumped all his other concerns. Even a limited Canadian independence might prevent Canada from possessing nuclear weapons. Compared with this issue, the social democracy of the NDP was nothing.

GRANT'S LATER POLITICAL THOUGHT

In the middle and late 1960s Grant was deeply involved in protests against the Vietnam War. His concerns were summed up briefly in a letter he wrote to the historian Kenneth McNaught in 1966: 'For whatever motives, it seems to me that the USA has got into a position where it is massacring masses of Vietnamese. Canada is more and more implicated in this, and the thought of us being implicated in a long and growing war between Asia and North America is too terrible to contemplate.'[54] Though civil disobedience was popular in the United States as a method of protest, Grant utterly rejected it in Canada. The Canadian government was not directly responsible for the evil war in Vietnam, and it was still open to reasoned persuasion.[55] Although Grant and the student radicals agreed in their opposition to the war and their objection to any Canadian involvement and support, Grant's opposition came from a conservative nationalist position and theirs from a leftist one. Although Grant deeply sympathized with the left, its position was not his. His Christian pacifism was miles away from the ideas that drove most of them.

After about 1970, Grant's enthusiasm for politics declined. When the Conservatives forced Diefenbaker from the leadership of the party in 1967, Grant expressed no regret. On the contrary, he wanted a new leader who was acceptable both to central Canada and to the west, someone who could force the Liberals to choose a replacement for Pearson. Grant had a long history with Pearson dating back at least to the Second World War and it would be fair, I think, to say that his attitude progressed from dislike to disgust to genuine loathing after the nuclear-arms crisis. The man to accomplish Pearson's removal was Duff Roblin of Manitoba. 'All his speeches and actions show him an intelligent and sane nationalist,' he wrote in the *Hamilton Spectator*.[56] It is not clear how much Grant really knew about Roblin, though his public reason for supporting him, his purported nationalism, is typical. Derek Bedson had left Diefenbaker's office in 1958 and, for the past decade, had worked as Roblin's principal adviser. Grant's friendship for Bedson was so great that alone it could explain Grant's public pronouncements on Roblin's behalf. Stanfield he dismissed as a 'rather ungenerous Whig of extremely limited horizon.' As for Trudeau, he distrusted his hostility to traditional French Canadian society and his naivety about English Canada. Nonetheless, he pronounced him 'a gentlemanly kind of person.'[57]

Grant continued to support the Conservatives in the 1972 federal election, but unenthusiastically. Although he thought that the Liberals had done better on French-English relations, he still preferred the Conservatives for their nationalism. 'Canada is a bourgeois country and nationalism has only hope if some of the bourgeois are with it and I trust the bourgeois in the PC party better than I trust the Liberals when they come to dealing with the US.'[58] If anything, this meant that small business supported the Conservatives while big business gave their support to the Liberals.

The next election came two years later. By this time, Grant had elevated his dislike of Trudeau to near Pearsonian levels. Southern Ontario, especially Toronto, was totally Americanized and there was little support for independence, whether traditional or radical. As for the Liberal leader: 'Trudeau is a kind of Canadian Kennedy – a shallow politician who makes people think this vulgar society has a slick patina to it.'[59]

Grant's assessment of Trudeau changed little over the next five years. He had happy memories of the time he spent in Quebec as a teenager; he respected Quebec's traditional culture and wanted it to survive. Trudeau, he said, had one unifying principle to his political career, 'bringing the French-Canadian people fully into the mainstream of North American life. This desire to homogenize made him truly a modern liberal. He had no sympathy for the powerful desire of some sections of Québécois to continue to exist as a people.' Trudeau was a cosmopolitan who was opposed to the parochial and did not understand, as nationalists did, 'that all human beings have a need for roots.' Cosmopolitanism threatened more than the survival of French Canada. 'Since 1918 cosmopolitanism has come to mean in the western world Americanism. Canadians, more than any other people, lived intimately with that modern cosmopolitanism. We therefore had to transcend that principle if we were going to continue to exist.'[60]

After the *Roe v. Wade* decision of the American Supreme Court in 1974, Grant and his wife, Sheila, became active in the Right to Life movement. Although Grant never linked his pro-Life position to his Christian pacifism, a common principle unites the two: a belief that it is morally unacceptable to take a human life. Grant sincerely believed, on religious and philosophical grounds, that the foetus was a human being. Thus, when in 1983 a *Globe and Mail* article linked him with the NDP, he was outraged. 'The NDP are absolutely out for me because of abortion, apart from my long time dislike of their utopian politics.'[61] However, when a small group of pro-life NDPers approached him in 1988, he encouraged them. 'I so dislike the exaltation of greed (in the name of liberty) which is so widespread in the English-speaking world that I would be glad to vote for a non-capitalist party.'[62]

Although he welcomed Brian Mulroney as the new Progressive Conservative leader and his landslide victory in the 1984 general election, he had low expectations. He did not expect the new government to address the politically controversial issue of abortion. 'Otherwise Mulroney just carries on the state capitalist machine in the way one would expect.'[63] 'I know the Tory party I cared about is largely gone – but I do not find Mulroney nearly as bad as all the old Liberal bagmen make out.'[64] Even when the Mulroney government raised the issue of free trade in 1986, Grant's initial response was neutral. He said he had no reason to be against the government and 'like some of the things they do.'[65]

Yet, by 1988, he had become hostile. He regretted that all parties seemed to have purged their nationalists, while the NDP were out of the question because of their stance on abortion. 'I find that abortion quite transcends any issue but nuclear disarmament.'[66] He was considering voting Liberal. As he wrote in a book review: 'Fata volentem ducunt, nolentem trahunt [fate leads the willing and drags the unwilling]. What is great about this book is that its writers are splendidly stating their unwillingness to be dragged. It is surely a nobler stance to go down with all flags flying (even our present Canadian one) and all guns blazing than to be acquiescently led, whether sadly or gladly, into the even greater homogenizing of our country into the American mass.'[67]

WAS GEORGE GRANT A RED TORY?

In 1967 Grant was asked if he were a Red Tory. He replied: 'The epithet "red tory" can only be used if you look at the practical part of my book [*Lament*] and not at the philosophical. [Gad] Horowitz was only concerned with the practical. I think philosophers are more likely to have sympathy with conservatives than with liberals, but, as I say in my book, modern conservatism comes out of modern assumptions as much as modern liberalism. Much of this labelling arises because peo-

ple cannot distinguish any longer between ideology and philosophy.
Ideology is the permitted form that philosophy often takes in this era.'[68]

How, then, do we evaluate the five grounds that Horowitz advanced
for considering Grant a Red Tory? These grounds were:

1 he had associations with both the Conservative Party and the NDP;
2 he published a book defending Diefenbaker;
3 he lamented the death of 'true' British conservatism in Canada;
4 he attacked the Liberals as individualists and Americanizers; and
5 he defined socialism as a variant of conservatism (each 'protects the
  public good against private freedom').

Grant followed politics closely for more than half a century. He knew
the score, as he liked to say about others. The score was that, for the
most part, social-democratic parties received a failing grade because
their belief in equality lacked grounding. They did not know that souls
were equal before God, and so they could support abortion. They did
not know that peace was, above all other things, important (although
J.S. Wordsworth had – he was the only MP to vote against Canada's
entry into the Second World War), so they brought down the Diefenbaker government on the nuclear-arms issue.

You could respect people who knew the score. Large concentrations of
power were a danger, and you supported anyone who could oppose
them, as long as they were not going to do it violently. You could even
grudgingly respect the Liberals: they were doing a good job selling out
the country to the Americans and it was a job that needed to be done.
You could sort of respect John Diefenbaker. He knew that the Liberals
had to be stopped – he felt it in his gut – but ultimately he did not know
how. When it came right down to it, he didn't really know the score at all.

Was Grant a Red Tory? At some point, he supported every major
party in the United States, the United Kingdom, and Canada. He published a book which said that John Diefenbaker's government had
largely been a failure, though he had enjoyed one truly glorious
moment, which was also a failure and which, in any case, was more
Howard Green's moment then Diefenbaker's. It is true that he lamented
the death of 'true' British conservatism, but he does not, at that point,
think that it made any difference. Dead is dead. Churchill handed over
the leadership of the English-speaking world to Roosevelt after the Second World War, because the British Empire was no longer up to the task.
Now there was a Conservative who really knew the score.

As for Grant's defence of 'true' British conservatism, this means, I think, two things. First, Grant genuinely did regret the passing of a vision of public life that he associated with his parents and his grandfathers. He did not think that it was true or good in any ultimate sense, but it was something that had meant a great deal to his family. It was also a civilized way of life and it was a pity to see it go, but gone it was. 'I lament it as a celebration of memory; in this case, the memory of that tenuous hope that was the principle of my ancestors.'[69] Second, this kind of conservatism was different from American conservatism. The views of Barry Goldwater, Grant contended, were a species of liberalism and had nothing to do with the British tradition that prevailed in Canada. Grant wanted to keep these views out the Canadian Progressive Conservative Party for a long as possible. He did not think that it was possible to keep them out forever. In this regard, we might label Grant a Tory, but only a nostalgic one. He did not intend it as a relevant contemporary political stance.

To attack the Liberals as individualists would be like condemning a cat for having a tail. Individualism is an essential characteristic of liberalism. As for them being Americanizers, they probably were. Grant had ambivalent feelings towards the United States, but, for most of his life, he was favourable. He opposed Kennedy on nuclear weapons and Johnson on the Vietnam War, but he seemed reasonably well disposed to most other American presidents on which we know his views. He did object when the United States took active steps to deprive Canada of its independence, and he said that he preferred a limited sovereignty to none. He also thought that Canada's eventual absorption by the United States was inevitable, though guns blazing and flags flying was always his preferred option to silent surrender.

As for socialism being a variant of conservatism, I do not think that this is what Grant meant. Both socialism and traditional (Tory) conservatism share in common the belief that it is necessary to use government 'to restrain greed in the name of social good.'[70] For Grant, socialism's failing was that, in the short run, it posed an unacceptable restraint on freedom to achieve this end. However, this comparison of socialism and conservatism has some validity. Grant had an enduring hostility to big business for its social, economic, and political influence. His 1935 letter complained that the fathers of the boys who intend to vote Conservative were industrialists. In *Lament*, Canada's most prominent industrialist, E.P. Taylor, was the object of his scorn. Part of Diefenbaker's nobility was that he had been patronized by the wealthy and the clever.[71] As for Brian Mulroney, he just carried 'on the state capitalist machine in the way one would expect.'[72]

It did not particularly matter to Grant which political party he supported; he had no particular loyalty to any. It was a matter of calculation, and circumstances vary. Tories and socialists can sometimes find themselves in alliance, although they may have nothing more in common than an enemy.

Towards the end of his life, when CBC interviewer David Cayley asked Grant if he would acknowledge himself a Red Tory, he replied: 'No, it's not a term I like very much ... what the term points to about me is my great resentment of the identification of the word *conservative* with the right of individuals, of private individuals to make money any way they want.'[73]

NOTES

1 Gad Horowitz, 'Conservatism, Liberalism and Socialism in Canada: An Interpretation,' in Hugh Thorburn, ed., *Party Politics in Canada*, 7th ed. (Scarborough, Ont.: Prentice Hall Canada, 1996), 154. For Horowitz, one of the Tory elements of Forsey's thought may have been his passionate concern for the conventions of parliamentary and democratic governance. He was a great admirer of that staunch Tory Arthur Meighen, and his book *The Royal Power of Dissolution in the British Commonwealth* remains the standard study of the reserve powers of the crown. However, other CCFers and NDPers, such as Stanley Knowles and Bill Blaikie, are just as committed to parliament, its spirit, and its rules. Without observance of parliamentary rules, how is a small party like the CCF or the NDP to protect itself from the governing majority?

The more abiding concern of Forsey's career, though, was the necessity of strong central government. Within a few weeks of its founding, he resigned from the NDP because he considered its decentralizing position with regard to Quebec fatal to national unity. He accepted Pierre Trudeau's offer of a seat in the Senate in 1970 because he knew that Trudeau was profoundly committed to a vision of Canada in which Ottawa took the lead. Was Forsey, then, on Horowitz's definition, a Red Tory? The answer would appear to be no. Forsey's socialism, which was sincere, was subordinate to his centralism. In this instance, he was, perhaps, a 'red liberal.' These developments took place after Horowitz wrote.

2 I have relied in this chapter mainly on Grant's contemporary statements about events and ideas. His memory was often unreliable.

3 Ibid.
4 GPG to Maude Grant (MEG), 1932, Library and Archives Canada (LAC), Grant-Parkin Papers, MG30 D59, vols. 38–40. All subsequent letters from GPG come from this source unless otherwise noted.
5 GPG, handwritten and undated, (LAC, MG30 D77, vol. 5, file: 1904–13.
6 GPG to MEG, September/October 1935.
7 GPG to MEG, September/October 1935.
8 GPG to MEG, 18 October 1937.
9 GPG to MEG, 24 July 1936, 7 July 1936.
10 GPG to MEG, 7 August 1936.
11 GPG to MEG, 1938.
12 GPG to MEG, 1939.
13 GPG to MEG, 19 May 1940.
14 GPG to MEG, 4 June 1940.
15 GPG to MEG, 17 June 1940.
16 GPG to Margaret Grant, 28 July 1940.
17 GPG to MEG, 4 December 1940.
18 GPG to MEG, 1941.
19 GPG to Dr Trotter, 26 December 1941.
20 GPG to MEG, 1942.
21 GPG to MEG, 21 August 1941.
22 GPG to Trotter, 3 November 1942.
23 GPG, Journal entry, 27 November 1942.
24 GPG to MEG, [August] 1944.
25 GPG to MEG, late 1944.
26 GPG to Alice Boissoneau, late 1945, LAC, Alice Boissoneau Personal Papers.
27 GPG to Alice Boissoneau, 1946, Alice Boissoneau Personal Papers.
28 GPG to MEG, 1946.
29 GPG to Alice Boissoneau, 3 March 1947, Alice Boissoneau Personal Papers.
30 GPG to MEG, 27 January 1948.
31 GPG to MEG, 1949.
32 GPG to MEG, 12 February 1948.
33 GPG to MEG, 7 November 1948.
34 GPG to MEG, 1950.
35 GPG to MEG, Christmas 1950.
36 GPG to MEG, 9 August 1952.
37 GPG to MEG, 27 October 1952.
38 GPG to MEG, 2 November 1956.
39 GPG to MEG, 2 November 1956.
40 Denis Smith, *Rogue Tory: The Life and Legend of John G. Diefenbaker* (Toronto: Macfarlene Walter and Ross, 1995), 244.

41 GPG to Derek Bedson, 2 April 1958, Bedson Papers, Province of Manitoba Archives. The verse quoted is from Milton's *Paradise Lost*, V, 893–4.

42 For a longer discussion, see William Christian, *George Grant: A Biography* (Toronto: University Press, 1993), 211–14.

43 George Grant, 'An Ethic of Community,' in Michael Oliver, ed., *Social Purpose for Canada* (Toronto: University of Toronto Press, 1961), 21.

44 Ibid.

45 GPG to Derek Bedson, 5 April 1962, Bedson Papers.

46 GPG to Derek Bedson, 18 June 1962, Bedson Papers.

47 GPG to Derek Bedson, 20 June 1962, Bedson Papers.

48 GPG to Derek Bedson, late 1962, Bedson Papers.

49 Hugh McLennan to GPG, 24 January 1966, George Grant Personal Papers, in the possession of Sheila Grant, Halifax.

50 GPG, 'The Future of Canadian Nationhood,' CBC radio 'Venture' series, 27 June 1965.

51 GPG to Derek Bedson, 2 July 1964, Bedson Papers.

52 George Grant, *Lament for a Nation* (Toronto: McClelland and Stewart, 1965), 69–70.

53 GPG, 'Diefenbaker: A Democrat in Theory and Soul,' *Globe and Mail*, 7 August 1979.

54 GPG to Kenneth McNaught, 11 February 1966, copy provided by Professor McNaught.

55 GPG to Peter Calamai, *Silhouette* (McMaster University student newspaper), 22 February 1966.

56 GPG, 'The Conservatives Must Put Canada First,' *Hamilton Spectator*, 30 August 1967.

57 GPG to Hugh McLennan, 27 March 1969, George Grant Personal Papers, Halifax.

58 GPG to Raleigh Parkin, 30 November 1972, George Grant Personal Papers, Halifax.

59 GPG to Derek Bedson, 2 July 1964, Bedson Papers.

60 GPG, 'Inconsistency Ruled in Canada's 70's,' *Globe and Mail*, 31 December 1979.

61 GPG to William Christian, 31 August 1983, William Christian Personal Papers, Guelph.

62 GPG to Terry Barker, 24 June 1988, George Grant Personal Papers, Halifax.

63 GPG to Joan O'Donovan, 8 November 1985, photocopy supplied.

64 GPG to Ed Andrew, 7 December 1985, photocopy supplied.

65 GPG to William Christian, 31 August 1983, William Christian Personal Papers, Guelph.

66 GPG to Dennis Duffy, 29 February 1988, Dennis Duffy Personal Papers.

67 George Grant, review of Laurier LaPierre, ed., *If You Love This Country: Facts and Feelings on Free Trade, Books in Canada* 17, no. 1 (1988): 19.

68 Stephen Bornstein to GPG, 20 February 1967, George Grant Personal Papers, Halifax.

69 Grant, *Lament* 1–2.

70 Ibid., 59.

71 Ibid., 1.

72 GPG to Joan O'Donovan, 8 November 1985, photocopy supplied.

73 David Cayley, *George Grant in Conservation* (Don Mills, ON: Anansi, 1995), 103.

4

Did George Grant Change His Politics?

ARTHUR DAVIS

Thus the real problem would now turn on the intimate relation which must be established between gift and freedom, between freedom and grace. Everything will depend on the answer we ultimately give to this most difficult of all questions ...

Gabriel Marcel[1]

George Grant allied himself with social-democratic politics when he published 'An Ethic of Community' in *Social Purpose for Canada*, a book intended to celebrate the founding of the New Party in 1960 and whose authors also included Pierre Trudeau.[2] During the 1960s Grant became known for confronting the American empire over the Vietnam War, and he found common cause with the New Left for a time in opposition to that conflict. After *Lament for a Nation*, he was identified as a Canadian nationalist, even though or perhaps because he had predicted the death of the country.

During the mid-1960s Grant's politics seemed to be changing. We know that he came to think that the nationalists and social democrats were naive and even deluded, albeit nobly, to think they could challenge our ignobly deluded leaders and convert the vast majority of us from our allegiance to science, capitalism, and empire. But was he giving up the modern goal of 'changing the world' to a more just place? Grant had argued in 'Acceptance and Rebellion' (1956) for 'the substantial truth' and 'great accomplishments' of the historical spirit. He applauded the 'history-makers' for rebelling against evils, but he urged rebels to accept divine and natural limits; that is, Grant supported limited history making in the 1950s. In *Philosophy in the Mass Age* (1959) he concluded with a call for thought in which the idea of limit includes within itself a doctrine that sees history as the sphere for the overcoming of evil.[3] In the mid-1960s, however, he began to call the modern project a giant mistake. Modern politics, like modern science and capitalism, had been fatally poisoned, he said, by the first principle of a radical human freedom that insisted on deciding for itself what is good while refusing to accept and obey any non-human limits. He defined modern liberalism as making the world as we want it.

Grant was raised a progressive and became a Christian Platonist. He sometimes appeared to want to erase the progressive upbringing that had shaped him, leading Charles Taylor, for one, to claim that Grant became an 'implacable pessimist' concerning the modern project.[4] Grant said he was a Christian and therefore not a pessimist. But did he abandon the modern hope that human efforts could change *this world* for the better? Did he come to the position, as Neil Robertson has said, that 'the realm of modern historical life cannot be a place of goodness and truth'?[5] According to Louis Greenspan, in the 1950s, Grant had combined 'spectacularly' an understanding of modern thinkers with an adherence to traditional religion. But Greenspan concluded that Grant had, in the 1970s, demonized human freedom as 'all is permitted.'[6]

To respond to this question about Grant's change of heart, I need to examine key moments in his life-long reflection on the difficult and contested principles of freedom and equality. He had a genius for seeing how these philosophical principles are at stake in our political and economic affairs. I am going to look at two passages from his later work where his definition of human freedom might seem to indicate an important change. One is from the 1988 addendum to 'Two Theological Languages' and the other is from 'Faith and the Multiversity' (1986). Next I argue that Grant's egalitarian political and economic principles, as laid out in 'An Ethic of Community' (1961), continue, with an important modification, to inform his later position. Finally, I will examine his changing assessment of the modern, history-making spirit in the 1960s. True, he seems to have decided that the modern turn towards human freedom and historical transformation was a fundamental mistake. But the important question is exactly what did he think was mistaken and where does that leave us in relation to the world we are in? Grant's solution was a Christianity purified of its triumphal elements, and a reinvigorated Platonic philosophy of eternal limits that could confront Heidegger's pure modern, historical thought. My own more specific question is: Did Grant's commitment to the goals of freedom and equality expressed in 'An Ethic of Community' change in his later conception of an engagement between history and eternity? Do those who wish to confront the American empire in the time of George W. Bush still have something to learn from George Grant? I obviously think they do, but there are many students of Grant who think he 'gave up' on the modern world as a field of positive change and thus lacked a ground from which to engage contemporary problems. I see a tendency both from the left and the right to exaggerate Grant's change, and to assume that he disavowed more of his earlier position than he did. I will conclude with my understanding of Grant's 'politics of the theology of the cross.'

HUMAN FREEDOM AS 'THE LIBERTY OF INDIFFERENCE TO THE GOOD'

In 'Faith and the Multiversity' (1986), Grant said he had come to define human freedom as 'the liberty of indifference; the ability to turn away from the light we have sighted.'[7] And he repeated the same definition in an Addendum (1988) that retracts his 'existential' account of biblical freedom in 'Two Theological Languages' (1953). At first sight, this revision seems to imply that human freedom consists only in turning towards or away from the light shed by Platonic reason and Christian revelation; he appeared to think that humans do not generate light of their own. The crucial question here is whether Grant changed his mind about the 'history-makers'? Did he abandon the freedom of conscience, the ability of humans to choose what is fitting in particular situations? An argument can be made that Grant came to believe that modern society could no longer accommodate the Good. Yet, in my view, a careful examination shows that Grant believed that modern society needed to change fundamentally for goodness to prevail. In the passage from the 'Addendum,' for example, Grant says that he had changed not his political goals but rather his philosophical understanding of freedom:

The chief mistake in this piece ['Two Theological Languages'] is that in describing what I called Biblical language, I was in fact describing the language of modern existentialism. The egregious confusion vitiates the substance of the paper. This is apparent in what I say about 'freedom.' To quote: 'The Biblical language rests upon a totally different use of the word freedom. Freedom in this (the Biblical) language is not the gift of truth.' But this is clearly not true. It is only necessary to quote: 'The truth shall make you free.'[8] Whatever differences there may be between Platonism and Christianity as to how and when truth is given us, it is clear that in both freedom is given us through truth ... Therefore, freedom cannot be used (as I did in this piece) as human absoluteness of choice, both in doing and making. For myself, I would now define 'freedom' as the liberty to be indifferent to good. This is of course a quite different use of the word from the authentic 'freedom' of modern existentialism which at its heart is an expression of heroic atheism.[9]

Existential freedom – as 'absoluteness of choice in doing and making' – is Sartre's extreme version of Rousseau's insight that we humans make ourselves in history. Grant was, I think, overstating the degree to which he was under the influence of this idea of radical freedom and its language in his original paper of 1953. It is true that he had embraced modern thinkers for their moral rebellion against evil in the world (especially Kant, and also Sartre) and that he now turned against Sartre's radical freedom. He had also begun to pay closer attention to the radical side of Kant's autonomy. But, to repeat, he was not suddenly defending limits on human freedom for the first time.

Grant was right to correct his earlier account of freedom and truth in the Bible. 'When truth is given us ... in both [Platonism and Christianity] freedom is given us.' But, along with this point, it is important to remember that the truth in both traditions is an ambiguous mystery, as Grant affirms in 'Faith and the Multiversity.' Because we must be *agnostic*, in part, about the truth that sets us free, we are also set free in the other human sense that we are given the responsibility to make difficult decisions and judgments. We are on our own, up to a point, and must look to our own lights to interpret and decide how to apply within our new situation what we inherit in our language and traditions.

Grant seems to have been so aware of the danger that the radical human freedom (in which we say 'we are our own') could eclipse the freedom which comes from the truth that is given (in which 'we are not our own') that he tended to see the two as unalterably opposed. He saw the opposition when he was focused on our failure to admit we are not our own. During times when he was frustrated by the failure of modern people to obey any limits, there is no doubt that he sometimes spoke as if he believed we have to choose one or the other. Modern historical or history-making thinking and its language seem to have no room for any action being categorically wrong, for example. All previously accepted limits can be rendered impotent by historical relativism. Modern people are triumphant creators of history and morally impotent creatures of history. This failure of modern thinking was something that always appalled and frustrated Grant. He saw it as a revelation of the inadequacy of the modern account of human freedom. So the question I am left with is this: If we take Grant's critique of modernity seriously, can we think it possible to reform or reconstitute the modern world in such a manner that a hope for greater justice can emerge once again? In any case, Grant clearly believed that those who embrace modernity *as presently constituted* are unwittingly giving up on the very freedom and equality they seek to achieve.

An instructive example of Grant's tendency to polarize or push intellectual alternatives to extremes can be found in his graduate lectures on Kant of 1973–4. By that time, he had come to emphasize Kant's *philosophical* denial of the possibility of deducing the content of the good will from revelation. *'Theologians,'* he says, 'must decide which side they are on, Kant's or the tradition's.' At the same time, however, Grant warned his students (who were not all theologically inclined) about seeing Kant only through his eyes or with his current preoccupations. Grant was, in the 1970s, drawing attention to Kant's radical modernity, something he had not appreciated in the 1950s when he had 'seen Socrates through Kantian eyes.'[10]

Grant embraced the two great traditions of order and limit coming from Socrates and Christ. But he also knew that the free man has to *learn* to praise (as he had); he did not think he should ever be forced to praise. He considered his work on abortion, for example, to be *education*, not a justification for the enforced prohibition of abortion. The political work Grant did with his wife on abortion, we should note, indicates that he did not give up on political work in this educational sense. This was an example of difficult and dangerous, but not impossible, politics. His work as a whole is about balancing one type of freedom with the other type, just as Kant was trying to to put together the human freedom of self-legislation with duty and biblical revelation.

EQUALITY IN 'AN ETHIC OF COMMUNITY' AND AFTER

Grant made it clear in 'An Ethic of Community' (1961) that his commitment to liberty and equality was based on his Christianity. Although he had egalitarian and democratic allies who were not Christians, Grant thought they were committed to secularized Christianity; they shared his conviction about the justice of the English-speaking institutions even if they had lost touch with part of the original intellectual roots of these institutions. He allied himself with social democrats (or democratic socialists) when he argued for a balance that included, alongside the principle of equality, a recognition that we have unequal talents. Grant embraced the liberal tradition that political equality, including the ballot and equality before the law, is necessary to safeguard economic equality of opportunity. But he also called for a 'richer conception of economic equality' than equality of opportunity, because in the new stratified mass society traditional political equality could no longer protect the many from the few. This 'richer conception' included the intervention of the state with social-democratic measures to counteract the power of corporate vested interests.

Grant defined the principle of equality as follows: 'Equality should be the central principle of society since all persons, whatever their condition, must freely choose to live by what is right or wrong. This act of choosing is the ultimate human act and is open to all. In this sense all persons are equal, and differences of talent are of petty significance.'[11] I think it is safe to assume that, had he subsequently been asked to revisit this essay, he would have revised his conception of the principle of equality away from the emphasis on human *will* that is assumed in the phrase, '*choosing* to live by what is right or wrong.' Judging from his later work, I suggest that he might have changed his definition of equality to a phrase like the following: what makes us all equal is that we are challenged to love what is good. Here, the important change is that love is given to us, at least in part, and thus it accompanies and tempers the will. The answer to my question as to whether or not Grant's egalitarian politics were abandoned, lies, I think, in a careful understanding of that change from willing to loving.

We should notice again that Grant's change from willing to loving is not as radical a change as it may seem at first glance. His earlier phrase, 'choosing what is right and wrong,' refers to morality that is *given*, not morality brought into being solely by the will or by choice. Grant believed that we choose from what is given to us, what we can know as our duty. It would be wrong to identify his early formulation with the radically modern conception of Rousseau that was taken up by Kant in his special way. Rousseau's insight that we make ourselves in our history led to his conception of the general will. What we are and what we will become is not given to us by nature. We, the people, use reason, but our sovereign will is not subject to it. Kant combined and modified Rousseau's radical idea with his own religious conception of morality as the categorical imperative, thereby retaining the ancient position that morality is given, although in the form of practical reason rather than as 'human nature.' For Kant, the prominence of the word *duty* (*Pflicht*) made it clear that he was talking about what is given even if he did not specify the content of the given. As Grant learned from Nietzsche in the late 1960s, Kant thereby *delayed* the coming of radical modernity. The point, for my purpose here, is that Grant's change from choosing to loving did not involve a change about morality being given us. He always saw it as given. Grant's early definition included free choice but he did not conceive it as complete *autonomy*, in which our choice creates and dictates what is right and wrong.

At the same time, however, Grant did side with the modern idea of changing the world to make it a more just place for the many. He agreed with the liberation of the instincts, for example, *up to a point*. This he made clear in his qualified support of Freud for liberating himself and others from excessive sexual repression. Grant agreed with Nietzsche that we should learn to love the earth, even if he opposed Nietzsche's rejection of Christian morality. Although he thought that moral limits were grounded in religion and philosophy, Grant also agreed with modern critics that religion and philosophy had been partly misused and misapplied in the tradition. There is a need to rebel and change the world if we can (again, within limits), as long as we do not use evil means to achieve good ends. Divine and natural law limits us, but we human beings are not programmed like computers or even regulated by instinct as are animals. We must interpret the demands of God and nature. When Grant came to speak of modernity as a 'mistake,' he therefore meant specifically that the radical turn to unlimited human freedom as the matrix of human nobility was a mistake. Such a turn abandons reverence (and obedience) as if humans cannot be truly free if they revere limits not subject to their own choosing. He did not mean that he had changed his mind about the good achievements of Freud, Nietzsche, and Marx. The question for Grant was whether and how freedom and reverence exist together in our human experience. Being free, we must acknowledge and revere what makes us free; being reverent, we have the freedom of responsibility for judgments and interpretation in our situation.

Our ability to love other people does seem to be a gift, not something that we can generate with our wills. And the blessing that others love us makes it possible for us to love in return. But is it not also true that love requires us to make efforts of our own? Are we not 'our own' as well as 'not our own' in this most important of experiences? The unity of 'the two freedoms' that Grant was trying to fathom is shown in the original meaning of the word 'free' in the Germanic languages. Ernest Klein, in his *Comprehensive Etymological Dictionary of the English Language,* states that the primary sense of the family of words around the Old and Middle English *freo* was 'beloved, friend; to love.'[12] 'The terms beloved and friend,' he says, 'were applied, as a rule, to the free members of the clan, and in contradistinction to slaves.' The original word 'free' carried within its meaning in a seamless unity what we call positive and negative freedom, now thought to be two different uses of the word freedom. The original word free literally meant 'loved,' referring to those individuals who were sheltered, protected, and thus given the leeway to live and carry out their responsibilities as loved members of the tribe, in contrast to the unloved, unfree slaves taken in battle. The two elements of freedom – that we are loved, ordered, and set free, on the one hand, and that we are responsible to think and to build, on the other – are present together in the original experience, as reflected in the word that first named it.

Did Grant mean to retain 'we are our own' when he embraced the truth that 'we are not our own'? Or did he believe, or come to believe, that our human freedom consists only of accepting or rejecting the gift of truth that sets us free? My answer is that he rejected 'we are our own' only if it excluded *in principle* all guidance from outside ourselves. Even when we recognize that 'we are not our own,' we will still experience also being our own. Grant believed that our human dispensation includes being and loving our own; we belong to particular traditions and communities and, even within these, each of us, as individuals, must also do our own thinking, believing, and dying. In 'Canadian Fate and Imperialism' he was clear on the place of 'our own' in our lives: 'In human life there must always be place for love of the good and love of one's own. Love of the good is man's highest end, but it is of the nature of things that we come to know and to love what is good by first meeting it in that which is our own – this particular body, this family, these friends, this woman, this part of the world, this set of traditions, this country, this civilisation.'[13] There is no reason to believe Grant changed his mind on this point in later years. To reiterate, his two great sources of 'the truth that sets us free,' namely Christian revelation and Platonic philosophy, are both agnostic. Philosophy, or love of wisdom, is not wisdom and faith is not knowledge. 'Without this agnosticism,' he said, 'humans tend to move to the great lie that evil is good and good evil.'[14] For Grant, the most telling contemporary examples of the lie were wars waged for 'progress' or 'freedom.' We do not know the truth of things in detail, and Grant rebelled against those who think they know the truth of the whole and the parts; he knew that they must not be allowed to threaten and curtail our human freedom and define our faith.

HUMAN FREEDOM, MAKING HISTORY, AND ETERNAL LIMITS

Grant's mission in 1956, then, was to persuade North American and European activists, whom he admired for *rebelling* against evil in the world, that they should *accept* eternal limits as guides of their history making.[15] He made three attempts to bring what he considered two truths together – the truth that we make history and the truth that we are given limits and are fitted for justice. His final plan, which he did not live long enough to complete, was to enlist Plato's philosophy (and Christianity) in a renewed contest with Heidegger.[16] His very precise account of the engagement makes it clear that he believed that each side had 'hit' parts of the truth and 'missed' others: 'To put it barely: the very clarity of Heidegger's incomparable thinking of historicism, from out of his assertion that human beings are only authentically free when they recognise that they are thrown into a particular historical existence, meets here the clarity of Plato's insistence that thought, at its purest, can rise above the particularities of any historical context, that indeed philosophy stands or falls by its ability to transcend the historical. Describing this as the central theoretical division in all western thought is perhaps a mere expression of my struggling uncertainty as to who misses what in this greatest of confrontations.'[17]

Grant believed that equality was rooted in Christianity and therefore in the eternal order, but moderns believed that we have moved beyond eternity, that we human beings are, or will be, the creators of equality. In Grant's account, Nietzsche and Heidegger were more consistent late-modern thinkers who saw that the rejection of God must be a rejection of equality as well.[18] Grant came to consider the commitment to equality on the part of earlier modern thinkers as part of Kant's 'great delay' of the coming of radical modernity. This was the delay, incidentally, that had anchored Grant's own teaching in his early years. In his Kant seminar of 1978, Grant explained how he had changed his mind about Kant's role:

Now it seems to me that this is what is so fascinating about Kant. As much as anybody he lays before us the new essence of truth in which humanity as subject installs itself as sovereign over all that is and in which humanity understands itself as autonomous legislator to master all that is and to enact what the world will be like – but then at the height of that new system of representation – namely in the question of justice, he does not cross the Rubicon to the new account of justice which is required of the new account of truth proceeding from the new account of reason. He offers the categorical imperative, that morality is the one fact of reason; he offers a fundamental equality of persons – that is, an account of justice which comes out of the older account of truth which was based not on the first principle of subjectivity – but on the eternal order.[19]

This point takes us to the heart of Grant's 'change.' He had come to see that the modern account was more profoundly mistaken than he had allowed himself to see in the 1950s. Nietzsche's explanation of Kant's tenuous compromise between the ancient and modern positions did not, however, lead Grant to abandon the modern world altogether. He did not lose hope that the world could ever move towards equality. Rather, he came to think that our commitment to radical human freedom had eroded our commitment to equality. He told his students of Greek religion and philosophy at McMaster that the catastrophe of Vietnam was forcing us to look beyond the modern for an understanding of what is wrong with the modern: 'In the light of this catastrophe [it is] very difficult to conceive turning one's mind to these ultimate issues. Yet we must. Indeed, just because of it, we must. If this is the upshot of what western civilization is, if this is the upshot of its religious, moral, [and] political assumptions – if this is American liberalism in the world, then one must say there is something [wrong] at the very roots of our society, that is, about its presuppositions. And those of us who live in its midst must try and give ourselves not only to the immediate – [to] hatred and fight against what is going on – but [to] try to see where our thought has been wrong.'[20]

When making notes in preparation for a discussion with a CBC producer in 1966, Grant planned to ask whether he should admit that he did not think it likely that equality would be achieved in an 'industrial' society.[21] Later, he wrote that 'the triumph of the will' had become the driving force at the heart of modern technological science and capital. Modern people would have to change fundamentally to a stance that includes obedience to divine and natural limits if we are to become able again to achieve what we are fitted for. Politics in the present day are difficult because such a sea change is so difficult to conceive, let alone enact. I take this need for fundamental change as an indication of our political task at its deepest level, something that is difficult, perhaps dangerous, but not impossible. Grant believed that the modern Western world had chosen time as history and become oblivious to the eternal order altogether, with the disastrous results that modern technology, once serving to relieve man's estate, had become an end in itself. We were now making history without the aims and guiding principles of justice.

Although he was a Christian Platonist, Grant criticized the Christian tradition, the Jewish tradition, and Platonic philosophy in the light of his own experience – with loved ones, in the university, in politics – and of his critical reading of other ancient and modern thinkers. He broke with Strauss, for example, on the question of the superiority of Plato's philosophy to religion; he believed that love and forgiveness were the 'highest truth,' though he did not think that *knowing* that truth made anyone superior to anyone else. Grant did not believe that people were equal because of their *knowledge* of the truth but rather because they were capable of loving what is good. Nor did he believe that human beings who lived before the time of the Christian revelation, or people in non-Christian traditions like Hinduism and Buddhism, did not find the truth of love in other ways.

Grant's strongest political assertion may have been his attack on the *allegiance* of North Americans to the purely historical technological-capitalist order. Our civilization, he said, has 'bought' 'a package deal' that keeps us locked inside the purely historical understanding of our existence: 'Western peoples (and perhaps soon all peoples) take themselves as subjects confronting otherness as objects – objects lying as raw material at the disposal of knowing and making subjects. Unless we comprehend the package deal we obscure from ourselves the central difficulty in our present destiny: we apprehend our destiny by forms of thought which are themselves the very core of that destiny.'[22] The essential requirement for change is that we change our minds about what we are here for, what we are fitted for as human beings and therefore what our stance or comportment should be inside modern technology and the empire where we find ourselves. A change in the way we act towards each other and towards the earth would flow naturally from our changed allegiance. Denise Levertov names our current allegiance, or our *daily reaffirmation*, in a wonderful poem in which she likens 'making peace' to the making of a poem:

> A line of peace might appear
> if we restructured the sentence our lives are making,
> revoked its reaffirmation of profit and power,

questioned our needs, allowed
long pauses ...[23]

CONCLUSION: THE WHOLE GRANT, NOT JUST THE MATURE GRANT

John Porter asserts in *Spirit Book Word* that Grant's most powerful insight is that what is given to us overwhelms what is made by us: 'There is more given in the world than is made in the world; we ourselves are more given than made. This, the one thought he was utterly obedient to: the power and glory of the Given. The Given which is given by grace, by God. The fitting response is gratitude and the will to give back to others – to give oneself away.'[24] Grant also argued (on the basis of what was given) that moderns had the right goals (genuine liberty and equality) but not the reverence to make it possible to achieve them. The rightness of their goals came, for him, out of the Christian account of human freedom and equality, adopted in a secular form as appropriate economic and political goals. What mattered was to relieve man's estate, to heal the sick and feed the hungry. The moderns who had secularized Christianity, he said, were superior to the ancients in this matter of basic justice. Did he decide that liberals and socialists were reaching for something that could not be achieved in this world? There is something to this point, but I think it would be better to say 'something that cannot be achieved in this industrial (or technological) world' if it holds fast to its current 'constitution.' Trying to control nature and human nature for mastery and profit is not going to achieve justice. Grant was not a Luddite and he did not think that we could return to an agrarian or hunting and gathering culture and economy. The reconstitution, if it happens, will be about changing our awareness of who we are and where we stand in relation to what is other than us – nature and other beings – inside the modern world where we are situated.

What are we to make of Grant's frequent attacks on the modern liberal progressive project? His animus against progressives does not make him an enemy of egalitarian politics. Rather, his attack on them was part of his critique of triumphal technology, which in turn was rooted, as he said, in triumphal Western Christianity. He followed Luther in siding with the theology of the cross against the theology of glory.[25] Is there, then, a 'politics of the theology of the cross,' a politics of love and forgiveness that alleviates human affliction, a politics of 'strength through weakness' that strengthens human effort by weakening the politics and economics of triumphal technology in its will to exploit the earth and other humans as resources?

Such a politics engages non-Christians as well as Christians, since Grant always spoke to the whole community on questions of justice and not just to the Christian fold. This remained true when, in his later work, he did speak more and more as a Christian. What we have lost in the West, he said in the 1980s, is 'a sense of grave limitation in human life.' 'Western Christianity' so emphasized the power of God in its teaching that it forgot 'the weakness of God.'[26] The weakness of God is demonstrated in the crucifixion: 'The history of western Christianity is strange when we consider that it centred around the rite of the Eucharist, surely a celebration of the weakness of God.' Our purposes, projects, and passions are doomed to remain 'incomplete,' and we must learn to accept our fragility and our vulnerability.

As well as posing some excellent questions, Grant gave us some answers about his position on liberal progressivism in 'A Platitude' (1969). Understanding how the modern project lost its bearings is obviously vital to asking whether it can regain them. Grant praised the aspiration of that modern project at its best. It was attempting to achieve freedom and equality with the motive of love: 'It might also be said that the older systems of meanings have simply been replaced by a new one. The enchantment of our souls by myth, philosophy or revelation has been replaced by a more immediate meaning – the building of the society of free and equal men by the overcoming of chance. For it is clear that the systematic interference with chance was not simply undertaken for its own sake but for the realisation of freedom. Indeed it was undertaken partly in the name of that charity which was held as the height in one of those ancient systems of meaning.'[27]

The problem came with the adoption of human freedom as the highest principle against the 'older systems of meaning.' Human freedom was no longer enfolded, measured, and defined. It was 'an unlimited freedom to make the world as we want in a universe indifferent to what purposes we choose.' We were left with no words for the Good that binds us, limits us, and sets us free: 'The drive to the planetary technical future is in any case inevitable; but those who would try to divert, to limit, or even simply to stand in fear before some of its applications find themselves defenceless, because of the disappearance of any speech by which the continual changes involved in that drive could ever be thought as deprivals. Every development of technique is an exercise of freedom by those who develop it, and the exercise of freedom is the only meaning, the changes can only be publicly known as the unfolding of meaning.'[28]

But there is no reason why we cannot learn from our mistake, as monumental as it certainly is. Grant asserts that the language of good is 'inescapable,' and it does seem unacceptable that our current ways of speaking cannot do justice to questions of good. Concerning judgments about what is good, we do have 'intimations of deprival'; we can see that our current language and way of being is depriving us of part of our humanity. Grant also drew attention to the fact that the language of good can sometimes be 'hidden' inside the language of freedom: 'But even among some of those who use the language of sheer freedom as protest, there seems to be heard something different than the words allow. Because they have been taught no language but the modern, they use it not only to insist that the promises of the modern be fulfilled, but also to express their anguish at its denials.'[29] Grant posed the task of 'the recollection of the language of good' in the middle of the world that denies it. He suggested to us what we should nurture when he asked: 'Is there some force in man which will rage against such division [between subjectivity and objectified world inhabited by increasingly objectifiable beings]: rage not only against a subjectivity which creates itself, but also against our own lives being so much at the disposal of the powerful objectifications of other freedoms?'[30]

In 'Faith and the Multiversity' (1986), Grant challenged the dominant technological and scientific paradigm of subjects controlling objects, asserting the counter-paradigm of faith and the primacy of love of the other in its being. He argued, following Simone Weil's statement that 'faith is the experience that intelligence is illuminated by love,' that the dominant paradigm informing science and capital cannot adequately measure our most important human experiences. We know our loved ones and the places where we are at home better because we love them, better than we would know them if we analysed them objectively.

I argue that Grant's new understanding of equality as our encounter with the Good, and his redefinition of freedom as the possibility of indifference to the Good, did not lead him to be anti-democratic or elitist. On the contrary, the change kept him in the camp of the democrats, despite his occasional despair about the prospects for humans loving the Good when it is so easy to affirm the direction of advanced industrial and imperial technological capitalism. This question is timely since some claim that a conservative elite, influenced by Leo Strauss, has captured the Pentagon and the White House.[31] Obviously, the influence of Strauss and some of his followers looms large in Grant's evolving thought. But it is also clear that Grant drew the line against the Straussians on the Vietnam War, on the need to defend liberal democracy with the sword, and on their account of religion as inferior to philosophy and as a means of deceiving the people to keep them in order.

Grant struggled with despair about the modern world and in 'A Platitude' he explained why in the end he rejected it. 'I have never found any who, in my understanding of them, have been able, through the length and breadth of their thought, to make the language of good secondary to freedom. It is for this reason that men find it difficult to take despair as the final stance in most circumstances.'[32] Gandhi made a similar claim: 'When I despair, I remember that all through history the way of truth and love has always won. There have been tyrants and murderers and for a time they seem invincible but in the end, they always fail – think of it, always!'[33] The current use of the language of 'values' combines good with freedom in a way that subordinates and weakens good. Grant was struggling to think through a combination of the two in which good is not undermined.

Grant was a master diviner of contending positions. His discrete insights came in staccato bursts that sometimes ignored the fear of contradiction in order to get at an indispensable part of the truth that needed uncovering. His responses to thinkers and events throughout his life were passionately driven by concerns of the day, by the demands of his path of thought, and by practical matters like the Vietnam War and abortion. In his later life, he was tired and sometimes embittered by what he saw as his failure at McMaster, as well as by his long struggle with the progressives. He then tended to move towards certain of the anti-progressive positions and to fall silent about his social-democratic convictions. Yet it would be wrong to consider the later Grant to be the 'mature' Grant, as if what went before had been transcended. Ironically, that would be a very 'historical' way of seeing his thought. There is indeed wisdom in the later work that had not yet unfolded in the earlier. But the early work boldly asserts the need for social change and Grant's thought, as a whole, stands up when we retain and reiterate his earlier insight and rebellion, which then were deepened and balanced by the wisdom of age and experience.

NOTES

1 Gabriel Marcel, *Mystery of Being*, vol 2, *Faith and Reality* (Chicago: H. Regenery, 1960), 122, quoted by Grant in his 1956 notebook with the question 'Is

he right?' Chapter 7, 121ff., of Marcel's work is entitled 'Freedom and Grace.' Two pages earlier, Marcel wrote: 'One may, in fact, say almost with certainty that there is nobody who has all his life been so unlucky as to have found it impossible ever to unite himself with another, or obliged to deny the other as a real presence.' Marcel, ibid., 120.

2 George Grant, 'An Ethic of Community' in Michael Oliver, ed., *Social Purpose for Canada* (Toronto: University of Toronto Press, 1961). The New Democratic Party was first named the New Party.

3 George Grant, *Philosophy in the Mass Age*, ed. William Christian (Toronto: University of Toronto Press, 1995), 102–3.

4 Charles Taylor's entry on George Grant in the *Canadian Encyclopedia*, 2nd ed., vol. 2, (Edmonton: Hurtig Publishers, 1988), 927, begins: 'A brooding philosopher of apparently implacable pessimism, Grant is one of the most influential thinkers of his era, having evolved from a nationalist and 'Red Tory' position to a concern with the fate of the entire Western world.'

5 Neil G. Robertson, review of Arthur Davis and Peter C. Emberley, eds., *Collected Works of George Grant, Volume 1 (1933–1950)*, in *Dalhousie Review* 83, no. 1 (2003): 146–9: 'One source of the lilting, lamenting, noble character of Grant's later writings gathered in this volume, is his sense that the realm of modern historical life ought to be a place of goodness and truth, and yet it is not and may not be; the other source arises in later years when he comes to see that, fatally, it cannot be.' (149).

6 For his case for and against Grant, see Louis Greenspan, 'The Unraveling of Liberalism,' in Arthur Davis, ed., *George Grant and the Subversion of Modernity: Art, Philosophy, Religion, Politics, and Education* (Toronto: University of Toronto Press, 1996), 201–19.

7 Grant, 'Faith and the Multiversity,' in *Technology and Justice* (Toronto: Anansi; 1986), 74–5. 'In much modern thought the core of being human is often affirmed as our freedom to make ourselves and the world. Whatever differences there may be among Christians about what it is to be human, finally there must be the denial of this account of freedom. Whatever we are called to do or to make in the world, the freedom to do or to make cannot be for us the final account of what we are. For Plato freedom is not our essence. It is simply the liberty of indifference; the ability to turn away from the light we have sighted.'

8 John 8:32.

9 George Grant, 'Two Theological Languages,' in Arthur Davis, ed., *Collected Works of George Grant, Volume 2 (1951–1959)* (Toronto: University of Toronto Press, 2002), 60.

10 Grant called himself a moral philosopher and later a political philosopher but he was reluctant to call himself a theologian. At this time, when he said he was 'no longer a modern philosopher,' he seemed to think that he had to admit that he was in some sense a theologian. In a mid-1960s lecture he said: 'It has taken me most of my life at this point to see that the very greatest formulations of the human condition by the moderns [Kant, Hegel, Marx] was somehow wrong. And when I say wrong I mean in my case not so much just philosophically wrong as theologically wrong. If I am honest what I found about modern philosophy was not only its results in the modern world – but the fact that it could not be reconciled with what I have called the perfection of Christ.'

11 George Grant, 'An Ethic of Community,' in Oliver, *Social Purpose for Canada*, 20.

12 Ernest Klein, *A Comprehensive Etymological Dictionary of the English Language: Dealing with the Origin of Words and Their Sense Development, thus Illustrating the History of Civilization and Culture* (New York: Elsevier Publishing Company, 1971), 295.

13 Grant, 'Canadian Fate and Imperialism,' in *Technology and Empire: Perspectives on North America* (Toronto: House of Anansi, 1969), 73.

14 Grant, 'Faith and the Multiversity,' 75.

15 See Grant, 'Acceptance and Rebellion' (1956) in Arthur Davis, ed., *Collected Works of George Grant, Volume 2 (1951–1959)*, 221ff.

16 Grant, 'Confronting Heidegger's *Nietzsche*' (1984), unpublished. See also Arthur Davis, 'Justice and Freedom: George Grant's Encounter with Martin Heidegger,' in Davis, *The Subversion of Modernity*, 139ff.

17 Grant, 'Confronting Heidegger's *Nietzsche*,' 10.

18 Heidegger claims that meditative thought is possible for everyone. See Martin Heidegger, 'Memorial Address,' in John M. Anderson and E. Hans Freund, *Discourse on Thinking* (New York: Harper and Row, 1966): 'Yet anyone can follow the path of meditative thinking in his own manner and within his own limits. Why? Because man is a *thinking*, that is, a *meditating* being' (47).

19 Grant, Lectures for Kant Seminar, McMaster University, 1978. In Notebook K, Grant Papers, in the possession of Sheila Grant, Halifax.

20 Arthus Davis and Henry Rogers, eds., *Collected Works of George Grant, Volume 3 (1960–1969)* (Toronto: University of Toronto Press, 2005), 696–7.

21 Roy Faibish of the CBC engaged Grant and Gad Horowitz to host several programs that were broadcast by the CBC early in 1966. These were a series of thirteen sessions, entitled as a whole 'Ideals of Democracy and Social Reality,' for the program *Extension*. Grant jotted down some 'notes for a con-

versation with Faibish,' declaring the most important point of the series to be 'how one combines the particular problems of Canadian nationhood with the universal problems of a technological society in which Canada is involved.' He wished to know whether Faibish wanted the particular or the universal emphasized and whether Faibish knew that he, Grant, 'was a conservative about modern social science,' 'not hopeful about technological society,' and held the view 'that no industrial society is likely to be egalitarian.' He wondered whether he could assert his position and perhaps 'attack' his guests or instead should confine himself to 'tentative discussing' of the issues. See Davis and Rogers, eds., *CollectedWorks of George Grant, Volume 3 (1960–1969)*, 431, 432, 452 n.2.

22 Grant, 'Thinking about Technology,' in *Technology and Justice*, 32.

23 Denise Levertov, 'Making Peace,' in *Breathing the Water* (New York: New Directions, 1984), 40.

24 J.S. Porter, *Spirit Book Word: An Inquiry into Literature and Spirituality* (Ottawa: Novalis, 2001), 167.

25 See Sheila Grant, 'George Grant and the Theology of the Cross,' in Davis, *The Subversion of Modernity*, and Harris Athanasiadis, *George Grant and the Theology of the Cross: The Christian Foundations of His Thought* (Toronto: University of Toronto Press, 2001).

26 Grant, 'Céline's Trilogy,' in Davis, *The Subversion of Modernity* 50–1.

27 Grant, 'A Platitude,' in *Technology and Empire*, 138.

28 Ibid., 139.

29 Ibid., 141.

30 Ibid., 142.

31 See, for example, Jim Lobe, 'Leo Strauss' Philosophy of Deception,' AlterNet (www.alternet.org/story/15935/), 19 May 2003, and Paul Knox, 'The Strauss Effect,' *Globe and Mail*, 12 July 2003, F9.

32 'A Platitude,' 141.

33 These words were spoken in Richard Attenborough's 1982 film *Gandhi*.

PART TWO

Modernity in North America

GEORGE GRANT'S ENCOUNTER with the thought of Leo Strauss is one of those rare moments of intellectual history in which are concentrated questions of great profundity and implication. As his lecture printed below shows, this encounter shifted Grant's uneasy modernism – which accepted modern metaphysics but rejected modern morality – towards an investigation of Plato as the highest synthetic understanding of metaphysics and morality. Between the first (1959) and second (1966) editions of *Philosophy in the Mass Age*, Grant engaged in a 'reassessment of the truth of modern philosophy.'[1] His earlier question was: 'How can we think a conception of law that does not deny the truth of our freedom or the truth of progress?'[2] By 1966, after his encounter with Strauss's work, he stated: 'If we question these presuppositions [of modern philosophy] ... the obvious place for a Western man to look is to the Greek philosophers – that is, to the political writings of Plato and Aristotle.'[3]

This section focuses on Grant's relation to Strauss and to Hegel as well as the related issues of the project of modernity in Quebec and the United States. As Robert Sibley shows, Hegel, as the greatest modern philosopher, has cast a long shadow across Canadian philosophy and Grant's early work partook of this tradition. However, we should note that his presentation of Hegel in *Philosophy in the Mass Age* (1959) already reflected ambivalence, wondering whether Hegel's historicism could adequately capture the love of eternity.[4] By the time of *Lament for a Nation* (1965), Grant had broken with Hegel. It was the influence of Leo Strauss that convinced him that modernity is necessarily a tyranny and thus turned him away from Hegel towards an appreciation of the truth in Platonic philosophy. Grant's account of the debate between Strauss and the Hegelian Alexandre Kojeve in 'Tyranny and Wisdom' (1964) is thus one of the key texts for analysing his account of modernity.

However, one should note that Grant was never an uncritical follower of Leo Strauss. Grant's lecture registers his religious difference with Strauss and the related point that, in Judaism and Islam, revelation comes as law whereas 'in Christianity it comes in a particular being.' Moreover, as both Sibley and Alexander Duff document, Hegel is retained in order to explain the spirit of modernity even while Grant denies that this spirit is the final truth. Despite the fact of Strauss's influence on Grant, then, one can easily overestimate its extent. Grant Havers shows that Grant's commitment to egalitarianism (which was based in his Christianity) never wavered, whereas Strauss's commitment to the natural reason of Greek philosophy supported elitism. Havers argues that this difference, or issue, was never explicitly posed as a question for Grant, indicating that Grant's reading of Strauss was oriented only to the claim that modern technology engenders a tyranny, and thus that the influence of Strauss was muted and not oriented to philosophical fundamentals. Alexander Duff agrees with Havers that a different evaluation of the relation between Greek philosophy and biblical religion explains the distance between Grant and Strauss. He argues that Grant's synthesis of Athens and Jerusalem requires that Christian and Platonic love be the same. This is the root of Grant's Christian Platonism, but it leaves open a tension of which Grant himself was aware: How can Christian charity be found within Platonic reason? This is not only a question of the interpretation of a philosopher but also a philosophical question of ultimate importance. For Strauss, it is clear that no such charity exists in Plato.

Grant's lecture suggests that Strauss's Jewishness had philosophical implications (even though it does not discuss them). As Duff points out, Strauss's very phrasing of the question of Western civilization as one of 'Athens and Jerusalem' implies a greater weight for Judaism than for Christianity. Strauss's investigations of medieval Jewish philosophy led him to the view that reason and belief were necessarily in tension, that 'no one can be both a philosopher and a theologian or, for that matter, a third which is beyond the conflict between philosophy and theology, or a synthesis of both. But every one of us can be and ought to be either one or the other, the philosopher open to the challenge of theology or the theologian open to the challenge of philosophy.'[5] Investigations of the difference between Grant and Strauss on the relation between Athens and Jerusalem must avoid assuming that because Strauss did not accept a synthesis between the two, he was simply hostile to biblical revelation.

The immense influence of Leo Strauss in turning Grant from an uneasy Hegelian modernism towards Christian Platonism cannot be over-emphasized, even if this does not mean that Grant followed Strauss on fundamentals concerning the relation between biblical revelation and Greek philosophy. Neil Robertson again takes up the issue of Grant's perspective on Hegelian modernism through an account of his relation to James Doull. Doull's Hegelianism allowed him to claim, contrary to Grant, that North American freedom is not just an expression of technology but equally co-exists with specific, particular institutions of sovereignty which can prevent Canada's assimilation into the United States. This returns us to exactly the point that Grant's lecture makes: for Grant, it is not possible for a technological modern science, oriented to the domination of nature, to contain any more profound or demanding morality than the convenience and well-being of individuals. It is this anti-Hegelian point that Grant learned from Leo Strauss and that required his turn towards Christian Platonism.

'"A Cow Is Just a Cow": George Grant and Eric Voegelin on the United States,' by John von Heyking and Barry Cooper, continues the questioning of Grant's view of the relation between Canada and the United States. Relying on the analyses of Eric Voegelin, von Heyking and Cooper argue that Grant misunderstood the nature of American political institutions. Grant viewed the United States as the most advanced form of liberalism in the world, and he had serious concerns about this. Voegelin, like Doull, was willing to embrace the United States whereas Grant thought Canada, as a country with a more conservative tradition, should play the gadfly to the empire. The discussion by Christian Roy of resonances of Grantian conservatism in current Quebec brings the critique of modernity back to Canada. 'Echoes of George Grant in Late Boomers' Critiques of Post–Quiet Revolution Quebec' documents the persistence of conservative anti-modernism in Canada, suggesting that Grant's view of the dilemma for Canada within North American modernity may be experiencing a resurgence.

NOTES

1 George Grant, 'Introduction to the 1966 Edition,' *Philosophy in the Mass Age*, ed. William Christian (Toronto: University of Toronto Press, 1995), 121.
2 Grant, *Philosophy in the Mass Age*, 90.
3 Grant, 'Introduction to the 1966 Edition,' 121.
4 Grant, *Philosophy in the Mass Age*, 99–102.
5 Leo Strauss, 'The Mutual Influence of Theology and Philosophy,' *Independent Journal of Philosophy* 3 (1979): 111.

5

Leo Strauss and Political Philosophy

GEORGE GRANT

This lecture, the full title of which was 'Excerpt on Leo Strauss and Political Philosophy from a Lecture on Technology and the Tradition,' is found in Notebook M and was delivered in 1972–3 to a graduate course on the relation of technology and the Western religious and philosophical tradition. While the lecture shows the degree to which Grant, at a particular moment, was deeply influenced by Strauss, it should be noted, as Grant himself points out, that he was not a 'Straussian,' there were important differences between Grant and Strauss about religion and therefore also about the relation of reason and revelation.

Now to turn to what we are going to discuss for several weeks, political philosophy. Let me speak about what it is and its relation to natural science and to philosophy in general. Let me say in parenthesis that what I am going to say about political philosophy obviously follows what is said by Leo Strauss. Late in life in my forties certain difficulties in my own thought as a philosopher became very pressing for me. These difficulties were that in general philosophy I believed the moderns – particularly Kant – to be true, but when I faced them clearly with political [questions] (or moral questions – the same) I found this same teaching unacceptable. How was I to face this contradiction? I accepted Kant's account of metaphysics rather than Plato's or Aristotle's and yet could not accept his account of the practical. For example, Kant defines marriage as 'a life-long contract for the mutual use of the genitals.'[1] I could not accept that. Or again I accepted Hegel's metaphysics and yet found in him the central assertion that the political good was to be achieved by bad means. I could not accept that – I had seen its effect too clearly in Hegel's great epigones, the Marxists. How was I to reconcile this obvious contradiction in my thought?

It was my great good fortune to find that these very difficulties were being discussed with consummate clarity by Strauss and through that discussion I have been able to bring political philosophy into my thought.

Let me say that in describing political philosophy in Strauss' language, I feel secure because over the last decade I have been able to think for myself what he has thought.

Let me also say that clearly in some points there must be differences between Strauss and myself – apprehended I hope in humility by myself. He is a Jew – albeit as he says an unorthodox one – I am a Christian and nobody has written more brilliantly than Strauss about the relation of philosophy to revelation. One of his most illuminating remarks is the difference in the relation between revelation and philosophy as it is found in Judaism and Islam on the one hand and Christianity on the other. In Judaism and Islam revelation comes as law – in Christianity it comes in a particular being – and Strauss has pointed out that that difference in revelation clearly leads to a difference in the formulation of the relation of philosophy to revelation.[2]

Be that as it may, it is clear that my account of political philosophy comes from Strauss. Now Strauss has written much but I would recommend as basic, two writings by him. In a book of his called *What Is Political Philosophy?* the first essay is of the same words. It is a careful extension of what I have given you in 'The Three Waves of Modernity.' [The second is a book] called *Natural Right and History.* My own commentary [on this is] 'Tyranny and Wisdom' which you will find in a book of mine *Technology and Empire* ...[3]

Philosophy is a Western activity which arises in Greece. Political philosophy as part of philosophy arises with Socrates. Previously to Socrates philosophy does not seem much concerned with the political things. But in Socrates there is a turn to the political things, an immense interest in the political things.

This seems to come from a great turn about in Socrates' own life – this turn in his own life is described in Plato's *Phaedo.* In prison because of censures, mechanical or moral.

This turn about can be seen from Aristophanes' account of Socrates in the *Clouds.* There Socrates [is] described as a man in a think-tank thinking only about what we would now call physical science – clouds, etc. Aristophanes attacks Socrates for not being interested in justice – outside the city.

Then the turn around towards the human things; he seeks knowledge of human ends – knowledge of what makes human life whole or complete – that is, human happiness, that is, knowledge of the human soul, *psyche*. And the human soul is seen as the only part of the whole which is open to the whole and therefore more like the whole than anything else. Therefore the whole is interpreted in terms of the highest we know in it. Nature is interpreted in terms of soul – the virtues – justice – moderation, courage, and wisdom are seen as natural.

Socrates' turning around to the human things[,] to the good[,] was for the West one of the great events in terms of which man's view of himself and his place in the whole was defined for a millennium. Christianity and Judaism may have modified that account – but basically the greatest Christian and Jewish thinkers interpreted revelation as at one with that account.

But one must see that that account of man in Greek political philosophy and its coming to be in Socrates has been seen in the modern West as a disaster. Both Marxists and positivists have said clearly that by turning to the question of man and man's ends – by judging the whole in terms of man and human ends – it turned men away from the objective science of nature and the control of nature – it led to an anthropomorphized view of nature in a way that prevented modern science and the modern control of nature from arising. The turn of Socrates is seen therefore as a disaster for Western man. One of the central historical doctrines of all modern thought is that this was a disaster – and whatever else may be different in the great modern philosophical systems – positivism, existentialism, Marxism – they are all agreed that Plato is a great obscurantist.

Now what is Strauss saying about modern political philosophy and why is he interested in looking at this turn of Socrates in a different way from other modern thinkers? It is clear from the history of the modern West that modern natural science and modern moral science both came to be as criticisms of Greek natural science and moral science. And the history of the modern West must be seen in terms of these criticisms. We have seen how the Newtonian science of nature required the withering of the Greek doctrine of substance. But equally it required the withering of the Greek moral and political philosophy. And the two criticisms go together. We can't have a moral science of one kind and a science of the non-human of another.

Clearly the question of the nature of man points to the question of the nature of the whole and the nature of the whole includes what the sciences of the non-human tell us of their part of the whole. A thinker who wants to think about the whole has to think both about the non-human world which in modern science is a world understood outside the idea of purpose and at the same time about the human world which is inevitably concerned with the question of purposes and ends.

Let me illustrate this in terms of the interpretation of Kant. It does not seem to me an exaggeration to say that in understanding modern thought there is no thinker who brings together in a greater synthesis the modern, than Kant – a stupendously comprehensive thinker. Now in understanding and interpreting Kant the interpreters have concentrated on the great tribute he paid to the Scottish thinker Hume. Hume taught him about the effect of modern science on metaphysics. He taught him, Kant says, the consequences of the Newtonian discoveries on philosophy. And these interpreters of Kant who concentrate on this side of Kant see his work as essentially work in the philosophy of science leading to positivism. But they often forget that Kant paid an even greater expression of debt to Rousseau – because where Newton taught him [?] about the science of non-human things, Rousseau taught him about the human things, and it is Kant's purpose as a philosopher to put together, to synthesize, what the modern is saying about the non-human world of purposeless mass and force with what we know of the human world of purposes and ends. And he puts these two worlds together in his great account of the whole.

Now Strauss says that there are three great waves in which the modern account of the human things comes to be: the first starts in a hidden way with Machiavelli (and if you are interested in that you can read his book called *Thoughts on Machiavelli* which is my favourite of all his books) and which comes out into the open world with the thought of Hobbes and Locke. It establishes itself particularly in the English-speaking world and as you will all know it is Locke's thought about the nature of the human things which above all is incarnated in the American revolution. (Let me say in parentheses to those of you who are Americans and probably those of you who are Americans and Catholics – one of the strangest parts of the Cold War era, theoretically, was when Father Courtney Murray wrote that the American Declaration of Independence was easily reconciled with the thought of Aquinas.[4] The difficulty was that Aquinas' political philosophy was based on Aristotle in which men by nature were directed to virtue – while in Locke's thought men are directed by nature to comfortable self-preservation and the virtues are not ends worth pursuing for their own purposes, but as means to that. Justice is not natural, but conventional – a means of achieving comfortable self-preservation.)

Be that as it may, I was unable to persuade any of you to write a paper on Hobbes or Locke – so we pass immediately to the second wave of modernity which Strauss takes as originating in Rousseau and the discovery of history – and which passes with the West through the great tradition of German idealism in Kant and Hegel and into the whole world through the greatest of their epigones, Marx. This is what we must discuss today, how in the thought of Rousseau the idea of history enters the West, so that in the West the central distinction becomes that between nature and history rather than the classical distinction between nature and convention – and in which man is seen as an historical being making his own history and in which, therefore, the virtues, and particularly justice, are not natural but historical – things that are coming to be in history.

Before proceeding to that discussion, I must just mention the third wave of modernity as political philosophy ... and which Strauss identifies with Nietzsche and of course his greatest epigone Heidegger.

Let me also say just an obvious word about the relation in Strauss' thought of this third wave of modernity and the return to look at Socrates. This is something I have never said or written before and it becomes increasingly clear to me. Let me put two points together: 1. Nietzsche's greatest exoteric book is called *Beyond Good and Evil*, *Gut und Böse – Beyond Moral Good and Evil*. And it is clear that this lies at the heart of this third wave of modern political philosophy. Nietzsche's great enemy was Rousseau and what Nietzsche is saying is that the attempt of Rousseau and his epigones to secularize Christianity – to make morality historical is just as much unthinkable as Christianity or classical morality. And Heidegger makes this equally clear – the impossibility of ethics.

Now if you put this fact together with another fact, which is that in the great modern thinkers who think in terms of Nietzsche – that is, above all, Heidegger – there is an increasing assertion of the impossibility of politics – this is particularly clear in Heidegger's writing since 1933 – that is, since he learnt the lesson of National Socialism. And it is also clear in the other great philosophers of this era – e.g. Whitehead. Modern thought at its height is led to be able to say nothing about how it is best for man to be together – it is led to have to be able to be silent before the most important question for man – what is the best life for man? – in what does human happiness consist? – in a more than private, in a public way.

Modern theory has been at one in discarding the Socratic turn towards the human things and the interpretation of the whole in the light of the human soul and its needs, but this has led it to be silent about something which is of the greatest importance for man – what is the political good? – what is the best form of political organization for man? Therefore perhaps there is something wrong in the long arguments of modern political philosophy against ancient political philosophy. Do we not now have a need to look again at classical political philosophy and see if there are not truths known that have been lost in the coming to be of modern thought. Read Strauss, pp. 39–40.[5]

NOTES

1 See 'The Natural Basis of Marriage,' in Kant's *The Science of Right*: 'Marriage is the union of two persons of different sex for life-long reciprocal possession of their sexual faculties.'

2 See Strauss, *Persecution and the Art of Writing* (Glencoe II: Free Press, 1952), 9: 'Revelation as understood by Jews and Muslims had the character of Law (*torah, shari'a*) rather than that of Faith.' See also 18–19: 'For the Christian, the sacred doctrine is revealed theology; for the Jew and the Muslim, the sacred doctrine is, at least primarily, the legal interpretation of the Divine Law (*talmud* or *fiqh*). The sacred doctrine in the latter sense has, to say the least, much less in common with philosophy than the sacred doctrine in the former sense.'

3 See Strauss, *Natural Right and History* (Chicago: University of Chicago Press, 1953) and *What Is Political Philosophy? And Other Studies* (Westport, CT: Greenwood Press, 1959). Grant refers to Strauss's essay 'The Three Waves of Modernity,' which he circulated in his graduate classes when it was not yet published. The essay can now be found in Halail Gildin, ed., *An Introduction to Political Philosophy: Ten Essays by Leo Strauss*, (Detroit: Wayne State University Press, 1989), 81–98. Grant's essay 'Tyranny and Wisdom' is in *Technology and Empire* (Toronto: House of Anansi, 1969), 81–109.

4 Father John Courtney Murray (1904–67), an American Roman Catholic theologian whose liberal views angered church conservatives, argued in *We Hold These Truths* (1961), according to Grant, that the American system of democratic and republican government finds its basic moral roots in the doctrine of natural law, which was justified by Aquinas, and that there are immutable standards of personal and public morality which are to be derived from the proper understanding of man's essential nature.

5 Strauss, *What Is Political Philosophy?*

6

Grant, Hegel, and the 'Impossibility of Canada'

ROBERT C. SIBLEY

The publication of George Grant's *Lament for a Nation* in 1965, it is said, sparked an intense period of nationalism in Canada.[1] Yet Grant consistently denied having nationalistic motives for the book. Indeed, he explicitly refers in *Lament* to 'the impossibility of Canada.'[2] Moreover, he is straightforward about why Canada has come to an 'end': the principles or ideas upon which the country was founded have given way to those of the American Republic. These 'American' principles promote social and political arrangements that make particular cultures and nations like Canada redundant. Since Canadians, on the whole, believe that the principles of modernity are right and proper, they have little reason to maintain an independent political existence. Hence, Grant concludes that Canada is impossible as a sovereign nation-state because of the 'character of the modern age.'[3]

How can the 'disappearance' of Canada be attributed to 'the character of the modern age'? The question brings forward the central concern of this chapter – how Grant's linkage of modernity and Canada's political fate is bound up with his philosophic relationship to Hegel. The German's influence on Grant is well known. So, too, is Grant's 'turn' from Hegel. However, insufficient consideration has been given to the connection between Grant's Hegelianism, both in its initial appeal and in its later repudiation, and Grant's claim about the impossibility of Canada. I argue that Grant's 'lament' is bound up with his interpretation of and response to the thinker he once described as the greatest philosopher.[4]

In the 1959 edition of *Philosophy in the Mass Age*, Grant praised Hegel as the one philosopher who had been able to synthesize classical reason, Christian theology, and modern freedom. Hegel, he said, reconciled the concept of modern man as an autonomous, history-making being with the pre-modern account of man as dwelling under the dispensation of an eternal, divinely given natural law. This optimistic appraisal of Hegel did not last long. Grant eventually recognized that it was impossible to bring together classical natural law with the modern ontological notion of time as the history created by men free to make of themselves what they will. Grant's 'turn' from Hegel and liberal progressivism has been called his 'era of retractions,'[5] that period when, under the influence of such thinkers as Leo Strauss, Jacques Ellul, Friedrich Nietzsche, Martin Heidegger, and Simone Weil, he reconsidered his attachments to the modern project. Seven years after *Philosophy in the Mass Age*, Grant had undergone an intellectual conversion: 'I came to the conclusion that Hegel was not correct in his claim to have taken the truth of antique thought and synthesised it with the modern to produce a higher (and perhaps highest) truth; that on many of the most important political matters Plato's teaching is truer than Hegel's. Particularly, I have come to the conclusion that Plato's account of what constitutes human excellence and the possibility of its realisation in the world is more valid than that of Hegel.'[6]

However, despite Grant's disavowal, Hegel continued to have an abiding influence on his thought, providing a theoretical perspective that enabled him to account for the character of the modern world. Grant implied as much in his 1966 repudiation of Hegel when he said that it is difficult for anyone who ascribes to 'the Western Christian doctrine of providence to avoid reaching the conclusion that Hegel has understood the implications of that doctrine better than any other thinker.'[7]

To the degree this comment demonstrates that Grant continued to regard Hegelian philosophy as the fullest expression of modernity, his subsequent thought constitutes an ongoing reappraisal of Hegel in light of what he saw as the failings of the modern project, especially as it was manifested in North American society. Even in rejecting Hegel, then, Grant could not excise the German's influence in any absolute sense because he retained throughout his work the 'truth' of the Hegelian account of modernity.[8] Grant's 'turn' from Hegel should therefore be interpreted not as a rejection of Hegel but as a shift in consciousness on Grant's part akin to the psychology reflected in Hegel's concept of *Aufheben*: that is, a conversion of consciousness that incorporates and sublates a previous mode of consciousness. In this light, the question becomes: What was it about Hegel's thought that Grant could not abide even though he recognized that it provided the most comprehensive account of the modern condition? Answering this question penetrates to the heart of Grant's judgment about the impossibility of Canada.

Before I approach this question, though, it is worthwhile to provide some context to Grant's Hegelianism through a brief comparison of Canadian and American appropriations of Hegelian thought, a comparison that underscores Grant's claim regarding the Canadian surrender to American principles.

HEGEL IN CANADA

Even a brief survey of the literature shows a long-standing interest in Canada in Hegel.[9] Hegelian philosophy was introduced into Canada through Scottish immigrants who imbibed the thought of the Scottish Enlightenment.[10] In the century after 1850, 'the mainstream of philosophy in English-speaking Canada was more often than not Hegelian.'[11] According to scholars, certain Hegelian principles have sunk deep roots in Canadian political culture because of this country's political and geographical circumstances. As Leslie Armour and Elizabeth Trott observe: 'We needed ideas that were capable of spanning spaces and which could link sub-cultures which, because of their distribution, tended to grow in significantly different ways.'[12] Indeed, with a population divided by language, religion, and culture, a vast territory that needed to be held together, and that territory's historical domination by other powers, the attractiveness of a philosophy that sought to reconcile such diversity was valuable in helping to comprehend the Canadian experience. Hegel appeared to provide a theoretical framework that allowed cultures to maintain and develop their distinctive features even while uniting them in a single political order.

Grant's initial employment of Hegelian thought reflects this attitude. Given Grant's concern with Canada maintaining its independence on a continent dominated by the United States, what perhaps most appealed to him about Hegel was the philosopher's understanding of how pluralistic societies can use legal and political systems and institutions to mitigate those forces that threaten to tear them apart. In the *Philosophy of Right*, for example, Hegel argues that modern societies are to be understood by reference to the fundamental concepts that guide them, and that the modern state seeks to enable citizens to assert those rights and freedoms that reflect the truest purposes of human life while, at the same time, reconciling them to a common good.[13] Grant asserts this sentiment in *Lament* when he says that 'a society only articulates itself as a nation through some common intention among its people.'[14] Canada existed as a nation state so long as its citizens held intentionally to the essential idea on which it was founded: 'an inchoate desire to build, in these cold and forbidding regions, a society with a greater sense of order and restraint than freedom-loving republicanism would allow.'[15]

Grant's initial appropriation of Hegel stands in sharp contrast to that of American thinkers, who tend to link Hegelian concepts to notions of manifest destiny. For example, Francis Fukuyama drew on Hegel's notion of historical progress to conclude that, with the collapse of communism, humanity had come to the end of its ideological evolution. The kind of liberal democracy practised in the United States was the final form of human government, the best way to organize human affairs, and it was destined to transform the globe into a homogeneous likeness of itself.[16]

This triumphalist appropriation of Hegel also appears in the nineteenth-century St Louis School whose members introduced the German philosopher to the United States. One of the founding members, Denton J. Snider, argued that the United States embodied the most recent form of World Spirit: 'The odyssey of the Hegelian World Spirit is clear – the United States has already arrived on the scene, bearing in its political structure the principle destined to become the *Begriff* of all future political reality.'[17] Others saw in Hegel's philosophy the means of fostering national unity. Josiah Royce recast Hegel's principle of reconciliation to replace the Hegelian Absolute with a community united by a common understanding of and feelings towards the world. That is to say, Royce sought to apply Hegelian concepts – the identity of identity and non-identity, for instance – to differences among people in such a way that these differences collapsed into a new identity, a new loyalty that transcended difference.[18]

Grant eventually saw this triumphalist appropriation of Hegel as the one that has the most meaning for the modern world, at least in the sense that the technological society of North America was the most complete embodiment of Hegel's thought. But what was it about the Hegelian project that Grant could not accept?

THE PROBLEM OF HISTORY: NECESSITY CONTRA THE GOOD

Grant's confrontation with Hegel begins in *Philosophy of the Mass Age* when he asserts the problematical nature of the concept of history. History, he says, presents difficulties for anyone attempting to make moral judgments about whether their actions are the right or wrong.[19] With this claim, Grant makes history a central concern of his thought. He seeks to show how history displaced the ancient understanding of nature as the overarching concept by which man comprehends himself and his world. History, according to Grant, is not one idea among others that shapes the modern world, but rather the core theoretical concept by which moderns understand themselves and their purposes. Historicism, in essence, posits the claim that man's knowledge and experience of that world are to be understood only in and through historical movement.

Grant contrasts historicist consciousness with ancient consciousness.[20] The former regards the world as an unending flow of unique and irreversible events that have to be dominated and controlled through creative will. The latter considers time "as the moving image of an unmoving eternity and in which the passing events of life only have meaning as they lead men to the unchanging reality of God.'[21] Ancient consciousness provided a doctrine of natural law by which man sought his perfectibility in a union of temporal and divine reason.

Grant, of course, stands against historicism. He cannot agree that man is ultimately knowable as an historical being, and much of his philosophic effort was devoted to countering this notion. In particular, his attempt to understand the significance of historicism reflects his confrontation with Hegel, who, for Grant, was the great exemplar of historicist thinking. What turned Grant from his initial acceptance of Hegel's notion of historical development was his recognition that it carried too much of the positivist idea of progress as the ultimate aim of man and, worse, made even evil a purposive good. Such a claim ignores the idea of man's existence having a given highest purpose or good that transcends time or history. According to Grant, Hegel's identification of necessity with goodness ultimately meant that history is the judgment of those possessed with the power to impose their will. For Grant, though, to make history 'the final court of appeal' for man's meanings is tantamount to 'worshipping force.'[22]

Grant's rejection of historicism is stated most clearly in the final chapter of *Lament for a Nation*:

I must dissociate myself from a common philosophic assumption. I do not identify necessity and goodness. This identification is widely assumed during an age of progress. Those who worship 'evolution' or 'history' consider that what must come in the future will be 'higher,' 'more developed,' 'better,' 'freer' than what has been in the past They identify necessity and good within the rubric of providence. From the assumption that God's purposes are unfolded in historical events, one may be led to view history as an ever-fuller manifestation of good.[23]

Against this historicist perspective, Grant sets Plato and classical philosophy. The ancients distinguished between eternity, or the Good, and Necessity, the realm of becoming that remains distinct from the Good even while participating in it. Only by maintaining this distinction between Necessity and the Good can we retain the distinction between good and evil. Grant, however, sees in Hegelian thought the collapse of this distinction. By identifying progress and providence, Hegel reduces all that is 'Other' to human subjectivity – that is, to historical development – and human willpower. The otherness of God that allows man to maintain a concept of goodness separate from and not subject to his history making is lost.

Adopting Martin Luther's terms, Grant describes Hegelian philosophy and its doctrine of progress as a theology of glory that exalts human will and makes the realm of necessity or history and not the Good or eternity (or nature) the arena for man's redemption. A theology of glory regards historical events as manifestations of divine will, setting up the claim that such events are unique and irreversible because their meaning is derived from God's will. This claim, in turn, tends to exalt human will and implies that action must be future-directed in that humans have their fulfilment not in the present but in the future.[24] For Grant, though, as he writes in the essay 'Faith and the Multiversity,' this was the fundamental 'mistake' of Western Christianity: It 'simplified divine love by identifying it too closely with immanent power in the world.'[25] That is to say, Christianity in the West became triumphalist because the historicist consciousness within which it came to function denied the infinite distance between necessity and good.

In Grant's view, this conflation of necessity and goodness received its fullest expression in Hegel and his notion of world history as the unfolding of Reason: 'Die Weltgeschichte ist das Weltgericht,' or 'World History is the world's judgement.'[26] Such a notion is anathema to Grant: 'Hegel makes God's providence scrutable, and that is a teaching that offended me then and now at the deepest level.'[27] In identifying progress and providence, Hegel effectively calls evil good and good evil in the sense that he casts the future as necessarily better than the past, thus justifying suffering as necessary for historical progress.

Grant thought this reliance on historical activity obscured the good and any genuine Otherness – including the 'Other' that was Canada. Indeed, Grant connects the conflation of progress and providence to his assertion regarding the 'impossibility' of Canada by arguing that nowhere has Hegel's doctrine of progress manifested itself more vigorously than in North America.

THE 'FATE' OF NORTH AMERICA

According to Grant, North American mass society epitomizes modernity's history-making consciousness. It incarnates more than any other society the values and principles of the age of progress, including an unquestioned subscription to mass production and its techniques, standardized consumption and education, wholesale entertainment, and almost wholesale medicine.

Grant identifies two basic characteristics of mass society: first, a scientific-technological epistemology and the attempt to apply that theory of knowledge to the domination of nature, including human nature; second, the use by an economic and political elite of various institutions and structures to extend this control, such that even the elite is subjected to technology's dominion. Under the sway of modern epistemology, reason itself comes to be an instrument to satisfy subjective purposes. Man's innate capacity for reason becomes part of the apparatus for enclosing him in an ever-tightening circle.[28]

Nowhere, Grant argues, does this technological encirclement reveal itself more completely than in the United States, making it the centre of the modern project. According to Grant, this makes the United States inherently imperialistic because it is technological in the deepest ontological sense. This imperialist intention does not necessarily express itself through colonies and territorial conquest; rather, it manifests itself through the imperatives of a technological society that gives priority to market forces, techniques of efficiency, and mass culture.

How did Grant see this 'American' technological imperialism reflected in the 'necessity' of Canada's disappearance, and how is that disappearance related to his confrontation with Hegel? Answering this question entails returning to *Lament for a Nation*. On the surface, *Lament* is the tale of how John Diefenbaker's Progressive Conservative government came under attack from Canada's political, corporate, and bureaucratic elite. It is a story of how a national debate about stationing U.S. nuclear warheads on Canadian soil turned into a conspiracy by

Canada's liberal establishment and business elite to defeat Diefenbaker in the 1963 election. Grant had little admiration for Diefenbaker – before the defence crisis he 'saw nothing in his [Diefenbaker's] favour,' as he said in a 1965 CBC interview[29] – but he regarded his electoral defeat as concrete evidence of the 'impossibility' of Canada and, by extension, 'the fate of any particularity in the technological age.'[30]

Furthermore, Grant saw in Diefenbaker a conservatism akin to his own. This conservatism should not be misconstrued; Grant was not hostile to change or opposed to technology.[31] Rather, his conservatism required maintaining connections to the older institutional orders and social traditions of Britain and, for Quebeckers, to France. So long as those connections and the traditions embedded in them held sway in Canadian society, particularly among the dominant elite, then Canada was possible. The fall of Diefenbaker's government revealed how tenuous these ties had become among that elite, especially in English-speaking Canada. They welcomed the influence of the United States as it expanded continent-wide and globally through the growth of corporate capitalism. Because expansion brought wealth, it was in the interests of Canada's ruling classes to attach themselves to the forces of continentalism, which, as one scholar observes, is a catchphrase that in the Canadian context 'signifies the loss of identity, sovereignty and distinctness.'[32] Or, as Grant puts it, 'the impossibility of conservatism in our era is the impossibility of Canada. As Canadians we attempted a ridiculous task in trying to build a conservative nation in the age of progress.'[33]

It is easy to understand why, for the sake of money, Canada's capitalists were so willing to forego the country's independence. As Grant sardonically states, 'no small country can depend for its existence on the loyalty of its capitalists.'[34] But even the federal public service 'did not have the stuff of loyalty' and, as a result, became the instrument of a policy that left Canada a satellite of the United States. To be sure, Grant knows that no modern state can function without the civil service having considerable authority. Especially in 'uncertain nations' such as Canada, 'the civil service is perhaps the essential instrument by which nationhood is preserved.' Nevertheless, Grant still asks why Canada's senior federal bureaucrats were so amenable to becoming 'more and more representative of a western empire rather than civil servants of a particular nation-state.'[35]

Grant may fault the elite for its betrayals, but he recognizes that the deeper sources of Canada's disappearance are rooted in the modern ontology. 'The confused strivings of politicians, businessmen and civil servants cannot alone account for Canada's collapse. This stems from the very character of the modern era.' Even if the bureaucrats, politicians, and businessmen had been more loyal, they could not have withstood the imperatives of the modern project. A conservative Canada is impossible because 'the aspirations of progress have made Canada redundant.'[36] Conservatism must give way to the imperatives of technology.

Grant sees that the essence of contemporary liberalism is the identification of freedom and technology. Secular man believes his freedom requires control of the world, and this is to be accomplished through technology. But it is this largely unthinking ascription to the technological imperative that fated Canada to disappear. When Grant declares 'the impossibility of Canada,' he means that the nation abandoned its former intention to preserve itself as conceptually different from the United States. Canada ceased to be a sovereign nation, not because its formal political existence had come to an end, but because the 'ideas' that provided its reasons for existence were no longer seen to be worth preserving in any substantive way. With no common intention beyond the liberal-progressivist promise of freedom and material goods, Canadians gave themselves over to the technological ethos exemplified in the American technological empire. The result was a 'country' that, as Donald Creighton put it, was merely 'a good place to live.'[37] Grant made much the same argument in later years about free trade between Canada and the United States. This, too, was another move toward Canada's economic and political integration into the United States. Such an integrative process was the fate of any particularity in the age of technology and there was little to stop it.[38]

Grant's understanding of Canada's fate is captured in the phrase 'the universal and homogeneous state'[39] that he appropriated from Alexandre Kojève, the French Hegel exegete. Kojève interpreted Hegel's philosophy to be a philosophy of Time as History, and, with this interpretation, originated the now famous end-of-history thesis, according to which the end of history is consistent with the universal and homogeneous state. It is through his appropriation of Kojève's end-of-history interpretation of Hegel as his own that Grant sees the 'impossibility' of Canada. Such a world state, if realized, requires an end to the idea of Canada as a sovereign nation state on the top half of the North American continent. In other words, 'conservative' Canada disappears with the fulfilment of the Hegelian project.

CONCLUSION: TYRANNY, PHILOSOPHY, AND THE 'END' OF CANADA

Grant was persuaded to this view of the universal and homogeneous state, in part at least, by his understanding of the debate between Leo Strauss and Kojève. Since a consideration of this debate is beyond the scope of this essay, I shall restrict myself to noting Grant's general acceptance of Strauss's judgment that the universal and homogeneous state would be a tyranny and not, as Kojève contended, the culmination of man's historical struggle for recognition.[40] As Grant puts it: 'If the best social order is the universal and homogeneous state, then the disappearance of Canada can be understood as a step towards that order. If the universal and homogeneous state would be a tyranny, then the disappearance of even this indigenous culture can be seen as the removal of a minor barrier on the road to that tyranny.'[41]

Beyond the social dimension, though, Grant also sees the establishment of the universal and homogeneous state in theological terms, recognizing that it necessitated the de-divinization of the 'Other' that is God. As Kojève argues, the universal and homogeneous state could be achieved only by secularizing Christian theism in favour of an anthropomorphic historicism in which Christian eschatological hopes for the perfection of humanity in a transcendent realm are recast as a goal to be realized in the here-and-now of this world. But this can be attempted, Grant argues, only if philosophy takes its ground not from 'an ahistorical eternal order,' but from an eternity that is 'the totality of all historical epochs.'[42]

For Grant, as an avowed Christian Platonist, such a goal is not one for which man is best fitted. The universal and homogeneous state, far from being the best social order, would, if actualized, result in a tyrannical order harmful to man, as conceived by classical philosophy. Hence, Grant follows Strauss's judgment on Kojève: 'Modern philosophy, which has substituted freedom for virtue, has as its chief ideal ... a social order which is destructive of humanity.'[43] Moreover, the universal and homogeneous state also means the end of philosophy, or, what is the same thing, the end of human excellence, since it is no longer acceptable to think that only a few are fitted for asking the most serious questions (never mind that there are no serious questions about human purposes to be asked at the end of history). For Kojève-Hegel, human satisfaction is grounded in historical recognition, or freedom and equality; for Grant-Strauss, human satisfaction is rooted in thought, in the contemplation of that which is unchanging: 'Philosophy is the excellence of the soul. There cannot be philosophy unless there is an eternal and unchangeable order.'[44] The coming-to-be of the technological order means the end of philosophy because the lowering of horizons that brings about the universal and homogenous state requires the denial of substantive distinctions among people, cultures, and even nations. The universal and homogeneous state, the end point of the Hegelian project, means the end of the 'distinct' political order that was Canada. Or, to put it differently, modern philosophy makes Canada impossible.

In conclusion, I have tried to show that, for Grant, the character of modernity means the end of a sovereign and independent Canada, and that this removal of what makes Canada 'Other' to the United States is but one example of the erasure of alternatives that results from the fulfilment of Hegelian philosophy. This is not anti-Americanism on Grant's part: he simply recognizes that, because of certain geo-political and economic realities, Americanization is the way modernization is unfolding. Americans were the first members of the planet to be fully modernized. Canadians came second.

By Grant's argument, then, we now dwell in a post-Canadian world. While we might retain the formal trappings of nationhood – a flag, a border, parliament, Canada Day – little of significant 'national' substance or sovereignty remains.[45] Nor can there be any serious prospect of recovering a substantively distinct Canada. As Grant learned from Nietzsche, all horizons are 'man-made perspectives by which the charismatic impose their will to power,' expressions of 'the values which our tortured instincts will to create.'[46] Our historicist consciousness tells us that nationalism is a fiction. So how can we sustain any authentic patriotism when we are self-consciously aware that our nation is an invention that exists at the sufferance (or indifference) of the modern project as embodied in the United States?

Hegel's thought, therefore, enabled Grant to comprehend what the modern project ultimately means. But this in turn means that he could not have rejected Hegel even if he so desired because his own thinking constitutes a response to Hegel. Grant's analysis of technology, his judgments on liberalism as a theology of glory, and his lament for Canada, all reflect variations on an ongoing confrontation with Hegel. As one critic puts it, Hegel is 'the true voice of all that Grant opposes.'[47] In this regard, Grant's reputation as a 'father of Canadian nationalism' needs to be re-evaluated. This reconsideration should be accompanied by a rejection of the notion that Grant's lament for the nation once known as Canada was little more than an indulgence in 'longing for the past,' an 'Anglo-Saxon lament,' or nostalgia for some pre-war myth of Canada's

Britishness.[48] Certainly, Grant knew that his thought was informed by his 'being part of a class which is disappearing.'[49] But he also insisted that only 'simple people' would settle for interpreting *Lament* as mere nostalgia for 'the passing of the British dream of Canada.'[50]

If Grant's views on the relationship between philosophy and the political reality of Canada can be parsed to a single statement, it is this: if modernity constitutes the end of philosophy in favour of technology, then Canada was fated to disappear. This might seems an outlandish notion to some, but it is what Grant's diagnosis of modernity implies. If Hegel is right, if necessity and goodness are identical, and the tyranny of the universal and homogeneous state is the political result of that identification, Grant is correct to pronounce Canada's impossibility.

NOTES

1 See, for example, Mel Hurtig, 'One Last Chance: The Legacy of Lament for a Nation,' in Peter Emberley, ed., *By Loving Our Own: George Grant and the Legacy of Lament for a Nation* (Ottawa: Carleton University Press, 1990), 44. Clifford Orwin refers to Grant as 'a father of Canadian nationalism.' Review of Grant's *English-Speaking Justice, University of Toronto Law Journal* 30 (1980): 106.

2 George Grant, *Lament for a Nation: The Defeat of Canadian Nationalism* (1965; repr. Ottawa: Carleton Library Series, 1989), 68. Even in later years, while acknowledging the 'traces of care' shown by Pierre Trudeau's nationalist policies, Grant maintained that 'below the surface the movement towards integration continues.' See ibid., 'Introduction,' viii–ix.' As late as 1985, Grant insisted that he had not been trying to promote the nationalist cause in *Lament*: 'Because people quite rightly want finite hopes, people have read a little book I wrote wrongly. I was talking about the *end* of Canadian nationalism. I was saying that this is over and people read it as if I was making an appeal for Canadian nationalism. I think that is just nonsense. I think they just read it wrongly.' Quoted by Larry Schmidt, 'An Interview with George Grant,' *Grail* 1 (March 1985): 36. Cited in William Christian, 'George Grant's Lament,' *Queen's Quarterly* 100, 1 (1993): 211.

3 Grant, *Lament*, 53.

4 Grant, *Philosophy in the Mass Age*, ed. William Christian (1959; rept. Toronto: University of Toronto Press, 1995), 120.

5 Frank Flinn, 'Bibliographical Introduction,' in Larry Schmidt, ed., *George Grant in Process* (Toronto: House of Anansi Press, 1978), 197.

6 Grant, *Philosophy in the Mass Age*, 121–2.
7 Ibid., 120.
8 George Grant, *Technology and Empire* (Toronto: House of Anansi Press, 1969), 104.
9 David MacGregor has written that, proportionately, 'Canada may produce more original work on Hegel than any other nation.' See 'Canada's Hegel,' *Literary Review of Canada*, February 1994, 18–29.
10 Leslie Armour and Elizabeth Trott, *The Faces of Reason: An Essay on Philosophy and Culture in English-Canada 1850–1950* (Waterloo, Ont.: Wilfrid Laurier University Press, 1981), 1–32.
11 Leslie Armour, *The Idea of Canada and the Crisis of Community* (Ottawa: Steel Rail Publishing, 1981), 79.
12 Armour and Trott, *The Faces of Reason*, 19.
13 Hegel, *Philosophy of Right* (no. 260), T.M. Knox translation (Oxford: Clarendon Press, 1952), 160–1.
14 Grant, *Lament*, 68. I have argued elsewhere that Grant may have absorbed Hegelian principles even before he read Hegel through the influence of his grandfather, George Monro Grant. As head of Queen's University in the later decades of the nineteenth century, G.M. Grant was a friend of the Idealist philosopher and Hegel scholar John Watson, who taught at Queen's for several decades. See Robert C. Sibley, 'Northern Spirits: Canadian Appropriations of Hegelian Political Thought,' PhD Thesis, Carleton University, 2002, 216–17.
15 Ibid., 70.
16 Francis Fukuyama, *The End of History and the Last Man* (New York: Free Press, 1992).
17 Quoted by James A. Good, 'A "World Historical Idea": The St. Louis Hegelians and the Civil War,' *Journal of American Studies* 34, 3 (2000): 450.
18 Josiah Royce, *The Philosophy of Loyalty* (New York: Macmillan, 1908).
19 Grant, *Philosophy in the Mass Age*, 3.
20 On this topic, I have greatly benefited from Harris Athanasiadis's study, *George Grant and the Theology of the Cross: The Christian Foundation of His Thought* (Toronto: University of Toronto Press, 2001), 112–15.
21 Grant, *Philosophy in the Mass Age*, 19.
22 Grant, *Lament*, 89.
23 Ibid., 88–9.
24 Athanasiadis, *George Grant and the Theology of the Cross*, 207–8.
25 George Grant, *Technology and Justice* (Toronto: Anansi, 1986), 76.
26 Grant, *Lament*, 89.
27 Grant, quoted by Schmidt, ed., *George Grant in Process*, 64.

28 Grant, *Philosophy in the Mass Age*, 4–8.

29 Cited by Christian, 'George Grant's Lament,' 205, 207–8.

30 Grant, 'Introduction,' *Lament*, ix.

31 As Grant writes in *Lament*: 'Those who criticize our age must at the same time contemplate pain, infant mortality, crop failures in isolated areas, and the sixteen-hour day' (94).

32 Yusuf Umar, 'George Grant's Political Philosophy,' in Yusuf Umar, ed., *George Grant and the Future of Canada* (Calgary: University of Calgary Press, 1992), 14–15.

33 Grant, *Lament*, 68.

34 Ibid., 69.

35 Ibid., 18, 51–2.

36 Ibid., 53.

37 Creighton's scathing statement needs to be quoted in full: 'Well, it's still a good place to live, but that's all Canada is now – just a good place to live.' Quoted by Charles Taylor, *Radical Tories* (Toronto: Anansi, 1982), 23. In short, Canada is a comfort zone for lifestyle consumers.

38 Monica Hall, 'Lament for a Nation Revisited: An Interview with George Grant,' by Monica Hall, *International Insights: A Dallhousie Journal on International Affairs* 4, no. 1 (1988): 7. Also: Tim Thomas, 'George Grant, the Free Trade Agreement and Contemporary Quebec,' *Journal of Canadian Studies* 27, no. 4 (1992–3): 180–96.

39 Grant, *Lament*, 53. This is Grant's first use of Kojève's phrase in *Lament* and it is worth quoting him on what he takes it to mean: 'The universal and homogeneous state is the pinnacle of political striving. "Universal" implies a world-wide state, which would eliminate the curse of war among nations; "homogeneous" means that all men would be equal, and war among classes would be eliminated.'

40 Grant's exposition of and commentary on the Strauss-Kojève debate is contained in his 1963 essay 'Tyranny and Wisdom.' See *Technology and Empire*, 81–109. The debate was raised in Strauss's book *On Tyranny: An Interpretation of Xenophon*, in which Strauss argues that Xenophon, in his dialogue *Hiero*, showed a better understanding of the relationship between politics and philosophy than modern thinkers. The book contains Kojève's response to Strauss and a rejoinder from Strauss to Kojève. In essence, Strauss claims that the philosopher can possess a knowledge that transcends particular historical circumstances. Kojève contends that philosophical knowledge and, hence, political order are dependent on and determined by the historical process, the end of which brings the universal and homogeneous states into being as the best and last political order. Grant accepts Strauss's refuta-

tion of Kojève's argument: the actualization of the universal and homogenous state would be a tyranny and not the culmination of man's historical
struggle for recognition. In this regard, it is understandable why Grant
describes the Strauss-Kojève debate as 'the most important controversy in
contemporary political philosophy,' *Technology and Empire*, 81.

41 Grant, *Lament*, 44.
42 Grant, *Technology and Empire*, 88–90.
43 Ibid., 92–3.
44 Ibid., 98.
45 Hans Hauge, 'George Grant's Critique of Modernity: Canadian Refractions
    of Continental Ideas,' *Canadian Issues* 12 (1990): 109–23.
46 George, Grant, *Time as History* (1969, rept.: Toronto: University of Toronto
    Press, 1995), 40.
47 Zdravko Planinc, 'Paradox and Polyphony in Grant's Critique of Moder-
    nity,' in Umar, ed., *George Grant and the Future of Canada*, 31.
48 Arthur Kroker, *Technology and the Canadian Mind* (Montreal: New World Per-
    spectives, 1984), 25, 50–1; R.K. Crook, 'Modernization and Nostalgia: A
    Note on the Sociology of Pessimism,' *Queen's Quarterly* 73 (1966): 269–84;
    Robert Blumstock, 'Anglo-Saxon Lament,' *Canadian Journal of Sociology and
    Anthropology* 3 (1966): 98–105; Abraham Rotstein, 'Running from Paradise,'
    Canadian Forum, (May 1969, 26; Dennis Duffy, 'The Ancestral Journeys:
    Travels with George Grant,' *Journal of Canadian Studies* 22, no. 3 (1987):
    90–103.
49 Grant, 'Conversation,' in Schmidt, ed., *George Grant in Process*, 63.
50 Grant, *Lament*, xi.

7

Response to the Strauss–Kojève Debate: Grant's Turn from Hegel to Christian Platonism

ALEXANDER DUFF

It is my aim in this chapter to discuss what I have called George Grant's turn from Hegel to Christian Platonism, particularly as it is illuminated by the place in his thought of the great twentieth-century Socratic, Leo Strauss. I shall endeavour to clarify the extent to which Grant's thought is less indebted to Strauss than challenged by it. I begin with and devote the larger part of this chapter to an exposition of Grant's essay 'Tyranny and Wisdom.'[1] This essay, Grant's discussion of the famous Strauss-Kojève debate, recommends itself as an especially useful entryway into our question.[2] It contains the core of Grant's response to (a) the problem of Hegel and (b) to where he differed with Strauss's reading of Plato. Then, by way of conclusion, I discuss in broader terms the questions raised by Grant in 'Tyranny and Wisdom'; here I have recourse to a frank later essay of his, 'Faith and the Multiversity.'[3] In this section, I intend to show that Grant was not, strictly speaking, indebted to Strauss for his understanding of classical philosophy; rather, he found in Strauss a powerful challenge to his own Christianity, one that had to be answered with great respect and that prepared the way for Grant's adoption of Christian Platonism.[4]

In the remarks that preface 'Tyranny and Wisdom' as the essay appears in *Technology and Empire*, Grant identifies it as his attempt 'to introduce what is for [him] the most important controversy in contemporary political philosophy' (81).[5] Namely, is 'the universal and homogenous state the best social order' (82)? Grant has structured the essay in two sections: first, he presents those parts of each interlocutor's argument that pertain to his interest; then, he formulates carefully constructed questions by way of commentary.

Grant enters the controversy 'at the point of a concrete political teaching' (86). He expresses this concrete teaching as Kojève's affirmation that the universal and homogenous state is 'the best social order and that mankind advances to the establishment of such an order' (86). Grant's choice of words here – 'best social order' – should alert us that he is evaluating this question in terms that will prove closer to Strauss's than to Kojève's.[6] Kojève, for one, would not presume to speak of the 'best' social order, accepting as he does no permanently self-identical standard by which to make such judgments of good. Let us assume, then, that Grant will not ultimately agree with Kojève. We might be prepared, however, for Grant to find some merit in Kojève's argument nonetheless.

Grant, following Kojève, proceeds to survey the relationship between tyranny and wisdom throughout Western history, identifying in earlier empires and epochs the seeds of universality and homogeneity. From this account of the history of the west, Grant isolates the implied teaching of what philosophy is, and from this he extracts what might be called, loosely speaking, the ontological premises of the argument. In Pauline Christianity, the natural master-slave distinctions of the universal Alexandrian empire are negated by Christian faith in the equal (i.e., homogenous) status of all before God. For this universal and homogenous church to, in turn, be overcome and replaced by the universal and homogenous state required the labour of the modern philosophers (Grant cites Hobbes and Spinoza) and their tyrannical 'students.' Naturally, this negative labour was completed by Napoleon and Hegel (86–8).

According to Kojève, the task of philosophy is to survey and then to put forth in discursive speech a complete account of the actual historical situation at a given moment, including all of its contradictions. In doing so, the philosopher distinguishes between the actual historical situation and the ideal and provides the necessary instruction to direct the negative 'struggle and work' of tyrants. This struggle and work, fomented by the utterances of the philosophers and executed by the tyrants, constitutes the progress of history. As Grant surmises, the 'dependence of philosophers on the activity of tyrants' (90), along with their complete attachment to their moment in history, is the political implication of the ontological premise that 'being creates itself throughout the course of history and that eternity is the totality of all historical epochs' – that is, not eternity (90).

Grant, as we shall see, subscribes to a different view of the task of philosophy, and accordingly a different view of ontology. Nonetheless, he finds Kojève's description of the universal and homogenous state accurate. In his words:

Indeed whatever else should be said of Kojève's sketch of western political history, it is surely accurate to affirm that the universal and homogenous state has been the dominant ideal in recent modern political thought, not only among many who would scorn Hegel's philosophy. Indeed the drive to the universal and homogenous state remains the dominant ethical 'ideal' to which our contemporary society appeals for meaning in its activity. In its terms our society legitimises itself to itself ... The need to think the truth of this ideal remains even as its content empties into little more than the pursuit of technical expansion. (88–9)

This is the merit that Grant sees in Kojève: that he accurately discerns the 'ideal' of all political thought that should properly be called modern; that this ideal and its corresponding ontology is what lurks behind the most serious modern thinkers (including, most important, Hegel); and that it should be described in much the manner adopted by Kojève.[7]

Grant approaches Strauss less directly or more circumspectly. Rather than beginning at the point of concrete political teaching, as with Kojève, Grant attends first to the form of Strauss's argument as a whole. He attributes to Strauss the general criticism of Kojève that his argument first assumes what it seeks to prove: that the universal and homogenous state is the 'best social order' (91). Grant remarks, however, that such an assertion is made from within the assumptions, not of Hegelian, Kojèvian, or, broadly speaking, modern political science, but of classical political science – that true statements about the best social order may be made independently of the historical epoch. Initially, then, Strauss does not meet Kojève on his own terms – this is what Grant means by the 'form' of Strauss's argument. Grant hypothesizes that this is because Strauss first wishes to establish the consistency and thus the relevance of classical political science; his objective is to treat classical political science as a viable alternative to the account offered by Kojève. Thus, before refuting Kojève, Strauss must first show that classical political philosophy is coherent on its own terms and not subject to the internal contradictions that would render it subject to the laborious movement of history (i.e., 'step one' in the dialectic), as in Kojève's account. Thus, Grant identifies Strauss's primary motive as political, or, as we might say, rhetorical: he wishes to propose the current, not to say permanent, viability of classical political philosophy as opposed to its alternatives, and therefore stresses its consistency, its internal coherence, and its enduring seriousness.

In this particular case, Strauss will perform his task by refuting Kojève's claim that the universal and homogenous state is the best social order. In this regard, the argument continues by asserting that, even on Kojèvian-Hegelian grounds, the universal and homogenous state will not provide 'reasonable satisfaction' (93). Grant mainly quotes Strauss at this point, citing long passages from the concluding pages of Strauss's restatement, where the broader implications are most clearly limned. Kojève's conclusions, according to Strauss, derive from the contradictory assertions that (a) the citizens of the universal and homogenous state are syntheses of masters and slaves, that is, warrior-workers; and that (b) war and work are over, completed. By this formulation, the satisfaction that is meant to be derived from war and work, and that is intended to distinguish man from the brutes, will have disappeared. And so, entailed in the withering away of this satisfaction is the withering away of man's humanity (94). Any alternative must look appealing.

Grant isolates the next step in Strauss's argument: once Strauss has shown, on Kojèvian-Hegelian terms, that the universal and homogenous state fails to satisfy, then he is free to refer outside those terms to his preferred alternative, that offered by classical political philosophy. In doing so, Grant points out, Strauss makes two points: first, he re-emphasizes the consistency of the classical position; and second, he shows that, on classical terms, the universal and homogenous state is 'destructive of humanity' (95) and that its practical import is tyranny, 'indeed, the most appalling tyranny in the story of the race' (95). The crucial distinction is the classical judgment that man's deepest satisfaction or happiness derives not from recognition but from philosophic thinking. In these terms, the universal and homogenous state would provide universal satisfaction only if it were the case that men universally were capable of philosophic thought. Strauss reminds us that this is not so, that, owing to the weakness of human nature, only the few are capable of the pursuit of wisdom. These recognized limits of human power inform the classical awareness that the best regime depends on chance and is therefore improbable. Yet, unlikely though it is, the best regime for the classics provides a natural standard by which to judge and to guide any actual political order.

Strauss contrasts this to the impossibility of actualizing, and the consequent destructiveness of attempting, the modern or Kojèvian scheme.

These three classical principles – that man's highest good or happiness is wisdom; that even its pursuit, let alone its realization, is available only to the few; and that the actualization of the accordingly best regime is dependent on chance – expose the truth that the universal and homogenous state is a tyranny. In the modern, Kojèvian instance, 'the goal of man is lowered' (95): universal recognition and its satisfactions are substituted for moral virtue and man's natural happiness. The goal is lowered, however, by the force of conquering and mastering nature, including that aspect of nature which is called chance. Thus, in the application of this new standard, which fails to satisfy even on its own terms (as Strauss has just pointed out), the former natural standard is obscured or obliterated, such that 'the very idea of a standard that is independent of actual situations' is destroyed (95). It is in the light of this obliteration of nature and the natural standard of the best regime that Strauss is able to call the universal and homogenous state a tyranny.

Upon concluding his brief summary of the controversy, Grant limits his comments to two matters: the standing of technology and its relation to biblical religion. On the whole, and as we have begun to see, Grant finds less merit in Kojève than in Strauss. But, in each of the two matters under consideration, he offers a carefully considered criticism of Strauss as well.

The question concerning technology comprises a few related issues. As a point of fact, what did the classical philosophers judge to be the proper relation between science or philosophy, on the one hand, and society or the city, on the other? Is such a judgment on their part right? And how might such a judgment rightly be applied now? Grant distils these into the *quaestio facti* and the *quaestio juris*, and he wisely attends to the distortion of a sound assessment of the *quaestio facti* effected by the great difference between classical and modern thinkers as to the *quaestio juris*: 'The fundamental nature of the presuppositions involved for a contemporary commentator in examining the "quaestio juris" may so dominate the mind as to make difficult the objective scrutiny of the "quaestio facti"' (99). Strauss's assertion of fact, the assertion in question, is that the classical political philosophers had considered the possibility of a science that issues in the conquest and mastery of nature but had rejected such a science as unnatural and destructive of humanity. In more penetrating terms, they did so for the reason that such a science would assert the illusory control of the realm of freedom over the realm of necessity. Such a wilful assertion would come at the cost of obscuring or perhaps somehow destroying the eternal unchanging order, the assumed existence of which is the necessary condition for the classical understanding of philosophy as the excellence of the soul, that is, for the contemplation of that eternal order. In short, a science issuing in the conquest of nature would amount to the denial of that human excellence which is the contemplation of nature. Hence its considered rejection by the classical philosophers. To substantiate this claim, Strauss cites one passage each from Xenophon, Empedocles, and Plato.

Grant finds Strauss's few references to classical political philosophers 'turning their back on' (99) the conquest of nature inadequate. He says so twice: 'Indeed it is clear that a matter of this consequence cannot be settled solely by an appeal to individual texts' (97); 'I must emphasise that the question of fact requires more elucidation than Strauss gives it' (100). Grant finds a possible justification for this in the fact that 'Strauss is reading into these references from the Greeks a clarity about their rejection of the conquest of nature which is not present in their writings, and that *he does so because of his concern to show a consistent alternative to the modern conception of the science of nature*' (99; emphasis added). Such an explanation seems more than possible Grant thought, in the light of what he adduced to be Strauss's rhetorical-political, primary intention: to show the consistency in the classical account of politics and the whole in order to present a clear alternative to the modern position. Still, Grant's explanation notwithstanding, it seems more likely, considering Strauss's remarks at the beginning of his 'Restatement,' that he regarded 'the attempt to restore classical social science' as 'utopian.'[8] Strauss's understanding of 'utopian' is set out in the final pages of his essay: 'Modern man, dissatisfied with utopias and scorning them, has tried to find a guarantee for the actualization of the best social order... The classical solution is utopian in the sense that its actualization is improbable. The modern solution is utopian in the sense that its actualization is impossible. The classical solution supplies a stable standard by which to judge of any actual order. The modern solution eventually destroys the very idea of a standard that is independent of actual situations.'[9] Grant is intimating this question: is Strauss failing to provide a more rigorous discussion of the classical philosophers' choice to reject a technological science in the interest of restoring classical political science as a salutary, utopian standard? The question becomes, then, whether Strauss is able to effect this task without giving a more satisfying account of the classical political philosophers' turning their back on a technological science. Or, to rephrase that question more strongly: How salutary a standard is Strauss supplying if it cannot suffer such questions?

Grant addresses himself to this subject in his treatment of the *quaestio juris*: were the classical philosophers right to consider a science issuing in the conquest of nature destructive of humanity? In the first place, Grant finds himself at the very disadvantage which he identified in the case of Strauss: he is surrounded by technological society, as it were, and consequently unable to distinguish clearly between the question of fact and the question of right in the matter of the relationship of science to society: 'My difficulty in comprehending Strauss' position lies not then in giving some meaning to the idea that the dominant leaders of our society are committed to unlimited technological progress, but rather in understanding what it meant to the classical political philosophers not to be so committed, and even more in understanding what it would mean not to be so committed in the contemporary world' (101). Nonetheless, Grant discerns, in remarks of Strauss found elsewhere, what Strauss thinks the more proper relation between science and society might be.[10] Strauss says that the classical position regarding science and society might be called conservative. It requires a strict distinction between the ends of the philosopher and the ends of the city, and; this in turn entails a strict moral-political – that is, above all prudent – supervision of technologies, or, as we might say, of the public face of science. This is required by the danger that 'man's inventions might become his masters and his destroyers' (102),[11] which would obscure the notion of the primacy of the Good. It is this notion, and the maintenance of the fundamental experience from which it is derived, that is the necessary condition for a healthy politics. And though a healthy politics is the end of the city, not the philosopher, it is the necessary condition for the practice of philosophy, and philosophers would do well to respect, even nurture, it (101–2).

It is the question of the present-day application of this classical, 'conservative' position (or Strauss's possibly misleading presentation thereof) that requires Grant to discuss compassion or charity and its elevated standing in the era of modern political science as compared to the classical. He writes movingly: 'no writing about technological progress and the rightness of imposing limits upon it should avoid expressing the fact that the poor, the diseased, the hungry and the tired can hardly be expected to contemplate any such limitation with the equanimity of the philosopher' (103). Grant recognizes that these chief benefits of technology, which can perhaps be summarized as the considerable easing of man's estate, would never have been realized had the 'conservative' classical understanding of the relation of science to society, which Strauss seems to prefer, obtained. It would seem, then, that according to the classics or at least according to Strauss, this understanding of the virtue of charity stands against the virtue of wisdom, and that, what is more, it obscures 'the fundamental experience from which [the notion of the primacy of the Good] is derived' (102).[12] On these premises, somehow, the benefits of charity contribute to the oblivion of eternity. This discussion of compassion or charity, the modern elevation of which derives from biblical origins, requires a consideration of biblical religion, the second of the questions that Grant poses to Strauss.

I think it would be fair to say that Grant finds Kojève's account of the relationship between the history of philosophy and biblical religion inadequate. He discerns Kojève's understanding of that relationship to be essentially Hegelian, whereby the thesis of classical master morality is synthesized with the antithesis of biblical slave morality to produce the absolute morality of the modern era. He finds Strauss's account, that Hegelian political science is derived from Hobbes, more apt. To this effect, he quotes Strauss: 'Syntheses effect miracles. Kojève's or Hegel's synthesis of classical and Biblical morality effects the miracle of producing an amazingly lax morality out of two moralities both of which made very strict demands on self-restraint' (105). Grant agrees with Strauss that biblical morality should not be identified with the emancipation of the passions but rather should be seen as a modern (i.e., Kojèvian-Hegelian-Hobbesian) phenomenon that cannot be reconciled with the restraint that characterizes both of the pre-modern moralities in question.

Yet Grant shrewdly observes that Strauss's reticence places him at a disadvantage in the discussion of this matter. That is to say, while Grant finds Strauss's criticism of Kojève's account of the relationship between biblical religion and the history of philosophy convincing, he recognizes that this criticism alone is inadequate as a positive account of that relationship: 'The rejection of the Hegelian account of the relation between modern philosophy and Biblical religion still leaves one with the question of what that relation has been' (106). The absence of a positive account prohibits Strauss from further clarifying Grant's inquiries: What does Strauss consider biblical religion to be? (107). And what, in his view, are the Bible's claims of authority over philosophers? (108) Grant himself is sympathetic to Strauss's likely reasons for remaining silent on the question of what authority the Bible claims (109). Still, he concludes that such silence cannot be maintained by one who seeks to restore classical social science, and, since this is what Grant identifies as Strauss's first aim, he fairly asks: 'How can [Strauss] maintain his reticence at this point?' (109).

To reiterate, Grant wishes that Strauss had treated more rigorously his claim that the classical philosophers gave some consideration to a technological science, including perhaps the charitable benefits of such a science, but rejected it as unnatural and destructive of man's humanity. He also wishes that Strauss had given a more forthright account of his implied position on the authority of biblical religion, especially in light of the apparent connection between Christian civilization in Western Europe and the coming to be of the universal and homogenous state.

Let us begin again where Grant finishes, with the question of Strauss's view of biblical religion. In several places in his writings published after his controversy with Kojève, Strauss claims to speak of the Bible or of Jerusalem, and hence of revelation.[13] But in identifying the Bible with Jerusalem, Strauss gives more weight to the claims of Judaism than to those of Christianity. This would seem to provide an answer to at least the second of Grant's questions: 'In asking what Strauss thinks about the role of Biblical religion in western history, I am also asking what he considers Biblical religion to be' (107). It will suffice to draw attention to one instance of Grant's explicit disagreement with Strauss. In a footnote to the essay 'In Defence of North America,' Grant writes of Strauss: 'To express my enormous debt to that great thinker must not, however, hide the fact that I interpret differently the relation of Christianity to the modern philosophers.'[14] To supplement this, consider the statements of Grant's biographer that Grant came to discern that Strauss's 'interpretation of Plato [and, we may surmise, the classics more generally] was an indirect attack on Christianity'[15] and that 'Strauss thought that each [of Platonism and Christianity] had been harmed by the encounter ... Strauss believed that Christianity led to an overextension of the soul, and Grant always considered this criticism worthy of close attention.'[16] In the light of these remarks, it seems that Christianity itself was subject to Strauss's criticism of Kojèvian modernity – that it is a miraculous synthesis which joined as one the two poles of Athens and Jerusalem. No wonder he was reticent. Thus, Strauss emerges as posing a serious challenge to Grant's understanding of the classics, Christianity, and modernity.

I shall conclude with a few remarks discussing Grant's considered position on these matters. It might first be germane to recall that in *Technology and Justice* Grant called himself a 'lover of Plato within Christianity.'[17] That is, for Grant, there is indeed an authority in the Christian Bible that applies to the philosopher, in this case the political philosopher. The differences between Strauss and Grant are here evidently more fundamental than any debt to Strauss. Indeed, whereas Strauss finds an irreducible opposition between philosophy and biblical religion at their heights, it is on that most high matter of love that Grant finds a point of contact between Plato and Christianity. However, this agreement of Plato and Christianity has not been wilfully tacked on to what Strauss identified as the broadly similar elements in the Bible and Greek philosophy, namely, morality or justice. Rather, though it goes to some degree without saying, Grant discerns that his sighting of the identity of Christianity and Plato at their heights exposes certain differences between himself and Strauss in more lowly matters of earthly justice. Here Grant's question to Strauss about the status of technology emerges again.

In the essay 'Faith and the Multiversity,' Grant's view of the connection between Christianity and Plato takes its starting point from the remark of Simone Weil's that 'Faith is the experience that the intelligence is enlightened by love' (38). The idea that intelligence and love are joined is by no means alien to classical thought, least of all to that of Plato; that this would be called faith, however, is surely a Christian notion. By now, it should come as no surprise that the place in Strauss's thought occupied by the great divide between Athens and Jerusalem is replaced in Grant's thinking by the closeness of Socrates and Christ:

This relation between Christ and Socrates is denied by those who would distinguish absolutely between two Greek words for love, *eros* and *agape*. Paul's hymn to love uses the word *agape* which is best translated charity; Plato's *Symposium* is concerned with *eros* which is best translated as desire ... Obviously it is the case that there is a great range between my liking for scrambled eggs and Francis loving the lepers ... There are clearly very different kinds and examples of love. But this does not seem reason to draw too sharp distinctions between them, and in so doing deny that all love is one. Eros not only goes around as a beggar but is in itself the activity of begetting upon the beautiful ... The philosophy of the dialogues is impregnated with the idea of receptivity or as was said in the old theological language, grace. What is given us and draws from us our loving is goodness itself; the perfection of all purposes which has been called God. We are hungry for the bread of eternity. In a way which is almost impossible to affirm, let alone describe, we can trust that we are offered such bread. (73–4)

The inapplicability of Straussian terms is illuminating. Strauss might say that this aspect of Grant's thought represents a synthesis of Athens and Jerusalem by means of *eros* and *agape*. Remembering, though, that it is characteristic of syntheses that they effect miracles, we may expect Grant perhaps to accept the characterization. For what greater miracle is there than the person of Christ?[18] Grant's account is only synthetic, however, if Strauss is correct that Athens and Jerusalem are irreducibly opposed in the way he says they are. This, not surprisingly, is the nub of the argument between them. I think it is not unreasonable to leave this question open for the time being; it is enough to indicate, as we have, that for Grant the matter is resolved in the person of Christ.

Just as Grant does not see a difference in kind between Christian and Platonic love, so he sees no more than a difference of degree in Christian and classical justice: 'What Christianity added to the classical account of justice was not any change in its definition but an extension of what was due to others and an account of how to fulfill that due' (54). It would be folly, however, to judge the implications of this difference to be small; in Grant's words: 'Indeed among all the western criticisms of Christianity the most substantial was that Christianity led to overextension of the soul. It was said that too much was demanded of human beings and this has made steady political orders impossible where the Gospel was influential. The call to perfection made difficult the handling of the necessities of the world, and laid too grave a burden upon individuals ... The call to perfected justice seemed to question the elementary justice possible in the world' (55). Grant is referring here, I think, to the Christian elevation of charity in its account of earthly justice. Guided as we are by the above-quoted remarks of Grant's biographer, we recognize this criticism as belonging to Strauss, to say nothing of several others. It would presumably proceed from something like the classical 'conservative' position limned by Strauss.[19] Thus, the elevation of charity or compassion, perhaps including a hesitation to shoulder or to face up to the burden that is the brutal arithmetic of political life, contributes to the destabilizing of otherwise decent and prudently or wisely ruled political orders. With its comparative elevation in the Christian scheme as opposed to the classical, compassion and thus compassionately arrayed technology might be loosed from the rule of prudence. Whatever merit there is in such a criticism might apply as much to an era where technology was long ago freed from moral-polit-ical restraint as it does to a pre-technological era. Thus, to Christianity today and to Grant himself, the question is how we should respond prudently and compassionately to the political issues of our age, shot through as they are with the products of technological science.[20]

If I am not mistaken, this way of posing the matter exposes a tension in George Grant's thought, though one of which I cannot think he was unaware. This tension may be expressed in the remark that compassion which slips the rule of reason is unreasonable and therefore not com-passionate. That there is no similar tension in Strauss is revealing of the differences between the two thinkers and the extent to which Strauss remains a challenge to Grant's Platonism. Along these lines, let me say that I do not see how Grant can, in the final analysis, find the identity he does in Plato and Christianity and at the same time agree with Strauss's judgement of the classical, 'conservative' understanding of science and society.[21] For Grant's reading of that great philosopher and that great religion to be true, it must be the case that the elevation of compassion or charity in the Christian scheme is somehow also implied in the Pla-tonic scheme. That is, accompanying the identity of reason and charity at the heights of Plato, there needs to be room for reasonable compas-sion at the political level. Implied in such room might be something like a technological science, a technological science that surely would not permit man's inventions to be his destroyers but that would rather have as its aim the easing of the burden of the poor, the diseased, the hungry and the tired. This might be called, at the risk of absurdity, a non-technological technological science, and whether or not it is present in Plato or the other classics must remain an open question for the time being.

NOTES

This study owes its beginnings to some provocative and instructive sugges-tions by Professor Tom Darby and much of its subsequent evolution to the help-ful criticism of Constantinos Konstantos and Stephen Head. It was first presented at the 2002 *Paideia* conference in Ottawa, Ontario, and has benefited, I think, from comments offered in that very collegial setting.

1 George Grant, 'Tyranny and Wisdom,' in *Technology and Empire: Perspective on North America* (House of Toronto: Anansi, 1969), 81–109.

2 This famous debate is best available in a revised and expanded edition which includes the correspondence between Strauss and Kojève: Leo Strauss, *On Tyranny*, ed. Michael Roth and Victor Gourevitch (Chicago: University of Chicago Press, 2000).

3 George Grant, 'Faith and the Multiversity,' in *Technology and Justice* (Toronto: Anansi, 1986), 35–77.

4 The secondary literature on the subject of Grant's relationship to Strauss is very good, but I disagree with the general emphasis on Grant's indebtedness to Strauss – usually understood as correcting his 'Hegelian' period. While there is more than something to this, I think that it mistakes the most important questions for both Grant and Strauss and underemphasizes the extent to which Grant fundamentally disagreed with Strauss. For this interpretation, see especially Michael Gillespie, 'George Grant and the Tradition of Political Philosophy,' and Barry Cooper, 'The Revival of Political Philosophy,' in *By Loving Our Own: George Grant and the Legacy of Lament for a Nation*, ed. Peter Emberley (Ottawa: Carleton University Press, 1990), 123–31, 97–121; Yusuf Umar, 'The Philosophical Context of George Grant's Political Thought,' and Zdravko Planinc, 'Paradox and Polyphony in Grant's Critique of Modernity,' in *George Grant and the Future of Canada*, ed. Yusuf Umar (Calgary: University of Calgary Press, 1992), 1–16, 17–45; Wayne Whillier, 'George Grant and Leo Strauss: A Parting of the Way,' and Ian Weeks, 'Two Uses of Secrecy: Leo Strauss and George Grant,' in *Two Theological Languages by George Grant; and Other Essays in Honour of His Work*, ed. Wayne Whillier (Lewiston, NY: Edwin Mellen Press, 1990), 63–81, 82–93; and Harris Athanasiadis, *George Grant and the Theology of the Cross: The Christian Foundation if His Thought* (Toronto, University of Toronto Press, 2001), 124–37. I find most congenial to my aims here the arguments of H.D. Forbes in 'George Grant and Leo Strauss,' in *George Grant and the Subversion of Modernity: Art, Philosophy, Religion, Politics, and Education*, ed. Arthur Davis (Toronto: University of Toronto Press, 1996), 169–98; Joan O'Donovan, *George Grant and the Twilight of Justice* (Toronto: University of Toronto Press, 1984), 50–60, 68–80; and Ian Angus, *A Border Within: National Identity, Cultural Plurality, and Wilderness* (Montreal and Kingston: McGill-Queen's University Press, 1997), 76–81.

5 Until otherwise noted, all parenthetical references are to pages in *Technology and Empire*.

6 Barry Cooper's remarks are indicative of the scholarly emphasis with which I should like to disagree: 'This way of posing the topic was non-Hegelian in the extreme, which is to say that Grant undertook a Straussian, not a Kojèvian reading of this controversy. This is not to say that Grant was a "Straus-

sian," which is a recondite term in any event. It is enough to say that Grant's relationship to the revival of political philosophy was mediated by Strauss' understanding of that revival.' Cooper, 'The Revival of Political Philosophy,' 112.

7 It is probably worth clarifying Grant's understanding of the relation between Kojève and Hegel, an understanding that is obscured by Grant's choice sometimes to refer to 'Hegel-Kojève,' rather than to one of them at a time. As he explains, he adopts this terminology in the present context because Strauss does not dispute that Kojève has correctly interpreted Hegel (84). To be most clear, I do not think that Grant misapprehends that the two thinkers are distinct, as he himself remarks in a footnote: 'As I write chiefly for English-speaking readers, it is necessary to state here that Kojève's Hegel is not the gentlemanly idealist of the nineteenth century who became the butt of the British "realists" in this century. To Kojève the essential work of Hegel is *The Phenomenology of Spirit*. His Hegel is atheist and his thought contains all the truth implicit in existentialism and Marxism ... I am not certain whether Kojève's interpretation is correct; but I am quite certain that Kojève's Hegel is incomparably nearer the original than such English interpretations as those of Caird, Bosanquet and Russell' (84). That Kojève's intent in his own writing is not at all to approximate Hegel's is not remarked upon by Grant, and perhaps deserves further attention. Moreover, his given reason for not himself distinguishing between Hegel and Kojève – that Strauss makes no such distinction – does not itself satisfy. As Grant discerns, Strauss has his own rhetorical purposes in his debate with Kojève. If, as we suspect, these are served by not marking the difference between the French, Heideggerian Marxist and the German Idealist, perhaps Grant's purposes – distinct though they are from those of Strauss – are equally well served. On the relation between Hegel and Kojève's interpretation of Hegel, see Stanley Rosen, *Hermeneutics as Politics* (Oxford: Oxford University Press 1987), chap. 3.

8 Leo Strauss, 'Restatement on Xenophon's *Hiero*,' in *On Tyranny*, 177.

9 Ibid., 210.

10 Grant cites passages from Strauss's *Thoughts on Machiavelli* (Chicago: University of Chicago Press, 1958) and the final paragraph of the French 'Restatement.'

11 Here Grant is quoting Strauss, *Thoughts on Machiavelli*, 299.

12 Grant is again quoting Strauss, *Thoughts on Machiavelli*, 299.

13 The following passages from Strauss must be relevant. 'There is a fundamental conflict or disagreement between the Bible and Greek philosophy. This fundamental conflict is blurred to a certain extent by the close similar-

ity in points ... One can begin to describe the fundamental disagreement between the Bible and Greek philosophy, and doing that from a purely historical point of view, from the fact that we observe a broad agreement between the Bible and Greek philosophy regarding both morality and the insufficiency of morality; the disagreement concerns that "x" which completes morality. According to Greek philosophy, that "x" is *theoria*, contemplation, and the biblical component we may call, I think without creating any misleading understanding, piety, the need of divine mercy or redemption, obedient love.' Leo Strauss, 'The Mutual Influence of Theology and Philosophy,' in *Faith and Political Philosophy,* ed. and trans. Peter C. Emberley and Barry Cooper (University Park: Pennsylvania State University Press 1993), 217–18. See also Strauss's essay 'Progress or Return,' where he discusses the broad similarities between the Bible and Greek philosophy with regard to justice. Leo Strauss, 'Progress or Return,' in *The Rebirth of Classical Political Rationalism*, ed. Thomas Pangle (Chicago: University of Chicago Press 1989), 248. In addition to these, there is Strauss's well-known essay 'Jerusalem and Athens: Some Preliminary Reflections,' where he sketches the stark opposition between these twin roots of Western civilization, and indeed, the opposition of what they represent, revelation and reason. In this essay he writes of the 'incompatible claims' of each, and even of 'the fundamental opposition of Athens at its peak to Jerusalem: the opposition of the God or gods of the philosophers to the God of Abraham, Isaac and Jacob, the opposition of Reason to Revelation.' Leo Strauss, *Studies in Platonic Political Philosophy* (Chicago: University of Chicago Press 1983), 149, 166. See also Leo Strauss, 'Thucydides: The Meaning of Political History,' in Pangle, *The Rebirth of Classical Political Rationalism*, 72–3.

14 Grant, *Technology and Empire*, 19.

15 William Christian, 'Introduction,' in *The George Grant Reader*, ed. Christian and Sheila Grant (Toronto: University of Toronto Press, 1998), 19.

16 Ibid., 19. It is worth remarking here that 'overextension of the soul' is one of the more cryptic turns of phrase attributed to Strauss. See n.19.

17 Geoge Grant, *Technology and Justice* (Toronto: Anansi, 1986), 90. The full quotation, discussing the difficulties involved in teaching Nietzsche, is: 'It is particularly difficult for somebody such as myself, who in political philosophy is above all a lover of Plato within Christianity.' It is followed by a reference to Leo Strauss. The parenthetical references that follow are to this work.

18 It may be worthwhile to consider here Grant's more explicit comparisons of Socrates and Christ. He writes that 'the two great deaths' of these figures 'stand at the origins of western life and thought.' Then he continues: 'Yet

those two deaths are very different. The calm, the wit, the practice of thought which are present at Socrates' death may be compared with the torture, the agony, the prayers, which are present in Christ's death. Just before drinking the hemlock Socrates makes a wonderful joke; in Gethsemane Christ's "sweat was, as it were, great drops of blood falling to the ground." Indeed the difference is also stated in the fact that where Socrates' wife is absent for most of *Phaedo*, the two Marys stand beneath the cross' (72).

19 The expression 'overextension of the soul' should not be understood as exclusively or even primarily having political implications, although that is our focus here.

20 With this in mind, I think it would be interesting to consider Strauss and Grant's different judgments of the American regime – Grant's characterization of it as the spearhead of the liberal, technological empire which is currently engulfing the world, and Strauss's own position as a friend, but not a flatterer, of liberal democracy; this discussion might include some consideration of the Cold War and the Soviet Union, for example, the war in Vietnam. Such a discussion, however, would lead too far beyond the limits of this chapter.

21 For a useful study of Plato that does not agree with the Straussian 'conservative' position, adducing a different understanding of *techne* and *poesis* in Plato, see Stanley Rosen, *Plato's Statesman: The Web of Politics* (New Haven, CT: Yale University Press, 1995).

8

Leo Strauss's Influence on George Grant

GRANT HAVERS

It is well known that Leo Strauss's critique of modern philosophy and his revival of classical political philosophy (or what he called the tradition of 'Athens') profoundly influenced the thought of George Grant. Both political philosophers critiqued and repudiated the triumph of the modern: the validation of the idea of progress (at the expense of timeless premodern wisdom), the hegemony of liberalism (and its defeat of conservative attempts to preserve tradition), and the technological conquest of nature (with its undermining of pagan teleology). Grant especially embraced Strauss's call to return to the great premodern texts to comprehend and overcome the most pernicious effects of modernity. In the texts of Plato, Aristotle, and their medieval heirs, both Strauss and Grant discovered a decisive alternative and solution to defective modern concepts of statecraft.

Yet it is also well known that Grant, a committed Christian philosopher, had misgivings about Strauss's views on faith. For Grant believed that Strauss showed 'contempt for certain forms of Biblical religion.'[1] Grant understood, unlike many of Strauss's supporters and detractors, that Strauss did not seek a return to that other great tradition of the West, the Bible (or what he called 'Jerusalem'). While Strauss throughout his writings took great pains to stress that both reason (Greek philosophy) and revelation (the Bible) must respect the claims of each other and not oppose each other (a truth that, Strauss believed, atheistic modern philosophers ignored), Grant thought that this recognition on Strauss's part did not translate into unconditional support for revelation itself. What are the implications of Strauss's views on revelation for Grant?

Answering this question requires an explanation of the very core of Strauss's philosophy. Strauss established a dualistic opposition between reason and revelation: reason was simply *philosophy,* and revelation was *faith.* There can be no synthesis between them. Socrates is not Christ. Reason must question the nature of things, and revelation must discourage such questions on the grounds of faith.[2] Yet Strauss, as a philosopher, was often coy about revealing his hostility to revelation in the context of his articulation of this dichotomy. It is unwise, in his view, for philosophers to express too openly their doubts about religion, since religion shapes the foundation of political regimes. Reason by itself cannot inspire loyalty or obedience, since reason is possessed by only a wise few, not the ignorant many. Given Strauss's famous commitment to esoteric writing, that secret premodern art of expression which concealed the most controversial truths of philosophy (such as the 'truth' that the real purpose of religion is to teach morality and obedience to the ignorant masses), why did Grant sense that Strauss was so *obviously* critical of revelation?

A careful reading of Strauss's work suggests that his adverse stance on revelation is not hard to spot. In *On Tyranny* (a commentary about Xenophon's *Hiero*), Strauss openly declares that the 'triumph of the biblical orientation' has impeded the return to classical antiquity.[3] Yet what was it in revelation that provoked Strauss's fears? Grant had an answer, which reflected his understanding of Strauss's esoteric bias. In his only essay on Strauss, a commentary on *On Tyranny,* Grant wrote: 'even if Strauss should in fact think that the Biblical categories have been in part responsible for a false and therefore dangerous concept of nature among modern philosophers, he would not necessarily think it wise to speak openly or forcibly about the matter.'[4] Within this brief passage, Grant astutely recognized two important facts about Strauss: first, that Strauss does not believe that philosophers should openly subvert the fragile sacred foundations of a civilization (lest they face the fate of Socrates, a theme to which I will return), and second, that the tradition of Jerusalem undermined the premodern concept of nature.

The first fact is well known to any reader of Strauss who has studied his *Persecution and the Art of Writing* (1952), where Strauss developed his now famous position that philosophers must be careful to keep their most sceptical uses of reason secret so that the irrational yet necessary foundations of a political order (such as religion and ethics) can function properly. For Grant, this position was not so shocking, since he was well aware of the 'conservative influences' of modernists who may think Christianity to be 'complete nonsense,' but are still hesitant in opposing it 'because they see the need of religion for social cohesion.'[5] Yet the second fact is not so well known, again because the majority of

Strauss's supporters and a few of his detractors accept Strauss's claim that, as a sign of heartfelt support for revelation, philosophy should leave it alone.[6]

Still, Grant knew that Strauss faulted Jerusalem for the decline of the premodern concept of nature. How did biblical revelation contribute to a 'false and dangerous conception of nature' among the moderns? Strauss openly answered this question in a 1958 lecture on Freud and Judaism: 'The Bible is the document of the greatest effort ever made to deprive all heavenly bodies of divine worship.'[7] Evidently, the Bible, in placing the authority of God above the heavenly bodies of nature, devalued premodern cosmology and ushered into being the modern scientific and technological assault on nature. God, not nature, is the foundation of all authority: with the triumph of the Bible, the teleological metaphysics that assigned natural purpose to all things collapses.

Despite his Christian faith, Grant was often sympathetic to Strauss's views on the impact of revelation on nature. Certainly, Grant faulted Calvinists for cutting 'themselves off from pure contemplation' (that is, Greek philosophy) in favour of the idea of progress and modern liberalism.[8] Calvinism unleashed capitalism and modern technology because its devotees were 'open to the new physical and moral science in a way the older Christianity was not.'[9] In short, Grant recognized that Protestant Christianity, in repudiating the older Thomistic tradition which was supportive of premodern teleology, had encouraged a destructive view of nature in modernity.

Grant's dislike of Calvinism, however, is not the same as Strauss's repudiation of revelation. For Strauss was faulting the *entire* biblical tradition, not just Protestantism, for the decline of premodern philosophy. Grant usually hesitated in joining Strauss's condemnation of Jerusalem altogether. Yet even he occasionally suggests that the entire tradition of Christianity opened up modernity long before the advent of Protestantism. It did so, he said, by introducing to humanity a particularly modern concept of time: 'we would have to examine how it was that Christianity so opened men to a particular consciousness of time, by opening them to anxiety and charity; how willing was exalted through the stamping proclamations of the creating Will.'[10] What is significant here is Grant's association of Christianity with the *Will*. Grant knew that the Will is not a premodern idea. The Will is symbolic of the modern conquest of nature through science and technology. Moreover, the Will creates rather than contemplates: it masters nature rather than accepts it. For Grant, the tradition of Christianity itself, not just its Protestant version, was the origin of the modern.

Nevertheless, Grant ultimately drew back from a full embrace of Strauss's dualistic opposition between reason and revelation. In his last work, an addendum to his essay 'Two Theological Languages,' Grant insists that the traditions of Athens and Jerusalem can be united. Indeed, both traditions speak with one voice on the meaning of freedom: 'Whatever differences there may be between Platonism and Christianity as to how and when truth is given us, it is clear that in both freedom is given us through truth. Therefore we do not stand before good and evil choosing as it were between equal alternatives ... To put the matter in language not easy for moderns, Platonism and Christianity are at their centre concerned with grief – if that word is given its literal meaning. Grace simply means that the great things of our existing are given us, not made by us and finally not to be understood as arbitrary accidents.'[11] It is significant that Grant reveals no concern over the Christian validation of the Will, as he did almost two decades before in *Time as History*. Gone is the angst over the Christian commitment to willing (or creating) reality and thus undermining the premodern contemplation of an unchanging natural order. Now Grant writes as if both Athens and Jerusalem are equally committed to the same unchanging order which assigns purposes to all things.

Earlier in 'Two Theological Languages,' Grant had already scorned Protestant theologians such as Reinhold Niebuhr or Anders Nygren who 'ask us to turn our back on rational theology and accept pure Biblical religion.'[12] Grant made no secret of his belief that medieval philosophers such as St Thomas Aquinas and Duns Scotus were essentially correct in insisting that Greek philosophy and the Bible speak with one voice of 'Man's proper end,' which is directed by nature.[13] Grant once again draws a dichotomy between premodern Thomistic Christianity and modern Protestant Christianity in their distinct treatments of nature.

Unlike Strauss, Grant clearly believed that the Christian tradition of revelation (minus its Protestant variants) was compatible with Greek philosophy and teleology. Modern Protestant Christianity is simply a distorted version of Jerusalem which fails to appreciate the unchanging natural order of things. To this extent, Grant on theological grounds could not fully accept Strauss's influence.

Yet how persuasive is Grant's unification of the two traditions? Does it escape a Straussian critique? In accepting the Platonic-Aristotelian view of nature, does Grant commit himself to a philosophy that is simply not compatible with fundamental biblical theology? Most important, what are the political consequences of accepting the premodern

view of nature (and rejecting modern Protestant Christianity)? I shall
address these questions in tandem.

In a letter to Eric Voegelin, another Christian philosopher committed to
the synthesis of Athens and Jerusalem, Strauss wrote: 'The classics
demonstrated that truly human life is a life dedicated to science, knowledge and the search for it. Coming from the Bible the *hen anagkaion* is
something completely different. No justifiable purpose is served by
obscuring this contradiction ... Every synthesis is actually an option
either for Jerusalem or for Athens.'[14]

What Strauss wrote to Voegelin easily applies to Grant as well. Typically, Strauss reiterates his position that Athens has nothing to do with
Jerusalem (ironically, the very position that Grant attributed to Protestant theologians like Niebuhr and Nygren, who also rejected a synthesis). Just as typically, Strauss repeats that philosophy is dedicated to
questioning through reason, which revelation can ill afford. Ultimately,
either reason masters revelation or the reverse, but there is no authentic
sharing of authority.

As we have seen, Grant respects Strauss's criticism of revelation for
undermining the premodern concept of nature, without endorsing it
wholesale. Yet did Grant fully appreciate *why* Strauss insisted on such a
dualism? Did Grant grasp what, for Strauss, were the political implications of repudiating this dualism?

I shall argue that Strauss's condemnation of revelation rests on his
profound *anti-egalitarianism*. Strauss lamented the decline of premodern teleology because it originally validated a *hierarchy* of the wise few
over the ignorant many.[15] The tradition of revelation, however, teaches
that all human beings are created equal in the eyes of God. This belief,
according to Strauss, is simply not compatible with the old premodern
wisdom. Ultimately, this defence of hierarchy is what Strauss meant by
'reason.' Only philosophy can protect and even understand this need
for hierarchy. As Strauss puts it, only the philosopher is 'closest' to
nature.[16] Ironically, Strauss offers no rational 'demonstration' for this
belief. (Indeed, significantly, Strauss elsewhere hints that reason itself
has no defence or foundation and that it is no less dogmatic than
revelation since it rests on an 'unevident premise.')[17]

Grant was obviously aware that Strauss was no egalitarian (given his
rejection of mass enlightenment in favour of esoteric writing), but he

did not deeply reflect on whether this anti-egalitarianism causes problems for his own synthesis of Athens and Jerusalem. Can the hierarchically driven teleology of the Greeks ever be consistent with the equality advanced within Jerusalem?

I believe that Grant's lack of reflection on the full implications of Srauss's elitism shows through in his all-too-easy acceptance of Strauss's critique of liberalism. *Lament for a Nation* (1965) clearly rests in part on Strauss's ideas of modern political philosophy. Grant looks to Strauss for his view that modern conservatism (especially in the United States) is but a pale imitation of the old Lockean progressivist liberalism and therefore an inappropriate pathway back to the classics.[18] Certainly, Strauss gives the impression that his main quarrel with both liberalism and conservatism is their common embrace of progress. Modern-day conservatives are just as committed to, or as uncritical of, the advent of 'technological change' as liberals are.[19] Still, is this the *only* reason that Strauss rejects liberalism (and its conservative variant)?

Despite Grant's reading of Strauss here, Strauss is not simply opposed to the progressivist elements of liberalism or to the liberal commitment to liberty. Strauss is also opposed to the egalitarian, leveling effects of liberalism; hence, he decries modern liberal education for embracing a philosophy that serves up ends to be 'pursued by all men.'[20] In declaring that 'the modern conception of philosophy is fundamentally democratic,' Strauss is clear on the origins of this conception. 'Philosophy thus understood could be presented with some plausibility as inspired by biblical charity, and accordingly philosophy in the classic sense could be disparaged as pagan and as sustained by sinful pride.'[21] What are the consequences of this biblically based modernism? In modernity, 'it became increasingly easy to argue from the premise that natural inequality has very little to do with social inequality, that practically or politically speaking one may safely assume that all men are by nature equal.'[22]

In short, the modern philosophical defeat of pagan hubris, resting on the belief in natural hierarchy, derives from the biblical concept of universal love (*agape*), which stresses that all are equal (in the eyes of God) and therefore should not be oppressed through a system of natural inequality. God loves *all* of humanity and therefore condemns the lack of love which human beings express for each other through oppression. If it is true, as I believe it is, that Strauss ultimately faults Jerusalem for the rise of modern egalitarianism, what does this mean for Grant's faith and philosophy and his appropriation of Strauss's ideas?

Grant, as a Christian, clearly could not accept Strauss's anti-egalitarianism. Indeed, Grant never abandoned his view, expressed in an essay on community in 1961, that equality is the 'central principle' of society. This biblical principle, Grant argues, recognizes the 'absolute worth of all men' and must check the principle of hierarchy.[23] Yet it is not clear that Grant reflected on how his own rejection of modern Western Christianity may also become a rejection of egalitarianism, especially the Calvinist insistence that all human authority be checked and restrained. When Calvin warns that the 'vices and defects of men' call for a political regime in which the many can censor authority for immoral 'excess,'[24] he is appealing to an egalitarian tradition in Christianity which recognizes that *all* human beings are equal in sin and therefore the rulers must be as restrained as the ruled. Strauss made no such allowance for his natural rulers, who need not be restrained, because they, like Plato's guardians, are not corruptible; they are naturally superior in their reason as long as they distance themselves from the inferior many.[25] In embracing a premodern version of Christianity, then, was Grant trying to reconcile premodern elitism with biblical equality? To my knowledge, there is no attempt in Grant's writings to resolve this tension.

Related to Grant's lack of reflection here is his failure to understand the most radical implications of Strauss's critique of liberalism. To be sure, Grant correctly understood Strauss's opposition to the liberal idea of progress. Yet did Strauss oppose liberalism for other reasons, which led him to a different conclusion about American politics and the alternative it offered to liberalism?

Usually, when Grant faults the United States, his comments reflect his disdain for the American celebration of progress and a liberalism untrammelled by all moral restraints. Yet Strauss believed that the United States is not entirely liberal or even unconditionally committed to freedom and equality for all. Strauss discovered, as he studied the American polity, that his newly adopted country had a conservative tradition that was not *merely* an older version of liberalism. Indeed, this tradition was staunchly anti-egalitarian. For this reason, Strauss had enormous respect for the American political theorist Willmoore Kendall (1909–67), whose work is dedicated to explicating the uniqueness of American conservatism. In order to stress the depth of Strauss's anti-liberalism (a depth that Grant failed to appreciate), I shall briefly discuss his interest in Kendall's work.

For Kendall, American conservatism is not a recycled version of English liberalism (despite the claims of Grant). It shares with traditional European conservatism a hatred of egalitarianism as levelling (the reduction of all human beings to a tyrannical sameness in status and power) and thus disputes much of liberal thought in the process. Yet it is also populist, unlike the old Burkean conservatism (which feared the role of the 'people' in unleashing the French revolution). Kendall believes that all sovereignty lies with the people (or at least the majority), but this populist order is deeply authoritarian. In his view, the true 'American people' have every right to be intolerant of dissent if the latter subverts the American way of life. Moreover, any attempts at levelling (such as Lincoln's emancipation of the slaves) contradict and subvert this way of life. In Kendall's philosophy, authoritarian populism met anti-egalitarianism.[26]

Obviously, an elitist like Strauss would have no patience with Kendall's populism. Yet three facts stand out about Strauss's relation to Kendall. First, Strauss praised Kendall as the most important political theorist of his generation.[27] Clearly, he had a degree of respect for this theorist that he did not have for many contemporaries (including Grant). Second, Kendall believed that anti-egalitarianism was embedded in the political traditions of the United States, a premise that attracted Strauss. Third, Kendall's view that a state, even a democratic populist one, has the right to suppress dissent contains echoes of Strauss (as I shall argue). Kendall contended that the Athenian people had the right to execute the 'revolutionary agitator' Socrates because of his overly bold subversion and rationalistic levelling of sacred and necessary conventions.[28]

This analysis is clearly compatible with Strauss's views that the real Socrates went too far in subverting the state and in forgetting, therefore, the necessity of concealing dangerous philosophical questioning of authority. Strauss believed in two versions of Socrates. The young Socrates, as portrayed in Aristophanes' *The Clouds*, had a 'youthful contempt for the political or moral things' that underlie a state. The older Socrates (as represented in Plato and Xenophon) possessed a 'mature concern' with the survival of these things. The older Socrates appreciates the need to be cautious and subtle, but the young Socrates is a brash, sceptical rationalist who fails to grasp the fragility of religion and morality.[29] For Strauss and Kendall, then, a state has no obligation to tolerate dissent over its most important noble fictions: every regime (even a popular one) has its breaking point, and philosophers need to become aware of this long before Socrates finally did (too late, as it were). Consistent with his views on revelation's undermining of hierarchy, Strauss believes that the state's ruler, not God (or an abstract principle of equality), decides the value and role of the citizen.

To my knowledge, Grant never knew of Kendall's work or Strauss's interest in it. Grant was usually more sympathetic to Louis Hartz's view that the United States was a wholly liberal nation (outside of the South),[30] a position that Kendall vigorously challenged. In accepting Strauss's critique of liberalism (including its American version), Grant accepted too quickly the impression that Strauss was simply denouncing the liberal idea of progress. It did not occur to Grant in this context that Strauss's anti-liberalism paralleled his anti-egalitarianism, and that this fact explained his greater sympathy for the United States, at least as Kendall portrays it.

I have argued that Strauss's anti-egalitarianism (and authoritarianism) runs more deeply than Grant himself understood, and that this outlook accounts for Strauss's true antipathy towards the biblical assault on natural teleology. Had Grant reflected on the depth of Strauss's views, would he have been more favourable to modern Protestant theology? Would the modernism of Calvinist theology have been more palatable to Grant had he pursued the egalitarian implications within this tradition?

As a Christian, Grant harboured an egalitarian bias. He was also committed to Christian *agape*. Unlike Strauss, Grant never supported the right of the state to suppress dissent (despite his critique of liberalism), and he believed in the primacy of God – not the ruling elite – over humanity. Yet he also embraced the rationalism of Greek philosophy and repudiated the impossibility of synthesizing Athens and Jerusalem. For this reason, Grant vigorously opposed Reform theologians who opposed reason to faith. Still, 'reason' here meant support for natural hierarchy, just as 'faith' meant a commitment to universal equality. Grant never related the ideals of equality or democracy to the Protestant (modern) tradition of Western Christianity which he repudiated, nor did he recognize the absence of a commitment to these ideals in the tradition of Athens (as Strauss did). Had he done so, would he have been more favourable to the Western Christian validation of the Will? For the very concept of the Will implies that humanity can become equal and free, through the grace of God. In sharp contrast to the teleology that Strauss supported, the Christian doctrine of the Will suggests that humanity need not resign itself to the inevitability of fate (or natural hierarchy). Humanity can be raised above the bonds of nature.

Moreover, Grant intimated in *Time and History* that Christianity opened humanity to both the Will and *agape*. Was Grant implying that universal love must be willed, because it is not natural? Did Athens fail to teach this because, as Strauss contended, natural teleology forbids both equality and love for the many? In contrast to Grant's commitment to *agape*, nowhere in Strauss is there the recognition that love of humanity (in his view, 'the many') is either possible or desirable in a regime dedicated to the rule of the enlightened few.

Strauss obviously rejects all of these premises, because of his commitment to Athens. His rulers do not love the ruled, nor do they consider them equal in any way. Strauss was consistent in eschewing any synthesis between Athens and Jerusalem. Yet Grant attempted no demonstration that Athens and Jerusalem are compatible. His mere assertion of a synthesis ultimately leaves his work vulnerable to the critique of his philosophical mentor, Leo Strauss.

NOTES

1 George Grant, 'Tyranny and Wisdom,' in *Technology and Empire: Perspectives on North America* (Toronto: House of Anansi Press, 1969), 108.

2 Leo Strauss, 'Progress or Return: The Contemporary Crisis in Western Civilization,' in *An Introduction to Political Philosophy: Ten Essays by Leo Strauss*, ed. Hilail Gildin (Detroit: Wayne State University Press, 1989), 273–98.

3 Leo Strauss, *On Tyranny, including the Strauss-Kojève Correspondence*, ed. Victor Gourevitch and Michael S. Roth (Chicago: University of Chicago Press, 2000), 178.

4 Grant, 'Tyranny and Wisdom,' 109.

5 George Grant, 'Religion and the State,' in *Technology and Empire*, 54.

6 See, for example, Kenneth Hart Green, *Jew and Philosopher: The Return to Maimonides in the Jewish Thought of Leo Strauss* (Albany: SUNY Press, 1993); Susan Orr, *Jerusalem and Athens: Reason and Revelation in the Work of Leo Strauss* (London: Rowman and Littlefield, 1995); David Novak, 'Philosophy and the Possibility of Revelation: A Theological Response to the Challenge of Leo Strauss,' in *Leo Strauss and Judaism: Jerusalem and Athens Critically Revisited*, ed. David Novak (London: Rowman and Littlefield, 1996). A few scholars recognize the anti-biblical strain in Strauss. See my 'Leo Strauss and the Politics of Biblical Religion,' *Studies in Religion* 30, nos. 3–4 (2001): 353–64; and Clark A. Merrill, 'Leo Strauss's Indictment of Christian Philosophy,' *Review of Politics* 62, no. 1 (2000): 77–106.

7 Leo Strauss, 'Freud on Moses and Monotheism,' in *Jewish Philosophy and the Crisis of Modernity: Essays and Lectures in Modern Jewish Thought by Leo Strauss*, ed. Kenneth Hart Green (Albany: SUNY Press, 1997), 293.

8 George Grant, 'In Defence of North America,' in *Technology and Empire*, 35–6.
9 George Grant, 'Canadian Fate and Imperialism,' in *Technology and Empire*, 66. For a detailed discussion of Grant's approach to Calvinism, see Harris Athanasiadis, *George Grant and the Theology of the Cross: The Christian Foundations of His Thought* (Toronto: University of Toronto Press, 2001).
10 George Grant, *Time as History* (Toronto: University of Toronto Press, 1995), 29.
11 'Two Theological Languages,' in *Two Theological Languages / by George Grant; and Other Essays in Honour of His Work*, ed. Wayne Whillier (Lewiston, NY: Edwin Mellen Press, 1990), 16.
12 Ibid., 11.
13 Ibid., 8.
14 Barry Cooper and Peter Emberley, eds., *Faith and Political Philosophy: The Correspondence between Leo Strauss and Eric Voegelin, 1934–1964* (University Park: Pennsylvania State University Press, 1993), 78.
15 Leo Strauss, *Natural Right and History* (Chicago: University of Chicago Press, 1953), 13–14.
16 Ibid., 81–9, 112–13.
17 Strauss, 'Progress or Return,' 310.
18 Grant, *Lament for a Nation: The Defeat of Canadian Nationalism* (Ottawa: Carleton University Press, 1991), 95–6.
19 Leo Strauss, *Thoughts on Machiavelli* (Chicago: University of Chicago Press, 1958), 298; 'Preface,' in *Liberalism Ancient and Modern* (Chicago: University of Chicago Press, 1968), ix.
20 Leo Strauss, 'Liberal Education and Responsibility,' in *Liberalism Ancient and Modern*, 19.
21 Ibid., 20.
22 Ibid., 21.
23 George Grant, 'An Ethic of Community,' in *The George Grant Reader*, ed. William Christian and Sheila Grant (Toronto: University of Toronto Press, 1998), 69.
24 John Calvin, *Institutes of the Christian Religion*, trans. Henry Beveridge (Grand Rapids, MI: Eerdmans, 1989), 657.
25 Strauss, *On Tyranny*, 201, stresses the importance of philosophers avoiding 'disordered souls' in the political realm.
26 Willmoore Kendall, *The Conservative Affirmation* (New York: Henry Regnery, 1963); *The Basic Symbols of the American Political Tradition*, with George W. Carey (Baton Rouge: Louisiana State University Press, 1970).
27 Willmoore Kendall, 'Willmoore Kendall–Leo Strauss Correspondence,' in

Willmoore Kendall: Maverick of American Conservatives, ed. John A. Murley and John E. Alvis (Lanham, KY: Lexington Books, 2002), 225, 237. Kendall in turn considered Strauss to be the greatest political teacher since Machiavelli. See *The Conservative Affirmation*, 260.

28 Willmoore Kendall, 'The People Versus Socrates Revisited,' in *Willmoore Kendall Contra Mundum*, ed. Nellie D. Kendall (New Rochelle, NY: Arlington House, 1971), 149–67.

29 Strauss, *Socrates and Aristophanes* (Chicago: University of Chicago Press, 1966), 314.

30 Louis Hartz, *The Liberal Tradition in America* (New York: Harcourt, Brace and World, 1955).

9

Freedom and the Tradition: George Grant, James Doull, and the Character of Modernity

NEIL ROBERTSON

With the publication in 1965 of *Lament for a Nation*, George Grant initiated a national debate about the nature, indeed the very reality, of Canada. Grant's own standpoint was captured succinctly in the subtitle to that book: 'The Defeat of Canadian Nationalism.' While it was the defeat of Diefenbaker's government in 1963 that clarified for Grant the desire of Canadians to give up their independence from the United States, the causes that he pointed to lay deeper than any particular political event. For Grant, the sources of Canada's demise lay in the forces at work in modernity and its expression in technology: the noble folly of Canadian nationalism rested in its belief that a more stable, conservative society could exist on the borders of the United States, the nation that more than any other embodied technological modernity.

In April 1965, George Grant's friend and former colleague, James Doull, wrote to him about the newly published work: 'Your book is as exasperating as it is brilliant. The worst is that you, incapable as any could be of inaction and mere lament, encourage Canadians to give up the battle before it has been fought.'[1] Three years later, Doull wrote again to Grant, now expressing how some of their differences over Canada had affected their friendship: 'Sometimes I have spoken or written harshly about your attachment to Upper Canadian conservatism, not evidently without giving offence I had not intended. What moved my comments was that you know young Canadians, can speak to them as no other: that this being so, you did not speak a little more hopefully to them – did not prepare them to resist a little more strongly absorption into the American Empire. For my part, I can only act as though resistance makes some sense.'[2] Doull would go on to refer to Grant's *Lament for a Nation* at a number of points in his own continuing reflections on

Canada. For example, in 1983, in an article published in a *Festschrift* for Grant, Doull again suggests that Grant is mistaken in his lament and by contrast argues for the possibility of a distinctive and independent Canada; even in the 1990s, after Grant's death, Doull is moved to distinguish his position from Grant's and suggest the insufficiency of Grant's account of Canada.[3]

This disagreement about the fate of Canada points to and opens up a set of deeper disagreements between Doull and Grant: the nature of the state, the essence of technology, the character of modernity, and the relation of God to history. If one wanted to sum up these disagreements in a phrase, it was a disagreement about the truth of Hegelian philosophy. However, Grant and Doull did not always have this disagreement. Though Doull and Grant's friendship pre-dates Doull's own immersion in Hegelian philosophy, according to Grant, it was he who introduced Grant to Hegel, and with such success that Grant was able to say concerning his first book, *Philosophy in the Mass Age* (1959): 'At the theoretical level, I considered Hegel the greatest of all philosophers. He had partaken of all that was true and beautiful and good in the Greek world and was able to synthesize it with Christianity and with the freedom of the enlightenment and modern science. It cannot be insisted too often how hard it is for anyone who believes the western Christian doctrine of providence to avoid reaching the conclusion that Hegel has understood the implications of that doctrine better than any other thinker. I therefore attempted to write down in non-professional language the substance of the vision that the age of reason was beginning to dawn and first in North America.'[4] However, by the time *Lament for a Nation* came to be written, Grant had broken his attachment to Hegel, and indeed he came in that work to define his own position in opposition to that of Hegel.[5] Grant's Hegelian-based hopes for the dawning of a new age in North America had turned to lamentation for the death of an independent Canada. Doull never shared Grant's rejection of Hegel nor his turn to resignation at the fate of a vanishing Canada.

In this chapter, I want to leave to one side the question of whether Grant's Hegel was the same as Doull's Hegel (and if they differ, which is a truer reflection of the historical Hegel) as well as the exact extent of Grant's 'Hegelianism' during the 1950s.[6] That is, while there is clearly a biographical context for a consideration of what distinguishes Grant's from Doull's position, it is to the substance of the thought of these two Canadian thinkers that I wish to turn, for it is here we can enter into a debate of a more universal concern. It can appear that Grant's passing

Hegelianism is indeed only of biographical interest, and yet the fact that he came to his later position through a rejection of Hegel is not without consequences for the shape and scope of that position: Grant came to see, as an implication of his mature position, the need to turn from the whole Western Christian standpoint which he saw expounded most fully in the thought of Hegel.[7] However, rather than turn directly to Doull's and Grant's differing assessments of Hegelian philosophy, a more approachable way into the substance of their disagreement might be to return to the question of Canada. For what distinguished Grant's position from Doull's was not simply a factual question – was Canada over or not? – but a substantive one: What is Canada? For both Doull and Grant (and this is a testimony to the depth and thoroughness of both thinkers), the substantive issue of Canada's nature was central.

GRANT AND DOULL ON CANADA

In *Lament for a Nation*, Grant argues that 'to be a Canadian was to build, along with the French, a more ordered and stable society than the liberal experiment in the United States.'[8] Canada was, for Grant, an inherently conservative society, and one built upon a rejection of the United States and its directly humanistic individualism. Through Canada's relation to Britain and France, a connection was maintained with a culture that preceded what Grant called 'the age of progress.' For Grant, this meant that English and French Canada sought to keep open through their institutions – above all, their institutions of higher learning, but also their political forms, their sense of what the economy was for, and the place of religion in society – a connection to the premodern cultures of Jerusalem and Athens, which saw human life in terms of purpose and goodness and not simply humanly enacted values and the individualistic pursuit of them. In Grant's view, a relation to the Good, a sense of one's 'creatureliness' and 'fellow-creatureliness,' belonged to this older European tradition with which Canada sought to keep connected.

The decision to build a nation more stable and less given to the illusions of modernity than was the case in the United States was a noble one, but destined for failure. The British connection (and, in Quebec's case, the French connection) was vital not because of its specific ethnic characteristic but because it was the only living connection Canadians had collectively and institutionally with this older European conception of society. Thus, for Grant, the failure of this connection, the decision of Liberal politicians to weaken rather than strengthen it, was equivalent to the end of Canada. Grant combines here a sense of *fate* – that Canada could not hope in the face of the dynamism and sheer massiveness of American modernity to be able to sustain this connection – with a sense of *betrayal*, that specific politicians and specific social groups acted, even underhandedly and manipulatively, to break the British connection.[9] For Grant, these two moments of fate and betrayal came together in the defeat of John Diefenbaker in 1963: the slick and ambitious in Canada's metropolitan centres turned against this apotheosis of pure loyalty, using his personal follies and weaknesses to ridicule his great and specifically Canadian virtue of loyalty – the attachment to the given, to one's own. When Canadians turned their backs on their own, their loyalty to the connection with an older European sense of stability, they gave up, except in name, all that distinguished them from the United States.[10]

Grant believed that the failure of Canada cannot be seen as merely the failure of a small cultural experiment. Rather, that failure is emblematic of the truth of modernity, the very vanishing of older, more sustaining forms: 'The impossibility of conservatism in our age is the impossibility of Canada. As Canadians we attempted a ridiculous task in trying to build a conservative nation in the age of progress, on a continent we share with the most dynamic nation on earth.'[11] And so, Grant tells us, 'the confused strivings of politicians, businessmen and civil servants cannot alone account for Canada's collapse. This stems from the very character of the modern era.'[12] The unravelling of Canada was the unravelling of the contradiction of conservatism in the modern age: Canada sought in its institutions both to retain a relation to the traditions of Jerusalem and Athens and, at the same time, to release and support its citizens in the pursuit of a modern dynamic society. The modern technological state in which, according to Grant, 'no appeal to human good, now or in the future, must be allowed to limit [individuals'] freedom to make the world as they choose'[13] was clearly incompatible with the desire of Canada's founders to 'build a society in which the right of the common good restrains the freedom of the individual.'[14] Canada was caught between attachment to older forms through the British and French traditions received from Europe, on the one hand, and participation in modernity in terms not only of the overwhelming presence of the United States but also of the inherent corruption of the British and French traditions insofar as they were already modern, on the other. In contrast to Doull, what Grant denied was that tradition and modernity, community and technology, could actually be united. The impossibility of this meant that, in Grant's eyes, Canada was a contradiction waiting to unravel; the defeat of Diefenbaker was merely the manifestation of this having, in fact, occurred.

According to Doull, however, Canada is not distinguished from the United States by an attachment to a conservative tradition. Doull does not deny that such a conservatism and attachment has been part of Canada's history and was vital to Canadian founders, both English and French; however, he argues that such a difference is passive and indefinite, making Canada's independence rest upon the external and – as it turned out – unstable realities of the British Empire and the Tridentine Catholic Church. Indeed, according to Doull, Grant may be right to lament, but his lamentation is not properly of Canada but of a specific British connection to Canada that Grant by education and family tradition saw as equivalent to Canada itself: 'Professor Grant calls his lament "the failure of a nation." There is much confusion in his use of the word "nation." What has failed in his account is British America ... The failure Professor Grant speaks of is of the effort to establish British culture directly in Canada from above through higher education and the arts. It would be better described as the failure of colonialism.'[15]

Doull agrees with Grant that the quiet revolutions of both Quebec and English Canada in the period after the Second World War destroyed the older forms of Canadian self-definition, but he thought this a positive development and not to be equated with absorption into American culture. For Doull, the death of the old Canadian culture is not to be equated with the death of Canada itself; he sees it, rather, as a development necessary for any possibility of real self-definition and independence on the part of Canadians. In his reaction to Grant's lament, Doull was by no means blind to the possibility that Canada could exchange its colonial relationship with Britain for a similar relationship with the United States, but he saw it as being in no way a necessity. This judgment was the source of Doull's opposition to Grant's stance: he saw Grant's fatalism as contributing to, rather than resisting, any tendency to absorption into American culture.

Doull argues that Canada's independence from the United States rests not upon certain qualitative measures (such as 'traditional' versus 'technological') but upon a substantial difference. Doull wants to press more firmly Grant's own point that Canada is distinguished from the United States in its history and its institutions by arguing that, if this difference is real, it cannot be a simply passively received difference, a difference resting on a colonial attachment to Europe. Rather, the demand is that Canadians appropriate these institutional and cultural forms as their own. Indeed, Doull would contend that, from the beginning, even in their colonialism, Canadians transformed what they received. As Doull once put it: 'The mere continuance of the old and customary has no power to educate, but can only impart an external order to the savagery of the natural will.'[16] Thus, for Doull, Canada must come to define itself, not principally through either Europe or the United States (though these are undoubtedly elements of Canada's self-definition), but through itself, and so bring these elements, and others, into a concrete relation. That is, Doull's contention is that Canada is substantial or real in its history and institutions and so is capable of relating and integrating seemingly opposed qualitative distinctions. In Doull's account, then, Canada is not – or at least need not be – a confusion or mixture of technology and tradition, but rather a certain form of the unity of the two.

A theme running throughout Doull's intellectual career – one resting, as we shall see, upon his larger Hegelian standpoint – was that Canada should not be consigned, as Grant claimed, to inevitable dissolution. What especially distinguishes Doull's political thought in the last decade and a half of his life (coincidentally, approximately from the death of Grant) is a clarification of his grounds for upholding his confidence in Canada as a sovereign state. Central to this clarification was a re-evaluation of the United States.

For a long time, Doull shared Grant's view that the United States was a technological empire. In the 1960s, 1970s, and much of the 1980s, Doull saw in the United States a technological naturalism liberated from the rationality and constraint of its older Enlightenment constitution: 'In place of the older order, one had come to assume in the later nineteenth century a naturalism and against it an abstract moralistic idealism. Marx and the socialists would draw these elements into one view: the free natural individuality they proposed combined these elements. Such in general is the technological culture of the present time. In the United States, where it occurs in its purest and simplest form, it is commonly assumed that technology and a free naturalistic individuality can sustain each other.'[17] Certainly, the New Deal and the emergence of the welfare-consumer state in the United States led Doull, as well as Grant, to see in that country the most complete embodiment of technology. So long as Doull held to this view, his account of Canada as at least implicitly beyond the opposition of technology and tradition was hard to justify: Why should Canada escape the corruption and revolution besetting the rest of the Western world? Grant's assessment that what remained of Canada's sense of its difference from the United States rested on a residual traditionalism was at least as plausible.

By the late 1980s, however, Doull broke with this account of the United States and, in doing so, reconfigured his interpretation of Canada and of the possibilities of the contemporary period. In a lecture Doull gave in 1992, he contrasted this new account to Grant's position in *Lament for a Nation*:

> Some years ago George Grant in a well-known book lamented the demise of Canada; a Canadian nation, betrayed by politicians, had fallen prey to the great technological empire to the south. But in truth neither was Canada a nation nor ... is the United States rightly defined as a centre of 'global technology.' What then were we to lament? George Grant grew up in the ruins of Victorian culture in Ontario and Heidegger was for him a principal interpreter of the culture which took its place. *Amicus Plato, sed magis amica veritas*. The effect on Canadians of this twofold relation to the Old World has been to make possible the question, what are we as a North American people, whose freedom and its political articulation has a different basis than for Europeans? [18]

Doull's reconsideration of the United States and regrounding of his hopes for Canada lay in his recognition of what he came to call 'North American freedom,' a freedom defining the character of these two 'post-national,' federal states. Doull's claim is that North American freedom can be put neither on the side of technology nor on that of tradition. Rather, it encompasses and integrates both sides: in North American freedom, Jerusalem and Athens come together with modernity. However, before we can make sense of Doull's account of North American freedom, it is necessary that we explore in more detail the character of technology and its relation to modernity. As is clear already, for Grant, technology is at the very centre of the modern and it is technology that renders conservatism (and, in turn, Canada) impossible. If Doull's account of Canada and of North American freedom is to have any plausibility, it must confront Grant's analysis of technology and modernity.

TECHNOLOGY AND MODERNITY

While it is possible to contrast Grant's and Doull's considerations of Canada in terms of lamentation and hope respectively, it is important to see that their differences are more deeply rooted than the emotional or subjective and that their disagreement is of wider than simply bio-graphical interest. Nor is it sufficient to argue that Doull's response is that of a naive liberalism or modernity and Grant's of a narrow tradi-tionalism. It cannot be said that Doull does not recognize the 'techno-logical' and its power to annihilate an apprehension of those sources upheld in the traditions of Jerusalem and Athens. Nor can it be said that Grant does not see the powerful appeal, and, indeed, claims to justice and legitimacy of the technological. Rather, the contrast between Doull and Grant is in a different assessment of the character and origins of 'technology' and its relation to modernity.

According to both Grant and Doull, the fundamental question of modernity is posed by the presence of technology. And according to both thinkers, technology is not to be understood simply as the devices before us, nor as the science that gave rise to those devices, nor even as the various developments in moral, political and religious thought that made possible the coming to be of that science. Deeper than these levels is the characterization of technology as a mode of being, what Heideg-ger characterizes as an ontology. Doull and Grant agree that the stand-point of technology involves a break with the European tradition of contemplation and a rise to the eternal. For both, technology is the asser-tion of a radical, 'this-worldly' mastering of nature and humanity that is essentially atheistic and destructive of the givenness of all traditional forms.

What principally distinguishes Doull's accounts from Grant's here is that Grant takes technology so understood as a complete or compre-hensive ontology, while Doull, though acknowledging the profound contemporary experience of technology as ontological, would question this status. That is, Doull fully accepts that the contemporary era encounters technology as the underlying standpoint that shapes all encounters with the world, that is, as an ontology; however, Doull also asserts that a deeper and historically informed analysis reveals this ontological experience to be, in fact, historically constructed or medi-ated. What we contemporaries experience as an all-pervasive immedi-ate ontology, is, in truth, a mediated relation. In short, Doull does not so much reject Grant's account of technology and its fundamental role in shaping the contemporary era as he does seek to place it in a larger con-text that frees our understanding from the apparent fatality of technol-ogy that Grant perceives. In Grant's view, Doull's claims fail to grasp the inner nature of technology and assert an Hegelian standpoint that makes the impossible claim to mediate technological ontology and the ontology of ancient and Christian accounts. To assess the relative merits of Grant and Doull's arguments, it is necessary to consider in more detail their respective views of technology.

The experience of the society he lived in as 'technological' was fundamental to Grant's thinking throughout his life, as the titles of a number of his writings make clear. For the purposes of this brief exploration of Grant's account of technology, it is useful to divide the development of his thinking, after his break with Hegel in the early 1960s, into two stages. The first stage comprises most of the 1960s, when his thinking about technology was principally guided by Jacques Ellul and Leo Strauss. The second stage began in the late 1960s with his exposure to the writings of Nietzsche and Heidegger. It should be said that, underlying these developments, there was a common structure to his thinking about technology, and one that relates him to a set of contemporary thinkers. Like Heidegger, Nietzsche, and Strauss, but also like figures such as Karl Löwith, Etienne Gilson, and Alisdair MacIntyre, Grant argues that technological modernity is nihilistic and that this nihilism reveals a suppressed, forgotten, or overlooked principle that we can now recover through a return to an older tradition or standpoint rejected by modernity, but nonetheless presupposed by it. For Heidegger or Nietzsche, this return is to the pre-Socratics: for Löwith, to the Stoics; for Strauss, to Plato; and for Gilson and MacIntyre, to Aquinas. In Grant's case, the return is to a Christian Platonism, especially as expounded in the writings of Simone Weil. This basic structure – the nihilism of technology and the corresponding return to a hidden Christian-Platonic standpoint – remained constant in Grant once he broke with the thought of Hegel. What developed in his thinking at that point was a deepening of the two sides: a deepening that involves a growing clarity about the irreconcilability of technology with Christian Platonism.

Grant began his account of this division through the work of Ellul and Strauss. What they taught Grant was to see the contemporary world, especially North America, as fundamentally given over to an order incompatible with ancient or Christian accounts of virtue or piety. Grant had learned from Strauss that a dynamic leading to the 'universal and homogeneous state' was built into all forms of modernity. Grant agreed with Strauss that the universal and homogeneous state that both liberalism and Marxism pursued would result, not in a liberated humanity released from all former limits and structures of oppression, but in a total tyranny inherently obstructive of all forms of higher life – religion, philosophy, and so on. Grant, however, disagreed with Strauss's assertion that the most completely modern forms were to be found in the second and third waves – those he associated with communism and national socialism respectively. Strauss saw the level of the political order and of the ideology underlying that order as fundamental. At that level, Grant agreed that communism and national socialism represented more 'advanced' forms of modernity. But, for Grant (and here he drew on Ellul), the actual dynamic of modernity, what underlay and informed its hold upon the world, was not at the level of political thought so much as at the level of 'technology.' For Grant, the contemporary era could best be characterized as, in Ellul's phrase, a 'technological society.' The principle articulated in this society is 'the conquest of human and non-human nature.'[19]

When the dynamic of modernity is understood in terms of the conquest of human and non-human nature, the analysis of the contemporary world is reconfigured in important ways. According to Strauss, but also according to Marxist analysis, communist regimes informed by the more developed thinking of figures from Rousseau to Marx are more modern than a regime such as the United States, informed as it is by the earlier thought of Hobbes and Locke with its emphasis on natural rights. However, in pointing to the deeper role of technology, Grant suggests that in fact American liberalism is the more modern form – not because it is a more advanced form politically, but because it is less developed and more pragmatic at the level of political thought, and is thus, ironically, more permissive of the unconstrained unfolding of technological dynamism: 'Liberalism is, then, the faith that can understand progress as an extension into the unlimited possibility of the future. It does this much better than Marxism, which still blocks progress by its old-fashioned ideas of the perfectibility of man.'[20] In liberalism, the dynamic modern account of man's essence as freedom is allowed untrammelled development.[21]

The implication of Grant's analysis of the role of technology as the dynamo of modernity is the recognition of the United States as the centre of modernity. This is obviously going to be a vital point when we turn to Grant's account of the impossibility of Canada. But here what is worth noting is that Grant sees that the United States is inherently imperialistic precisely because of its technological character. American imperialism, however, while sharing many similarities with traditional European imperialism, is distinctive in its fundamentally technological character. American imperialism is not primarily realized through conquest and colonial expansion, as were the older European empires;

rather, it is accomplished by the willing or coerced accession of other peoples and civilizations to the expansion of technological civilization. For Grant, in the 1960s, the clearest expression of American technological imperialism was the Vietnam War. As he put it, in that conflict the Americans were willing to commit genocide rather than allow the Vietnamese to stand apart from the American liberal technological empire.

What the reading of Nietzsche and Heidegger brought to Grant was not so much a revision of his earlier conception of technology as a deepening of that conception. One way to refer to the account Grant held of technology while he was writing *Lament for a Nation* was that it was fundamentally a 'civilizational' account. Technology was, centrally, a certain civilizational form given over to the mastery of human and non-human nature. Following *Lament*, Grant's reading of Nietzsche and Heidegger allowed him to see the ground of this civilization as 'ontological.' What makes technology so enveloping and fateful is that it enfolds the very fundamental ways of our thinking and being:

To put the matter crudely; when we represent technology to ourselves through its common sense we think of ourselves as picking and choosing in a supermarket, rather than within the analogy of a package deal. We have bought a package deal of far more fundamental novelness than simply a set of instruments under our control. It is a destiny which enfolds us in its own conceptions of instrumentality, neutrality and purposiveness. It is in this sense that it has been truthfully said: technology is the ontology of the age. Western peoples (and perhaps soon all peoples) take themselves as subjects confronting otherness as objects – objects lying as raw material at the disposal of knowing and making subjects. Unless we comprehend the package deal we obscure from ourselves the central difficulty in our present destiny: we apprehend our destiny by forms of thought which are themselves the very core of the destiny.[22]

How this ontology of technology came to be is a real question for Grant. Precisely because it is nihilistic and historically specific, technology cannot be seen as belonging simply to the nature of things, but neither can it, as ontological, be attributed to a self-conscious human agency. The ontology of technology arises specifically out of the historical development of the West, but not as willed or consciously constructed. In this sense, the origins of technology are inherently obscure. Certainly, modernity is, for Grant, technological through and through. But the roots of technology lie deeper than modernity, which, Grant argues (with Heidegger), presupposes technological ontology rather than initiates it. Grant points to these deeper roots in a late essay:

I do not mean by 'technology' the sum of all modern techniques, but that unique co-penetration of knowing and making, of the arts and sciences which originated in Western Europe and has now become worldwide. Behind such descriptions lies the fact that 'technology' is an affirmation concerning what is; it remains unfathomed, but is very closely interwoven with that primal affirmation made by medieval Westerners as they accepted their Christianity in a new set of apperceptions. That affirmation had something to do with a new content given by Western people to the activity of 'willing.' 'Technology' is the closest, yet inadequate word for what that new affirmation has become as it is now worked out in us and around us.[23]

What Grant chiefly learned from reading Nietzsche was that the heart of technological ontology was what Nietzsche characterized as the will to power: a will to mastery, a will to more free and creative willing in which all otherness or givenness is reduced to being but a moment of the will. As the above quotation suggests, Grant saw the roots of this pure willing in the Western Augustinian turn to the will. It is in reaction to this development of the Western tradition that Grant turns to a Christian Platonism more consonant – in his eyes – with the Eastern tradition of Christianity.[24] What this non-Western tradition preserved was a sense of the Good or God as participatively, but not wilfully, present in the world. God and the order of creation, especially the order of justice, were present in the very being of the world, not through a self-active will – whether divine or human. All of this is clearly related to Grant's break with the Hegelian account of history as God's activity.

The centrality of the will in the West, Grant suggests, is ultimately generative of the standpoint of technology, of an ontology of the will to power that necessarily, as Grant puts it, 'has meant for all of us a very dimming of our ability to think justice lucidly.'[25] What Nietzsche clarified, above all, for Grant was that the ontology of technology was inherently incompatible with the ancient accounts of justice and the Good: 'Nietzsche's writings may be singled out as a Rubicon, because more than a hundred years ago he laid down with incomparable lucidity that which is now publicly open: what is given about the whole in technological science cannot be thought together with what is given us concerning justice and truth, reverence and beauty, from our tradition.'[26] In the older account, there is an order 'we do not measure and define, but by which we are measured and defined.'[27] The standpoint of technology necessarily must elide this order: the very possibility of a self-active will requires a break from the given order. The very being of technology, of modernity, of a self-contained secularity can be ontologically established only by a negating or occluding of the order of what is. For Grant, the very nihilism that is manifested in pure technological willing brings to light the negativity present in the essence of technology.

A crucial implication of the ontological character of technology is that it cannot be itself mastered or taken in hand or subordinated to higher human ends. All such efforts to get control of technology are themselves technological, not only in the obvious sense that one cannot master mastery, but in the more deep-seated sense that, for the contemporary person, the viable forms of moral and political thought that are supposed to give direction and purpose to technology are themselves implicated in technological modernity: 'The result of this is that when we are deliberating in any practical situation our judgement acts rather like a mirror, which throws back the very metaphysics of the technology which we are supposed to be deliberating about in detail.'[28] For Grant, the only possibility for getting 'beyond' technology is, on the one hand, through the recollection of a pre-technological ethic evoked by those remnants of premodernity still present (this is Grant's conservatism), and, on the other hand, through the radicalizing of technological civilization to the point of its collapse from its own inner nihilism (here appears Grant's extremism). What is crucial in this prognosis is that Grant's account of technology allows no mediation between technology and a humanly livable order. As ontological, technology is corruptive of all efforts to humanize it by relating it to human ends. Technology must rather be allowed to fulfil its self-dissolution, which will purge the Western tradition of all voluntarism and open us to a participatory and receptive relation to the divine.

For James Doull, Grant is right in characterizing technology as ontological – but only in a relative and conditional sense. Doull argues that technology in the ontological sense is not to be seen as modern or premodern in its origins – though he would certainly concede that technology is not possible without the whole development of modernity. Rather, Doull argues that 'technology' in the sense Grant intends is a nineteenth- and twentieth-century phenomenon. According to Doull, technology arises out of the collapse of the nineteenth-century nation-state and in fact is one aspect of a two-sided corruption of the that state; the other side is nationalism, existentialism, or fascism. Doull contends that technology is in truth an element of the nation-state, but an element that takes itself to be self-complete and immediately actual. The other element, the existentialist or nationalist, suffers the same immediacy. In the nineteenth century, these two elements had their radical and revolutionary theorists, the most developed of whom were Marx, on the one side, and Nietzsche, on the other. Doull suggests the twentieth century is where these elements took on a life of their own as the European nation-state was destroyed in the trenches of the First World War. The history of twentieth-century Europe is a gradual development from the two elements assuming themselves to be self-constituted wholes, in the forms of communism and fascism, to the dissolution of this assumption as reflected in the present European Union, in which the two sides remain as irresolvable but restrained aspects of European life.[29]

What is crucial to grasp in Doull's analysis of technology is that he places technology in a wider context in which it can be seen not as the whole reality but as one element of a more comprehensive dialectic. There is alongside technology (to which it is necessarily related) the existential or nationalist aspect, which, for lack of a better term, I will call the 'communitarian' aspect. The communitarian side of the contemporary, like the technological, takes on a variety of forms. Some of the anti-technological positions are religious and traditionalist, others more radical and revolutionary. However, according to Doull, they share a common logical and structural character informed through the relation to technology: to preserve a realm of being from the technological reduction, there is the need to uncover a principle whose being is beyond the technological. From Doull's perspective, then, Grant himself takes up just such an anti-technological account and so occupies a one-sided aspect of the contemporary. Grant thus dogmatically asserts the radical difference of technology from the standpoint that would recognize the Good and the order of justice that informs the world. Doull would allow that this is a true perception so long as one leaves undisturbed the immediate distinction of the forms in which the contemporary experiences itself. But it is Doull's argument that this assumption is misplaced. These forms that take themselves to be directly what they claim to be – and this is what it is to speak of them as ontological – are in fact dialectically related to one another in three senses.

First, according to Doull, the two sides of the contemporary are forms historically derived from the nation-state, where, so long as the nation-state had life, they could be related and connected to one another. This especially took the form of the relation between civil society and the state, where universality and particularity were able to be concretely related and united. In the dissolved state of the twentieth century, there tends to be either the collapse of the state into civil society in communism, socialism, or liberalism, and later in a global economy, or the separation of the two in nationalism, fascism, or Nazism and later in communitarianism. As Doull states:

In their time the thought of Marx and Nietzsche was not of general interest. Both perceived the national political community in a partial and unbalanced way through one of its elements. With the decline of the national state their thought came into its own, since the decline is nothing else than that elements contained before in the whole came to have rather a life of their own. The assumption on which the independence and completion of the national state rested was that life and nature were capable of containing technology – that the concreteness of the Christian principle existed naturally in the state. The history of these communities has been rather the disintegration of these elements.[30]

Doull maintains that what each side of the contemporary takes as immediate, the free individuals of the technological society or the rooted individuals of the particular community, are, in truth, historical results which do not know themselves as such. Indeed, according to Doull, not only are the two sides results of the whole development of the nation-state, but also the very immediacy that hides this history is itself a historical result. In his view, it belongs to the inadequately self-conscious character of the nineteenth-century nation-state that it should so readily collapse at the point that it is fully developed into opposed forms.

There is a second sense in which there is an undisclosed dialectic at work in the relation of technology to community. Doull's claim is not only that the two sides share a common origin, but that, even in their claim to be self-grounded, they are in fact defined negatively through one another. The technological defines its activity relative to an anti-technological standpoint that resists the freedom of technological universality by holding, for 'superstitious' reasons, to a particularity that can be understood only as oppressive and limiting. Equally, the communitarian standpoint is drawn to a principle that is defined precisely in its being beyond the technological – whether this be Heideggerian Being, Straussian nature, or Gilsonian God. Further, the immediacy of the one side is precisely necessary to the self-grounding of the other. In each case, the immediacy of the opposed standpoint turns out to be false: a false particularity or a false universality. For the technological will, the attachment to the particular is simply a negation of the universal and the attachment to what is in truth nothing. For the communitarian, the attachment to technology is a nihilism premised on negating rootedness and so is, in truth, the attachment to nothing. So long as these forms – the technological and the communitarian – remain distinct from one another, they can at best be alternately balanced but not related or reconciled. Doull argues that this describes the contemporary state of the European Union.[31]

This leads to the third form of dialectic that Doull points to: precisely because of the two earlier forms of dialectic, there is both the possibility and the need to move beyond the contemporary opposition of the sides of technology and community to an actual relating between and uniting of them. Not technology simply, but the relation of technology to community through the institutional order of the state, Doull took to be the question before the contemporary era: 'The practical interest of the present age is transparently that science and technology be brought under universal will, and that individuals have their particular freedom explicitly and primarily therein – not through the blind conflict of aggressive wills.'[32] By contrast with Grant, Doull contends that technology can and must be subordinated to human ends. He states: 'In antiquity Prometheus could be subdued and taught to live under the power of Zeus. But now he has captured the citadel of Zeus and founded technology on the sovereign right of the individual. The principle of the modern age is the unity of theoretical and practical. A more dangerous principle there could not be. But Hegel would, as before, see no other course than to awaken in men a clearer knowledge of this principle. Danger he would see to lie exactly in a seeming modesty which left open to human passions and false certainties to seduce reason and science from their natural end of serving humanity.'[33]

For Doull, the course of the twentieth century in Europe, from the rise of fascism and communism, where community and technology took themselves to be complete wholes and gathered to themselves the whole power of the state, through to the unstable relation of global technology and community in the European Union, there has been a growing recognition of the truth that both sides of the contemporary are in themselves nothing. This result is already evident, in Doull's eyes, in postmodernity, where the instability of both universal and particular is known in an all-dissolving scepticism. Doull sees postmodernity as the philosophy proper to the European Union. Thus, the nothingness that each side of the contemporary took to be the truth of the other side is found to be its own truth. But this is to suggest a purely negative result.

For Doull, this negative postmodern result is one aspect of the contemporary, that it comes to nothing in its effort to establish itself in itself. But equally for Doull, the contemporary is the fullness of historical development. What Doull takes to be at work in the period between the Hegelian nation-state and a return to the fullness of historical development is not simply revolt, corruption, and denial. That is to say, the return to the lost content of the European nation-state is not simply a return. The old nation-states are, in Doull's eyes, gone for good. What the collapse of the older European order has accomplished is the liberation from received forms that can readily lose their actuality as forms of spirit. The contemporary has been, according to Doull, a painful education beyond the immediacies that the old Europeans fell prey to. Doull suggests, especially in his last political writings, that it belongs to North America, and its more directly universal and self-conscious forms of polity, to realize the returned dialectic that knows technology and community as aspects of one totality in a freer and more complete form than even the nation-states of Hegel's time could offer.

But, from Grant's perspective, Doull's claim is contradictory. On the one hand, Doull argues that the state – that is, the Hegelian concept of the state – can comprehend the difference between technology and community, and yet the historical realization of this in the nineteenth-century nation-state was in fact unable to hold together these 'elements' and suffered disintegration. Grant's argument is that, given the actually experienced division of technology and community, it is more compelling to see in technology a principle destructive of community, virtue, religion, and life than to suppose there can be a uniting of technology and community, freedom and virtue, secularity and religion. Doull insists that this sense of division is in fact the true experience of contemporary Europe and sees, in Heidegger especially, its most powerful and profound articulation. But what undergirds Doull's whole account are two claims: 1) that even in the division of technology and community, the Idea of the State is still effective (this is what allows him to articulate a threefold dialectic even in the very opposition of technology and community in contemporary life); and 2) that the nineteenth-century European state was only an immediate instantiation of the Idea, and its more universal and adequate realization is in the New World and especially the federations of North America.[34]

For Doull, North American states are to be differentiated from European nation-states because they are founded explicitly on rational principles and have not been subject to a radical division between the Enlightenment principles of universal freedom and equality and attachment to a particular culture and language. As a result, whereas the European nation-states suffered in the Second World War the virtual destruction of independent sovereignty and required a European Union to secure political life in the global technological economy, the states of North America are in principle beyond the nation-state and not subject to its history. The United States is, for Doull, in his later political writings, the most well-developed example of North American freedom, a freedom that retains the concreteness that Hegel thought belonged to the nineteenth-century nation-state while at the same time realized in a more universal and self-conscious form. This freedom can hold together as one reality what contemporary Europe assumes only in a divided form: technology and tradition, the particularity of community and the universality of rights and liberties. Because these North American states are federations, they are capable of uniting and drawing into a common life a multicultural, multi-ethnic populace and yet able to retain local distinctions – and, in the case of Canada, even national differences.

It is this North American freedom that, Doull suggests, Grant does not sufficiently recognize. From Doull's perspective, Grant is still thinking in a European context when he puts on one side the 'nation' of British North America and, on the other, the technological 'empire' of the United States. Put in these terms, Doull would certainly allow, Grant's analysis was correct. Canada has experienced the dissolution of British North America and, equally, of French Catholic Quebec. But Doull's argument is that these terms are insufficient to the reality of Canada as a form of North American freedom. To get hold of Doull's argument, it is not enough to say that North American states, in contrast to the European nation-states, escaped the direct destruction of institutions and culture wrought by the World Wars – this is largely true of Great Britain also, especially if one finds, as Doull does, the imperial expansion of nineteenth-century Europe to be a corruption and not an essential aspect of those states. But Britain, as much as the other nations of the European Union, has found itself incapable of holding together technology and tradition. What is distinctive about North American forms is that they are post-nation-states and, as such, are not technological empires that dissolve and destroy particularity and tradition. Rather, the federal structure of these states, their capacity to promote and uphold local differences which are not at the same time simply frozen into external givenness of pure custom, points to a concreteness, a holding together of technology and community, that is beyond and yet comprehensive of the dividedness that contemporary Europe experiences.

This distinctive character of North American freedom is crucial to Doull's critique of Grant's account of Canada. Grant sees Canada's distinctiveness to lie in its determination to conserve the presence of English and French culture in Canada and so to have access to a tradition of contemplation, virtue, and political stability. The role of Canada is to act as a means to defend the institutions and ways of being that sustain this culture, which is received by Canadians as received forms they are to participate in. Since Grant understands the heart of English and French culture to be a participation in the Good, there is a coherence to this receptive or passive attitude. But Doull disagrees with Grant, not only as to the content of Anglo/French culture, but also as to the Canadian relation to it. Doull outlines a history of Canada whose purpose is to question the claim that English and French culture was ever simply participatory and conservative. Rather, Doull wants to argue that, from its beginning, Canada appropriated and transformed its received cultural forms in the new context of North America.[35]

What Doull's account means for Canada is that its technological and traditional sides need not be seen as ultimately opposed. Canada, and North American federations generally, are capable of containing and mediating technology together with a preservation of a specific sovereignty. This active uniting of past and present, universal and particular, is, according to Doull, the very character of North American freedom: the actuality of the state as explicated in Hegelian philosophy. For Doull, at the heart of Grant's account of Canada is a colonial passivity where tradition can be preserved only when it is not actively appropriated through a self-determining freedom. This contrast takes us to the theological-philosophical heart of the debate: the truth of Heglian philosophy, the claim that in the modern state – which for both Doull and Grant, from their opposed perspectives, is most fully realized in the North American state – there is a uniting of God and history, of human self-activity and the eternal, of freedom and the traditions of Jerusalem and Athens.

DOULL AND GRANT ON GOD AND HISTORY

Grant tells us that his lament for the demise of Canadian nationhood rested on an understanding of history fundamentally opposed to the liberal conception of history as the development of freedom and equality. By the time he wrote *Lament for a Nation*, Grant had broken with the doctrine of progress in which he had been raised and to which in his first book, *Philosophy in the Mass Age* (1959), he subscribed, in what he believed was the form articulated by Hegel. In the concluding chapter of *Lament for a Nation*, Grant turned explicitly against what he found most disturbing in the Hegelian doctrine of progress, namely, the claim that '*Die Weltgeschichte ist das Weltgericht.*' Here Grant argued that 'the doctrines of progress and providence have been brought together.'[36] Historical development was both directed towards higher forms of human life and at the same time made God's will scrutable as it was accomplished through these higher forms. This doctrine of progress was connected to Grant's account of Canada because he saw in its hold upon Canadians a source of their blindness to what was being lost in the passing away of what was specifically Canadian through ever greater integration with the United States and its dynamic modernity. In this doctrine, Canadians could see continental integration not as loss but rather as part of the beneficent, liberating movement of history, a stage in the fuller realization of freedom. In portraying the future as a necessarily higher stage than the past, the doctrine of progress, in Grant's eyes, reconfigures evil, loss, destruction, and the whole suffering of historical life, as good, thereby redeeming itself through its role in the higher achievement of future development: 'But if history is the final court of appeal, force is the final argument. Is it possible to look at history and deny that within its dimension force is the supreme ruler? To take a progressive view of providence is to come close to worshiping force. Does this not make us cavalier about evil? The screams of the tortured child can be justified by the achievements of history. How pleasant for the achievers, but how meaningless for the child. As a believer, I must then reject these Western interpretations of providence. Belief is blasphemy if it rests on any easy identification of necessity and good.'[37]

Grant saw in the doctrine of progress, and most fully in the Hegelian expression of it, a confusion between what he referred to as the order of necessity and the order of the Good. Grant argued that Plato, and the ancients generally, preserved a distinction between the eternal or the Good and necessity, a realm of becoming that participates in the eternal but remains as other to it. It was only by so distinguishing the historical and the eternal that the distinction of good and evil could be retained. Grant found the same distinction in Christianity that he found in Platonism – the notion that, for Christianity, God's will, providence, is not scrutable, and so we are called to look not to human history but to Christ, and particularly, to his crucifixion, for our theology. Using Luther's terms, Grant distinguished a theology of glory – above all embodied in the doctrine of progress – from a theology of the cross. In the one, Grant saw a triumphalism where human will or subjectivity was seen as an agent of divine activity in the world; in the other, he saw the deep humiliation of Christ in not asserting his will but rather giving it away both to his Father and, in forgiveness and love, to those who had persecuted him. For Grant, Christ's greatness lay in his surrendering will to the eternal order and, even in the face of extreme affliction, in the very abandonment of God, not conforming to the wilfulness of the realm of necessity and historical life.

Grant saw in the Hegelian uniting of progress and providence a radical reduction of all otherness to human historical life, ultimately to human subjectivity and will. For his part, he thought that otherness – both the otherness of God and of other beings – was preservable only in the recognition of an order of the Good, an order of justice, that precedes human willing and activity. Grant here saw two levels of recognition: 1) a Platonic recognition that affirmed justice as the love of the beautiful in otherness and so the limitation of one's will through the virtues made possible by the illumination of one's intelligence by the Good; 2) the still more radical Christian form of love of otherness in the giving away of one's self for the sake of otherness in the face of radical affliction or the experience of the absence of the Good. In spite of these distinctions between what Grant took to be the Platonic and Christian accounts of the Good, what they together affirmed was a relation of the human to the good as receptive or participatory and not as generative or determining. For Grant, religion, art, and philosophy are all forms of participation and so, in a broader sense, they are all religious. There is certainly a human activity in each, but only as responsive to and within a 'gift' from the eternal source. It is only this standpoint of receptivity or openness, as Strauss and a number of other contemporary thinkers also suggest, that makes possible an apprehension of the eternal as eternal and not simply as a moment of human self-activity.

Doull argues on the basis of Hegel's philosophy of religion that Grant's account of the separation of God and history, or necessity, is neither true nor Christian. In Hegel's account, the full philosophical articulation of the Christian *Vorstellung* sees the human relation to God as mediated by the activity of the thinking subject and by the development of history. The contemplation of God, from an initial withdrawal from the world in early Christianity, is inwardly transformed so as to bring forth a recognition of the *logos* present in human activity, both in its contemplative and in its practical dimensions. History is conceived, then, not as a merely external necessity or Fate but as the activity of an infinite actuality, a necessity that has as its *telos* the Good conceived as self-conscious freedom, what Hegel calls Spirit. In Hegelian philosophy, the Trinitarian God revealed in Christianity is at the same time the ground of historical, worldly existence. Doull makes this point relative to the Hegelian position: 'The movement of this thought, as in the *Vorstellung*, is to a relation of equal "persons" within which are contained all subjective and objective concepts. On this foundation rests a *Sittlichkeit* in which "life" or the immediate existence of spirit, and its relation of individuals in their particularity, are comprehended in a self-governing community wherein the unity of freedom and nature in family, society and state is equally the unfolding of an objective end, and, from the side of individuals, the realizing of that end is their concrete good.'[38]

It is the state, and above all the modern state, that is, according to both Doull and Hegel, the focus of God's relation to historical life and, as such, the precise object of world history in general and so also the substance of Hegel's theodicy.[39] Doull wrote to Grant in 1956: 'Hegel is able to say with perfect accuracy that the state is the *civitas dei* on earth; for what was for Augustine, as far as practice goes, a regulative idea, is in the state, so far as true to its idea, the practical good.'[40] In his final publication, some forty-five years later, Doull expands on the point that the Augustinian *civitas dei*, which relates, as Doull puts it, 'the absolute creative God of Judaism and the subjective freedom mediated by the Greek world,' is made historically actual in the state:

Christian history mediates between Augustine's *civitas dei* – as possessing the absolute truth in separation – and historical existence. There takes shape a world more and more conformed in its institutions, and in the spirit moving in them, to the unchanging belief of all peoples. And philosophy, in responding to the reason of the world that has broken from the *Vorstellung*, gives to its religious content the form of thought. At first in this work one drew on the ancient philosophy. Then, finding that this could not contain the concreteness of the *Vorstellung*, the need of which the structure of medieval institutions made felt, a new philosophy emerged founded on the religious belief itself and able to relate that belief to a secularity apparently radically opposed to it. And from that modern world in turn has emerged a more deeply Christianized secularity and a new philosophy.[41]

Doull argues that this historically real *civitas dei*, the state in its full development, comprehends modern freedom so that this freedom is not corrupting of premodern virtue and piety but is rather the fulfilling of the promise of the ancient world: 'In Plato's polities the ruling power was freed from the special interests of classes. The difficulty then occurred how the ruling part could be in the state. How this uncorrupted independence of the ruler could move effectively the classes to the realization of the good is shown in Hegel's concept of the state.'[42]

But this is just what George Grant denies. Fundamental to Grant's denial of the Hegelian account of history is his claim that modernity is fundamentally corruptive of virtue and the human participation in justice, and thus, rather than fulfilling the Platonic philosophy, is its ruination. For Grant, the synthesis of ancient and modern, of Christian and secular, that Hegel claimed to have achieved is impossible. The ancient account that preserves the distinction between the necessary and the Good cannot, with integrity, be united with an account that dissolves this distinction. In the doctrine of progress and its turn to human historical activity, Grant sees not a realization of the divine but rather an obscuring of the divine and of genuine otherness – their reduction to moments of the will. For Grant, otherness is preserved as otherness by being seen as grounded in the Good as its source and so as having a being apart from human willing. The destruction of otherness, however much it belongs to the order of necessity to bring this about, is therefore secured as irreducibly evil. In the doctrine of progress, both the realm of natural and human otherness and that of divine otherness or the order of the Good are drawn into human will and subjectivity and so obscured. From this perspective, Hegel's understanding of history must be seen, if not in intention, at least in result, to involve the dissolution not only of religion but of every relation – philosophic, artistic, civic, or moral – of the human to an order transcending and defining the human. Grant sees built into the modern conception of the state not, as Doull and Hegel would have it, a fulfilling of the ancient forms but their dissolution.

We seem to have arrived at an impasse, or at least at the limits of this discussion. Judging the validity of Grant's or of Doull's account would seem to rest on an ability to determine rightly the relation of God to historical life. Indeed, its full exploration would require as a beginning an inquiry into the Hegelian system as a whole as (both Doull and Grant agree) the most comprehensive consideration of this question in the Western tradition. But there would also be the need for further reflection on whether the history of the West since Hegel has revealed the underlying falsity or truth of this account.[43] Are we left, then, with nothing more than our various intuitions, experiences, and inclinations about these issues?

Throughout his career, Doull could defend his claims by referring to the Hegelian system, and he could explicate – with a depth of knowledge that astonished Grant – the history of philosophy and of the West more generally and so display the historical reality of the Hegelian system and the inadequacy of accounts of that history that assumed one or another of the aspects of the contemporary standpoint. He could also point to the experience of the contemporary, which seemed to undermine the Hegelian position but in fact confirmed it. For, while each side of the contemporary divide between technology and community recognized the divide, they could not do more than explain it one-sidedly; nor could they explain the ground of their own position or its relation to the whole history it nonetheless presupposed. But, of course, the claim to be able to rise to a standpoint beyond the opposition of technology and community, one that can be 'objective' and that can mediate in thought their division, is precisely what Grant denies.[44] In the last decade and a half of his life, Doull argued that the Idea of the State is not only available to a philosophical comprehension of the divisions of contemporary European culture but is in fact actual and effective in the societies of the New World, especially in the United States and (somewhat more obscurely) in Canada. During Grant's life, Doull and Grant tended to agree that the United States was a technological empire as much given over to one-sided contemporary corruption and revolution as Europe was in the era of disintegrating nation-states. In the period after Grant's death, however, Doull began to see in the United States an actual integration of technology and community.[45] From this standpoint, Doull could not only point above contemporary life to the Idea, which comprehended in wholeness what was experienced dividedly, but argue that this division was being actually and effectively overcome not in Europe but in the New World.

Equally, for Grant, there is a connection between the truth of Hegel's philosophy and the possibility of Canada in the modern age. His turn away from Hegel in the early 1960s gave birth to a deepening insight into the fragility, indeed the impossibility, of Canada – or perhaps it was a deepening sense of the impossibility of Canada in the context of North America that gave him insight into the problematic character of the Hegelian philosophy.[46] The point that, for Grant, fused these two insights was the question of modernity. Grant 'came to the conclusion that Hegel was not correct in his claim to have taken the truth of antique thought and synthesized it with the modern to produce a higher (and perhaps highest) truth.'[47] For Grant, Jerusalem and Athens, Christ and Socrates, while they could be brought together in some manner, could not, without corruption and distortion, come together in and with modernity. Grant's turning away from the claim in Hegel that the modern and ancient are not, in the end, opposed but rather united and completed in one another, was part and parcel of his turning from hope to lamentation about the fate of Canada. Grant saw the coming to Canada of technological modernism as one with the occluding of the light cast by the contemplation of Athens and the piety of Jerusalem. For Grant, as much as for Doull, the possibility of Canada and the reality of Hegelian philosophy were interconnected.[48]

We have, then, a more direct, if also limited, route by which to consider the debate between Doull and Grant, and this is to return to the question of Canada. For Doull, the actuality of Spirit is present to the Hegelian philosopher, but, precisely if it is Spirit, it is also present – no doubt incompletely and inarticulately – in the institutions and social life of Canadians and North Americans generally. For Doull, because of the confusion of post-Hegelian culture, we tend to see this reality one-sidedly: we view Canada either as liberal and progressive or as conservative and traditional. Canada is portrayed as a nation built either on universal rights or on specific communities. Grant, by contrast opposes these two sides. On this ground, Canada as traditional cannot be united with Canada as liberal and progressive. But Doull suggests that, while Canadians tend to take up one side in opposition to the other, the country from its beginning could not be simply one side or the other. An implication of this more self-active account of Canadian history sketched by Doull is the claim that Canada's history cannot be understood as the histories of two distinct 'nations' – British and French – which, out of a shared determination to avoid assimilation into the United States have formed a marriage of convenience. As Doull puts this, 'were the history of the "two nations" such as nationalists recount, they would already have separated painlessly enough, seeing mutual benefit and little loss in their separation.'[49] Doull's criticism of Grant is that he in fact leaves Canada as just such a compact, without real unity.[50] However, Grant argues that what unites Canadians, whether French or English, is an attachment to the universality of the premodern tradition that is instantiated in differing forms in Quebec and in English Canada – a shared standpoint deeper than the differences of culture and equally opposed to American modernity. Doull, in one sense, does not disagree, but he says that if such a universal culture is the truth of Canada, then the national forms become secondary and in fact this is what the history of Canada has been. As Doull puts it, 'there is not only a separate history of Quebec and another of a British "nation"; there is also a common Canadian history more basic than either of these abstractions.'[51] It is this common history that Canadians have made to which Doull wishes to turn our attention, and which, for him, points to a reality that escapes Grant's account.

The very confusion and indecision of Canadians suggests this larger reality. Canadians can neither agree to separate along linguistic lines, and thereby dissolve what appears a marriage of convenience, nor accept the constitution as settled and Quebec separatism put to rest by the patriation of the constitution and the Charter of Rights. In this incapacity of Canada to settle into one or other side of our current self-understandings, Doull suggests that there is present a deeper truth: Canada comprehends both universal rights and specific community. Canadians would not feel caught in indecision, Doull argues, unless they knew implicitly that the truth is on both sides: we belong to received traditions, which we also transcend in a comprehensive universality. The same ambiguity can be seen, according to Doull, in Canada's vexed relation to the United States.[52] Through the Free Trade Agreement, Canada seems to have given itself over wholly to American technological consumerism and 'globalization,' and yet it still appears to be distinct from the United States in the area social programs, in the relation of provinces and regions to one another, and in foreign policy. For Grant, such distinctions can be understood as only the last glowing embers of an extinguished fire. What is the truth here?

For both Doull and Grant, contemporary Canadians live in ambiguous times: we are either a state unable to articulate the sovereignty we in fact possesses (Doull) or we are a people without sovereignty and independence and yet still think ourselves a state (Grant). For both there is a problem of articulation or recognition, since what is required for an articulation adequate to our situation is not only a recollection of the whole history of Canada, nor only an understanding of its constitutional order, but also a reflection on the character of the contemporary as a whole – on the nature of technology and its relation to the sovereignty of political institutions in this era. This latter reflection, in turn, requires a consideration of how higher ends and human freedom and self-activity relate: how God can be present or absent in historical life. It is a testimony to the depth of both thinkers that they are opposed to one another consistently and at the same points. To put the matter in its simplest form, Grant argues that there is a fundamental divide at each level, whereas Doull acknowledges this division at every point but argues that it is overcome. Beyond the division between the British/French connection and American technology, Doull argues for the possibility of a sovereign, post-national Canada. Beyond the division between community and technology, between tradition and modernity, Doull argues for the possibility of a sovereignty in the state capable of uniting these aspects. Beyond the division between God and human historical life, Doull argues for the possibility of their effective and scrutable unity. Grant denies such possibilities on the basis of both an experience of their total division and a philosophical analysis that argues for the irreconcilability of these divisions. Doull, in his turn, allows that, short of the absolute standpoint of Hegelian philosophy, there can be no known overcoming of these opposed aspects. It is not my purpose here to decide which account is valid. Rather, I wish to suggest that, both in their similarities and in their differences, the two men pose the most fundamental questions: through them, the reader can experience in contrasting ways the deep presence and absence of Jerusalem and Athens in our contemporary life.

NOTES

This chapter owes a great deal to the collaborative work I have done with David Peddle and, in particular, to our paper 'Lamentation and Speculation: George Grant, James Doull and the Possibility of Canada' in *Animus* 7 (2002).

1 Letter to George Grant, 26 April 1965, George's Grant Personal Papers, in the possession of Sheila Grant, Halifax.
2 Letter to George Grant, 11 October 1968, ibid.
3 James Doull, 'Naturalistic Individualism: Quebec Independence and an Independent Canada,' in Eugene Coombs, ed., *Modernity and Responsibility: Essays for George Grant* (Toronto: University of Toronto Press, 1983), 29; Doull in David G. Peddle and Neil G. Robertson eds., *Philosophy and Freedom: The Legacy of James Doull* (Toronto: University of Toronto Press, 2003), 375 and 395–6.
4 George Grant, *Philosophy in the Mass Age* [hereafter *PMA*], (Toronto: Copp-Clark, 1959, 1966), vii.
5 George Grant, *Lament for a Nation* [hereafter *LN*], (Toronto: McClelland and Stewart, 1965, 1978), 89.

6 There is good reason to think two things: 1) Grant never fully internalized the Hegelian position in the way Doull did; and 2) Doull thought Grant had an inadequate understanding of Hegel. See Grant 'Comments on Hegel' (1956–7) in Arthur Davis, ed., *Collected Works of George Grant, Volume 2 (1951–1959)* (Toronto: University of Toronto Press, 2002), 521–6; Grant letter to Sheila Grant (August 1957), in William Christian, ed., *George Grant: Selected Letters* (Toronto: University of Toronto Press, 1996), 194–5; Larry Schmidt, ed., *George Grant in Process* (Toronto: House of Anansi Press, 1978), 64; Doull letter to George Grant, 26 April 1965, George Grant Personal Papers.

7 Grant, *PMA*, vii, and *LN*, 89.

8 *LN*, 4.

9 Grant made himself clear in his 1970 foreword to a reissuing of *Lament for a Nation*, that he: a) was not attached to the British connection ethnically – indeed he saw such unthinking attachment as part of the demise of that connection; b) viewed the collapse of this connection with equanimity – especially given the British abasement before the United States in the twentieth century. As Grant states, 'I emphasise this failure in irony because many simple people (particularly journalists and professors) took it to be a lament for the passing of a British dream of Canada. It was rather a lament for the romanticism of the original dream.' *LN*, xi.

10 'The argument that Canada, a local culture, must disappear can, therefore, be stated in three steps. First, men everywhere move ineluctably toward membership in the universal and homogeneous state. Second, Canadians live next to a society that is the heart of modernity. Third, nearly all Canadians think that modernity is good, so nothing essential distinguishes Canadians from Americans. When they oblate themselves before "the American way of life," they offer themselves on the altar of the reigning western goddess.' *LN*, 54.

11 *LN*, 68.

12 *LN*, 69.

13 *LN*, 70.

14 *LN*, 87.

15 Notes to a lecture on *LN* (unpublished, Doull Archive, Sir Wilfred Grenfell College, Corner Brook, Nfld.), 3.

16 Doull, 'Naturalistic Individualism,' 44.

17 Ibid., 39.

18 James Doull, 'Heidegger and the State,' in Peddle and Robertson, *Philosophy and Freedom*, 357–77.

19 *LN*, 70.

20 *LN*, 71.

21 *LN*, 71.

22 George Grant, *Technology and Justice* (Toronto: Anansi, 1986), 32.
23 William Christian and Sheila Grant, eds., *The George Grant Reader* (Toronto: University of Toronto Press 1998), 435–6.
24 On Grant's relation to Eastern Christianity, especially through the work of Philip Sherrard, see Harris Athanasiadis, *George Grant and the Theology of the Cross: The Christian Foundation of the Thought* (Toronto: University of Toronto Press, 2001), 134–7 and 168–71.
25 Christian and Grant, eds., *Grant Reader*, 437.
26 George Grant, *English Speaking Justice* (1974; repr.: Toronto: Anansi/South Bend, IN: University of Notre Dame Press 1985), 77.
27 David Caley, *George Grant in Conversation* (Don Mills, ON: Anansi, 1995), 82.
28 Grant, *Technology and Justice*, 33.
29 See Doull, in Peddle and Robertson, eds., *Philosophy and Freedom*, 360–70 and 399–402.
30 James Doull, 'Augustinian Trinitarianism and Existential Theology,' *Dionysius* 3 (1979): 121.
31 Doull, in Peddle and Robertson, eds., *Philosophy and Freedom*, 399–402.
32 James Doull, 'Hegel and Contemporary Liberalism, Anarchism, Socialism: A Defense of the *Rechtsphilosophie* against Marx and His Contemporary Followers,' in J.J. O'Malley et al., *The Legacy of Hegel* (The Hague: Nijhoff, 1973), 229.
33 Doull, in Peddle and Robertson, eds., *Philosophy and Freedom*, 341.
34 For Doull on Latin America, see ibid., 406–7.
35 Doull's history of Canada is found in ibid., 434–59. For a fuller discussion of Doull's history of Canada in contrast to Grant's, see David Peddle and Neil Robertson, 'Lamentation and Speculation: George Grant, James Doull and the Possibility of Canada,' *Animus* 7 (2002): 16–19.
36 *LN*, 99. That Doull disagreed with Grant's portrayal of Hegel's argument is an understatement. In a letter he wrote to Grant: 'When Hegel writes that 'die Weltgeschichte ist das Weltgericht' he means nothing remotely resembling the sense his words have in your quotation of them. It would be easy to find statements in Aquinas and Hooker equivalent to Hegel's. You and Strauss in turning from Hegel show yourselves still liberals at heart. America is omnipotent, you think, because its virtues of direct concerns for individuals are also for you the highest virtues. Whatever one may think about this, classical conservatism was on the other side.' Letter, 26 April 1965, George Grant Personal Papers.
37 *LN*, 100.
38 Doull, in Peddle and Robertson, *Philosophy and Freedom*, 288.
39 Hegel, *Introduction to The Philosophy of History*, trans. Leo Rauch (Indianapolis: Hackett, 1988), 18 and 42.

40 Doull letter to George Grant, December 1956, George Grant Personal Papers.

41 Doull, in Peddle and Robertson, eds., *Philosophy and Freedom*, 298–9.

42 James Doull, 'Hegel's Critique of Hellenic Virtue,' *Dionysius* 9 (1985): 14. For Doull's summary of Hegel's concept of the state, see ibid., 14–15.

43 See the Doull-Fackenheim debate and Ken Kieran's commentary on this debate in Peddle and Robertson, eds., *Philosophy and Freedom*, 330–53, as a beginning to this reflection.

44 Indeed, from Grant's position, Doull is not beyond the division but has rather sided with modernity. This is clear from Grant's comments about Hegel in the new introduction to *PMA*, viii.

45 Doull did not see the United States as the most perfect form of this integration, but he nevertheless regarded the integrity achieved there as real and as capable of further development. See James Doull, 'The Philosophical Basis of the Constitutional Discussion in Canada,' in Peddle and Robertson, *Philosophy and Freedom*, 393–465.

46 In his new preface to *Philosophy in the Mass Age*, Grant wrote, 'To state quickly why one has changed one's mind is always difficult. Experience and reflection are too intricately bound for any ease of intellectual relation,' *PMA*, x–xi.

47 Ibid., viii.

48 But, it should be said, not united: neither thinker would confuse the limited question of Canada's reality with the absolute question of the relation of God to the world.

49 Doull, in Peddle and Robertson, *Philosophy and Freedom*, 396.

50 Doull, ibid., 395–8.

51 Doull, ibid., 398.

52 Doull, ibid., 455–6.

10

'A Cow Is Just a Cow': George Grant and Eric Voegelin on the United States

JOHN VON HEYKING AND BARRY COOPER

George Grant and Eric Voegelin both invoked the stories and the symbols of 'Jerusalem and Athens' – to use a trope made famous by Leo Strauss[1] – as aids to understanding modern life. Grant often described himself as a Christian Platonist whose reflections on technology, the good life, beauty, and Canada were informed by a mixture of Platonic rationalism and Christian exegesis of the depths of meaning symbolized by the cross. Voegelin's reflections on history, modernity, and ideology, featured most prominently in his *New Science of Politics* and *Order and History*, were formed by his understanding of the Platonic or 'noetic' quest for order – Athens – as well as the biblical, Israelite, Christian, 'pneumatic' quest for order – Jerusalem.

A systematic comparison of Voegelin and Grant could be likened to retrieving an imaginary conversation they never held. Voegelin and Grant never met, nor did they make much use of each other's writings. Voegelin seems never to have read Grant. Grant, on the other hand, referred to Voegelin on a few occasions. Grant admired *Order and History* and often recommended volume one, *Israel and Revelation*, to his students as the best study on understanding the Bible in the modern age.[2] He referred to Voegelin's account of representation in the *New Science of Politics* as an antidote to an anachronistic conservatism that would confine Canadian nationalism to memories of the past.[3] Late in his life, he wrote in a letter that he found Voegelin's understanding of the relationship between philosophy and faith more profound than that of Strauss.[4] However, in his praise of Simone Weil as a 'Gnostic saint,' Grant offered the opinion that Voegelin erred in his understanding of Gnosticism.[5] Regrettably, he did not elaborate this view.

Common themes in their writings that would provide points of contact include their interpretations of Plato, their interpretations of Christian revelation, their perspectives on the work of Leo Strauss, and their views on the relationship between poetry, myth, and philosophy, on gnosticism, theodicy, and suffering, on twentieth-century ideological mass movements, and on technology and scientism. These are large and complex problems involving grand questions of interpretation. The question we raise in this chapter is more concrete, pragmatic, and empirical: What did they think of the United States? Whatever the extent of their agreement regarding Athens and Jerusalem and the great issues of noetic and pneumatic symbolism, Voegelin and Grant held widely divergent, even antithetical, views of the principles and practices of American politics and founding principles. Grant regarded the liberal-democratic United States as the clearest manifestation of technological, imperial modernity, more seductive and ultimately more destructive than even the ideological empires of international and national socialists. From his early writings on the fate of Canada through his late reflections on technology, Grant applied his Christian Platonism to view the United States as the vanguard of technology, the moloch to which it was necessary to sacrifice 'one's own,' to repudiate the love of one's own, and thus as well to repudiate the image in the world of the Good and even the love of the Good. In short, to Grant, the moloch-face of America was satanic.[6]

In contrast, Voegelin consistently viewed the United States as having maintained sufficient substance from the classical-Judaeo-Christian heritage of the West to preserve itself against the more virulent of the ideological onslaughts of modernity that had engulfed Europe. Voegelin's first book was on the United States, in which he drew a distinction between the ideological self-interpretations of Americans and the actual, although less conscious, practices of the polity that occur through its institutions, which he regarded as a better way to understand the principles of a regime.[7] Voegelin's writings on scientism indicate that he, too, was aware of the dangers of technology that so worried Grant. However, like Leo Strauss, but unlike Grant, Voegelin saw the United States as endowed with a spiritual and intellectual substance that enabled it to resist the limitless claims of technology.[8]

As we shall see, biographical accident played a part in conditioning the two men's respective interpretations of the principles and practices of the United States. Their differences, however, have more than biographical significance. To begin with, their accounts indicate the way that each thinker understood the possibility of a good polity enduring modernity. An analysis of their respective views of the United States provides a lens through which we can see, not simply their opinions of a particular regime, but the ability of the great issues of Jerusalem and Athens to inform a polity within modernity. To use the kind of dramatic language that Grant favoured on such occasions: at issue is the degree to which either man considered the Good or even the good regime to be capable of manifestation in history. Our analysis aims to uncover or 'enucleate' (one of Grant's favourite words) the 'fundamental experiences' (Voegelin) or the 'primal' (Grant) that each author regarded as the core of the American experience. Both, for example, understood the importance of 'the frontier.' For Voegelin, the experience of the frontier shaped the American understanding of the biblical realities of equality and freedom. For Grant, the 'frontier' symbolized the lonely and alienated will of liberal and Calvinist modernity bent on the exploitation of nature. As we shall see, their explications of the United States reveal as much about themselves and their respective experiences of order in history as about the United States.

'EXPERIENCES' OF THE UNITED STATES

Voegelin and Grant had in common the biographically unique encounter of a foreigner with the United States. For both men, that experience was critical and significant. Moreover, both were aware of the link between biography and philosophy; both knew that philosophical consciousness was *somebody's* philosophical consciousness. That is, concrete human beings, with specific and identifiable names such as George Grant and Eric Voegelin, participate in the order and disorder of particular times and places. Their reflections are already under way in their pre-reflective experiences of participation in the here and now of the America they knew. Looked at in terms of the accounts they rendered of their participation in the reality of America, what they said was also an account of how they understood themselves. In order to see their respective assessments of the United States, it is first necessary to consider where they were standing and where they were going.

Born in Cologne, Germany, Voegelin first encountered the United States as part of his professional career. At the age of twenty-four, he spent two years on a study trip immediately after he earned his doctorate at the University of Vienna under the supervision of the great legal scholar Hans Kelsen. During that time, he heard A.N. Whitehead and John Dewey lecture at Harvard; he worked in the genetics lab of Thomas Hunt Morgan at Columbia but also took courses from John Dewey, F.H. Giddings, Irwin Edman, and J.W. Macmahon. Perhaps most important, he spent time in Wisconsin, where he learned American government and economics from John R. Commons, an economist who was influential among the Progressives. Upon returning to central Europe, he spent the next decade immersed in the ideological struggles surrounding the rise of Nazi Germany. In 1938 he barely escaped from Nazism and fled to the United States. He taught at several American universities before settling for sixteen years at Louisiana State University in Baton Rouge. In 1958 he returned to Europe as professor and director of the Institute for Political Science at the University of Munich, where, among other things, he taught American government and politics to German students as part of what he called his belated post-war reconstruction effort. He retired to the United States in 1969 to work at the Hoover Institution in Palo Alto, California, and died there in 1985.

The effect of the United States on Voegelin's thought has been well documented. He stated in an extended interview in 1973 that his two-year study trip in the 1920s taught him common sense philosophy, which inoculated him against the ideological disorders plaguing Europe at the time.[9] Unlike Grant, however, Voegelin regarded this philosophy as congruent with, and ultimately based upon, the classical Greek and biblical principles that sustain existential resistance to the deleterious effects of modernity. The other thing that Voegelin learned from that two-year study trip was the primacy to be accorded to the practice and self-understanding of practitioners. That is, Voegelin learned from his experience of the United States that political science begins from an understanding of the self-interpretation of those individuals who actually participate in any particular political order, and not from an elaborate 'scientific' understanding. The specific and particular character of American democracy (or of any other regime), with its complex manifold of political, spiritual, intellectual, legal, and economic forms, made it impossible to analyse it through the lens of externally imposed, aprioristic categories (as positivists of various stripes did then, and continue to do at present).

Instead, Voegelin developed a technical, though still commonsensical, method of studying American society. He found that particular 'forms' such as laws or economics exist in a social space that gives them their shape but that this social space is, in turn, informed by them: 'The fact that a necessary structure with variable themes can be combined into an unbroken unity of an intellectual form presupposes that the structure itself contains a point of departure for variability. When the topic contains such a point, only a variation can of necessity be described; it cannot be described "in itself." Thus the only way to clarify its essence is precisely through comparison of a number of these variations.'[10] The unifying form and the 'variations' of that form exist in a dialectical relationship whereby each engages the other in historical time. This insight would lead Voegelin to become sceptical of doctrines that simply incorporate empirical materials into an a priori interpretation. His early work on the United States, therefore, contains several studies of American institutions, including the Federal Reserve Board and the Supreme Court, that draw from scholars of American institutions; it also includes studies of representative figures, including William James, Samuel Gompers, Robert La Follette, Jonathan Edwards, and John R. Commons, who typify what Voegelin, borrowing from Henri Bergson, referred to as the 'open self.'[11] Finally, these studies reflect his view that liberal democracy and the Anglo-American tradition within which it arose is, because it is a tradition, never fully present or conscious to itself. Accordingly, all the arguments and 'philosophies' of the American tradition are necessarily incomplete precisely because they are merely traditions, that is, accounts and stories that are handed down or handed over unreflectively between generations. At the same time, however, these traditions can express a truth of existence or, to use a favourite, though far from idiomatic, expression of Voegelin, are luminous towards the divine ground.[12]

Voegelin's attention to 'variations' and empirical materials is not simply the result of his scholarly contentiousness but is integral to the self-understanding of his or anyone's participation in reality. Recall the famous opening statement of *Order and History*: 'the order of history emerges from the history of order.' This means, among other things, that Voegelin saw his own scholarship as the result of his participation in history, which includes his resistance to disorder. Put another way, Voegelin's scholarship is the result of his participation in order and of his own ability to transcend disorder, which is made possible because of the nature of the order within which he (as all human beings) participates and of which he (as a singular human being) is conscious. Moreover, to return to the approach outlined in our introduction, Voegelin's self-understanding as participant informs his position regarding the face of the Good in the world, whether (or the extent to which) a good regime can appear in the world, and thus whether (or the extent to which) the United States is so informed.

The contingencies of George Parkin Grant's life were rather different. Grant belonged to a well-connected family who saw themselves as members of the British Empire and who happened to dwell in Canada. His grandfather, George Monro Grant, presided over Queen's University; his grandfather, George Parkin, directed the Rhodes Trust; his uncle, Vincent Massey, was the first Canadian-born governor general; and his father, William Grant, was principal of Upper Canada College in Toronto. Grant understood that he and his distinguished family were charged with the duty of maintaining Canada's Britishness through the imperial connection; when that option was no longer possible, they adopted the view that it was of overriding importance to maintain whatever it was that made Canada distinct from the United States. George Grant personally felt extraordinary pressure, from his mother in particular, to succeed in the world of affairs; he seemed to reciprocate with worldly ambition and pragmatism, at least until his time at Oxford on a Rhodes scholarship in 1939–40.[13]

Whatever one may think of such a family,[14] there is a sense of homelessness that pervades Grant's biography and his writings. For example, he speaks of his father's family as Highland Scots and evokes an image of the Clearances and the Highlanders' forcible expulsion as if it were yesterday or the day before, not a century and a half earlier.[15] Likewise, Grant recalled the experiences of the Loyalists, men and women driven from the America colonies and made homeless by the young republic, as if those experiences still burned in the souls of yeomen along the Niagara frontier. Grant, in short, lived within a powerful tradition: the experiences of exile of the Scots following the Clearances and of the Loyalists following the American revolution were crucial to his identity in the present. In both instances, Grant saw that a significant part of what he was charged to maintain was defined as resistance to imperial ruthlessness: the memory of Culloden appeared through the image of Uncle Sam. More poignant still, homelessness was part of Grant's internal landscape, a lonely, alienated self trapped within modernity.

Notwithstanding a keen nostalgia for Oxford and for England, and a great pride in his lineage, Grant came to reject many of the assumptions of his family history. He would make light of his own Oedipal problems and claim that he had moved beyond the stifling conventions of Upper Canada. He said that he found the liberal Protestantism embodied in Upper Canada 'oblivious of the eternal,' of world-transcendent experiences and realities, just as worldly American Puritanism, which transformed itself into capitalism and liberal pragmatism, had become blind to those same realities. Thus, the key part of Grant's biography consisted of what he and his biographer called a basic reorientation of his outlook on the divine whereby he focused his spiritual and intellectual energies on the meaning of the mystery of the cross. William Christian notes that this event took place following a long process of rethinking his own faith and moving away from that of his family's: 'His experience of God at the bleakest moment of the war was less a rejection of his past than it was the culmination of a long development.'[16] His conversion – on 11 or 12 December 1941 – came at a difficult time: he was convalescing the country while London was undergoing the crucible of the Blitz. As with many such accounts, he says that his conversion came about after a great suffering that ground him down to nearly nothing.

However important the long preparatory suffering may have been, it is important to note as well that it occurred only a few days after the Japanese bombing of Pearl Harbor. News of the bombing, and of the U.S. entry into the war, drove him to despair and thoughts of suicide. That is, American entry into the war, which Grant, a pacifist, knew would turn the tide against Hitler, did not end his suffering. On the contrary, the decision of a nation of 130 million people to join the conflict would be 'an experience which will only create greater ill will, greater misunderstanding that will take them farther from the face of God.'[17] It was not simply that the participation in the war of a large and powerful state would ensure that the killing would continue. Grant also opposed the 'dehumanized' way the Americans practised war.[18] In short, the conversion experience that constitutes the centerpiece of his life, and the centerpiece of his philosophizing, was occasioned by his view that the American entry into the war would worsen world relations instead of improving them – even though he recognized that it would also mean eventual victory over Nazi Germany. The deep ambivalence Grant experienced towards his family was reinforced by his ambivalence towards war and by his own pacifism, feelings that became even more intense after Pearl Harbor.

Grant's deepening personal depression was resolved with his conversion a few days later when he was reminded that God exists. His descent paralleled the abyss into which he thought the world had sunk. The individual may be redeemed, he concluded, but civilization is not. Writing to his mother a few years earlier, Grant had stated, 'My trouble is that I am a true Lutheran in that I seek out my own personal salvation and don't try to affect others.'[19] The difference between personal salvation and a political sphere that is not saved, perhaps not even improved, was later decisive in his understanding of political order in the modern technological world. Thus, the same event, the U.S. entry into the war, both intensified Grant's purgatorial experience and led him to divide even more radically than he had in his letter to his mother the question of personal salvation and his place in the modern world.

Grant's conversion directed him away from the pragmatic, worldly Protestant faith of his family, but evidence suggests the theologico-political stance towards which he gravitated is characterized more by intracosmic Manichean tendencies than by a full movement of transcendence. He reflects upon the connection between his personal search for meaning and the state of civilization in a 1988 'Addendum' to the reissue of 'Two Theological Languages,' first published in 1947.[20] The article deals with the relationship between rationality and freedom and for the first time invokes Martin Luther's Twenty-First Heidelberg thesis to emphasize Grant's preference for the biblical account of the two: 'The "theologian of glory" calls the bad good and the good bad. The "theologian of the cross" says what a thing is.'[21] The essay represents an early, comparatively unrefined attempt by Grant to articulate the difference between reason and revelation and the relationship between freedom and necessity. In 1988 he corrected his previous articulation by claiming that it had conflated the biblical account of freedom with the modern existential one: 'I had been brought up in secularized Protestantism which in the English-speaking world generally expressed itself in some form of liberal progressivism. Canadians held on to that latter faith much longer than people in more sophisticated centers.' He thus revised his understanding of freedom as 'the liberty to be indifferent to good' in order to move it away from the freedom of modern existentialism, which he viewed as 'an expression of heroic atheism.'

His revised definition of freedom, however, is closer to that of Lockean liberalism, as well as to late-medieval nominalist accounts of freedom, than it is to Augustine's view. He invokes Augustine's view of evil as the 'absence' of good to avoid falling into the false dualism that he thought his earlier view had included. However, Augustine's view of evil is better described as a 'deformation' of good than as an absence. Absence entails waiting for something that may never arrive – the darkness experienced by the romantic as well as the theologian of the cross, who can overlook the intimations that St Paul mentions when he speaks of faith as evidence of things unseen.[22] Grant's writings on technology, and his general rejection of Augustine's account of theodicy, which he regarded as inspiring the modern progress, suggest that he really did mean to say 'absence' of the Good. Despite invoking Augustine in the 'Addendum,' Grant maintained the categories of the theology of the cross along with the romantic qualities of a beautiful soul in order to articulate his own version of the theodicy problem whereby the beautiful soul waits in the darkness – and perhaps with indifference – for the irruption of God's grace. In this respect, he may have been closer to the Manicheans than to Augustine, because, for Grant, the regime of technology, as embodied by the United States, stands in for theological darkness. Furthermore, his view of Canadians as bumpkins living outside unnamed 'sophisticated centers' that were both attractive and unsavory is yet another expression of Grant's longing and homelessness.

While Grant waited for grace personally, in politics there can be a real 'absence' of good, that is, a world that is dominated by technology, which, even though it is bounded by the givenness of creation, so darkens everything that good becomes altogether obscured (just as the world was for Grant from 7 December 1941 until the moment of his conversion a few days later). Personally, Grant waited for his grace; politically, he was a romantic, a Hegelian beautiful soul. His attitude is most forcefully expressed in the way he chose to understand the United States.

ELEMENTAL AND EXISTENTIAL REPRESENTATION

Our analysis of each thinker's view of the United States is guided by Voegelin's theory of representation, which, as noted above, Grant also found useful. Each political society understands itself in its own unique way and explains itself to itself in order to make its own particular existence intelligible. Voegelin identified three levels of representation: elemental, existential, and transcendental. Elemental representation refers to the external existence of society, to the various agents that hold society together physically, including, for example, the laws, the institutions, the mechanics of voting, and geographical districts.[23] Existential representation signifies an idea, spirit, or political culture that animates a society. If the elemental representative does not match the existential reality of a society, then the institution that embodies the representative will atrophy into irrelevance. A country may have a beautiful constitution – the former Soviet Union, for example – but, because this institution did not correspond to the existential reality of a one-party totalitarian regime, one would learn nothing of the reality of

Soviet politics by reading the Soviet constitution. Beyond existential and elemental representation lies what Voegelin called transcendent representation, which reflects the attempts by a society to interpret itself as representative of something beyond, or transcendent to, itself. Generally speaking, transcendent representations provide a given political society with an account of its meaningfulness, justice, divinely appointed mission, and so on. In this section we compare the way Grant and Voegelin discussed the elemental and existential modes of American representation; the following section considers transcendent representation, although the treatments of each overlap.

Beginning with his visit to the United States and the publication of *On the Form of the American Mind*, Voegelin viewed the United States as a political society informed fundamentally by classical and Judeo-Christian ideas of liberty, equality, and even solidarity, which he identified with Henri Bergson's concept of the 'open self' and John Dewey's solidarist idea of 'like-mindedness,' where members of a community 'can advance equally to the essence of their person and whom the individual who has reached his goal through the advantage of circumstances is obliged to help.'[24] This substance was expressed by a pervasive common-sense attitude in American thought, which Voegelin analysed in empirical studies of political practices (elemental representation). Such practices, he believed, often convey the moral substance of American thought (existential representation) better than reflective theoretical treatments. In this context, the concepts of the 'open self' and of solidarity fit easily into Voegelin's interpretive strategy for studying 'institutions,' including the U.S. Supreme Court, property, and economics, because he found that no a priori theoretical concept could adequately explain what was going on, for example, in the Supreme Court jurisprudence on property or even in the way the constitution manifests the moral substance of American society. The 'openness' towards inarticulate and intimated meanings that lay just beyond the consciousness of practitioners had to be recaptured in Voegelin's scholarly analysis of the various elements of the American institutional structure.

For Voegelin, American economic thinking had been formed out of the frontier experience, an experience that also permeated the ideas of the Progressives.[25] However, American political society was able to move beyond the limitations of that view in the transition to industrialization. Voegelin pointed to various examples of how liberty and solidarity endured through industrialization, including Samuel Gompers and the American Federation of Labor (AFL).[26] Gompers's labour politics was distinctly American in that his pragmatism led him to distrust socialist theories of capitalist exploitations, thus, he spoke of 'wage consciousness' instead of 'class consciousness,' and, despite the abuses that accompanied business practices, viewed employer/employee negotiations within the broader political like-mindedness that is expressed through the constitution. Such like-mindedness is not simply a consequence of the constitution. Throughout his writings, Voegelin argued that socialist theories pitting entrepreneur against worker never really obtained salience in industrial society because such theories were derived from feudal, agrarian experiences.[27] Political conflict within industrial society is based not on employer-employee cleavages but on the exploitation of technological productivity, where both employees and employers share common and overlapping interests as well as differing ones. Thus, Voegelin saw Gompers and the AFL in terms comparable to a Tocquevillian exercise in self-government, which contained implicitly within it the Judaeo-Christian notion of like-mindedness.[28]

Voegelin realized that industrial society raises the standard of living for all, a moral undertaking that, to him, was consistent with classical and Judaeo-Christian principles of order. He thought that surplus wealth, especially that generated in the post-war period, enabled individuals to obtain economic security, once it was understood that security depends on viewing individuals as components of a larger web of relations, and not as the self-sufficient farmer challenged only by nature rather than by the numerous decisions made by other actors in the economy:

When I went to America in 1938, nonessential income, the phenomenon that today puzzles economists, sociologists, and politicians, did not exist. On this new productivity-basis, it has come within the reach of the possible and even become reality what Jefferson foresaw as possible only under the conditions of an old-fashioned agrarian economy: the material security for all, but with a far higher level of consumer and capital goods within modern industrial society. The possibility of a civil government in an industrial society can, based upon the American experience, be considered as assured.[29]

His assessment of industrial society in this 1959 essay thus differs from that of agrarians including Thomas Jefferson (and, it appears, Grant), who thought that only a society of austere, publicly minded farmers could secure self-sufficiency for themselves and practise patriotism. Voegelin's assessment derives in part from his view that webs of interdependencies characterize industrial society, including that of entrepreneur and labour with rationalized expertise in relevant sectors:

> Modern industrial society is a total enterprise that disperses entrepreneurial initiatives among persons and associations, industrial entrepreneurship in the stricter sense and unions, public and private bureaucracies, managers, services for recruiting, information and communication, commercial organizations, school systems, the organization of research by universities, economic enterprises and also government, laws governing social and economic orders, and many similar institutions. In this sense we have been speaking about a democratization of the entrepreneurial function.[30]

Civil government, based on liberty, equality, and solidarity, remains possible in the industrial period so long as governments appreciate the fluidity and mobility of the industrial economy and the need to ensure worker retraining so they can sustain their reciprocal entrepreneurial status.

Voegelin's conclusions regarding American economics are fairly consistent with the moral and economic arguments made by democratic capitalists who emphasize wealth-creation. Unlike laissez-faire libertarians, however, Voegelin found that citizens in an industrial society cannot be viewed as isolated actors whose only challenges derive solely from their own initiative and from nature; the complexities and interdependence of mass-industrial society require governments to acknowledge that workers may be put out of work as a result of a decision made elsewhere in the economic system, which in turn requires an adequate view of property and personhood. According to Voegelin, the American polity contained within it the moral and spiritual substance needed to navigate successfully the move between agrarian and industrial society.

Voegelin's early direct encounter with the United States enabled him to see how this political substance was retained. His empirical approach in studying America differed from Grant's because Voegelin viewed doctrinal self-interpretation as subordinate to actual political practices, whereas Grant emphasized doctrine as the determining factor. As we saw with Gompers, Voegelin, unlike most other European students of the United States at the time, noticed how the workings of institutions under the constitution preserved the moral substance of the regime despite the self-interpretations given to it by its partisans.[31]

In contrast to Voegelin, Grant viewed the United States as an oligarchy run by the wealthy and the technocratic elite. Between the end of the Second World War and the Vietnam War, which he described as having shed a 'searchlight' on the structure of its society,[32] the United States had also become imperialistic. Its elemental representation may have been liberal and democratic, but, for Grant, its existential representation had become (or always was) oligarchic and imperialistic, two realities that liberal democrats tended to overlook.[33] Grant drew his conclusions about the regime from his own observations and from his reading of the texts of American liberalism. Both of these modes stemmed from his purpose of understanding the United States so as to understand how Canada relates to it, which at one point he compared to the relationship between a crooked stockbroker and his son.[34]

Grant's critique of the United States was fairly consistent throughout his career. Before the 1960s, when he turned his attention to technology, his criticisms were what one would expect of a Canadian conservative. The United State is too individualistic and so less concerned about the common good than is Canada. The lawless American frontier contrasted with the Canadian frontier, where the North-West Mounted Police preceded settlement.[35] Via their Britishness, Canadian conservatives preserved ordered liberty because, unlike the American revolutionaries, 'these men and women ... feel that a break with the past may endanger the future.'[36] Grant regarded the American revolution, which derived from natural rights, in terms similar to Burke's view of the French revolution: in both instances, reference to abstract natural rights produced an unstable political order because it undermined tradition and community. The bearers of the American Revolution in the contemporary context consist of the technological elites, including the corporations, the 'progressive intellectuals,' and the politicians who pander to the former and embody the ideas of the latter. The post-war transition to a full-blown industrial state turned power over completely to the corporations, thus making Jefferson's dream of a society of small property owners a long-distant memory.[37] The corporations work with the scientists to implement the technological society over and above the protestations of dissenters, whose own viewpoint becomes 'bureaucratized,' 'normalized,' and thus negated by the logic of the technological society. The oligarchic technological society that Grant saw south of the border, towards which Canadian elites (the metaphorical sons of the corrupt stockbroker) were pushing Canada, was characterized by the dominance of urban and wealthy elites over ignorant, unsophisticated rural populations whose livelihoods were rooted on the land and, by extension, constituted a truer embodiment of conservatism. What remained of public life for the masses in this society consisted of little more than sexually driven entertainment and political demagoguery, which was also served up as titillation and entertainment. Grant had in mind the Kennedys and Trudeau, icons that threatened to deprive public discourse of meaning.[38] Such manipulation of the masses in the welfare state included as well the application of the social sciences such as psychology and sociology.[39]

Despite the homogeneity of thought that Grant ascribed to technological society, he at times noticed a greater pluralism in the United States than in Canada while also recognizing that, in some regards, non-technological political positions showed greater effectiveness in public life there. In *Lament for a Nation* he observed how a deeper experience of technology in the United States than in Canada had produced a more firmly defined opposition to it: 'Not so many of us have been forced to look unflinchingly into the face of Moloch.'[40] Similarly, late in life, Grant expressed in a letter his admiration for the greater political effectiveness of U.S. anti-abortion movement compared to that of its Canadian counterpart, which he took as a sign of vitality in the American polity: 'My sense of the greatness of the U.S.A. has been greatly raised by the presence of this anti-abortion movement.'[41]

Grant noticed another strength in the U.S. regime when he praised the staying power of social-contract thinking over utilitarianism. Utilitarianism, which he dismissed as hedonistic and as majoritarian, may have a hold over the masses; social-contract thinking, he said, has a greater hold over practising politicians. Although Grant ultimately rejected social-contract thinking, the reason he noted for its hold over practising politicians was that it provided them with a better guide than utilitarianism in negotiating the details of an American constitutional structure that preserved the rights of individuals: 'The politicians had to come to terms with the details of justice in terms of individuals. Therefore when John Rawls insists on the superiority of Locke to Hume, we seem to be entering a world which is much less flaccid about what can be done to individuals than the world called forth by the successors of Hume ... Rawls gives us hope that we will meet the complexities and difficulties of political justice in a way that is not possible under the principles of mass hedonism.'[42] In a passage that echoes Tocqueville's admiration of the genius of democratic institutions, Grant observed that the American constitution required politicians to attend to the nitty-gritty of preserving rights and freedoms, even when their public philosophies eventually dissolved those rights and freedoms in the vacuous air of principles rooted in abstract notions of the will. Grant thus recognized that the American constitution preserved ordered liberty, perhaps in a way he thought Canadian Burkean conservatism had done, but he lamented that the ideological liberal underpinnings of United States, tied as they are to the modern notion of the will, ultimately collapsed under the weight of technology.[43]

Grant's analysis of the United States consisted of a critique more of liberalism than of its constitution, which is one of the weaknesses of his account. Unlike Strauss, whom he so admired, and the followers of Strauss, Grant never provided an analysis of the American founders or of the U.S. constitutional structure, with the exception of his critique of *Roe v. Wade*, which he also treated more as an occasion to criticize liberalism. Further, he ignored the debate between liberalism and republican civic virtue that began in the 1960s with the publication of Bernard Bailyn's *Ideological Origins of the American Revolution* and Gordon S. Wood's *The Creation of the American Republic*, not to mention the works of Strauss's students such as Harry Jaffa.[44] Instead, the nucleus of Grant's ideological critique of the United States could be found in his comparison of the Calvinist and liberal accounts of freedom, the conjunction of which prepared the ground for the technological society, just as that conjunction formed the soul of Grant himself in his early days and against which he struggled throughout his life.

TRANSCENDENT REPRESENTATION

According to Grant, the confusion of the West, and of North America in particular, is a result of the 'dialectic' between Calvinism and secular liberalism, which constitutes the West's 'transcendent' representation. The two have cooperated historically in maintaining the liberal state: liberalism provides principles of consent and Protestantism provides the moral glue that holds society together. Grant distinguished the two by observing how Protestants have always hesitated to accept the view of secular liberalism that avoidance of violent death is man's greatest purpose; in this way, Protestantism provided a justification for self-sacrifice when liberalism fell short.[45] Grant characterized the relationship between the two as 'dialectic' because Protestantism was not a passive partner in the relationship. The dynamo of secular liberalism did not simply roll over a passive Protestantism. Rather, Protestantism, in its Calvinist form, has been a willing partner because, fundamentally, in the 'primal' of the West, the Calvinist understanding of the human will, which derives from late-medieval nominalist views of God as will, harmonizes with a secular view of the will that postulates man as maker of his own laws. Calvinism and liberalism constitute a tandem that provides the foundation for the technological society, where freedom is understood as the freedom to remake nature and to remake man. In fact, however, there is no 'dialectic' or tandem because both share the same 'primal.' Secular liberalism, according to Grant, is the anthropomorphic side of the Calvinist theology of the will.

Further, Grant did not treat the Calvinist/liberal view of the will as one option among alternate understandings, including the Augustinian, Thomist, and so forth. Instead, Grant considered the entry of this understanding of the will into the West as inevitable, as part of the 'primal' that all westerners share:

This is the attempt to articulate that primal western affirmation which stands shaping our whole civilization, before modern science and technology, before liberalism and capitalism, before our philosophies and theologies. It is present in all of us, and yet hidden to all of us; it originates somewhere and sometime which nobody seems quite to know. Nobody has been able to bring it into the full light of understanding. In all its unfathomedness, the closest I can come to it is the affirmation of human beings as 'will,' the content of which word has something to do with how westerners took the Bible as a certain kind of exclusivity.[46]

Beneath the procrustean bed of liberalism, science, Calvinism, and technology lies the 'primal' that is the will. With the exception of his reference to Hooker's Thomistic criticism of Calvinist voluntarism, Grant did not offer a non-Calvinist Christian account of the will in *English-Speaking Justice*. One would have to turn to his criticisms of Western Christianity, especially of Augustine and Thomas Aquinas, to see how their errors, typical of those made by theologians of glory, had led Western Christianity towards Calvinism/liberalism and thus modern science and technology.[47] In particular, Augustine's allegedly triumphalist view of Christianity had prepared the way somehow for the triumphalism of modern progress and technology.[48] This is a far different 'primal' than the one Voegelin at times invoked in his writings on the United States and democracy when he referred to the democratic faith in equality and its rootedness in classical and Judaeo-Christian sources.[49]

Indeed, Grant's invocation of the 'primal' differed from the 'primal' that he himself had invoked a few years earlier in *Technology and Empire* when he spoke of Greece as another 'primal' in the context of North

America's lack of the 'chthonic.'[50] For North Americans, as opposed to Europeans, the 'primal' lay not in its 'chthonic' root in Christianity and Greece but in the 'meeting of the alien and yet conquerable land with English-speaking Protestants,' as if the migration to the New World differed in an experiential sense from the expansion of the Roman Empire northward into the barbarian frontier. The 'primal' that Grant saw for North America was the equivalent of Voegelin's references to the frontier experience that lay behind formulations of property and community. However, for Voegelin, North Americans have made a home, whereas for Grant, the frontier was an experience of homelessness, which Calvinists met with their already homeless will.[51] Given this understanding of frontier experience, it is no wonder that Grant's experience of Canada, in contrast to Voegelin's experience of the United States to which he immigrated, is one of homelessness: 'When we go into the Rockies we may have the sense that gods are there. But if so, they cannot manifest themselves to us as ours.'[52] Whether those of us who live near the Rockies share that experience is certainly questionable.[53] For Grant, however, Canada, as well as the United States, is technological because the fundamental encounter by Protestants was one of homelessness. Hence, Grant's lament for what has passed is in fact a lament for something that can never have existed.

Even the British conservatism that was alleged to distinguish the Loyalists from the American revolutionaries, because of the inchoate desire of the former 'to build, in these cold and forbidding regions, a society with a greater sense of order and restraint than freedom-loving republicanism would allow,' was as much the expression of homelessness and alienation from the 'primal' as the latter's liberalism. Canadians apparently experienced that homelessness with greater 'stodginess,' a 'simplicity, formality, and perhaps even [greater] innocence than the people to the south.'[54] Then why did Grant regard the United States as a threat to something that never existed? Since one could not find a 'primal' home in Canada, in North America, or in modernity, Grant believed that the only choice was to bear the weight of suffering in the world, living in hope that redemption occurs outside time. He concludes *Lament* with a quotation from the part of Virgil's *Aeneid* where Aeneas is ferried with the dead across the river Acheron: '*Tendebantque manus ripae ulterioris amore.*'[55] Grant's forsaken cry from within the bowels of modernity and of the United States is also the call of the theologian of the cross for whom the Good is radically separate from the necessary, and for whom the realm of the necessary, namely the world, can no longer be a home.

The satanic United States entraps the homeless soul, suffering in the darkness of technological modernity, for whom the Good can manifest itself only through God's direct intervention. Grant's United States comes close to serving as the evil god of intracosmic Gnostic myths that entraps the pure soul in darkness and prevents it from reaching its homeland. Grant's moderation, which he symbolized as his 'Lutheranism,' ensured that he did not expand his personal quasi-Gnostic psychodrama into a metastatic faith in political redemption. His view of the United States, 'enucleated' in his treatment of the will as symbolized by Calvinism, was ultimately his view of the West, and of himself.

Voegelin's view of the transcendent representation of the United States is markedly different and reflects his position that, despite the ideological disorders of the twentieth century, the Good as symbolized by Jerusalem and Athens manifests itself despite those disorders. In documents such as the Declaration of Independence and Lincoln's Second Inaugural, he saw proof that the United States understood itself as a nation under God. Its civil religion constitutes a 'minimum dogma' (in the sense used by Plato and Spinoza, for example) whereby nationhood is secured by a general belief in God and by God's concern for human affairs, which serves as a model of solidarity for its citizens. Voegelin thought that this spiritual substance provided glue for the otherwise individualistic and spiritually thin doctrines of modern liberalism, and so he disagreed with Grant, who identified the two. Even so, Voegelin noticed, as Grant might have as well, a this-worldly, pantheistic, or Lucretian dimension to the American civil religion and to its representative thinkers such as William James and Jonathan Edwards. Voegelin drew different conclusions from these observations than Grant would have done, because the methodology he developed in the 1920s led him to be aware of the inarticulate dimensions of speeches and actions (which he would later develop in his theory of experience and symbolization in *Order and History*) that Grant often overlooked. Voegelin saw in thinkers such as James and Edwards examples of the 'open self' that is turned towards the divine ground and, like all human beings, articulates that orientation in necessarily inadequate and imprecise symbols that require continuous reworking. The determining feature of those articulations is their democratic commitment to equality, implying the necessity of symbolizing the open self in terms that everyone can understand. This democratic symbolization was something that Grant, who frequently used the noble example of Mozart to symbolize the Good and Céline to symbolize beauty alienated from the

Good, never really grasped. Conversely, Voegelin concluded his book on the United States with a quotation from John R. Commons's essay 'Utilitarian Idealism,' regarding the paradox of democratic symbolizations of order:

I do not see why there is not much idealism of its kind in breeding a perfect animal or a Wisconsin No. 7 ear of corn, or in devising an absolutely exact instrument for measuring a thousand cubic feet of gas, or for measuring exactly the amount of butter or casein in milk, as there is in chipping out a Venus de Milo or erecting a Parthenon ... Of course a cow is just a cow, and can never become a Winged Victory. But within her field of human endeavor she is capable of approaching an ideal. And, more than that, she is an ideal that every farmer and farmer's boy – the despised slaves and helots of Greece – can aspire to.[56]

CONCLUSION

With the democratic revolution of modernity, the 'despised slaves and helots' have become incorporated into the spiritual life of the modern state, thus altering its transcendent representation. The open-ended and paradoxical process of symbolizing the New World order corresponds to the open self that Voegelin saw as its representative. Of course, Mozart is Mozart and a cow is just a cow, but Voegelin, like Tocqueville, saw a fundamental decency in the openness of this order to the divine ground that Grant did not. Voegelin regarded the 'variations' of U.S. symbolizations as part of a historical process, while Grant, in Voegelin's terms, ascribed a priori categories to his commonsensical but yet inadequate observations on American politics. Grant did point to historical practices when he spoke in a Tocquevillian manner of the attention that politicians must give to the technicalities of law and rights, but practice played no determining role in his method for studying the United States. Further, Grant's a priori categories played a part in his understanding of his own role, and the role of nations, in the 'fate' of technological modernity, whereas Voegelin, who was no less critical of elements of modernity, saw it as having no such fate, but rather regarded history as a process of order arising out of disorder. If Grant's alleged pessimism regarding the fate of modernity was tempered by an eschatological hope in personal salvation, in the sense of waiting for God, then Voegelin's understanding of disorder was leavened by his hope in the incarnation of order in history, which he saw in the details and fragments, the 'variations,' of history that he observed.

NOTES .

1 Leo Strauss, 'What Is Political Philosophy?' in *What Is Political Philosophy? and Other Studies* (Glencoe, IL: The Free Press, 1959), 7ff.
2 William Christian, *George Grant: A Biography* (Toronto: University of Toronto Press, 1993), 210.
3 George Grant, *Lament for a Nation* (Ottawa: Carleton University Press, 1988), 12. Hereafter *LN*.
4 Grant, letter to David Bovenizer, in *George Grant: Selected Letters*, ed. William Christian (Toronto: University of Toronto Press, 1996), 359.
5 George Grant, 'Simone Weil,' in *The George Grant Reader*, ed. William Christian and Sheila Grant (Toronto: University of Toronto Press, 1998), 259.
6 *LN*, x. The ancient idolatrous Israelites sacrificed children to Moloch (see Lev. 18:21, 1 Kings 11:7, and Acts 7:43).
7 Eric Voegelin, *On the Form of the American Mind: Collected Works* [hereafter *CW*] *of Eric Voegelin*, vol. 1, trans. Ruth Hein, ed. Jürgen Gebhardt and Barry Cooper (Baton Rouge: Louisiana State University Press, 1995) [hereafter *OFAM*]. See also the essays on 'stateform' and the United States in *Published Essays, 1922–1928, CW 7*, trans. M.J. Hanak, ed. Thomas W. Heilke and John von Heyking (Columbia: University of Missouri Press, 2003), and *Published Essays, 1928–1933, CW 8*, trans. M.J. Hanak and Jodi Cockerill, ed. Thomas W. Heilke and John von Heyking (Columbia: University of Missouri Press).
8 See Eric Voegelin, 'Origins of Scientism,' in *Published Essays, 1940–1952, CW* 10, ed. Ellis Sandoz (Columbia: University of Missouri Press, 2000), 168–97; on Grant's disagreement with Strauss on technology, see Christian, *George Grant*, 293. 'The United States of America may be said to be the only country in the world which was founded in explicit opposition to Machiavellian principles.' Leo Strauss, *Thoughts on Machiavelli* (Chicago: University of Chicago Press, 1958), 13.
9 Eric Voegelin, *Autobiographical Reflections*, ed. with an introduction by Ellis Sandoz (Baton Rouge: Louisiana State University Press, 1989), chapter 10.
10 Voegelin, *OFAM*, 19.
11 See *OFAM* and the essays in *CW 7* and 8. For an overview of Voegelin's empirical method, see Barry Cooper, *Eric Voegelin and the Foundations of Political Science* (Columbia: University of Missouri Press, 1999), chapters 7–8.
12 See Eric Voegelin, 'Max Weber,' *CW 8*, 132.
13 Christian, *George Grant*, chapter 5.
14 See Barry Cooper, 'Did George Grant's Canada Ever Exist?' in *George Grant and the Future of Canada*, ed. Yusuf K. Umar (Calgary: University of Calgary Press, 1992), 151–64.

15 In Christian, *George Grant*, xxiii.
16 Ibid., 92.
17 Quoted in ibid., 85. He told the CBC in 1979 that the subsequent Allied victory in 1945 produced similar despair: 'I never really cried so much ... I felt very far from rejoicing at the end of the war.' Quoted in Dennis Duffy, 'The Ancestral Journey: Travels with George Grant,' *Journal of Canadian Studies* 22, no. 3 (1987): 102 n.10.
18 Christian, *George Grant*, 72.
19 Quoted in ibid., 251.
20 Or 1953. See 'Two Theological Languages,' in *Collected Works of George Grant, Volume 2 (1951–1959)*, ed. Arthur Davis (Toronto: University of Toronto Press, 2002), 49–65. The 'Addendum' is reprinted starting on 59.
21 Paraphrased in 'Two Theological Languages,' 57. Quotation from Martin Luther, 'Theses for the Heidelberg Disputation,' Thesis 21, in *Martin Luther: Selections from His Writings*, trans. John Dillenberger (New York: Doubleday, 1961), 503. On Grant's view of the 'theology of the cross,' see Sheila Grant, 'George Grant and the Theology of the Cross,' in *George Grant and the Subversion of Modernity: Art, Philosophy, Politics, Religion, and Education*, ed. Arthur Davis (Toronto: University of Toronto Press, 1996), 243–62, and Harris Athanasiadis, *George Grant and the Theology of the Cross: The Christian Foundation of His Thought* (Toronto: University of Toronto Press, 2001).
22 Hebrews 11:1. Voegelin invokes the latter Pauline sense in the *New Science of Politics*, and also cites St Thomas Aquinas, *Summa Theologiae*, II-II.4.1, in *Modernity without Restraint*, ed. Manfred Henningsen, CW 5 (Columbia: University of Missouri Press, 1999), 187. Edward Andrew criticizes Grant's understanding of faith by showing Grant's temptation towards beautiful untruth in modernity: 'Gerald Owen has brilliantly elucidated Grant's attraction to Céline in terms of the choice of lying and dying, and why living in our graceless and God-forsaken world requires untruth. The impossibility of truth in our world perhaps suggested to Grant an otherworldly truth to anchor our turbulence in this imperfect world.' 'Grant's Céline,' in Davis, ed., *George Grant and the Subversion of Modernity*, 79.
23 Voegelin, *The New Science of Politics*, CW 5, 112–28.
24 '"Postscript" to *The Art of Thinking*,' CW 8, 233.
25 *OFAM*, chapter 5; 'La Follette and the Wisconsin Idea,' CW 7, chapter 8.
26 *OFAM*, 231–5.
27 See 'The Research of Business Cycles and the Stabilization of Capitalism,' CW 7, chapter 12; 'Democracy and Industrial Society,' CW 11, ed. Ellis Sandoz (Columbia: University of Missouri Press, 2000), 208.
28 *OFAM*, 239. Voegelin also notes the opportunities for leisure – even a degree

of contemplation – within the working conditions of the working trades: 'The skilled practice of a manual trade left the mind free for conversation: the workers chose a good reader from their midst and compensated him for the loss in work; the reading was followed by discussions, and the workers came to know one another better and became friends' (*OFAM*, 233). Compare this with Grant's perplexities concerning whether industrial or Neolithic society provided for greater opportunities for leisure: 'The anthropologist Lévi-Strauss says that the best order for man was what we call the Neolithic era in which man had gained sufficient control to build organic communities and to give him time to contemplate. I do not know what the answer is' ('The Great Society,' in Christian and Grant, eds., *The George Grant Reader*, 100). This is a shocking statement by someone who so closely studied Plato and Nietzsche, not to mention Rousseau's *Discourse on the Origin and Foundations of Inequality*. For a recent treatment of American economic and business practices that cultivate solidarity and trust within the market framework, see Francis Fukuyama, *Trust: The Social Virtues and the Creation of Prosperity* (New York: Free Press, 1996).

29 Eric Voegelin, 'Democracy in the New Europe,' *CW* 11, 68.

30 Eric Voegelin, 'Democracy and Industrial Society,' *CW* 11, 221. Voegelin's view on the interdependence and equality of labour in industrial society, with its concomitant principle of equality, draws from Emile Durkheim ('"Postscript" to *The Art of Thinking*,' *CW* 8, 232). See Durkheim, *The Division of Labor in Society*, trans. George Simpson (1933; repr., New York: Free Press, 1964).

31 Voegelin claimed that most of those works failed to examine American problems for their own sake 'were written in the shadow of an upheaval that has shifted the center of gravity of the world economy toward the West, and in almost all one can sense a more or less veiled *ressentiment*' (*Selected Book Reviews*, *CW* 13, trans. Jodi Cockerill and Barry Cooper, 19). Similarly, James Ceaser finds that the failure to examine the United States according to political considerations is the key failing of most European approaches. As examples of non-political premises, he cites the Count de Buffon's physiological writings on climatic and biological causes of American degeneracy, the metaphysics of the French revolutionaries (and their descendents) who dismissed the American revolution on aesthetic grounds because it failed to produce great works of art, Arthur de Gobineau's race theories, postmodern theories of multiculturalism whose contradictory ideas about culture hold priority over political considerations, Jünger's and Spengler's apocalyptic theories of technology, Heidegger's invocation of Hölderin's poetry as a means of founding a nontechnological politics, and Kojève's view of the

United States as the 'universal, homogeneous state.' By implication, the technological approach of Grant, who follows Heidegger and Kojève, misunderstands what is essential to politics. Ceaser's study omits Voegelin's scholarship. James W. Ceaser, *Reconstructing America: The Symbol of America in Modern Thought* (New Haven, CT: Yale University Press, 1997).

32 George Grant, *Technology and Empire* (Toronto: House of Anansi Press, 1969), 75 [hereafter *TE*].

33 Grant, *English-Speaking Justice* (1974; repr., Toronto: Anansi/South Bend, Ind.: University of Notre Dame Press, 1985), 42 [hereafter *ESJ*].

34 *LN*, ix.

35 George Grant, 'The Empire: Yes or No?' in *Collected Works of George Grant, Volume 1 (1933–1950)*, ed. Arthur Davis and Peter C. Emberley (Toronto: University of Toronto Press, 2000), 120–1.

36 Ibid., 116.

37 *LN*, 63.

38 See 'Nationalism and Rationality,' in Christian and Grant, *The George Grant Reader*, 103–7. Voegelin points to propaganda ('pragmatic communication') and entertainment as corrosive characteristics in industrial society, going so far as to call both an 'intoxicant' and a Pascalian 'divertissment' ('Necessary Moral Bases for Communication in a Democracy,' *CW* 11, 48–50). However, he takes a more benign view of propaganda and entertainment than Grant does, arguing for its inevitability in organizing human beings on a massive scale and, more important, that it does not *necessarily* serve as a placebo replacement for a society's moral substance.

39 *ESJ*, 39.

40 *LN*, x.

41 Grant letter to David Bovenizer, in Christian, *Selected Letters*, 359.

42 *ESJ*, 14–15.

43 Grant's emphasis on doctrine over practice is seen also in his criticism of Winston Churchill's compact defence of liberty, the theoretical incoherence of which Grant regarded as too rooted in technology. His attitude differs from Strauss's assessment of Churchill as well as Voegelin's method of analysing the speeches as well as actions of political actors.

44 Gordon Wood, *The Creation of the American Republic* (Chapel Hill: University of North Carolina Press, 1969); Bernard Bailyn, *The Ideological Origins of the American Revolution* (Cambridge, MA: Harvard University Press, 1967); and Harry V. Jaffa, *The Crisis of the House Divided: An Interpretation of the Issues in the Lincoln-Douglas Debates*, 1st ed. (Seattle: University of Washington Press, 1959). Grant's failure to consider the American constitution thus led him to exaggerate the way that it subordinates virtue to interest. As Harvey Mans-

field, Jr noted: 'a certain understatement may be more effective and appropriate than exhortation' (*America's Constitutional Soul* [Baltimore: Johns Hopkins University Press, 1991], 216). If understatement is a Canadian virtue, then Grant never learned to see the Canadianness of the American constitution.

45 *ESJ*, 62.
46 *ESJ*, 63–4.
47 George Grant, *Technology and Justice* (Toronto: Anansi, 1986), 43–4; 'St. Augustine,' lecture in Davis ed., *Collected Works*, 476–89.
48 Recent research shows Augustine less triumphalist than Grant's interpretation permits. See John von Heyking, *Augustine and Politics as Longing in the World* (Columbia: University of Missouri Press, 2001).
49 See also David Walsh on the tradition of liberalism: *The Growth of the Liberal Soul* (Columbia: University of Missouri Press, 1997).
50 Grant, *TE*, 18–19.
51 See *TE*, 23: 'Where the ordinary Catholic might restrain the body with a corporatively ordained tradition of a liturgy rhythmic in its changes between control and release, the Protestant had solitary responsibility all the time to impose restraint.'
52 *TE*, 17.
53 See Cooper, 'Did George Grant's Canada Ever Exist?' 151–64.
54 *LN*, 70.
55 Ibid., 97. 'They were holding their arms outstretched in love toward the further shore' (*Aeneid*, VI.314).
56 *OFAM*, 282, quoting Commons, 'Utilitarian Idealism,' *Western Collegiate Magazine*, December 1909, 267–9. (Reprinted in *Labor and Administration* (New York: A.M. Kelley, 1964 [1913]), chapter 1.

11

Echoes of George Grant in 'Late Boomer' Critiques of Post–Quiet Revolution Quebec

CHRISTIAN ROY

The time for a proper reception of Grant's thought seems to have finally arrived in Quebec. Upon submitting the idea of a presentation of it in the review *Argument* a couple of years ago,[1] I discovered that the editors had been looking for somebody to write such an essay since the journal's launching in 1998 as the main organ of an emerging *nouvelle sensibilité* among Quebec intellectuals. At this writing, a symposium on thinkers from the past is being organized for the May 2004 ACFAS meeting (a Quebec-based francophone equivalent of the annual Learned Societies conference in Canada) at the Université du Québec à Montréal (UQAM); the session on Grant has attracted more proposals than those on Hannah Arendt or Emmanuel Mounier. This may be seen as part of a significant trend among young scholars, who now often display a remarkable familiarity with English Canadian historiography and political traditions in a wider Anglo-American context, within which they do not hesitate to place Quebec in a comparative perspective, assessing this dimension of its make-up as an integral part of its identity, with all its flaws and its merits, rather than just a colonial imposition on a victimized populace. This sober, balanced attitude has, for instance, yielded a long-overdue study of the similarities and differences between the classic French and English expressions of Canadian nationalism that George Grant drew from – showing the stumbling blocks to their meeting on conservative and spiritualist common ground: sociologist Sylvie Lacombe's book about Henri Bourassa and the Canadian imperialists.[2]

Carl Berger's classic study of these early English Canadian nationalists, *The Sense of Power*,[3] had already been an eye-opener for the young historian Éric Bédard, a specialist of both the October Crisis[4] and nineteenth-century French Canadian conservatism, who also edits the correspondence of Louis-Hippolyte Lafontaine.[5] As a prominent militant of the Parti Québécois (he was president of its youth wing from 1994 to 1996), Bédard has also been much inspired by Grant's *Lament for a Nation*. In notes he kindly provided me, this committed Quebec nationalist confesses he could well have been able to live within Grant's Canada, thinking, like Grant, that if only Diefenbaker had found a solid French Canadian lieutenant, the wrong turn of Trudeau's dogmatic liberal project could have been avoided and Canada would have been refounded on the sounder basis of a more comprehensive, binational understanding of its roots, rather than on an artificial constitutional patriotism that pretends to ignore them.[6] Diefenbaker's own brand of 'unhyphenated Canadianism' already suffers from the same defects, according to Grant, since 'his interpretation of federalism is basically American. It could not encompass those who were concerned with being a nation, only those who wanted to preserve charming residual customs. This failure to recognize the rights of French Canadians, *qua* community, was inconsistent with the roots of Canadian nationalism ... in the belief that Canada was predicated on the rights of nations as well as on the rights of individuals.' Otherwise, 'the French Canadians might as well be asked to be homogenized straight into the American Republic. In so far as he did not distinguish between the rights of individuals and the rights of nations, Diefenbaker showed himself to be a liberal rather than a conservative,'[7] actually prefiguring Trudeau.

RECLAIMING TEMPORAL CONTINUITY FROM CONTINENTAL SPACE

In Bédard's opinion, Trudeau's conception of Canada as the vanguard of cosmopolitan humanity in the overcoming of nationalism, rather than as an alliance between nations faithful to their own traditions reaching before the age of progress, has led to the country's dissolution into a magma of undifferentiated individuals ruled by an all-powerful Charter of Rights that makes no reference to the country's origins. Its top-down application to a society understood in contractual terms turns out to be perfectly consonant with the all-pervasive market model of an integrated North America, as well as with the managerial model that reduces government to the role of a mere service-provider. 'For Quebecers who dream of being recognized as a "people" – worse: as a "founding people" – Trudeau's Canada no longer offers any horizon for the future ...' 'Canada is no longer an alternative for anyone claiming a heritage other than that of the Enlightenment and of Technique ...'

Ironically, it might seem that neither is Quebec, judging not only from the much touted 'Quebec model' of government but also from the dominant discourse among sovereignist intellectuals in urban professional/ progressive circles (a class of which Gilles Duceppe is as representative in Quebec as Jack Layton is of its English-Canadian counterpart in the New Democratic Party). According to Bédard, they have become so wary of the trap of 'ethnicism' since Jacques Parizeau's unhappy dismissal of the ethnic vote on referendum night in 1995 that 'they cut themselves off from the deep meaning of Quebec's struggle, which has its basis in the preservation of a heritage – still deemed sacred by more grassroots militants,' who dare not speak up and break the politically correct official consensus about their cause. Bédard is one of the few voices to do it (alongside older authors like Jacques Beauchemin[8] and the Acadian Joseph-Yvon Thériault),[9] by forcefully criticizing the likes of Gérard Bouchard, brother of former Parti Québecois (PQ) premier Lucien Bouchard and a social historian whose *Genèse des nations et cultures du Nouveau Monde*[10] is a significant contribution to the comparative study of nation-building in what he terms 'new societies.' Bédard writes:

He and many others believe that the truth of the Quebec nation is its 'Americanness' ... and that only a 'break' with the (French) metropolis will allow the Country to emerge ... These intellectuals want to create a Quebec mini-republic with the same values and the same principles as those now prevailing on the continent ... It is no longer a question of preserving a community of destiny and meaning rooted in time, but of denoting the originality of a mere idiom of communication between 'individuals' on a certain 'territory' ... If a sovereign Quebec only seeks to reproduce the spirit of Trudeau's institutions for Quebec, then the mountain will have given birth to a rather tiny mouse indeed ...

For, as Edmund Burke said in his 1782 Speech on Reform of Representation of the Commons, 'a nation is not an idea only of local extent and individual momentary aggregation, but it is an idea of continuity which extends in time as well as in numbers and space.'[11] Yet there is even a movement around sovereignist intellectuals like Jocelyn Maclure (see their slick, 'politically correct' review *Cahiers du 27 juin*) that takes the adoption of Quebec's own Charter of Rights on 27 June 1974 as a foundational event, on a par with the enshrining of Canada's charter in the 1982 constitution – which just happens to be the ultimate expression of Trudeau's dream of overcoming nationhood and attaining freedom from the weight of history and memory in the French Canadian heritage, the better to claim direct access to the universal liberal values of human rights. But if the 'Quebec model' of the welfare state championed by establishment progressives is also criticized by the '*nouvelle sensibilité*,' the criticism does not arise – as is often assumed – from the kind of neo-liberal pan-capitalist perspective that passes for conservatism south of the border. As if to confirm the 'Red Tory' paradigm of Canadian political thought devised by Gad Horowitz to account for George Grant's *Lament for a Nation*,[12] it must also be remembered that 'historically, the main criticisms of the Quiet Revolution and the Quebec model have first been raised by Marxist or conservative intellectuals, critical of radical individualism: Hubert Guindon, Dorval Brunelle, Jacques Grand'Maison, Gary Caldwell, Nicole Laurin, Fernand Dumont, Jean-Jacques Simard.'[13]

Grant was sympathetic towards the Quebec sovereignist movement precisely because he saw it as rooted in a healthy reaction of French Canadian communitarianism against the universal homogeneous state prepared by continental liberalism. Not unlike René Lévesque's vice-premier, Jacques-Yvan Morin, whose family Grant spent time with in his youth,[14] Éric Bédard views Grant's thought as a rich, potent source of inspiration for those who would remind this movement of its *raison d'être*, although he has never cited him explicitly until now. A more common (indeed constant) reference point for all those who would see in Quebec's nationhood not just some blandly generic civic allegiance but a cultural heritage transmitted through a living community of memory is the thought of Fernand Dumont (1927–97).[15] This prominent, politically committed sociologist, inspired by a Christian socialist vision, helped draft the PQ's *Charte de la langue française* and may be viewed as a kind of counterpart of Grant among Quebec nationalist intellectuals. Aside from his *La Vigile* du Québec,[16] he is especially known for his seminal book *Genèse de la nation québécoise*,[17] which was prompted by the October Crisis of 1970, just as Grant's *Lament for a Nation* stemmed from the 'Defeat of Canadian Nationalism' marked by the fall of the Diefenbaker government in 1963.

LATE BOOMERS – A LOST GENERATION?

It is surely no coincidence that Serge Cantin, a student of Dumont's thought, also seems in his latest book to be echoing Grant in his concern to prevent the complete disenchantment of the world, whereby 'the question that man is for himself could only arise in the private sphere, a sphere itself subject to the reign of Technique, subject to the good offices of a medical science entrusted with regulating the functioning of a world that produces itself and consumes itself without any other purpose.'[18] Aside from criticizing the therapeutic management of the human condition,[19] the writers of the review *Argument* precisely aim to raise the philosophical 'question that man is for himself' in the public sphere. The areas encompassed in its subtitle, *Politique, société et histoire*, therefore always overlap in the reflections of the political philosophers, sociologists, and historians who mostly make up the new intellectual current it represents. Like Grant, they are critical of the subsidy-driven research imperatives and narrow scientific specialization of a 'multiversity' that has lost sight of the university's humanist purpose and of the critical distance it requires from the pragmatic requirements of the social system within which it is embedded. Most of them are 'thirty-somethings' who, despite their often substantial achievements, and owing to the entrenched position of baby boomers in universities,[20] have only belatedly (if at all) found any kind of professional footing within academic institutions – often in English-language or bilingual ones in Quebec and Ontario, where their questioning of the standard *doxa* about the Quiet Revolution and its outcome finds fewer feathers to ruffle. I propose to refer to them as 'late boomers,' as a deliberate pun on 'late bloomers' – which they are, professionally speaking, and because many of them were born at the tail end of the post-war baby boom in the 1960s, though they feel they have a lot more in common with 'Generation X' than with the baby boomers who still dominate public life and discourse. The late boomers' criticisms of their parents' generation and the society they shaped is sometimes reduced by boomer critics to envy of their own positions – just as Grant's criticisms occasionally were attributed to a dying class's resentment at the loss of its status and associated values. Fortunately, the late boomers do have a handful of vocal allies among more established boomer academics in their late forties or fifties who share their spirit.

The *nouvelle sensibilité* is thus only in part the stance of the first generation to have been born during or after the Quiet Revolution and who find the society built on a wholesale negation of French Canada's past to be wanting in many respects. If late boomers aim to give their society a fresh look, it is not out of any facile nostalgia for previous conditions they never knew, the agenda of 'a generation that dreams of possessing what its predecessors have failed to transmit to them and has received from them a society driven by a ceaseless motion nobody dares to slow down – on pains of being deemed an antimodernist,' as the young jurist and political scientist Marc Chevrier puts it.[21] Rather the outlook of late boomers reflects a conviction that traces of the kind of timeless goods which they were not taught to honour need to be recovered before the full closure of thought by technological discourse. In the same way, it can be said that 'Grant respects the past, not because it is the past, but because it puts us in touch with an account of reality that embodies a greater truth than the nihilism of modern thought.'[22] If recent expressions of such a relation to our times and previous ones in Quebec echo certain insights of George Grant about Canada and the world, and may even take them further, their direct sources of inspiration usually lie elsewhere. For instance, the young sociologist Jean Gould, host of a famed salon at his apartment in Montreal's Mile End district that may be seen as an informal crucible of the *nouvelle sensibilité*, acknowledges the debt he and others owe to a recently retired, Swiss-born UQAM sociologist who summarized late boomers' assumptions at the end of his contribution to the proceedings of a conference held at McGill University in the winter of 2000: *Les idées mènent le Québec. Essais sur une sensibilité historique*:

It is by way of the opposition 'institution/organization,' which we borrow from Michel Freitag, rather than the pairs 'tradition/modernity' or yet 'Liberal State/Welfare State,' that we are trying to reflect on the nature and the genesis of contemporary Quebec. The transformation of public administration into vast administrative apparatuses conceived as systems meant to adapt to the environment jettisons any political dimension in what has become the management of social and educational executive functions. Issues are always discussed at a subpolitical level, in technical terms, between experts, managers, and client groups. This dissolves the public administration's capacity for normative reflection and for action, which ought to be based on a distance between institutions and civil society.[23]

HISTORIC HERITAGE AND CRITICAL JUDGMENT

This distance defines the political dimension, and normative reflection goes hand in hand with it, so that citizenship ultimately depends on philosophy, as has been argued in an eloquent plea for the centrality of philosophy in the school curriculum by *Argument*'s director, the political philosopher Daniel Jacques.[24] Now disdained as élitist and impractical by educational authorities, the teaching of philosophy is vital to the formation of political judgment, so that citizens can live up to what is their duty even more than their right in a democratic society: active participation in the public affairs of a particular polity, which is not the same thing as training individuals for specialized functions within an economic system, as has been done since the educational reforms of the Quiet Revolution. But, as Grant observed at the time in *Lament for a Nation*, 'even when much of the economy is socialized, the managers will gradually become indistinguishable from their international counterparts. To run a modern economy, men must be trained in the new technology over human and non-human nature. Such training cannot be reconciled with French-Canadian classical education. An élite trained in the modern way may speak French for many generations, but what other traditions will it uphold? The new social sciences are dissolvents of the family of Catholicism, of classical education.'[25]

For Jacques as for a host of like-minded critics – including several disillusioned early promoters of this unavoidable turn, Quebec's educational project has been built – in a radical break in the transmission of values needed for meaningful judgment – on the symbolic vacuum created by the liquidation of the French Canadian past, with its moorings in Christian tradition and classical humanism. Far from questioning the Enlightenment ideal of freedom of conscience, the older critics often cited by late boomers[26] deplore its betrayal with the collapse of all judgment and the trivialization of conscience in mindless adherence to a liberal consensus on democratic commonplaces and politically correct dogmas. Jacques sees whatever political freedoms we have enjoyed as dependent on a certain understanding of our humanity – which Grant also saw rooted in Christian assumptions and classical ideas. If the breakdown in this humanist transmission is final, it may not be possible to maintain a form of political allegiance that can be called citizenship, or, as Grant once put it in 'Nietzsche and the Ancients: Philosophy and Scholarship' 'Why should constitutional regimes be considered superior to their alternatives if human beings are basically "*ids*"?'[27] We then had better reflect on the consequences of using a technology of knowledge to mobilize humans for the production of things, as Peter Sloterdijk has dared to do in his controversial essay on the 'management of the human park' that is set to take over from humanist education.[28] Social science may actually be enough if the modern individual is the ultimate expression of human nature, as can be argued in a line of thinking that goes from Hegel to Kojève to Fukuyama. If democratic man is instead seen to be just one particular expression of the human phenomenon, critical reflection is called for about what we are becoming, and philosophy can draw on a variety of other configurations of our condition to allow this vital process to take place. Except for religious assumptions which late boomers mostly seem unable to share, this may not be so far from the task Grant ascribed to philosophy in the first sentence of his report about its place in English Canada for the 1951 Massey Commission (which was much better received in French Canada at the time): 'The study of philosophy is the analysis of the traditions of our society and the judgment of those traditions against our varying intuitions of the Perfection of God.'[29]

It is, at any rate, consistent with a defining trait of the *nouvelle sensibilité*, as highlighted by the political philosopher Daniel Tanguay, author of an intellectual biography of Leo Strauss,[30] in his capacity as editor of *Argument*. In the same issue as the one cotaining Jacques's essay, Tanguay urges a relationship to the past, to historical memory, that is less judgmental, dismissive, and dogmatic than has long been customary in public and academic discourse in Quebec, where current generations like to see themselves as paragons of enlightened virtue and all those that came before them as shamefully benighted. Be it as a radical break with a pre-modern past in canonical accounts, or as the culmination of a fairly standard process of modernization in more recent 'revisionist' accounts, the Quiet Revolution is always taken to be a '*happy ending* which we are never through celebrating,' even though neither version of the 'modernist grand narrative allows us to understand certain failures of Quebec's modernity,' such as 'the suicide rate, technocratic rigidity, corporatism,' as Bédard explains in an interview with *L'Action nationale*.[31] The late boomers' approach to the past as well as the future is more free, inclined to accept neither the way things were nor the way they have turned out. Always looking for aspects of our history and to ideas from the past that could bring new impulses and fresh perspectives to reflections about the present time, they draw on horizons of thought that have been lost sight of with the advent of full-fledged modernity.

In my postscript to *Les idées mènent le Québec*,[32] I tried to conceptualize this emerging new temporal paradigm in opposition to the utopianism of the ideology of progress that triumphed with the Quiet Revolution and in its aftermath. I did so by appropriating the concept of 'uchronia' from science-fiction studies, where it refers to alternate accounts of history – the way things might have turned out if a slightly different path had been taken at a critical point of the past.[33] This kind of lateral thinking about discarded historical possibilities allows a liberating distance from the arrow of time that is presumed to always bring us back to the present situation as the best of all possible worlds. Yet that is because it takes seriously, and with a new respect, the indeterminacy and unpredictability of past and present events, so that timeless values are seen to come into play in the concrete ethical choices of situated human agents, irreducible to the determinism of social pressures and economic forces. Some late boomers have even taken to apply the label *uchronistes* to representatives of their *nouvelle sensibilité* who display an openly idealist approach (generally tempered by a sound hermeneutic sense).

PARADOXES OF CATHOLIC MODERNIZATION

One of the main preoccupations of the *uchronistes* is the genesis and unfolding of the Quiet Revolution – not surprisingly for a generation that envies the ethical certainties and humanist commitments of the largely Christian intellectuals who prepared the Quiet Revolution in the 1950s and presided over it in the 1960s, but that loathes the self-satisfaction of the baby boomers who came of age at that time and to power in the 1970s. Like the Napoleonic Empire did with the French Revolution, they are seen as having perverted the Quiet Revolution's intentions even as they claimed to embody them and monopolized its institutions, with the simultaneous and interdependent appearance of a technocratic welfare state and a typically North American hedonist ethic, at the leading edge of a post-human age of universal cybernetics. Where, how, and why did things go so wrong, and what other paths might have been taken (and may still be groped towards) that did not necessarily lead to the dead end we find ourselves in? These are the queries haunting the *uchronistes*. They keep on contemplating their own version of the paradox of the heterogeneity of intentions and results, observed by Weber about the road from the Puritan spirit to the 'iron cage' of advanced capitalism. Jean Gould could thus explain in similar terms 'la genèse catholique d'une modernisation bureaucratique'[34] within the Catholic Church even under the so-called 'Grande Noirceur' of the Duplessis years after the Second World War, as it adopted the paradigms of North American social science and psychological pedagogy with the view of adapting its structures to the affluent society emerging in Quebec as on the rest of the continent. At the same time, as part of a worldwide process that remade the church at the Second Vatican Council, Christian militants were promoting a shift from a clericalist Tridentine morality based on authority to a newfangled personalist ethic centred on freedom, as the young sociologists Jean-Philippe Warren and É.-Martin Meunier have established in their groundbreaking studies.[35] But in *Lament for a Nation*, Grant was already formulating some of the tough questions raised by the transformation under way, as he pondered the prospects envisioned by the progressive Catholicism that engineered it: 'What is the status of Catholicism in the age of progress? Will a liberalized Catholicism accept industrialism and still be able to shape it to a more human end? In Quebec, Catholicism will no longer be "*Je me souviens*," but a Catholicism appropriate to a vital present. Lay education will not destroy the Church, but enable her to become the spiritual leader of a free people. Accepting the age of progress, the Church will give leadership to a more humane industrialism than has arisen elsewhere in North America. It will provide the spiritual basis for a continuing Franco-American civilization.' 'The possibility of such a Catholicism in Quebec cannot be discussed apart from the relation of Catholicism to technology throughout the world,' Grant continued, leaving 'open the question whether Catholicism will be able to humanize mass Western society or be swept into the catacombs. What happens to the Catholic view of man, when Catholics are asked to shape society through the new sciences of biochemistry, physiological psychology, and sociology?'[36] Grant foresaw that, in Quebec at least, 'as traditional Catholicism breaks up, there will be some exciting moments. A Catholic society cannot be modernized as easily as a Protestant one. When the dam breaks the flood will be furious. Nevertheless, the young intellectuals of the upper-middle class will gradually desert their existentialist nationalism and take the places made for them in the continental corporations. The enormity of the break will arouse in the dispossessed youth intense forms of beatness' – though the spiritually dispossessed upper and middle classes would hardly be immune from them either. For Grant, 'dissent is built into the fabric of the modern system. We bureaucratize it as much as everything else. Is there any reason to believe that French Canada will be different? A majority of the young is gradually patterned for its place in the bureaucracies. Those who resist such shaping will retreat into a fringe world of pseudo-revolt.'[37]

'INTENSE FORMS OF BEATNESS'

As it turns out, 'beatniks' and 'hippies' were eventually to find their way to the very centre of state and corporate bureaucracies by way of academia and culture. Grant would no doubt agree with the explanation for this convergence provided by the political scientist Gilles Labelle (a relative senior to the late boomers), who points to something like the Heideggerian *Gestell* or the 'standing reserve' of possibility that is the real aim for technological man, which is the background of Grant's sense that today 'we discount what is, in favour of what can be; actuality is less than potentiality.'[38] Labelle begins by establishing that, enshrined in educational and cultural institutions, 'the questioning of the difference between generations carried out by yesterday's protesters like that of gender differences carried out by differentialists nowadays is ... radical, even revolutionary, in that it affects the very conditions that make humanity what it is. But is it a coincidence,' he asks rhetorically, 'if this questioning has been deployed and is being deployed at the very moment when an almost unquestioned domination of commercial logic is getting established?'

If nothing is prohibited or forbidden in principle to subjectivity, then it follows that for it, which is defined by its pure freedom and is indeed identified with this freedom, there can only be the possible – which, by definition, is only ever the impossible that it can and must constantly push back. This is precisely the logic of the functioning of the market, which totally ignores the 'moral' or 'ethical' categories of the permitted and the prohibited and is entirely based on pushing away the frontiers of what is traditionally held to be possible ... The driving force of globalized neo-liberalism is not to be found in the abandonment of left-wing ideals (why then did people abandon them?), nor in the manipulation of the masses by the media (are people rats that can be conditioned?); it is there, in this soft figure of the subject, this 'destructured' subject as Grand'Maison says, that was born some thirty or thirty-five years ago.[39]

But Jacques Grand'Maison would not be the only Christian – or humanist-inspired early 'quiet revolutionary' to deplore the situation Grant sensed was around the corner in *Lament for a Nation*, as Jean-Philippe Warren has also pointed out: 'To the narcissism of the generation of the *baby boomers* corresponds a technocratic and cybernetic State as purveyor of the needs of the different corporatist groups demanding their well-being from it, pragmatic in its operative logic, instrumental in its means of action on the real. This State, neither Dumont nor Vadeboncoeur could be satisfied with it, since for so many years they had fought for a management of society in which charity would inform technique as much as technique would enlighten charity.'

Contrary to the sanguine hopes of these Catholic progressives, in Quebec as in the rest of North America, 'all coherent languages beyond those which serve the drive to unlimited freedom through technique have been broken up in the coming to be of what we are,'[40] for, as Grant saw in his essay 'A Platitude,' 'our vision of ourselves as freedom in an indifferent world could only have arisen in so far as we had analysed to disintegration those systems of meaning, given in myth, philosophy and revelation, which had held sway over our progenitors.'[41] In perhaps more Dionysian fashion in Quebec,

that modernity which the first-born of the *baby boom* have celebrated in their collective jamborees and their artificial paradises has ended up, according to [François] Ricard [in his 1991 essay devoted to *La génération lyrique*], 'in the disqualification of all that which limits, orders, and devalues present existence in the name of some meaning imposed from outside: myth, divinity, transcendence, past, authority.' Thus, the pleasure of projecting oneself into a limitless horizon of desires ends up in the withdrawal of the individual upon himself, upon an inside inhabited by the primal impulses of a life without otherness. The freedom that each individual claims for herself transmutes itself into a pretext to shield oneself against the experience of difference.[42]

Grant's famous question in 'A Platitude' – namely, 'How far will the race be able to carry the divided state which characterises individuals in modernity: the plush patina of hectic subjectivity lived out in the iron maiden of an objectified world inhabited by increasingly objectified beings?'[43] – is echoed in Marc Chevrier's diagnosis of the depressive personality of contemporary man, who 'hangs on to an idealized ego that provides him a feeling of omnipotence, albeit without any hold on reality. Having failed to discover ideals in society, tradition or religion, he remains in his primal narcissism, without any reference point, haunted by death. Encouraged by the permissiveness of our era, he thinks he can become his own ideal unto himself and determine his own value.'[44]

But what, then, might the *parvenu* veterans of the 'intense forms of beatness' Grant talked about have to pass on to their children, who fend for themselves amidst the looted stores of human experience left in the boomers' wake? That is the question confronting Denys Arcand's somewhat pathetic group of 'bourgeois bohemian' history professors – first introduced in the 1986 film *The Decline of the American Empire* (whose very title could be that of a Grant essay!) – as they come to terms with the terminal illness of one of their circle, Rémi, the philanderer who had been the life of the party, in the recent sequel *The Barbarian Invasions*. The spiritual goods they have been taught about are of no possible help at this point, buried as they are deeper than the catacombs in which Grant thought Catholicism was bound to retreat: in the dusty cellar of an irrelevant, incomprehensible past, like the ghostly crowds of discarded religious statues that the old cleric Father Leclerc (played by Gilles Pelletier), in a poignant subplot, vainly tries to pawn off for whatever artistic value he was hoping they might have to foreign collectors. As he explains to a European auctioneer (in a striking – if inaccurate – oversimplification): 'You know, it used to be that everybody was Catholic, as in Spain or in Ireland. And at a very precise moment, in fact during the year 1966, the churches suddenly emptied, in the space of a few months. A strange phenomenon, that no one has ever been able to account for.'[45]

POST-CATHOLIC NIHILISM SYNDROME

A plausible answer seems to have just emerged in late-boomer publications with the rediscovery by Gilles Labelle of the fictional priest's homonym Gilles Leclerc – a prophet in the desert who died in 1999 a complete unknown, having foreseen in the 1950s in his *Journal d'un inquisiteur* how the particular kind of Catholicism still prevalent in Quebec under Duplessis could lead overnight to its remorseless reversal in the perfected form of American nihilism. (His thesis might therefore illuminate a wider 'Post-Catholic Nihilism Syndrome' that also seems to be affecting the cultural climate of countries like Portugal and Spain in the aftermath of the collapse of their own heavy-handed clerical regimes.) The only non-traditionalist, post-Christian agnostic to voice grave doubts about the prospects of the post-clerical society still in the offing, 'Gilles Leclerc defends a thesis that probably could not be understood or heard at the beginning of the 1960s, but which sounds uncanny to contemporary ears. For him, it is what he calls the "ethno-theologico-political" regime that has led us to historical existence, that made us enter an era of radical modernity ... By constantly invoking our "French and Catholic heritage" over everything and nothing, the theologico-political regime has actually killed at their root the values it claimed to embody.'[46] For the church had itself profaned this heritage by instrumentalizing absolute values under cover of Roman ownership of the truth – a 'lowering of the sights' in which Machiavelli's secular theory was long preceded by Pope Gregory VII's theocratic practice when 'he turned the church from its traditional role of holding forth the mystery of perfection, to the role of control in worldly affairs,'[47] just as Grant has suggested in 'Faith and the Multiversity.' The church thus led the people to the logical conclusion that 'all values are equivalent, or more precisely, to deduce that they only have the value we decide to give them, and that, consequently, what is noblest and what is basest can be interchanged, or even identified.'[48] Democracy can then easily allow the people to question this monopoly and take over the arbitrary assignment of value, since it enshrines everybody's right to be what he is or what she wants to be. This marks the passage to a 'fragmented society, ever more incapable of determining what could be shared in common,' aside from the 'mental and moral lowest common denominator' of the 'mass-man': 'possessing, consuming, enjoying. In reaction to the freedom of choosing between Good and Evil which the theologico-political regime never stopped speaking about, democratic citizens reduce freedom to "the faculty of choosing between two goods," thus confusing liberty with "licence"' in a way that defines with crystal clarity the market model governing both consumer society and liberal democracy.

Far from allowing virtue to flower in freedom, the joint advent of consumerism and liberalism feeds into what Leclerc calls 'prométhéisme.' 'By this should be understood the blossoming of the "technical genius" aiming to reduce everything to the state of materials available for a humanity determined essentially by its passions and its desires,' that is, to a commodity under the 'ecumenical dictatorship of Money' which consecrates and enacts human mastery of the world.[49] Thus, beyond the mirages of the ideology of progress, 'at the end of the ethno-theologico-political regime and at the end of the monstrosities it has spawned, there is no History announcing a radiant future, no *telos*, but only a modern being – absolutely modern, that is decidedly "atheistic" in that s/he has not only ceased to believe in God, but also to "believe altogether," in anything at all' – except perhaps in 'anti-normativity,' whose concrete implications have been documented by Jacques Grand'Maison in his essay *Quand le jugement fout le camp* (1999).[50] And so, there arose this other monster: 'a society, isolated in North America because it is French and Catholic, but which passionately hates France (the French spirit) and Catholicism' and eagerly embraces 'what Leclerc has called "*panaméricanisme*" – the *American way of life* being the most explicit negation of a past which its élites had conceived to be ascetic:' 'a society defined in purely materialistic and utilitarian terms, devoid of any ends other than the accumulation of wealth for wealth's sake and pleasure for pleasure's sake.'[51]

Like the mature Grant (for example, in his 1969 Massey Lectures on *Time as History*[52]), Gilles Leclerc fought the 'generalized Hegelianism' of the modern religion of material success. Gilles Labelle also feels it would be hard to deny that 'the Quiet Revolution has enshrined *historical existence* in Quebec as the only legitimate mode of being in the world. Federalists or sovereignists, liberals, personalists or socialists, believers, agnostics or atheists – after 1960 there is no one left who might appear to question that our habitat be history and only history. From now on, we will be nowhere else than in this present, with behind us a past to disenchant and before us a future we will seek to forecast precisely because it will seem open to us.'[53] Even transcendence could no longer be sought anywhere other than within history as the self-making of humanity, whether or not it was still experienced as a divine call, as it was in the new 'Incarnation theology' (weaving revelation into the secular historical process as such) that had come to dominate Catholic discourse and played such a role in the motivation of those Quiet Revolution militants in the once thriving Catholic Action lay movements, as Meunier and Warren have shown.

Infatuation with the Philosophy of History has constituted the concrete form taken by the metaphysics of autonomy in Quebec ... Whether or not they have pondered Hegel or Marx, reformers after 1960 reason in essentially Hegelian or Marxian terms. On one side, the political class and the technocracy work at the consolidation or the building of a modern and enlightened state bureaucracy. Located by some in Ottawa (where it will be a matter of perfecting it, since the federal government has been building it up since 1945 at least), for others in Quebec City, this bureaucracy calls on a faith and on efforts that are only justified by the hope of seeing it realize what Hegel calls the 'ethical moment', namely the reconciliation by the State of a humanity torn by the conflicts inherent in civil society and called to freedom. As late as 1977 [in *La Presse* on 10 March], Pierre Elliott Trudeau could declare: 'I myself am not particularly Hegelian, but I share the opinion of a vision of history as a march towards freedom. Freedom is respect for the other in society, it is the possibility for each person to blossom independently of his or her historical, blood, language ties, etc.' Minus the reference to Hegel, one could easily find a related discourse with Claude Morin or Jacques Parizeau.[54]

THE APOLITICAL TOTALITARIANISM OF TECHNOLOGY'S 'CIVIL SOCIETY'

But Michel Freitag has insisted on the vital importance to democracy of these very social ties Trudeau wanted to make irrelevant (witness what struck Grant – like young Quebec historians today – as Trudeau's 'evident distaste for what was by tradition his own,' coupled with his view that the universal goods of liberalism would dissolve this heritage by integrating French Canada into the Canadian structure, itself a mere stage on the road to the total integration of the Western system[55]). For with the process of '"asymptotic" liquidation of *common* sense, which modernity enters into when it undertakes the critique, *sub specie aeternitatis*, of the substantial contents of inherited traditions and values,' all the unencumbered individual of liberalism is left with is 'in-dependence' from anything that 'situates and constitutes him as a real and concrete subject, endowed with his own inexhaustible richness and depth.' The paradoxical result is 'immediate dependence on determinism' in a 'pure relation to reason that boils down in practice to the free quest of individual interest.' If, in other words, intelligence is not enlightened by love for the other in its very autonomy as other –as Grant insisted after Weil, 'external necessity replaces inner demands. Otherness is reduced to constraint undergone and resistance overcome: "Man is a wolf to man!".' The human being, 'already virtually a computer, becomes the calculator of self-interest imagined by liberal thought since the seventeenth century. This rhetorical figure of the individual was largely prevented from dominating social life as long as it was actually applied to

the individual understood as *human person*, for, whether we like it or not, such a person is always of necessity also already fashioned by social ties, be it only by those of language, family, daily interactions, and of course countless other things of a moral, cultural, political and aesthetic nature. But this weapon of ideological combat that was utilitarian doctrine could turn into a reality only when the subject to which it applied ceased to be a human person, and the principle of the autonomy of calculating subjectivity was extended to what we now call organizations, corporations, and finally totally impersonal systems (such as the self-regulated market, for instance, when we speak of the freedom of markets) ... The modalities of operational functioning then overtake, by absorbing it, the whole logic of interest: the only logic they obey is that of effectiveness and power, that of the unlimited increase of their hold and their self-reproduction without purpose.[56]

It is easy to recognize here Jacques Ellul's understanding of technique as an all-encompassing system focussed only on at its own functional efficiency and the removal of all obstacles to its unfolding, an outlook that decisively influenced Grant and remains a reference for many Quebec writers who share in the *'nouvelle sensibilité.'* Widely respected among them, Freitag has even worked out an Ellulian type of analysis of postmodern technologism as a totalitarian system comparable in certain ways to Nazism. Of course, it already was exactly that for Grant, who saw the logic of liberalism (i.e., the gutting out of all accounts of goodness as something found and not made and that might stand in the way of the emancipated subject's mastery over human and non-human nature) culminate in such a 'Triumph of the Will,' to quote the title of Leni Riefenstahl's infamous Nazi propaganda film. (Grant liked to quote that title too, since he thought that it encapsulated the modern project.)[57] Where Grant spoke of modern man as 'a predicate of the subject technology' that takes over liberalism's assumption of 'an unlimited freedom to make the world as we want in a universe indifferent to what purpose we choose,'[58] for Freitag, 'the real has become "what we do," it is no longer what already is, outside of us, on its own, be it at the level of the objective existent or at the level of the way of life.'[59] 'There is therefore no longer anything either that could resist us, oppose its own being to our will'[60] – except perhaps within us and between us, where the 'omnipotence of impersonal technical systems' may still be met with 'the self-restraint and the wisdom of subjects ... if they unite for them.'[61] For 'it is on the defeat of common sense that totalitarianism is established, reproducing it as it enlarges without cease the invasive empire of non-sense. To resist it, we must reconquer the freedom of thinking the ideas of the true, the just, and the beautiful, and start again to seriously confront each other about them,'[62] as Christopher Lasch (a disgruntled American progressive intellectual much cited by Quebec's late boomers)[63] and other communitarian critics of liberalism have also insisted. Grant could have related to the connection made here by Freitag between contemplation of the Platonic triad and the political action of citizens as they strive to live by the light of these things they have in common – that is, for the *res publica.*

Gilles Labelle likewise comes back to the task of 'rethinking the political,' that is to say: 'what verticality can be, for it is inseparable from the political, in a universe where, however, horizontality is irreversible.' This is the case because, after forty years of Quiet Revolution, no other model of relationships is tolerated beside 'those woven by free, unfettered individuals, in function of mutual interests. This contractualist model needs a guarantor, and that is law. The name of this relation of one with another, when it is generalized, is civil society,' defined by 'contract, market, and law' – the same 'regulating parameters' on which 'globalized capitalism feeds.'[64] Thus, just as Grant had to recognize that the 1960s protesters he admired for standing up to the one-dimensional society created by capitalism and technology were still beholden to the liberal assumptions of the ideology of progress at its core, Labelle sees the same problem in today's protest movements, which cannot think of society in any way other than as an association of individuals for the furtherance of their freedom of choice in self-making, independently of overarching, historically rooted institutions that could command their allegiance to objective norms of life in common. His assessment of the political task facing Quebec in this context is eerily reminiscent of Grant's dire pronouncements in *Lament for a Nation* about the impossibility of conservatism in our era also being the impossibility of Canada – except that the modernist ideology of the Quiet Revolution appears to him equally untenable in the postmodern situation it ushered in: 'To think the political in Quebec, from now on, is, before anything else, to take stock of two impossibilities. It is impossible to think of resurrecting what is dead for good. The Philosophy of History, capitals [for words like Humanity, Progress, etc.], all that is over and done with. Scepticism is in a sense irreversible. Conservatism thus has no chance. Transcendence is no more going to come back than the Law of the Father in the families. But it is just as impossible to blissfully consent to the reign of civil society, to the refusal of the political it embodies.'[65]

TOWARDS A POSTMODERN CONSERVATISM

And yet, by the same token, there might also still be something ethically imperative about the practically impossible stances of both pre-modern conservatism and modern progressivism in the face of the postmodern 'civil society' of human rights. At the risk of sounding partisan (the author is, after all, a committed 'Red/Green' Tory), I would even venture to describe the underlying common aspirations of Quebec's late-boomer intellectuals in terms of a postmodern 'progressive conservatism.' This would encompass in a new symbiosis both the modern freedoms obtained in the name of progress and the pre-modern horizons out of (even if often against) which they arose. For both belong to the human heritage which needs to be preserved from the rising tide of a post-human process that is all that is left once progress has been emptied out by the collapse of any principled, substantial resistance to it. The triumph over human and non-human nature means that the political life of conflict and judgment characteristic of the human animal according to Aristotle no longer has a significant place in technology's 'civil society.' Today, therefore, a genuine conservative can hope to preserve time-honored goods only by actively taking up the freedoms secured by liberalism to defend social justice, while a thoughtful liberal or progressive can hope to preserve these modern gains and give them content only by rooting them in an older heritage, beyond calls for the liberation of all passions and mindless change for its own sake.

Such a 'disposition to preserve and an ability to improve' (following Edmund Burke's 'standard of a statesman'[66]) modern as well as pre-modern goods first requires a postmodern ethical defence of the idea of conservatism, which has been attempted by the *nouvelle sensibilité* in close association with certain theoretical developments in France. Thus, a recent book by one of France's foremost public intellectuals, Alain Finkielkraut, entitled *L'Ingratitude*, took the form of a conversation with Antoine Robitaille, a young journalist at *Le Devoir* who is on the editorial council of *Argument*.[67] Its themes were first developed as part of a prestigious new lecture series sponsored by the Caisses populaires Desjardins at McGill University's Redpath Museum. In the lecture he devoted to conservatism (or the unthinkability thereof) in contemporary societies on 26 May 1998,[68] Finkielkraut appealed to both Edmund Burke and Hannah Arendt to argue for the need to respect the heritage of those who came before us and not instantly dismiss it as dead baggage in the now triumphant posture of modernity, that even so-called political conservatives are most ready to adopt as they push for a bold embrace of the permanent revolution wrought by globalized capitalism and technological change. Unfortunately, given the strictures of political correctness, it does not go without saying that Arendt, Finkielkraut, and those in Quebec who think along the same lines do not have in mind an idea of the fixed forms of a past society of estates.

According to Éric Bédard, even in the nineteenth century, conservatism should not be confused with a reactionary or fundamentalist ideology that denies the dynamics and dialectics of history, such as ultramontanism. The 'conservative synthesis' represented by Quebec's *bleus* acknowledges the revolution of human rights but does not share the liberal faith that law will change people into the manifestation of the rational perfectibility of mankind. Together with the best minds of the era of progress (be it Comte, Tocqueville, Marx, or Durkheim) that also saw the birth of sociology, conservatism is keenly aware of the new forms of servitude that have come with the shedding of the weight of tradition by liberal modernity in politics and economics. 'For the liberal 'individual,' happy or anguished, and the uprooted and alienated worker threaten social bonds ... One does not want to give up liberal and technical progress, but at the same time, one fears these advances may bring the dissolution of the community.' This concern not to allow the fabric of an organically conceived society to fray under the stress of industrialization and capitalism has always been at the root of the kind of Red Toryism embodied by George Grant, which can be traced back to Disraeli, Shaftesbury, and beyond (to say nothing of French Legitimists like the Marquis de Villeneuve). But even more perhaps than in Grant's Canadian Loyalist tradition, 'it is self-evident that at the heart of French Canadian conservatism, there is the awareness of a nation's fragility, and this certainly cannot be said of the French or English cases. "*Survi- vance*" is conservative disappearance anxiety,'[69] which, however, as we know since Margaret Atwood's *Survival*,[70] is also a defining trait of the Canadian identity generally. How else could it find its most powerful expression in a *Lament for a Nation*?

A FRESH LOOK AT LIBERALISM, OLD AND NEW

However, according to the young sociologist Stéphane Kelly, 'if Canada is threatened today, it is less because it is inspired from the American model than because the United States is ever more Hamiltonian. The dilemma facing Canadians is not that of choosing between liberalism and conservatism, as Grant thought. In *Lament for a Nation*, Grant accused Mackenzie King of having broken with Canadian political tra- dition. Since 1982, the same accusation has been levelled at Trudeau. And yet Canada has actually been faithful to the Hamiltonian ideal ever since its foundation,'[71] by promoting at all times and by every means the central consolidation and the temporal duration of political authority around an 'imperial-monarchical' pole – much like the Feder- alists who are known to have made a lasting impression on Canadian Loyalists even after they parted ways in the American Revolution, and whose ideals of stability and nationalism came to prevail in the long run over the Jeffersonian ideals of grassroots democracy and local autonomy. 'While the United States was founded on a tension between the two ideals, Canada on its part was created more purely following the Hamiltonian ideal. For the Jeffersonian ideal has been less popular in British North America.'[72] The Jeffersonian tradition, Kelly suggested, was increasingly downplayed and eventually abandoned in favour of the Hamiltonian tradition by Canada's Liberal Party, which was heir to its modest influence north of the border.

Kelly examines the careers of four prime ministers whose long reigns – covering over half of Canadian history since Confederation – demonstrate the importance of the Hamiltonian tradition in their country already by their sheer duration. His essay explicitly aims to follow in the footsteps of *Lament for a Nation* by 'thinking with Grant against Grant' to address 'a point on which a large majority of Canadians would agree' namely: 'that something is out of order with our experience of democratic life.'[73] The book's title, *Les Fins du Canada selon Macdonald, Laurier, Mackenzie King et Trudeau*, is a deliberate answer to the French title of Grant's *Lament: Est-ce la fin du Canada?*[74] Instead of wondering whether the end has come for Canada, Kelly prefers to investigate the ends pursued by Canada's political leaders. In the *uchronian* spirit of the *nouvelle sensibilité*, he questions a line of thinking determined by time's arrow – whether it is supposed to lead upwards or downwards, and holds up the timeless ideals that can orient human judgment at any given time. 'The two main dominant ideologies of our time, liberalism and conservatism, are based on the idea of irreversible historical movement. The liberal sees in this movement a progress of freedom. The conservative, on his part, perceives instead in this movement a decline of authority.'[75] Hence Grant's fatalistic pessimism about conservatism and his country, an altitude that Kelly (somewhat unfairly – witness the galvanizing effect *Lament for a Nation* has had on succeeding generations of Canadian nationalists) sees as feeding into the malaise of postmodern public life. 'Thus, liberals and conservatives, thinking in terms of "progress" or "decline,"' disqualify the legitimacy of concrete action in the polity. This way of reasoning has been given credence by contemporary political parties, which also seem to have given up on defending political ideals,' content instead to play 'the role of mouthpiece for the new trends before which they claim we are supposed to bow down.'[76]

And yet Grant's appeal to transcendent goods over against progressive historicism is echoed in Kelly's insistence that 'it is impossible to speak of progress if we have not defined beforehand the ideal or the end against which it is to be measured. There is no progress if there is not a common ideal that is inspiring us.'[77] Kelly and others thus oppose the communitarian republicanism of early liberals (based on civic virtue for self-government) to the social-democratic 'New Liberalism' (centred on the creation, distribution, and consumption of wealth) that gradually supplanted it over the course of the twentieth century. 'The history of how modern liberalism has replaced older republican traditions cannot be given in detail'[78] by Grant in his *Lament*, but Kelly, for his part, always returns to this theme in his writings[79] in an attempt to recover those older traditions and to turn republican ideals against opportunistic liberal subservience to social trends. For the New Liberalism was the ideology of an ascendant new class of managers and professional experts who favoured a therapeutic model of self-improvement and social engineering, eventually collapsing class relations into cultural-identity politics. In the process, economic growth and the redistribution of wealth (aiming at material comfort) overshadowed self-government (a question of moral character) as liberal and progressive concerns, so that Hamiltonian top-down models came to displace Jeffersonian elements. Kelly admits having portrayed the latter more empathetically, in the hope of reinfusing them into our political tradition and thus restoring a fruitful tension to public life, in the absence of which citizens are losing interest in politics. 'Since the end of the 1960s, with the triumph of the Hamiltonian ideal in North America, 'Quebec nationalists and Canadian nationalists, in their joint struggle, have strongly contributed to petrifying our political regime and degrading public space.'[80] Thus, Trudeau has consolidated the imperial synthesis achieved by Macdonald – except that, in the latter's day, political freedom was still part of the Hamiltonian ideal while Jeffersonian principles aimed against both 'big business' and 'big government,' such as provincial autonomy, have in effect been jettisoned since then by their traditional Liberal champions. If provincial autonomy otherwise remains 'one of the few republican aspects to have survived in political debates,'

in the hands of Western regionalists and Quebec nationalists, this principle has been shorn of its original humanism. Calls for the decentralization of federalism are rarely associated today with a project for the democratization of political and civic institutions or a struggle against economic concentration. What their different advocates want is instead to recover powers and put them at the service of a State that is just as Hamiltonian as the federal government. Contemporary provincialists seek to create an *Alberta Inc.* or a *Quebec Inc.*, just as in the past Alexander Hamilton dreamed of creating an *America Inc.* and John Macdonald a *Canada Inc.*[81]

As a Canadian nationalist, George Grant clearly had more trust in the central government's ability to act as a check on particular interests straying from the public good. Though Grant's assumptions about federalism at the time of *Lament for a Nation* were distinctly Hamiltonian, his practical objections to provincial autonomy overlapped with Kelly's own Jeffersonian regrets about its concrete content nowadays, thereby uncovering common ground in an ideal of active citizenship: 'Any federal system of government strengthens the power of the corporations. The division of powers weakens the ability of public authority to control private governments; the size of the provinces allows them to be controlled by private economic power. The espousing by American or Canadian "conservatives" of greater authority for the local states has always a phony ring about it, unless it is coupled with an appeal for the break-up of continental corporations. Decentralized government and continental corporations can lead in only one direction.'[82]

A NEO-REPUBLICAN COUNTRY PARTY

Be that as it may, all roads seem to be leading to the new Rome south of the border anyway, so that 'the question of the hour is not knowing whether French Canada exists with its "ethnic" nationalism or whether Quebec's independence is possible with an inclusive nationalism, but whether political and school institutions can be preserved from federal, national, militant, or globalizing technocracy,' as Jean Gould writes. Gould describes *nouvelle sensibilité* as 'neo-republican' – in contrast to both the 'neo-federalist' sensibility of the chief architects of the Quiet Revolution and the 'neo-nationalist' sensibility of its chief beneficiaries.[83] Eloquent cases for republican as opposed to monarchical institutions have actually been made by some of the authors discussed here,[84] but though there are also a few (including this writer) who lean the other way,[85] it should be clear by now that if they can all be said to share in a republican sensibility, the latter has little to do with a regime consisting of unencumbered individuals pursuing their private happiness in a polite society and everything to do with a political community rooted in shared memories – perhaps a 'community of communities,' to borrow Joe Clark's classic formula for the Canadian identity, as Éric Bédard is wont to do when he tries to describe the vision of a sovereign Quebec that he draws from Fernand Dumont.

This *res publica* is therefore not fundamentally different from the commonweal Red Tories such as George Grant often like to see symbolized in the crown. A more significant opposition than that between monarchy and republic, or that between conservatism and liberalism, and even that between federalism and separatism, which are all more like poles within the continuum of the same 'new sensibility,' may be the one between 'Court' and 'Country' that underlies Stéphane Kelly's analyses

– as in the Hamiltonian/Jeffersonian polarity he relies on in *Les fins du Canada*. Drawn from the historiography of eighteenth-century Britain,[86] this idea is applied by Peter J. Smith[87] to the ideological origins of Canadian confederation (Smith believes that the Loyalists and their heirs are better described as Court Whigs than as principled Tories), and by others to the 'Court Party' established by Trudeau as he concentrated absolutist power in the Prime Minister's Office and the Supreme Court – the executive and the judiciary – thus usurping the sovereign authority of crown and parliament and undermining democracy.[88] In Hanoverian England, a Country Party arose to defend civic virtue – as a pervasive sense of duty to the commonwealth – against the court's use of patronage to ensure the stability of a commercial society based on the pursuit of private interests and ambitions, all justified in the name of the 'possessive individualism' of classical liberal theory, as we know from C.B. Macpherson.[89] Yet there were Tories and Whigs on both sides of this divide who placed principles – whether conservative or liberal – above interests and for whom, therefore, a corrupt regime was an affront. Likewise in today's Quebec, progressive and conservative personalities and sensibilities seem to be meeting and meshing, in the intellectual equivalent of a Country Party, to take on the continental Court Party of globalized technocracy. These intellectuals are clarifying issues raised by Grant's thought – like the ambivalent relation between political freedom and timeless goods – in addition to bringing to light a paradox he overlooked: the ambiguous role of throne and altar in actually easing the transition to modernity, by fostering passive acquiescence to 'consensus' as something decreed from on high. Thus, the fond hope Grant placed in Quebec may yet be rewarded – even after the realization of his dire prophecies – by a 'neo-republican' party composed of all those who still insist on having a country, in defiance of the universal homogeneous state. For they are bent on taking up a challenge that Grant saw as the vocation and justification of Canadian nationhood – a challenge that is nowhere so clear as in Quebec, whether inside or outside Confederation.

NOTES

1 C. Roy, 'George Grant: L'identité canadienne face à l'empire de la technique,' *Argument: Politique, société et histoire* [hereafter *Argument*], 5, no. 1 (2002): 181–9. Tables of contents and excerpts of every issue of *Argument* are available on its website: www.pol.ulaval.ca/argument.

2 See Damien-Claude Bélanger's review of Sylvie Lacombe, *La rencontre de*

deux peuples élus. Comparaison des ambitions nationale et impériale au Canada entre 1896 et 1920 (Quebec: Presses de l'Université Laval, 2002), in *Mens: Revue d'histoire intellectuelle de l'Amérique française* 3, no. 1 (2002): 99–102.

3 C. Berger, *The Sense of Power: Studies in the Ideas of Canadian Imperialism, 1867–1914.* (Toronto: University of Toronto Press, 1970).

4 É. Bédard, *Chronique d'une insurrection appréhendée: La Crise d'Octobre et le milieu universitaire.* (Quebec: Septentrion, 1998).

5 L.-H. La Fontaine, *Correspondance générale*, trans. Nicole Panet-Raymond Roy and Suzanne Manseau de Grandmont, revised and annotated by Georges Aubin, presented by Éric Bédard (Montreal: Varia, 2002).

6 This analysis of the early derailing and ultimate fiasco of constitutional-reform policies, as detailed in Kenneth McRoberts's book *Misconceiving Canada: The Struggle for National Unity* (Toronto: Oxford University Press, 1997), is widely shared in Quebec intellectual and political circles.

7 G. Grant, *Lament for a Nation: The Defeat of Canadian Nationalism* (Toronto: McClelland and Stewart, 1970), 21–2.

8 J. Beauchemin, *L'histoire en trop* (Montreal: VLB, 2002).

9 J.-Y. Thériault, *Critique de l'américanité* (Montreal: Québec-Amérique, 2002). See also his article 'L'américanité comme effacement du sujet québécois,' *Argument* 3, no. 1 (2000–2001): 136–44.

10 G. Bouchard, *Genèse des nations et cultures du Nouveau Monde* (Montreal: Boréal, 2000). See Bédard's review 'Genèse des nations et cultures du Nouveau Monde: le magnum opus de l'historiographie moderniste,' *Bulletin d'histoire politique*, 9, no. 2 (2001): 160–74, preceded on 144–59 by Bouchard's essay 'Sur le modèle de la nation québécoise et la conception de la nation chez Fernand Dumont.'

11 Cited in I. Gilmour, *Inside Right: A Study of Conservatism* (London: Quartet Books, 1978), 62.

12 G. Horowitz, 'Conservatism, Liberalism, and Socialism in Canada: An Interpretation,' *Canadian Journal of Economics and Political Science* 32, no. 2 (1966): 143–71.

13 S. Kelly, in his introduction to *Les idées mènent le Québec: Essais sur une sensibilité historique* (Quebec: Presses de l'Université Laval, 2003), 9.

14 See C. Roy, 'Le Québec et le Canada au regard du fédéralisme européen et du nationalisme canadien: un entretien avec Jacques-Yvan Morin,' *Argument* 5, no. 1 (2002): 115–30.

15 See especially Jean-Philippe Warren's much discussed study *Un supplément d'âme: Les intentions primordiales de Fernand Dumont (1947–1970)* (Quebec: Presses de l'Université Laval, 1998), and his contribution entitled 'L'état de

la nation' to a theme section devoted to Dumont's current relevance in the *Bulletin d'histoire politique* 9, no. 1 (2000): 60–70.

16 F. Dumont, *The Vigil of Quebec*, trans. Sheila Fischman and Richard Howard (Toronto: University of Toronto Press, 1974).

17 F. Dumont, *Genèse de la nation québécoise* (Montreal: Boréal, 1993).

18 S. Cantin, in an interview with Antoine Robitaille entitled 'Face au désenchantement,' in *Le Devoir*, 29–30 November 2003, about his book *Nous voilà rendus au sol. Essai sur le désenchantement du monde* (Montreal: Bellarmin, 2003) www.vigile.net/auteurs/c/cantins.html

19 See S. Kelly, 'Initiation à la société thérapeutique,' in Kelly, ed., *Les idées mènent le Québec*, 175–95.

20 The recurring theme of intergenerational justice, related to the baby boomers' refusal of any debt to those who came before them and of any heritage to transmit to those who will follow, has been treated at length in É. Bédard's book (titled after the working group led by Jacques Grand'Maison whose research and reflections it presents) *Le Pont entre les générations* (Montreal: Les Intouchables, 1998).

21 M. Chevrier, 'Le temps de l'homme fini,' *Argument* 5, no. 2 (2003): 113.

22 Nick Loenen, 'George Grant's Conservatism,' *The Friend: The Red Tory Review* 4, no. 4 (2002–2003): 14.

23 J. Gould, 'La genèse catholique d'une modernisation bureaucratique,' in Kelly, ed., *Les idées mènent le Québec*, 174. See also the editorial: 'Le principe d'institution,' in *Argument* 4, no. 2 (2002): 3–6, and the winner of the Governor General's Prize in the Essay category for 1996: Michel Freitag, *Le Naufrage de l'Université et autres essais d'épistémologie politique* (Montreal: Éditions Nota bene, 1998).

24 D. Jacques, 'Une vérité utile: Philosophie et citoyenneté,' *Argument* 3, no. 2 (2001): 3–12.

25 Grant, *Lament for a Nation*, 79.

26 Jacques mentions the following books in 'Une vérité utile,' 6n.1: Jacques Grand'Maison, *Quand le jugement fout le camp: Essai sur la déculturation* (Montreal: Fides, 1999); Pierre Vadeboncoeur, *L'Humanité improvisée* (Montreal: Bellarmin, 2000); and Paul Chamberland, *En nouvelle barbarie* (Montreal: L'Hexagone, 1999).

27 G. Grant, *Technology and Justice* (Toronto: Anansi, 1986), 85.

28 Aside from a concluding mention in Jacques's article, Sloterdijk's lecture *Regeln für den Menschenpark: Ein Antwortschreiben zum Brief über den Humanismus* (Frankfurt: Suhrkamp, 1999) has been more fully discussed by Daniel Tanguay, 'De l'impasse nihiliste à l'utopie biogénétique: Remarques sur une rétractation de Francis Fukuyama, un roman de Michel Houellebecq, une

conférence de Peter Sloterdijk et l'âme humaine,' *Argument* 3, no. 1 (2000): 32–57.

29 Cited in W. Christian, *George Grant: A Biography* (Toronto: University of Toronto Press, 1993), 153.

30 See D. Tanguay's introduction to a theme section on the Quiet Revolution: 'La Révolution tranquille: un héritage en discussion,' *Argument* 3, no. 2 (2001): 13–15, and his *Leo Strauss : une biographie intellectuelle* (Paris: Grasset 2003).

31 Mathieu Bock-Côté, 'Entretien avec Éric Bédard,' *L'Action nationale* 93, nos. 9–10 (2003) (www.action-nationale.qc.ca/03-11/bock-cote.html).

32 C. Roy, 'Épilogue – De l'utopie à l'uchronie,' in Kelly, ed., *Les idées mènent le Québec*, 197–219.

33 Among the best-known examples of this genre in English-language science fiction (though the credentials of *uchronian* speculation reach much further in the past and wider across genres, disciplines, and cultures) are Philip K. Dick's 1962 novel *The Man in the High Castle*, set after the Axis victory in the Second World War, and Robert Silverberg's 1967 novel *The Gate of Worlds*, set in a twentieth century when Western Europe has not only never conquered the New World but has itself long been part of the Ottoman Empire.

34 Gould, 'Lagenèse catholique d'une modernisation bureaucratique.'

35 See É.-M. Meunier and J. Ph. Warren, *Sortir de la 'Grande Noirceur': L'horizon 'personnaliste' de la Révolution tranquille* (Québec: Septentrion, 2002). Éric Bédard wrote the foreword to this book version of a text first published in a landmark special issue of the review *Société* nos. 20/21 (1999) entitled *Le chaînon manquant* – after the 'missing link' in the origins of the Quiet Revolution that accounts for its suddenness and smoothness: it had been prepared since the war within the Catholic Church itself – hence its lack of resistance to the secularization of institutions – that had the unintended result of bringing about its demise rather than its revival. For a strikingly parallel analysis of the wider North American context of these kinds of sociological and ideological transformations among both Protestants and Catholics, see E. McCarraher, *Christian Critics: Religion and the Impasse in Modern American Social Thought* (Ithaca, NY: Cornell University Press, 2000).

36 Grant, *Lament for a Nation*, 82–3.

37 Ibid., 79–80.

38 Loenen, 'George Grant's Conservatism,' 11.

39 Labelle, 'L'université et la déstructuration de la subjectivité,' *Argument* 3, no. 2 (2001): 82–3.

40 G. Grant, *Technology and Empire: Perspectives on North America* (Toronto: House of Anansi, 1969), 139.

41 Ibid., 137.

42 Chevrier, 'Le temps de l'homme fini,' 94.

43 Grant, *Technology and Empire*, 142.

44 Chevrier, 'Le temps de l'homme fini,' 109–10.

45 D. Arcand, *Les Invasions barbares: Scénario* (Montreal: Boréal, 2003), 154.

46 G. Labelle, 'Gilles Leclerc, inquisiteur et prophète,' *Argument* 5, no. 1 (2003): 167.

47 Grant, *Technology and Justice*, 58.

48 G. Labelle, 'Gilles Leclerc, un inquisiteur oublié,' *Mens* 3, no. 2 (2003): 201.

49 Ibid., 204.

50 G. Labelle, 'Gilles Leclerc, inquisiteur et prophète,' *Argument* 5, no. 1 (2003): 168.

51 Ibid., 167.

52 G. Grant, *Time as History* (Toronto: University of Toronto Press, 1995).

53 Labelle, 'Gilles Leclerc, inquisiteur et prophète,' 164.

54 G. Labelle, 'De la Philosophie de l'Histoire au règne de la société civile,' *Argument* 5, no. 2 (2003): 77.

55 G. Grant, 'Nationalism and Modernity,' *Canadian Forum*, January 1971, in W. Christian and S. Grant, eds., *The George Grant Reader* (Toronto: University of Toronto Press, 1998), 104.

56 M. Freitag, 'De la terreur nazie au meilleur des mondes cybernétique. Réflexions sociologiques sur les tendances totalitaires de notre époque,' *Argument* 5, no. 1 (2003): 80–1.

57 G. Grant, 'The Triumph of the Will,' in D. O'Leary, *The Issue is Life: A Christian Response to Abortion in Canada* (Burlington, ON: Welsh Publishing, 1988).

58 Grant, *Technology and Empire*, 138.

59 Freitag, 'De la terreur nazie,' 95.

60 Ibid., 94.

61 Ibid., 83.

62 Ibid., 82.

63 For example, Lasch's *The Culture of Narcissism* (New York: Warner, 1979).

64 Labelle, 'L'université et la déstructuration de la subjectivité,' 81.

65 Ibid., 81.

66 Edmund Burke, *Reflections on the Revolution in France*, ed. Conor Cruise O'Brien. (Harmondsworth, UK: Penguin Books, 1969), 267.

67 A. Finkielkraut, with A. Robitaille, *L'Ingratitude: conversation sur notre temps* (Montréal: Québec/Amérique, 1999).

68 The lecture's text has been published as a pamphlet entitled *Le conservatisme*

à l'aube du XXIe siècle (Montreal: Programme d'études sur le Québec de l'Université McGill, 'Grandes conférences Desjardins,' no. 2 [1998]). See M. Chevrier's review: 'L'empire de l'écran total – Ce que conserver veut dire d'après Alain Finkielkraut,' *L'Agora* 5, no. 4 (1998) (agora.qc.ca/textes/chevrier.html).

69 M. Bock-Côté, 'Entretien avec É. Bédard,'

70 M. Atwood, *Survival* (Toronto: House of Anansi Press, 1972).

71 S. Kelly, *Les Fins du Canada selon Macdonald, Laurier, Mackenzie King et Trudeau* (Montreal: Boréal, 2001), 12.

72 Ibid., 250.

73 Ibid., 9.

74 George Grant, *Est-ce la fin du Canada? Lamentation sur l'échec du nationalisme canadien*, foreword by Jacques-Yvan Morin, translated by Gaston Laurion (Montreal: Hurtubise HMH, 'Cahiers du Québec [Sociologie],' 1987).

75 Ibid., 253.

76 Ibid., 254.

77 Ibid., 255.

78 Grant, *Lament for a Nation*, 64.

79 See for instance 'Initiation à la société thérapeutique,' or Kelly's presentation of the 'conservative' champion of an older liberalism after his taste in the regular 'Figure de pensée' segment of *Argument* 3, no. 1 (2000–2001): 145–54: 'La dignité de posséder son chapeau: Gilbert Keith Chesterton, 1874–1936.'

80 Kelly, *Les Fins du Canada*, 251.

81 Ibid., 252–53.

82 Grant, *Lament for a Nation*, 77.

83 See Gould, 'La genèse catholique d'une modernisation bureaucratique,' 174.

84 Many of them are by Marc Chevrier, whose texts can be read on the Internet version of the journal *L'Agora* (http://agora.qc.ca/textes/chevrier.html) and in the evolving on-line *Encyclopédie de l'Agora*, both works-in-progress of the established philosopher Jacques Dufresne, who has voiced concerns similar to Grant's about the technological society in books such as *Après l'homme ... le cyborg?* (Montreal: Multimondes, 1999), discussed by him and several other thinkers in a theme section of *Argument* 2, no. 2 (2000): 104–33. Dufresne himself has also written 'Simone Weil ou la synthèse de la méthode et de la purification,' in the 'Figure de pensée' section of *Argument* 3, no. 2 (2001): 160–7.

85 See, for instance, the provocative case that French Canadians always defended the 'rights of Englishmen' as their own under the Canadian crown, despite the latter's absolutist tendencies: Frédéric Demers (author of

Céline Dion et l'identité québécoise [Montreal: VLB, 1999]), 'Les 'monarchistes' québécois,' *Argument* 3, no. 2 (2001): 85–101.

86 See J.G.A. Pocock, *The Machiavellian Moment: Florentine Political Thought and the Atlantic Republican Tradition* (Princeton, NJ: Princeton University Press, 1975), and Bonnelyn Young Kunze and Dwight D. Brautigam, eds., *Court, Country, and Culture: Essays on Early Modern British History in Honor of Perez Zagorin*, preface by Donald R. Kelley (Rochester, NY: University of Rochester Press, 1992).

87 Peter J. Smith, 'The Ideological Origins of Canadian Confederation,' *Canadian Journal of Political Science* 20, no. 1 (1987): 5–29.

88 See Rainer Knopff and F.L. Morton, *The Charter Revolution and the Court Party* (Toronto: Broadview, 2000), and Donald J. Savoie, *Governing from the Centre: The Concentration of Power in Canadian Politics* (Toronto: University of Toronto Press, 1999).

89 C.B. Macpherson, *The Political Theory of Possessive Individualism: Hobbes to Locke* (Oxford: Oxford University Press, 1962).

PART THREE

Christian Commitments and Theological Questions

GRANT BELIEVED that the questions of modernity and liberalism could be adequately answered only by drawing on the rich tradition of the Christian faith. This section begins with unpublished notes for a series of five lectures on Christianity that Grant gave at McMaster University in 1976. In these lectures, Grant outlined why he believed that the teachings of Christ could enable us to understand how Christianity was, at its inception, very different from the Western forms of Christianity we see today. Using the Gospels as his starting place, Grant develops a complex critique of Western Christianity and its stepchild, modernity.

The central concern of Grant's thought was to show that God and justice are one and thereby to distinguish God from necessity. Grant believed that there was a version of Christianity adequate to address this theological problem but that the Christian West had ignored it. This forgotten strain of Christianity was what he called Platonic Christianity, and he drew from many traditions to piece it together. The dominant Christian tradition of the West, caught up in a faulty teaching on divine providence, had placed all events either for good or evil at the door of God's will. Grant thought that, if one equates God's will with the course of natural events, then theology has no moral response to the suffering of the innocent.

In the lecture notes reproduced here, Grant argues that the Gospels teach that the place of charity is higher than that of contemplation. Whereas in Plato's dialogues contemplation and charity are equal, the Christian Gospels surpass Plato in describing God's love as his willingness to sacrifice himself for all human kind. To demonstrate that the Gospels present an alternate account of Christian faith, Grant shows how western Christianity has missed the essence of Christ's teaching on justice, his suffering, and the account of the resurrection. Grant then argues that St Augustine's stands at the turning point in Christian history between the two traditions of Eastern and Western Christianity. He finishes off his lectures with a detailed exposition of Dostoevsky's parable on the Grand Inquisitor in which Western Christianity, with its dedication to power, politics, and reason, is confronted by the foolishness of Christ. These lectures notes, published here for the first time, give the reader an excellent insight into the complexity of Grant's struggle between Athens and Jerusalem.

In this section, the complexity of Grant's thought on the competing claims of Athens and Jerusalem is illustrated by three authors who each present a different side of Grant's theological understanding. Grant saw in the Anglican way an opportunity to retrieve the best from all the Christian traditions in order to allow a way of thinking and living distinct from the Nietzchean will to power that was inherent in modern technology. Grant also drew from other traditions such as the Eastern Orthodox Church, as seen in his work on Philip Sherrard and Dostovesky, Roman Catholicism, as seen in his affinity with Simone Weil and her sacramental theology, and Protestantism as demonstrated in his appropriations of Martin Luther and the theology of the cross. Each of these three great traditions is represented in this chapter. It begins with Randy Peg Peters's account of Grant's appreciation of Orthodox Christianity, entitled 'Three Wise Men from the East.' After reading Heidegger, Grant agreed that the modern eclipse of meaning was a result of Western forms of Christianity that had elevated the human will (and its ability to know something by creating and making it) to a position of primacy. Grant saw in Orthodoxy a way to speak about faith and theology that was free of Heidegger's devastating critique of Western Christianity and the rise of modern technological ways of knowing. It was by reading and drawing from these Eastern theologians that he learned how Christian Platonists understood knowing as loving rather than as power. For Grant, Eastern Orthodoxy was a theological tradition that had been nourished outside the West and therefore was devoid of modernity's most devastating effects.

Not only did Grant use Orthodoxy to further his theological thinking, but he also began to go back through the Western tradition and find pockets of theological resistance that refused to be assimilated by modernity. This led him to Martin Luther's notion of the theology of the cross as an antidote to the typical Western Christian theology of glory. The theology of glory uses religion for power, domination, and control, whereas the theology of the cross says that God does not reveal himself in power but in brokenness and pain, as seen in Christ on the cross. Harris Athanasiadis takes the reader into the depths of this distinction and articulates a spirituality that is centred around the broken, the marginalized, and the weak. One can see here the theological underpinnings of Grant's critique of modern liberalism and the marginalizing effects of the American Empire.

Grant also drew from the Catholic thinker and writer Simone Weil. For Grant, Weil represented another theological light in the darkness of modernity. Her political engagement, her socialistic economics, and her concern for poor factory workers revealed a depth of meaning in her theological writings that Grant had rarely seen before. Grant was not interested in disengaged, erudite theology. In his mind, theology needed to engage the issues of the day. The essay by Pam McCarroll, entitled 'The Whole as Love,' explores Grant's affinity with Weil's notion of knowing through love. The sacramental way of knowing, rooted in the idea that God reveals his divine grace through matter, allowed Grant to see the connection between the Good, the Beautiful, and the Just. Grant believed that, when you love and stand for justice – such as when he criticized the American war in Vietnam – the beauty of the divine is most revealed. One cannot know something like justice unless you love it and you can never love something if you stand over it to control it. The act of knowing *is* an act of love, the act of entering and embracing the reality of the other, of allowing the other to enter and embrace us. In this way, Grant brought Athens towards Jerusalem.

12

Five Lectures on Christianity

GEORGE GRANT

These lectures are found in Notebook A. Delivered in 1976 to a graduate course on Plato and is published here for the first time, they show how Grant tried to open up a way of understanding Christianity outside its modern Western expressions. Although he referred to this as Platonic Christianity, he drew from various Christian traditions and sources to help him outline what it might look like.

THE GOSPELS

Today we come to the thing itself. The supreme figure, Jesus Christ, and to understand what Christianity is one must understand why for those of us who are Christians this is the supreme figure. That is what I am going to talk about today, and please stop me because it is hard to describe what one loves. One of my sons thinks the music of a group called the Grateful Dead is very beautiful, and he has succeeded in showing me why that is so – but it has been hard.

Now the Gospels are to me where one finds the entirely beautiful and it is hard to describe. By the beautiful I mean the image of the Good in the world. The answer to this is in the title we give the books. The Gospels, written by what one calls the Evangelists, are the good news. This is the good news – the good news about the whole, not about this or that, but about the whole – the news that 'to *be* is good.' Now why does one need such news?

All of us from the earliest days suffer – things go wrong, people we love die, and we come to think that to be is not good. It is only good under some circumstances. If somebody came through that door now and told me my wife had been killed, I would not think it good to be.

But we pass beyond ourselves in this matter. The terrible things that happen to others, in general and in detail, the enslavement of whole peoples, the victory of the unjust and the conquerors in history – the earthquakes, etc., etc. I need not pile it on. Suffering is the very heart of human life, and animal life.

Now in the face of that there are two responses. (1) Those who say that world is a mad chaos and there is no purpose to anything, that God is not. That is despair, and despair has always been considered the greatest evil for a human being. The second response is to be continually thinking for our adult lives how one puts together the perfection of God and the sufferings of the world. Can I believe that justice is good, and that God is just? The study is called theodicy (*theo dike*). Trying to understand how we can think God is just in the light of the terrible afflictions of human beings.

Now Christ's life is the Gospel, is the good news, because it answers the contradiction (contra diction – speaking against) between the justice of God and the sufferings of human beings. Now if you want to overcome a contradiction falsely you wipe one side away and then there is no contradiction. But that is not an overcoming of the contradiction, that is just a denial of it. In this case, if you deny the perfection of God you are left with the contradiction of atheism. If you deny the suffering of human beings you just pretend that the world is other than it is.

Now Christianity does not deny either side of the contradiction, but answers it by taking suffering up into God. Here is this entirely beautiful, absolutely just, that is *perfect* being – that is God, who is afflicted by the worst suffering life has to offer, and overcomes that suffering. That is, the supreme contradiction of life between the perfection of God and the suffering of human beings is overcome, not in the general principles of thought – but in the actual here and now events of the world. This is what is meant by saying these writings are Gospels, they are the good news of a completely concrete (if you like the word, existential) kind that justice is good. To use the language of Paul in the New Testament, what the Gospels are about is the self-emptying of God. We all know that suffering, any real suffering, is self-emptying. People in mental hospitals experience this.

THE PASSION AND SUFFERING

Now in the terms of that statement, how is that carried out in the Gospels? First of all through the teaching and life of Jesus and secondly through his Passion or Suffering.

Let's start with the teaching from the Sermon on the Mount. Matthew chapter[s] 5 to 7 reveal a perfect account of justice or righteousness. These are called the Beatitudes. Jesus says 'Blessed are the meek' and 'Blessed are those who hunger and thirst for righteousness or justice.' I prefer the word 'happy' to 'blessed' – the union of happiness and justice. Happiness is what we are fitted for. What is breathtaking also in the teaching is its immediate clarity and comprehensibility. Take the great parables or stories, for example, the Good Samaritan, Luke chapter 12, or the Prodigal Son, Luke 15. What is wonderful about the Prodigal Son, for example, is that it is profoundly clear on the surface and profoundly deep however many times one reads it. Now this combination of clarity and depth meant that Christianity was equally open to all human beings. Why it spread so quickly through the Roman Empire was just that. The parable of the Prodigal Son just lays before people in the simplest story the truth of the relations between God and human beings, yet that very simplicity is absolutely profound, so that the greatest thinker can never come to the bottom of it. This is why 'equality' has been central to Christianity. The cleverest of the most powerful ruler, or the greatest artist, are in the same position before that story as the simplest non-literate. All can learn from it equally.

But of course the life and teaching of Christ is but a preparation for what has been called the Passion of Christ. This is true of all of us, our deeds are more important than our words. As was once said about another human being, – 'what you do speaks so loudly that I can't hear what you say.' Christ said it very clearly. See above and read Matt. 25:34–35.

Why these deeds of Christ have been at the centre of Western history is because they are the supreme drama – drama is just the Greek word for deeds done. That is why I think the most important readings for this part of the course, on Christianity, is an account of the deeds in Matthew's Gospel, chapter 26 and following.

Now let's talk about Gethsemane and Golgotha. The greatest commentary on this is not in words – but in music, Bach's Passion according to St Matthew. I chose this rendering of the events because of that commentary. It is much better than words – the great art which combines most profoundly the abstract and the erotic. I will nevertheless try some words to describe those deeds. Here is the entirely beautiful being destroyed by the forces of the great authorities of his day, and by the religious authorities of his day, and that destruction was met with complete justice by the one who is being destroyed. At the height of his destruction on the Cross, in the midst of extreme physical pain, he says about those who are destroying him, 'Father forgive them, for they know not what they do' (Luke, 23, 24). This remark of Christ's is the completely just remark. Justice, as I have said, is to render each human being their due. Here he says what is his torturers' due – to be forgiven because they are fools – they do not know what they are doing. They do not know the way things are, therefore they torture him. Here is the perfect living out of justice by good, even under extreme affliction.

I think one first has to see the extremity of that suffering. To compare, I said last day that two deaths have dominated the thought of the Western world, that of Socrates and that of Christ. Now it is the extremity of the suffering in Christ's death which has made these events more dominating in the Western world than the death of Socrates. Socrates had a calm, serene death. He tells a joke just before he takes the hemlock. But the death of Christ is a death of such blackness. The scene in Gethsemane describes this. St Luke reports that He sweated blood. We all sweat when we are scared out of wits. It is above all the destruction of our prestige. All of us are able to maintain ourselves in life above all by some form of prestige. We convince ourselves we *are* something by how others see us in the world. (I have been much flattered in the last years, and what is so horrible is how one eats it up. Flattery will get you everywhere.) Now what is so staggering in the Gospels is the complete destruction of Christ's prestige. Here is this beautiful being coming into Jerusalem in great acclaim and then days later his destruction, including the destruction of his prestige. This is in the cry of dereliction on the Cross, Matthew 27:41. My God, my God, why hast thou forsaken me? Even the very foundation of his life, the relation of God to God, is destroyed. Cry of desolation – a psalm, yes indeed. But it is the very absence of God from God. Suffering is absence.

THE RESURRECTION

I am still lecturing on the Gospels because I haven't dealt with what is given us in the Resurrection of Christ – later in the lecture I will go on to St Augustine. Now in the modern world there is a thing that stands in the way of getting near what is given in the Resurrection, and that is our modern account of miracles. Therefore I have to start from a description of that to clear it out of the way. We all think that the world is a great network of causes. What we are doing in science is trying to understand that network of causes. Now those of us who assert that God or Good exist believe He has set up this great network of causes.

He is the first cause of these secondary causes. We often call God the First Cause. But it is also clear that there is a great independence of this network of secondary causes – we call the world the cosmos.

Now the modern account of miracles is that a miracle occurs when the First cause interferes with the usual network of secondary causes and makes something happen that would not otherwise happen. Now this account of miracles is nonsense for the following reason. It makes of God an arbitrary and immoral tyrant. Why, if God can interfere arbitrarily with the great network of secondary causes, does he not do so – when people are being tortured, or when babies are born defective? This modern view of miracles was invented by those who wanted to hold apart science and religious truth – but it is quite unthinkable when one starts to think it – because it makes God or Good arbitrary and wicked.

If that kind of nonsense [is] now cleared out of our minds, we are able to think about the wonders that have occurred throughout history of all civilizations, and happen to this day. All over the world in any society there are certain powers associated with those who love greatly. What does the word 'charity' mean? It is much abused these days. What charity means is those people who give themselves away to other people. The powers granted to such people are fantastic. I have seen such powers.

There is a ghastly way of speaking about the resurrection in the modern world which I call the fairy-tale way. A prince (or princess) is dressed in rags and everybody scorns him, and suddenly the clothes are pulled off and he appears in his prince's costume and everybody treats him well. Let's apply this to Christianity. The central symbol of Christianity has always been the Cross. Clearly in some sense the Resurrection takes place on the Cross. We see it in all the language of St John about Christ being lifted up and elevated. Christ says on the cross, 'It is consummated.' Marriage is consummated, sexually fulfilled. As I have said, on the Cross justice is consummated – because the absolute absence of justice is met with justice. Let me put it another way. At the height of the dinner Christ has with his friends just before he is arrested, He says (St John's Gospel, 16:33) don't be afraid of what is going to happen, 'I have overcome the world' – or better translated, 'I have been victorious over the cosmos.' Now the cosmos or the world just means that network of necessary secondary causes of which we are part. Now what do these words mean? Justice is always in a certain sense absent from that order of necessity of secondary causes. But in Christ's life and death these causes have been made to serve justice. He has conquered the cosmos because he has submitted to all the injustice of the cosmos – justly. Now of course one of the central things of the order of the cosmos is death. In that sense the Resurrection means that by being victorious over the cosmos on the Cross he overcomes death, in a way that people have always known since that time.

ST AUGUSTINE

Now we get on to the history of Christianity since that date. We will skip immediately to St Augustine, who more than any figure is the founder of Western Christianity. The great division in Christianity is between Western and Eastern Christianity. With Western Christianity there came to be closely associated what we call the Reformation. But these divisions are minor compared with the great division between east and west. Now what do we mean by two statements: (a) what is Western Christianity? and (b) what do we mean by saying that Augustine is the central figure in its foundation? Western civilization is that which arose in Western Europe after the fall of classical Mediterranean civilization. It spread its roots outside of Europe in the Americas, ourselves included; this civilization was held together above all by a certain account of Christianity. In recent years this civilization has spread its power out into the other civilizations of the world, China, India, Russia etc. so that it is in some sense now world wide, but in becoming world wide it is now dying.

History is certainly a great story of the rise and fall of civilizations, and of one thing I am certain – we are now living at the time of the end of Western civilization. It is clearly dying all around us. What does it mean to say that St Augustine was as much as anybody the founder of Western civilization? The extract which you are being asked to read is from his book, 'The City of God.' That book was written just after the sack of Rome – 410 A.D. Think what it meant – the sack of Rome – the sack of civilization (a modern day equivalent would be New York etc.). We are reading a small part of the 14th book – but the book as a whole is 22 books, just describing why Roman civilization was inadequate and therefore why it doesn't matter that its empire is falling. Why Augustine fascinates modern western people – the study of him is enormously popular in our world – is that people see a great similarity between his situation and our own. He lived at the end of Roman civilization as we live at the end of Western civilization.

Now let me say that I am rather sad that I chose this extract from him. It is a great extract, but it is a rather negative one. To understand Western Christianity we had to have something from Augustine, but this extract is fairly negative, because he is turning back to say what was wrong with classical civilization and classical philosophy. If you want to read him in his more positive mood, read his 'Confessions.' Read it in a modern translation. Augustine has been called the first modern man because of the Confessions. One thing that makes Western civilization is our tendency to self-analysis, and there is no more staggering book of self-analysis than Augustine's 'Confessions.'

Now in this extract which you are asked to read, why is Augustine shown to be the founder of Western Christianity? First, go back to Plato. The good means what we are fitted for. And the Good (capital G) means what fits us for what we a fitted for, namely God. What Augustine says in this extract is that classical philosophy has been enormously divided about the human good – He says that according to the famous Roman philosopher, Varro, there are 288 possible accounts of human good, and he shows how that division has taken place. What he says about Christianity is that against that uncertainty about human good Christianity declares unequivocally what human good consists in – Peace in Eternal Life.

Now I think that you should get two things that in my opinion have above all characterized western Christianity, Certainty and Transcendence. It was 'certainty' in Christianity that life has a purpose, and what that purpose is. Certainty – both for good and ill; for good in the terrible uncertainty of life – for ill in the ability of Christianity to move out into other civilizations of the world. Western Christianity is 'so certain.' Exclusivity gave it that certainty which is less pleasant.

What about Western Christianity's second idea, transcendence, which means standing above. What Augustine says in unequivocal terms is that the purpose of this life is in the world – but quite transcends the world. This has been the enormous power of Christianity – transcendence and immanence. What modern people mean by the death of God is that transcendence has gone.

Certainty and transcendence weigh against each other – but this is a strength.

DOSTOEVSKY'S CHRISTIANITY

That question 'What is Christianity' is not easy in 5 lectures; or for you to have to try to come upon it for the purposes of a class. I have not said much about the history of Christianity and simply ... [say now] that in the history of Christianity there was to be, with St Augustine as the elemental founder, a particular species of Christianity – Western Christianity.

Now by Western Christianity I mean by way of civilization – the civilization which centres in the North Atlantic, France, Germany Holland, England. The dynamic heart of civilization is from the Mediterranean (just look at the map) Greece and Rome, to the North Atlantic countries and their chief extensions abroad in North America. Probably the origin of the word 'religion' is 'what binds together' (Latin word) and what binds together that North Atlantic civilization is what I call Western Christianity, that is, both Protestantism and Catholicism. It was the destiny of that civilization to be world wide.

Take Marxism, which is a kind of public religion in Russia and China, a totally Western product – a product of Western Biblical religion – part Christianity, part Judaism. It is impossible to think of Marx's view of history without seeing it as coming out of Biblical religion. It is 'the secular Biblical religion.' Indeed the two great public religions of the world today are Marxism and American progressivism; these two religions are late outcrops of that civilization, founded on Western Christianity, [which] seems now to be tottering to its end. Therefore in asking the question, 'What is Christianity?' we have to make a careful distinction between Christianity and Western Christianity. It is for this reason that I choose as the last piece of the readings the extract from Dostoevsky's 'The Brother's Karamazov,' The Grand Inquisitor – because that writing is a criticism of Western Christianity in the name of Christ.

I might have used this last lecture to talk of the history of Western Christianity, such questions as the Protestant Reformation – the great break within Western Christianity between Protestant and Catholics. Such questions are important and I hope you have discussed them in your tutorials. But I am going to use this last lecture to talk about Dostoevsky's attack on Western Christianity in the name of Christ.

Who was Dostoevsky? A Russian novelist writing in late 19th Century. No doubt Dostoevsky and Tolstoy are the supreme writers of fiction and Shakespeare the great playwright. Dostoevsky lived in the West, but turned back to assert Eastern Christianity – what is known as Orthodoxy. His writing is a great attack on Russia being westernized. For example, 'The Possessed' (or 'The Devils') is a great prophecy against the Western revolutionaries who are going to take over Russia in the coming revolution. If God is not, anything is permissible; there is no reason we can't do anything, however brutal. This thought leads us to think of Stalin and his ferocious tyranny under Marxism where 16 million Kulaks were killed. This novel 'The Brothers Karamazov' is the last, and his great masterpiece. I hope someday some of you will read it.

This small extract is a story one brother tells another. It is about the meeting of the Grand Inquisitor and Christ, and it turns on an account of Christ's temptations in the wilderness which describe three great temptations (see Matthew chap 4). Now to face this writing of Dostoevsky's, I would say two things. First of all, you need to understand ambiguity. Dostoevsky is saying something that points in two or more directions. He [says] there are double meanings to everything. He was the great master of what we call today black comedy. This makes his writing difficult to read. Secondly, all the words are put in the mouth of the Grand Inquisitor. Christ only does two things – he heals somebody at the beginning, and kisses the Grand Inquisitor at the end. This represents the silence of truth. We live in a world dominated by words and pictures, the media dominates our lives. We live in a world in which there is little silence and yet the Old Testament reminds us to 'Be still and know that I am God.' Dostoevsky is emphasizing the silence of truth.

But Dostoevsky also puts a very powerful case in the mouth of the Grand Inquisitor, and to see what is being said in this passage you must see the strength and persuasiveness of what is being said by the Grand Inquisitor. His case is to Dostoevsky the case of Western Christianity in all its dynamism, and attraction and exclusivity – put forward most clearly. Let me say how important this is in life. If you are going to show what is untrue about any opinion, you must see that opinion at its best, not at its worst. Otherwise you cannot refute it. In the American view of Russia or the Russian view of America, both pretend the other has a weak case. Therefore they can never see the other person's case. Unless one is really touched by the possible truth one will never really look at it. You must see the great strength of the Grand Inquisitor's case, because it is a case which most of us often really think is true.

Now the Grand Inquisitor uses the three temptations of Christ to make his case. After his meeting with John the Baptist, Christ went into the wilderness, and his three temptations are described as turning stones into bread, jumping off the temple, a public miracle, and taking over all the powers of the state. Now the Grand Inquisitor says that Christ was wrong not to have done these things. Why was Christ wrong? According to the Grand Inquisitor, if Christ had done these things he would have built a world where all people were comfortable and happy on earth, and that is what human beings want and need.

Therefore Christ led human beings away from worldly happiness and that was a great evil. Western Christianity, according to the Grand Inquisitor, has corrected that mistake of Christ's. It has made human beings happy, by giving them bread and miracles and authority. Those are what human beings want and need, and Western Christianity has provided them with that. It took over the power of the state and gave them what they wanted. What they wanted was to live in a harmonious ant-hill, and this is what Western Christianity has achieved – and what Christ threatened by offering them freedom.

What men wanted was to get rid of their freedom – to give up their freedom of conscience – so that they would have the comfort of living securely in the world – where they do not need to think or to be uncertain, and here they live with the certainty of authority. Human beings are just too weak to want what Christ offers them. It was therefore foolish to offer them this, and Western Christianity has got over that mistake of Christ's. The only way Christ could have united all human beings in worship for ever was by giving them earthly bread, and earthly authority and earthly entertainment (miracles), and he threw away the chance.

Now there are three things I would like to say by way of commentary. First of all, I want to note the sheer strength of the Grand Inquisitor's case. Is it not a fact that what men both want and need most is a comfortable life here on earth? In terms of the language I used earlier for Plato and Augustine – is this not man's highest good, the purpose of life? Is not man's chief purpose to have a comfortable life here on earth? To get that does he not need bread? To get that does he not need beyond bread – entertainment, the mass entertainment which is now so much the centre of our lives? To get that does he not need authority, to keep things in order, so that he can enjoy things here on earth? Take, for example, the fact of war. Isn't life here on earth particularly ruined for human beings by war, and isn't above all authority necessary, the authority of the state, and finally the authority of the state to eliminate war? What I am saying is that the Grand Inquisitor's case is very strong. How can we doubt that the purpose of life is a comfortable life on earth and this requires bread and entertainment and authority. Anyway, this is what most human beings want. As the Grand Inquisitor says to Christ, 'You will only have the few; we will give peace to all.'

Secondly, I would like to say, isn't the picture of what the Grand Inquisitor says that Western civilization under the drive of western Christianity has offered human beings – a very accurate picture of the ideals that this civilization has offered the rest of the world, that it is best to have the harmonious ant-heap?

This is surely why North America is the centre of the world – because it is the society where that is most completely realized. Think about the Great Lakes' region which is representative of our world. In that sense, when you think of what Dostoevsky is offering through the words of the Grand Inquisitor, you should think above all of the society you inhabit. Think also about the mental health state – the next stage of capitalist society. We have conquered the question of bread; beyond bread is a happy sexual life, and that is arranged by the psychiatrists. If people step out of line, the mental health apparatus will bring them back into line.

Thirdly, what does Dostoevsky mean by the freedom that Christ offered them, and which the Grand Inquisitor says a good society must get rid of? This is difficult for us to understand, because we live in the society the Grand Inquisitor offers and therefore it is hard to see what is absent in that society. Freedom means for us external freedom. We mean by freedom when we want to do something, nothing stands in the way of us doing it, and that political freedom is surely a great good. To put it at its crudest: if I want to do it with a girl or a boy or an animal, there is an identical Holiday Inn everywhere in North America for me to do it in.

Now clearly this external freedom is not what Dostoevsky means by freedom. The Russian word for freedom is 'sroboden', and it is nearly the same as the word for God. I would think what he means by freedom or 'sroboden' is best translated as openness to eternity. But you must think about that. What the Grand Inquisitor offers human beings is everything except that freedom which I have translated as openness to eternity.

13

Three Wise Men from the East: Eastern Orthodox Influences on George Grant

RANDY PEG PETERS

Political philosophy grew out of the idea that the most important thing for the philosopher to do was to think what was the best regime under which human beings could live. The two main people who came out of this were Plato and Aristotle, and this has led to a great division in the West. The Catholic West, to a very great extent, accepted Aristotle, both in natural science and in political science, and this is one of the reasons there is such a difference between the Eastern church and the Western church. The Western church fundamentally chose Aristotle; the Eastern church fundamentally chose Plato. As far as my own thought goes, I have fundamentally chosen Plato.

George Grant in Conversation

In this chapter, I will explore why Grant believed there was a major distinction between Western and Eastern Christianity. For him, this was rooted in a foundational difference between Plato, whom he considered Eastern, and Aristotle, whom he considered Western. As Grant puts it in one of his personal journals, 'I have to face the question whether Plato stands at the end of a long tradition which is broken by Aristotle, this is what Sherrard and Simone Weil say, or whether western metaphysics began with Plato. This is what Heidegger seems to be saying.'[1]

George Grant believed that the modern world is committed to the objectification of everything with the aim of controlling it. He also believed that Western metaphysics, namely Western Christianity, was the force behind this objectification. In light of this, Grant saw in Eastern Orthodoxy theological concepts that had not fallen prey to the 'onto-theology' of the West. Grant argued that the technological way of knowing dominant in the West brings about a certain loss. For Grant, the blame lay with the Western Christian preoccupation with human will as it evolved in the difference between the Platonic Eastern church and the more Aristotelian Western church. In this chapter I will explicate Grant's reading of three different 'Eastern' thinkers, Dostoyevsky, Erick Frank, and Philip Sherrard, who helped him formulate a response to what he believed was a flawed Western form of Christianity. I will discuss each of these thinkers by drawing on three unpublished sources in Grant's private journals. In doing so, I hope to deepen Grantian scholarship by introducing new influences on George Grant's theological legacy. The first thinker, Philip Sherrard, an Eastern Orthodox theologian from Greece, allowed Grant to see for the first time that there was an Eastern version of Christianity, drawing from Plato, that offered a way past Heidegger's critique of the Latin Western, more Aristotelian church. The second writer I want to explore, Erich Frank, was a Jewish philosopher who had taken over the philosophy chair from Martin Heidegger at the University of Freiburg in 1928. It was a few of his essays that helped Grant understand, in more philosophical detail, the difference between Aristotle and Plato. If Grant read Sherrard for the theological framework, he read Frank for the philosophical. My final source of Eastern inspiration, the Russian Dostoevsky, allowed Grant to work out his final position on how to live his faith in the midst of the Western dynamo. Dostoevsky's notion that faith was not about controlling people but about freeing people to love justice buttressed Grant's deep sense of the equality of all people.

PHILIP SHERRARD: THE GREEK ORTHODOX WISE MAN

In order to understand Grant's interest in the Greek Orthodox writer Philip Sherrard, one must first appreciate the context of Grant's theological interest. For this we turn to Grant's interpretation of Martin Heidegger. In his essay 'What Is Metaphysics?,' Heidegger says that the word 'metaphysics derives from the Greek which means to inquire in a way that extends out "over" beings as such. Metaphysics is inquiry beyond or over beings, which aims to recover them as such and as a whole for our grasp.'[2] For Heidegger, then, metaphysics stands for a way of thinking that seeks to 'grasp' and stand 'over' and it is this way of thinking that has developed into modern scientific rationality, or what Heidegger calls 'calculative thinking.' Grant agreed with Heidegger that the Enlightenment has seen modern science reduce all thinking to calculative thought. Calculative thought is the human way of thinking that construes reality as material for human control. As such, reality becomes value-free material. We have purposes to impose on it, but it imposes no purposes on us. Grant agreed with Heidegger's Nietzschean analysis that there was a controlling motive behind all human attempts to know the world.

The calculative thinking that characterizes modern science is itself only possible on the basis of having a subject that can calculate and a 'world' or object that is 'placed before' it, a world that is easily manipulated, controlled, and contained. Heidegger called this world technology. For Grant, metaphysics, calculative thought, and technology were all words and concepts to describe the modern paradigm of knowing which assumes that the subject (me) is able to see everything as an object for consumption and control.[3] If theology meant the study of God and ontology was the philosophical study of Being, then to mix God into philosophy was to undertake the damning practice of 'onto-theology.' Heidegger uses this word 'onto-theology' in his book *Identity and Difference*[4] to describe the effect calculative thinking has on the understanding of God. The onto-theological constitution of metaphysics means that God enters into philosophy but only on philosophy's terms. God becomes the *causa sui*, the logos, the prime ratio – all of which are totalizing projects of human thought. Even the act of 'placing' God at the top of all beings or declaring God to be the highest value is still part of the metaphysical language that sees the human as subject and all else as objects to be controlled. Onto-theology, in short, is simply religion as technology. Grant's reading of Heidegger led him to understand technology as the ontology of the age. But how could Grant maintain his Christian faith and still accept Heidegger's interpretation of the history of Western metaphysics if it all seemed to point to Christianity as the source of modern calculative thought?

It was not until Grant read *The Greek East and Latin West*, a book by a Eastern Orthodox theologian named Philip Sherrard, that he had the theological framework to be able to make sense of Heidegger's critique of Western theology. This book confirmed Grant's view that the ontological errors that corrupted Christianity in modernity were rooted in Western scholastic theology. Grant took fifteen pages of notes while reading Sherrard's study.[5] By drawing from these handwritten notes and from Sherrard's book itself, I will highlight what aspects of the book that Grant found most helpful.

Grant's notes on Sherrard begin by indicating the difference he sees between Aristotle and Plato. Sherrard's book takes us into a discussion of the metaphysical distinction between Being and essence in God and the interrelation of the three persons of the Trinity. From Sherrard, Grant learnt that scholastic metaphysics articulated the nature of the Godhead and the structure of the Trinity in terms that equated God with Being. It was this notion that allowed Grant to wed Heidegger's critique of onto-theology with the Eastern Christian critique of God as pure Being. He also learnt that the doctrinal formulation of God in Greek Christendom, at least of the Patristic period, did not make this same move. Sherrard's book gave Grant additional proof of a latent theology in Eastern Christianity which is Platonic in origin and amenable to his own theological concerns.

In particular, Sherrard's analysis led Grant to think that the Aristotelian version of Christianity dominant in the West had made God too immanent in the world and identified God too closely with necessity, emphasizing his role primarily as first cause and Being himself. This error in the West made God's will scrutable. If God was seen as primarily the first cause, this led to two errors. The first was that the mystery and transcendence of God disappears in favour God's immanence and his knowability through human reason. The second error was that humans see themselves in the image of God as co-creators or masters of their own wills. Sherrard distinguishes Greek and Latin Trinitarian theology along the following lines. Latin Christendom emphasizes, in a non-Platonic fashion, that God as Trinity is both Being and essence undivided and simple. The essential nature of God is not described in scholastic thought as 'pre-ontological, but as a purely ontological, reality – as, in fact, Being itself.'[6] This meant that the scholastic theologians of Latin Christianity took Being and essence in God to refer to the same indistinguishable reality.[7] For this reason, Latin Christianity used philosophical categories such as Being and essence to define the nature of God. They did not take God to be beyond such categories. Sherrard thought that this marked a fundamental difference between Eastern and Western theology. In the East, God's nature transcended any philosophical principle that we may rationally develop to explain the world around us. God's nature was so different and transcendent that it could not ultimately be described by philosophy. In the West, on the other hand, theologians were inclined to reject any 'metaphysical and totally unqualified principle'[8] to describe God because that made God too transcendent.

This disagreement about God's transcendence prejudiced Western theology, Sherrard wrote. Furthermore, it resulted in a 'limitation of vision': 'It cannot be pretended that it does not represent a limitation of vision, in the sense that it implies a far too rational, almost "monist" conception of the divine Unity, and one that excludes, and does not include, the idea of the infinite and inexhaustible profusion of the divine powers and of the multitudinous modes of existence in which they manifest themselves.'[9] In sum, to identify Being and essence in God, and to formulate the divine nature as divine simplicity made God too much the subject of rationality and, in Heidegger's words, committed the error of onto-theology.

Having overemphasized God's immanence in the world, in Sherrard's opinion, the Latin church argued that God revealed himself to us as Being in creation. Because Sherrard drew attention to the fact that scholastic theologians had said that God was primarily the creator, 'the ontological principle of Creation – as, in fact, Being itself,'[10] Grant took it as given that scholastic theology had laid the groundwork for modernity, although perhaps without intent. In emphasizing God's simplicity and expressing a strong inclination towards a theology of divine immanence, the Latin church had set the stage for the fundamental error of modernity, which was to join in rational thought the ontological nature of God with the ontological structure of creation. This was the obvious root of the idea that God's will was scrutable. It was because God's essence and powers were separate that the Greek church could hold, as the Latin church could not, that God was both creator and transcendent.

In Grant's private journal on Sherrard, he speaks much of the importance of guarding against speaking of God as a being like other beings, which was Heidegger's criticism of Western onto-theology. Byzantine Christianity is heir to the apophatic tradition in which contemplation and vision, not intellection and analysis, characterize the theological task. In this apophatic orientation the mystery of God leads to mystical union with him. This negative orientation (apophasis, denial) of unknowing (agnosia) or of learned ignorance begins with the celebration, rather than the rationalistic extermination or explanation, of divine mystery. This Eastern approach to God, which refused to make God into a Being, was another reason why Grant tended to side with Eastern Orthodox theology. God, for the Eastern theologians, was beyond knowing and beyond Being. By making God beyond all Being, they were guarding against any idea of insufficiency in, or limitation of, the divine infinity, falsely imposed by the human intelligence. They were also saying that there was no way of systemizing or completely understanding God's nature. The Patristic fathers, wanting to maintain both God's transcendence and his immanence, taught that one must recognize that in God there must be a distinction between his ultimate nature, or essence, and his uncreated powers and energies. The essence of God is infinite and unknowable; it is entirely simple, totally transcendent of all qualities and determinations, exempt from all change and multiplicity, and, in fact, from all such relative oppositions as those between creator and created, non-existence and existence, Being and Becoming, and so on. It is not according to his essence that God has any relationship with creation, or manifests himself in the multiplicity of created things; it is, on the contrary, according to his essence that he is totally transcendent. Eastern theologians conveyed the immanence of God by talking about his uncreated powers and energies, through which he manifests himself in creation and is present in all that he creates.

Grant learnt from this book how to understand God's essence apart from his hypostatic powers, as do Eastern theologians. He liked the complexity of the Greek account, I believe, because Sherrard's view of the Trinity assisted him in explaining how the first person of the Trinity could be both beyond Being and, through his hypostatic powers, a creator. Thus, it seems that Sherrard's book reinforced his sense that Eastern Christianity was less responsible for the errors of modernity than other schools of Christianity. Insofar as Sherrard indicates why God is not simply Being, in the philosophical sense, he affords Grant a theology of a God who is beyond Being in the Christian tradition and thus shielded from Heidegger's onto-theological critique.

ERICH FRANK: THE JEWISH WISE MAN

Latin Christianity, Sherrard argued, was more deeply imbued with Aristotelianism than with Platonism. Aristotelianism, he said, had drawn Christian theology towards a greater emphasis on God as first cause and, therefore, as immanent in the world. By this reasoning, Grant takes Sherrard to suggest that, through scholastic theology, Aristotelianism is a probable, albeit remote, source of the theoretical errors of modern metaphysical reasoning.

Grant never wrote a piece on the difference between the philosophies of Plato and Aristotle; however, he does make reference in his notes to an author who had. In his private journals he praised an article written by Erich Frank[11] entitled 'The Fundamental Opposition of Plato and Aristotle,'[12] stating that Frank had 'put his own opinion quite well.'[13]

Grant likes Frank's article because it places Plato and Aristotle on opposite sides of a debate about the ability of the philosopher to know the nature of the divine. Frank begins the article by repeating Aristo-

tle's well-known criticism of Plato's ideas: 'Aristotle rejects the transcendence, the *chorismos*, of the ideas, i.e. Plato's conviction that the
true existence, the idea is absolutely separated from the objects of the
world; in their finite, particular, and perishable existence these objects
reflect only in an image, as it were, the eternal and universal subsis-
tence of an unique idea; they "imitate it" and "partake of it" (Aristotle,
Metaphysics, 987b10), without ever being able to reproduce it themselves.'[14] Frank states that Plato considered the forms or ideas to exist in
separation from objects in the world, and that Aristotle took this to be
incorrect because he thought it impossible for the universal nature of a
thing to exist in separation from its particular manifestation and still be
related. (Aristotle argues that the universal concept of dog could not
exist in complete separation from all particular and existent dogs.)
Aristotle, therefore, concludes that the idea is not transcendent, and
places the essential nature of a thing, or its idea, in the thing itself – only
the activity of thought separates the essence of a particular from its
being.[15] From the Aristotelian point of view, knowing the true nature of
something begins with apprehending its phenomenal appearance, and
membership in a genus or species is made apparent upon examination
of the particularities of a substance.

Frank argues that Aristotle's criticism of Platonic metaphysics misses
or dismisses Plato's careful use of the concept of the idea. Plato con-
ceives of the idea as neither universal nor particular, in the sense that
Aristotle used those terms. For one thing, the subsisting idea does not
require unity with existence to be because the subsisting idea has its
own realm of existence that is not subject to the same kind of apprehension which allows one to encounter things in the world. Plato sets up,
in fact, three separate realms of existence: 'the true existence of the idea,
the empirical existence of the sensible world, and between the two the
realm of the mathematical.'[16] To know something by its idea rather
than its material existence requires a specific type of cognitive activity
on the part of the knower. So to know objects that belong to the mathematical realm requires mathematical thinking, and to know ideas
requires dialectic.

In Frank's account, Plato said that the three spheres of existence are
related analogically rather than existentially. This means that the idea
and its reflection are related through their essential nature rather than
their mode of existence. For example, according to Plato, the mathema-
tician knows that the geometrically conceived triangle is related to the
drawn triangle by analogy, despite the fact that one exists only in

thought and the other is apprehended by the senses. The two triangles correspond to each other in name only; Frank states that for Plato 'it is the name alone that [the three modes of existence] have in common; they are "homonymous" as Plato himself says (*Parmenides* 133d; *Phaedrus* 266a, *Philebus* 57b–d).'[17] The example from geometry is important to understanding Plato since the Good is related to ideas in the same way as a triangle in thought is related to a drawn triangle. Frank comments that 'it is only by "analogy" (*Republic* 534a) with the objects of Pythagorean mathematics that Socrates can explain the ontological character of the idea of the *agathon*. As the mathematical ideas, apprehensible in the thinking of the *dianoia*, stand to the perceptible, so the ideas and the agathon ... stand to the mathematical objects.'[18] Plato applies the principle active in geometrical reasoning across the board to all forms of knowledge. The importance of defining reason as analogical allows Plato to talk of the Good as 'true being' and at the same time not deny the existence or being of things in the material world.

By this adaptation of the principles of analogical reasoning, Plato distinguishes 'true being' or the Good from the world. 'True being' exists but is known by analogy to the forms that are eternal, immaterial, and intelligible. Aristotle, on the other hand, applies the principles of logic to the nature of being. That means that Aristotle applies one type of reasoning to all existing things and makes the first principle more intelligible to logos than had Plato in speaking of the Idea of the Good. This difference between Plato's multiform use of the word being and Aristotle's uniform use is important to Frank because he argues that Aristotle's use of logical reasoning marks a major difference from Plato. Plato and Aristotle differ, therefore, as to whether Good or true being is made comprehensible by simple apprehension of the material world. As Frank puts the question, they force one to consider 'whether the true being, God, is beyond this world and therefore also beyond the being of the philosopher himself or whether it is within himself, adequately intelligible to his own thought and intuition.'[19]

Whether or not Frank's analysis is entirely fair to the subtlety of Aristotle's thought may be a matter of debate, but from it he drew certain conclusions. Frank argues that, as a result of their difference about the relation of form/idea to matter, a tension existed between Plato and Aristotle as to how the philosopher can know the divine. Frank said that, in comparing their work, one finds a contrast between philosophy described as 'theoretical objectivity' and philosophy described as an 'ethico-religious experience.'[20] If true knowledge results from 'theoretical objectivity,' then the philosopher should strive primarily to understand phenomena by placing it in categories amenable to logos. On the other hand, to speak of philosophy as an 'ethico-religious experience' implies that the knower must dispose his soul towards the ideas and the Good prior to knowing; the knower must adapt his way of knowing to the thing known. For Plato, logos must include the category of ethics.

Frank concludes that, because Aristotle takes *ousia* or substance to be a combination of essence and existence, he has greater confidence in the ability of the human mind to know the essential nature of things than Plato. That means that Aristotle considers the idea or divine source of life to be sufficiently immanent in the world to be intelligible to the philosopher. Because Aristotle places the universal 'in the seed itself,'[21] as Frank puts it, he changes the relation of mind to nature in the philosophical quest; nature is made an object of theory rather than theory being a source of revelatory experience through participation in the divine. For Grant, we have in this difference between Plato and Aristotle a diverting of the ethical content of Greek philosophy. This is important for the later question of where metaphysics/technology begins.

Frank's argument about the fundamental difference between Plato and Aristotle's account of essence or form suggested to Grant that Aristotle took an important step towards making the divine principle adequate to human reason. The argument undoubtedly impressed Grant and made him wonder if Aristotle's notion of substance could be linked to the rise of technological modernity. At the very least, Grant would have noticed that Aristotle, as described by Frank, held a metaphysical account of the divine which was antithetical to the Good as beyond being.

As a Platonist, Grant found himself drawn to an understanding of the Good that gave ethical content to Being and provided limits for unaided human reason. Grant would often quote from Plato's *Republic* that the Good is 'beyond Being' (*epekena tes ousias*) [509B].[22] He said that he interpreted 'Plato as unequivocally believing in the One or the Good as transcendent – that which is the supreme object of our love is absent. Let me quote to you the Republic 508–509. What does it mean to say that the highest object of desire and of intellect is ultimately unknowable? God's essence is unknowable. The One or the Good or God is beyond knowledge.'[23]

For Grant, it is only when the Good is understood as 'beyond' and uniting both Being and reason that love rather than science or an ethically neutral openness to Being can be understood as the height of humanity. If Plato argues, as Grant suggests, that the Good is 'beyond Being' and that which one seeks through love, then to seek the Good by objective reasoning would be to miss it. For Grant, the Good is not subject to human reasoning; instead we are subject to its rule. It is both the author of the human constitution and its end.

This is also why, for Grant, Heidegger sides with Aristotle on this distinction.[24] It is also the case that, whereas Heidegger's account of the idea of the Good 'asserts an ontology which excludes what is essential about justice,'[25] our task as thinkers, at least following Plato's *Republic*, surely is, says Grant, not only to develop an ontology, but to develop an ontology that carries in itself the essence of justice.[26] Grant takes the *Republic* to teach that, if there were no Good that orders all Being, there would be no possibility of justice between people. He points out how the moderns use the word Good: 'Goodness is now apprehended as a way which excludes from it all "owingness." The traditional western view of goodness is that which meets us with an excluding claim and persuades us that in obedience to that claim we will find what we are fitted for. The modern view of goodness is that which is advantageous to our creating richness of life or ... 'quality of life.' What is true of the modern conception of goodness ... is that it does not include the assertion of an owed claim which is intrinsic to our desiring. Owing is always provisory upon what we desire to create.'[27]

In a personal letter to a friend concerning his upcoming sabbatical, Grant writes that during his leave he planned on writing about 'the reasons why Plato's account of good seems preferable to Aristotle's.'[28] If Frank is correct, then from the beginning of Western thought there is a deep divide about the relation of philosophy to justice, and Grant would clearly side with Plato in such a debate.

DOSTOVESKY: THE RUSSIAN WISE MAN

I end this chapter with an explication of a lecture that Grant gave on Christianity in 1976. Until this point in his career, Grant had avoided giving explicit content to his own theological position. The lecture was the fifth in a series of five addressing the question 'What Is Christianity?'[29] and focused on Grant's reading of Dostoevsky's passage on the Grand Inquisitor in the novel *The Brothers Karamazov*.

In this lecture Grant begins by stressing the distinction between Christianity and 'a particular species of Christianity – Western Christianity' (15). In his mind, this species of Christianity stands for a 'way of civilization which centres in the North Atlantic, France, Germany, Holland, England' (15) and is bound together by a way of thinking that has arisen from both Catholicism and Protestantism. According to Grant, the passage dealing with the Grand Inquisitor in *The Brother Karamazov* is about 'Dostoevsky's attack on Western Christianity in the name of Christ' (16). Grant is drawn to Dostoevsky because he sees in the Russian novelist's Eastern Orthodoxy a way to critique Western Christianity while still holding on to his faith in Christ.

'The Grand Inquisitor' is the fifth chapter of Book V of *The Brothers Karamazov*. Set in Seville during the days of the Inquisition, the story describes how Jesus himself comes back to earth the day after a hundred heretics have been burned in his own name.[30] Even though he arrived quietly, people are inexplicably drawn to him. He begins to attract crowds and is eventually noticed by the Grand Inquisitor, an old man of almost ninety. The Inquisitor recognizes Jesus at once and has him arrested, thrown in jail, and scheduled to be burned as a heretic. Why was Jesus to be killed again? He should be killed, according to the Inquisitor, because he would have hindered the church's work.

The Grand Inquisitor extract is a story one brother tells another. As Grant says, it is about 'the meeting of the Grand Inquisitor and Christ, and it turns on an account of Christ's temptation in the wilderness, the three great temptations from Matthew chapter 4' (235). Grant notes that, before reading the passage, you must be aware that Dostoevsky intentionally uses ambiguity and double meanings to make his point. Grant points out that in the passage 'Christ only does two things – he heals somebody at the beginning, and kisses the Grand Inquisitor at the end' (235). There are no words spoken, only silence. This understanding of the 'silence of truth' (235) was important for Grant because it represented the apophathic theological tradition that begins with a conscious awareness of God's radical transcendence and the total inadequacy of linguistic concepts to apprehend his essential nature. Grant, affirming the Eastern Orthodox position, said that he interpreted 'Plato as unequivocally believing in the One or the Good as transcendent – that which is the supreme object of our love is absent ... To put it in theological terms, God's essence is unknowable. This is the idea that the One or the Good or God is beyond knowledge.'[31] For Grant, Aristotle represents the beginning of the scholastic tradition that would flower in Middle Ages, be furthered by Descartes, achieve dominance through the scientific method during the Enlightenment, and find its final expression in modern technology.

As Grant moves further in his explication of the Grand Inquisitor, he notes that Dostoevsky puts a powerful case in the mouth of his character. This case, he says, 'is to Dostoevsky the case of Western Christianity in all its dynamism, and attraction and exclusivity – put forward most clearly' (235). The Grand Inquisitor uses the three temptations of Christ (turning stones to bread, jumping off the temple, and taking over all the powers of the state) to show how Christ was wrong not to have done these things. Grant argues that, according to the Grand Inquisitor, if Christ had given into these temptations he would have 'built a world where all people were comfortable and happy' (235). The great mistake and evil was that Christ tried to lead human beings away from worldly happiness by saying that there is something deeper than the pleasure that is being lost. Grant explains:

Western Christianity, according to the Grand Inquisitor, has corrected that mistake of Christ's. It has made human beings happy, by giving them bread and miracles, and authority. Those are what human beings want and need, and Western Christianity has provided them with that. It took over the power of the state and gave them what they wanted. What they wanted was to live in a harmonious ant-hill, and this is what Western Christianity has achieved – and what Christ threatened by offering them freedom. What men wanted was to get rid of their freedom – to give up their freedom of conscience – so that they would have the comfort of living securely in the world – where they do not need to think or to be uncertain, and where they live with the certainty of authority. (236)

The Grand Inquisitor says that Christ was wrong not to give people earthly bread, earthly authority, and earthly entertainment. Grant notes that the power of the Grand Inquisitor's case lies in his understanding of the power of technology. For Grant, technology as a way of thinking arose because of Western Christianity's goal of easing man's burden. He struggled with the hegemonous power of technology as a force that silenced all other ways of thinking; he would often comment that he found it hard to critique technology as ontology when it produced something so helpful as the machine that allowed his wife to wash the clothes of their six children.[32] Grant was not a Luddite; instead, he held that technology as ontology produced a way of thinking that sought only man's comfort through control. To get that, Grant notes, 'does he not need bread, and to get that does he not need beyond bread, entertainment, and to achieve that does he not need authority to keep things in order, so that he can enjoy things on earth?' (236). Grant saw the modern way of life as rooted in modern Western liberal capitalism, itself a product of Western Christianity. Drawing from Alexander Kojève,[33] he refers to this as the 'universal homogenous state' where all are equal and everyone's needs are met. In Grant's most mature position on Hegel's notion of the 'End of History,' as seen in his addendum to his essay *Two Theological Languages*, he recognized just how destructive to faith Western metaphysics and technology really are.[34]

Grant's main argument is that, although the onto-theology of Western Christianity has produced the universal homogenous state, it is still associated with power and will, and although it seeks to address all of the human needs, it ends up enslaving humans by taking their freedom. It is on this point that Grant asks, 'What does Dostoevsky mean by the freedom that Christ offered them, and which the Grand Inquisitor says a good society must get rid of?' (237). Grant believes that the Grand Inquisitor needs to mask the fact that freedom is being taken away. He notes that, because we live within the society that the Grand Inquisitor offers us, it is hard to see what is absent.

For Grant, the most important concept for humans to understand is freedom.[35] In the West, he says, freedom means something external. It is a notion deeply connected with will and the absence of anything blocking our will or choice. In a modern liberal-capitalist society, the language of individual freedom and rights is ultimate. This is what is at the core of liberalism – external freedom to do and make yourself in any way you choose. Grant states that the modern notion of freedom is about 'calculation of self-interest.'[36] As epitomized by the Grand Inquisitor it means 'an unlimited freedom to make the world as we want in a universe indifferent to what purposes we choose.'[37] It is a freedom *from* something. It is this notion of freedom that Grant sees as problematic and eventually producing a form of tyranny and slavery where all individuals are subject to sameness and mediocrity. Even modernity's sharpest critiques, such as Nietzsche and Heidegger, still end up rejecting Enlightenment rationality in the name of the individual's right to be free from control or power. For Grant, this radical anarchist tradition was just another form of modern liberalism with its pursuit of individual freedom. Such a freedom was false and did not necessarily produce justice.

Grant saw that the Eastern, more Platonic tradition regarded freedom in a different way. It spoke of the *freedom for* something, that humans are free to live within an order, whereas, Grant notes, within 'the universal homogeneous state ... people would still be left with a question, unanswerable in its own terms: how do we know what is worth doing with our freedom?'[38] What was the modern person lacked was true freedom. It was on this question that we can most clearly see Grant's position regarding the distance between Athens and Jerusalem. In the end he sided with Jerusalem and Christ because he believed that only Christ could offer an understanding of freedom that was beyond modern notions of individual rights and autonomy. Western calculative technology is the human answer to suffering. Christ's solution, in contrast to the Inquisitor's, is one of co-suffering love. There is no direct doctrinal answer to this issue. Instead, Christ approaches the old man in silence and kisses him on the lips. Commenting on this passage, Travis Kroeker notes that 'the response required is to hand the self over in an obedient trust that temporally embraces the offering of eternal, divine love, offering in turn to share it actively with others in the superabundant economy of divine fullness.'[39] This is the kind of freedom that Christ offers, one that is gained only through loss. Or, to put the matter another way, it is found only when it is lost. In handing over the self to the mystery of God, one finds a freedom to love.

Grant argues that what Christ offers is freedom for love and the other rather than freedom for self. For Grant, freedom often makes many demands on us. It is full of responsibilities. The freedom that had been lost in the modern world was the freedom for Good. It was an ethical freedom that was rooted in notions of justice and responsibility to the 'other.' Justice was treated and defined under the calculative thinking of the West according to what each individual saw as being in his or her self-interest. Modern liberalism has defined freedom in an external way, referring to one's power to make and control.[40] But, argues Grant, 'this external freedom is not what Dostoevsky means by freedom. The Russian word for freedom is "sroboden," and it is nearly the same as the word for God' (237). Grant goes on to end his final lecture on Christianity with an explanation of what he thinks the freedom that Christ offers really is. He says, 'I think what he means by freedom or sroboden is best translated as "openness to eternity." But you must think about that. What the Grant Inquisitor offers humans beings is everything except that freedom which I have translated as openness to eternity'[41] (237). Here we have Grant's most mature understanding of the relation between Athens and Jerusalem. In contrast to Heidegger, who would argue that the problem of Western metaphysics began with Plato, Grant would defend Plato and instead say that the problem began with Aristotle. This is why Grant believes that Eastern Christianity was superior: it synthesized Plato and Christian Orthodoxy without falling prey to Heidegger's critique of onto-theology. In contrast to Athens and its progeny – the West – Grant looked to the kenotic, self-emptying love that he believed characterized Jerusalem and the East.

I have argued that Grant, drawing from Heidegger's critique of Western metaphysics, finds in the Eastern Christian tradition a corrective to the practice of religion in our modern or postmodern era. By moving away from onto-theological expressions of power, and avoiding Nietzschean religions of violence and will, Grant ends up with a faith guided by a love that expresses itself in self-emptying justice. It is through the living out of this corrective that Grant seeks to create space for a language and understanding of the 'Other.'[42] Overcoming Western metaphysics or onto-theology in such a way, Grant believed, offers a renewed place for ethics, God, and the Good. By rooting his thinking in the Eastern Orthodox notions of co-suffering love, Grant is able to ward off the calculative reductionism of modern science and the morally neutral response that leaves no place for justice. His understanding of justice leads one to obedience but this is not an obedience that is blind and destructive to individual freedom. Instead, it is obedience to that which is lovable. It consents to otherness because it sees the other as lovable.

Grant says that 'for Plato the opposite of knowledge is not ignorance, but madness, and the nearest he can come to an example of complete madness is the tyrant, because in that case otherness has disappeared as much as can be imagined.'[43] The religious tyrant is the embodiment of onto-theological systems of power and control, of a religion of violence, a self-serving religion that fails to value otherness and practise justice. Grant used three wise men from the East – Sherrard, Frank, and Dostoyevsky – to mount a defence against the religious madness of Western onto-theology.

NOTES

1 This is the opening line in Grant's notes on Philip Sherrard's book *The Greek East and Latin West* (Oxford: Oxford University Press, 1959).
2 Martin Heidegger, *Basic Writings* (San Francisco: Harper Collins, 1993), 106.
3 George Grant, 'Thinking about Technology,' in *Technology and Justice* (Toronto: Anansi, 1986), 32.

4 See Martin Heidegger, *Identity and Difference* (Chicago: University of Chicago Press, 2002), 54.

5 I obtained these unpublished notes from Mrs Sheila Grant's private collection in May 2002.

6 Sherrard, *The Greek East and the Latin West*, 68

7 The term 'being' refers to that which is, the individuality of a thing. 'Essence' refers to the type of thing something is. Plato's term 'form' is used interchangeably with 'essence.' Thus, for Latin theology, God is essentially divine in nature but also is or exists, a being.

8 Sherrard, *The Greek East and the Latin West*, 60

9 Ibid., 71.

10 Ibid., 60.

11 Erich Frank had taken over the chair of philosophy at the University of Marburg in 1928 when it was vacated by Heidegger. Hans-Georg Gadamer succeeded Frank after Frank, a Jew, was forced to resign in 1935 on account of Nazi pressure. Frank then moved to Harvard where he ended his career.

12 Erich Frank, 'The Fundamental Opposition between Plato and Aristotle,' *American Journal of Philology*, 61/1, no. 241 (1940): 34–43, and 2, no. 242 (1940): 168–85.

13 George Grant, 'Notebook for a class on Simone Weil,' McMaster University, 1975–6. I surmise that he first learned of this article upon seeing a reference to it in Leo Strauss's 'On a New Interpretation of Plato's Political Philosophy,' *Social Research* 13, no. 3 (1946): 348.

14 Frank, 'The Fundamental Opposition between Plato and Aristotle,' *American Journal of Philology* 61/1, no. 241, 34.

15 Ibid., 38.

16 Frank, 'The Fundamental Opposition between Plato and Aristotle,' *American Journal of Philology* 61/2, no. 242, 174.

17 Ibid., 169.

18 Frank, 'The Fundamental Opposition between Plato and Aristotle,' *American Journal of Philology* 61/1, no. 241, 50.

19 Ibid., 35.

20 Frank, 'The Fundamental Opposition between Plato and Aristotle,' *American Journal of Philology* 61/2, no. 242, 182.

21 Frank, 'The Fundamental Opposition between Plato and Aristotle,' *American Journal of Philology* 61/1, no. 241, 53.

22 G.M.A. Grube, in *Plato: Republic* (Indianapolis, IN: Hackett Publishing, 1992) translates 509b as: 'Therefore, you should also say that not only do the objects of knowledge owe their being known to the good, but their beings is also due it, although the good is not being, but superior to it in rank and

power' (182). *In the Republic of Plato* (Oxford: Oxford University Press, 1945). Francis MacDonald Cornford translates 509b as 'And so with the objects of knowledge: these derive from the Good not only their power of being known, but their very being and reality; and Goodness is not the same thing as being, but even beyond being, surpassing it in dignity and power' (220). George Grant often quoted from Eric Voeglin's book, *Plato* (Baton Rouge: Louisana State University Press, 1966), where he says, 'The Agathon (good) not only makes objects knowable, but provides them with their existence and essence, though it is itself beyond (epekeina) essence in dignity and power. The epekeina is Plato's term for "beyond" or "transcendent"' (113).

23 George Grant, *The George Grant Reader*, ed. William Christian and Sheila Grant (Toronto: University of Toronto Press, 1998), 209–10.

24 Frank's conclusions about Aristotle were reinforced by Grant's reading of Martin Heidegger because both Aristotle and Heidegger did not place the Good beyond Being. See the discussion later in this essay.

25 George Grant, 'Justice and Technology,' in *Theology and Technology: Essays in Christian Analysis and Exegesis*, ed. Carl Mitcham and Jim Grote (Lanham, MD: University Press of America, 1984), 243.

26 Ibid., 243.

27 George Grant, 'The computer does not impose ...' in Christian and Grant, *George Grant Reader*, 429.

28 Collected letters (in author's possession), 21 October 1975.

29 George Grant, 'What Is Christianity?' Notebook F, George Grant Personal Papers, in the possession of Sheila Grant, Halifax. These notes are included in the current volume as chapter 12. The page numbers in brackets refer to this version.

30 Jesus is never addressed by name. The Inquisitor always refers to him as 'thee' or 'thou.'

31 Christian and Grant, eds., *The George Grant Reader*, 209–10.

32 See David Cayley, *George Grant in Conversation* (Don Mills, ON: Anansi, 1995), 78.

33 See Grant's essay 'Tyranny and Wisdom,' in *Technology and Empire: Perspectives on North America* (Toronto: House of Anansi, 1969).

34 See Grant's addendum in 1988 to his article 'Two Theological Languages' where he reverses his prior acceptance of Hegel's notion of the end of history. The article is found in *Two Theological Languages / by George Grant; and Other Essays in Honour of His Work*, ed. Wayne Whillier (Lewiston, NY: Edwin Mellen Press, 1990).

35 'Lectures on Christianity,' 1976, Notebook A, 24, McMaster University.

36 George Grant, *English-Speaking Justice* (Toronto: Anansi, 1998), 45.

37 *Technology and Empire*, 138.

38 Ibid.

39 Travis Kroeker, *Remembering the End: Dostoevsky as Prophet to Modernity* (Boulder, CO: Westview Press, 2001), 260.

40 See Grant's essay 'Abortion and Rights,' in *Technology and Justice*, 177–85.

41 Although Grant appears to use Dostevesky's phrase 'openness to eternity' interchangeably throughout his journals with Heidegger's phrase 'openness to mystery' he believed that Heidegger did not place enough ethical content into this phrase. See his journal on Simone Weil, (George Grant Personal Papers), 11, 15, 33. This phrase 'openness to mystery,' from the German *die Offenheit für das Geheimnis*, appears throughout Heidegger's essay *What Is thinking?*

42 Grant's turn to the writings of Simone Weil echoes his desire to ground his thinking in Jerusalem and kenotic notions of love. His use of words like attention, owingness, and obedience was his attempt to find a language that was not grounded in Western metaphysical notions of control and objectification. See Pam McCaroll's chapter in this volume.

43 George Grant, 'Faith and the Multiversity,' in *Technology and Justice*, 467.

14

Waiting at the Foot of the Cross: The Spirituality of George Grant

HARRIS ATHANASIADIS

George Grant is well known as a political philosopher, a Canadian nationalist, a critic of technological globalization, and an activist on certain social and ethical issues. More recently, the significance of Grant's Christianity and the theological foundations of his Christianity have become the subject of writing and reflection. But what about George Grant's spirituality? Does Grant have a spirituality, and, if so, how is it manifested? Is it the kind of spirituality that influences his thought and perspective on the world and life as a whole? This chapter is intended to offer an answer to such questions. I maintain that George Grant does have a spirituality, and it is the type of spirituality that undergirds his thought and the ways his thought shapes his perspective on being and acting in the world. More than this, Grant's spirituality grounds him and nourishes him with the kind of hope rooted in love which helps him exist in a world alienated from the divine.

But in order to begin to understand and appreciate Grant's spirituality, we need to understand what spirituality is and to appreciate the particular roots of Grant's spirituality. Spirituality is about experiencing the sacred and the sacred is something that is known as other than us while at the same time penetrating us. We encounter the sacred within us but the sacred we encounter within us is greater than us, transcending us and opening us to otherness as that which is beautiful and good. George Grant has such an experience of the sacred and this experience shapes his thought as well as the critical and practical implications of his thought.

Experiencing the sacred, however, is not enough. In addition to establishing the experience of the sacred as the basis for genuine contemplation, it is essential that there be critical contemplation on the experience of the sacred. How does one know one's experience of the sacred to be true? What are the criteria? Grant not only experiences the sacred in a powerful and dramatic way, he also derives important criteria that help define the true nature of the sacred and, therefore, the true content of the experience of the sacred. But in order to situate Grant's experience of the sacred and the critical criteria he derives for such experience, we must distinguish Grant's spirituality from two alternative spiritualities that continue to find advocates in the world today.

The first type of spirituality has broad roots in Neoplatonism, Epicureanism, and certain forms of Gnosticism such as Manichaeism. This type of spirituality believes that evil and suffering in the world are to be identified with the material and physical dimensions of reality. In order to overcome evil and suffering, and in order to be wedded to the sacred, one must find ways to escape, transcend, overcome, or become detached from the material, social world with all its volatile and unpredictable ebb and flow. In modern expressions of such a spirituality, be they of a 'new age' or religious/fundamentalist variety, the goal of union with the sacred must involve the discovery of a level of peace or love that is not shaken or affected by the behaviour and attitudes of others or the conflicts and tragedies of the world. Grant, as we shall see below, cannot contemplate a peace, love, or union with the sacred that involves any movement away from the 'messiness' of life lived fully in a world made up of 'botched and bungled' human beings of which he is one. Quite the contrary. He comes to discover the truth of love as our spiritual vocation as human beings, focused on 'otherness' in all its specificity, with a spirit of openness, attention, and consent. He comes to such a place, moreover, through an intentional movement in spirit and thought towards the messiness of the world rather than away from it. Often referring to Plato's 'allegory of the cave,'[1] Grant believes that, as a person is enlightened and refreshed in the sunlight of the Good (Plato) or God (the Bible) through a spiritual ascent, he or she is then compelled to descend once again into the cave in order to 'bring to light the darkness as darkness'[2] and to reflect *via negativa* the source of the light which can never ultimately be extinguished by the darkness.

A second type of spirituality is exemplified by modern Western liberalism in its many theological and philosophical forms, with some roots in ancient mystery religions and the Greek Dionysian cult. This type of spirituality represents an uncritical embrace of the world 'as it is'[3] by portraying it and believing it to be otherwise than it is. Whether expressed in culture through various art forms, political and social movements, the expansion of science and technology, or a certain progressive optimism and triumphalism about the historical flow of civilization, the sacred is believed to be progressively realized in history and represented in various cultural, practical, and intellectual achievements in the here and now. The benefits of such a 'faith,' and the spiritual expressions to which it has given birth, are that it has been the source for many a justice movement as well as the basis for changing the status quo and overcoming age-old oppressions rooted in age-old beliefs about nature and human society. Nonetheless, the uncritical embrace of a progressively evolving culture, society, history, or world has also led to a fearful blindness to new forms of oppression and injustice of immense proportions, a blindness that has unwittingly precipitated new arteries for the very evils sought to be overcome. Grant, as we shall also see below, is not only committed to bringing to light the darkness as darkness in the world, because this is the way the world is and there is no authentic way to the sacred without passing through the world as it is; he is also committed to bringing to light the darkness as darkness because this is the only way to avoid the kind of illusory optimism and false triumphalism that has led, and promises to lead even further, towards fearfully destructive directions for the individual and the collective whole.[4] The experience of the sacred must be true to reality if it is to be true to the 'whole.'[5]

Thus, even though Grant agrees with any form of thought that places the experience of the sacred as fundamental for thinking about the truth of the whole, the content of such experience is another matter. From his earliest years as a graduate student, Grant struggled to come to terms with the liberal heritage of his progenitors in the face of twentieth-century war. In selecting a thesis topic for his doctoral dissertation, Grant focused on the best that liberalism has to offer to a world which cannot make sense of optimistic appraisals of human nature and destiny. John Oman was liberal in spirit and a theologian in mind and heart who took the experience of the sacred as fundamental for thought about the truth of the whole. But, as a disciple of Friederich Schliermacher, Oman tended towards the second type of spirituality described above, although he also wrestled with the difficulty of experiencing divine redemption in a world that so often crushed the human spirit. In spite of Oman's wrestling, however, Grant criticizes him as having failed, just as liberalism in general has failed, to do justice to the human condition in the world and therefore, to the content of the authentic experience of the sacred. This view is especially evident in Grant's criticism of Oman's interpretation of the crucifixion of Christ as the experience of divine redemption. Grant accuses Oman of not appreciating the experience of the afflicted, the sceptic, and the defeated. To speak about Christ offering the forgiveness of God as something those at the foot of the cross can simply embrace by an act of the will, Grant believed, does violence to the truth of experience wherein a person can become so crushed by circumstances that forgiveness or the larger love of God – in whatever form it can be appropriated and known – cannot be touched in a way that heals and redeems.[6] The focus on the cross, then, becomes a key means for Grant to speak about the primacy of experience for knowing and doing, as well as the critical content of such experience.

This perspective is well reflected in comments that Grant made in an interview with David Cayley: 'It has been my life to ask about the best way to think the truth of the gospels ... Obviously, we don't know what the life of Christ may have had that we are not given in the gospels, but going to the cross is not an act of philosophy, is it? There doesn't seem to be much philosophy in the gospels; and if you want to think of the gospels in relation to the rest of the world, you at least need some coherent discourse with which to think about it. This is why theologians have used philosophy, isn't it?'[7] Philosophy or thought, then, is second-order reflection on a more first-order experience of the Good. The experience of the Good, moreover, must itself be shaped critically and inspired constructively by a 'going' to and abiding at the foot of the cross.

The focus of faith's experience on Christ and the cross is highly significant for Grant. It is in Christ crucified that the sacred/Good that is God is most powerfully experienced, and it is in Christ crucified that the criteria for critical reflection on experience are derived. How so? Grant's appreciation for Christ's journey culminating at 'Gethsemane and Golgotha'[8] as the basis for an authentic experience of faith in the Good/God is tied up with his own personal experience during the Second World War. Grant grew up as part of an educated Canadian elite in the first half of the twentieth century. As British imperialists, the members of this elite saw the fate of Europe during the two World Wars as deeply intertwined with their own sense of destiny and hope for the world. This hope was an amalgam of secularized Christian progressivism, evolutionary theory, and a Calvinist sense of the destiny of the elect to create the conditions for God's kingdom to come and God's will to be done on earth as it was in heaven. From the highpoint of British power and social optimism at the beginning of the century, however, the World Wars had the effect of eating into the progressive optimism so inherent among a significant segment of the Canadian educated elite, and leaving in its place a mix of anxious urgency and fearful responsibility, on the one hand, and a growing cynicism and disillusionment, on the other. For a sensitive soul such as Grant, the World Wars had the cumulative effect of bringing him to his knees spiritually. The progressive faith of his progenitors in a world of peace and stability, under the political and spiritual leadership of a British imperial federation of nations, gave way to an overwhelming sense of dread because of the capability and inclination of corruptible human beings to destroy the earth many times over with the new powers of science and technology in their grasp.

How this manifested itself personally in Grant's life was through his involvement in the war effort. Even though he himself participated in a non-violent way as an air raids precaution officer, what he witnessed during the bombing of London left him shattered in body and in spirit.[9] The shocking and unexpected experience in Grant's interior life, however, was not so much the truth of human suffering and anguish to which he was opened up in a first-hand way. Rather, at the very point he was breaking up internally into pieces, he was opened up to a powerful and overwhelming experience of the sacred. After the air raids ended, Grant's job was no longer necessary and his health became fragile. He got a job making deliveries, which kept him busy in spite of the inner disorientation and helplessness that possessed him. One day he was riding a bicycle, making a delivery to a farm in the countryside outside London. As he entered the farm, he opened the front gate and suddenly, he said, it came to him that 'God is.' But what did this revelation or insight mean? Reflecting on this experience later in life, Grant explained that he was given to trust deep within that 'all was finally well, that 'beyond time and space there is order,' that 'ultimately the world is not a maniacal chaos.' It was the realization that 'I am not my own' but belong to an "Other."' Writing to his mother, he spoke about experiencing a new birth, of being grasped and taken by mysterious, tremendous, loving forces, drawing him to ecstatic places beyond his control.[10] To trust such an experience as an experience of the Other, and to experience the surge of love flowing through his spiritual veins, becomes an experience that is not easily forgotten or dismissed.

At the same time, this experience does not shift Grant's painful preoccupation with the misery and suffering in the world as he had absorbed it first-hand during the war. He understands early on that there was no rational or causal connection between the experience of suffering and the experience of God. But he also comes to experience how the two together are the fundamental means through which truth about the whole is opened up. Without being opened to the experiential truth of God, the experience of deep suffering is singularly destructive and demeaning. Without entering the experiential truth of suffering to its depths, the experience of God cannot be trusted as real as opposed to some purely subjective world-escapism or a wishful projection of the self. To put it in more Christian revelational terms, the experience of the cross without the resurrection leads to despair, and the experience of the resurrection without the cross cannot but lead to false, triumphalistic, and escapist hope. Given the progressively optimistic liberalism so prevalent around him, the bulk of Grant's work is focused on the prophetic unmasking of false, triumphalistic, escapist hopes, hopes that are dangerous because they are dishonest. But this does not mean, as some have suggested, that Grant does not hold the other side of the experience as true, namely, the experience of resurrection. His concern, consistently, is to open up a way towards such experience that is true to the hard data of the reality of suffering and tragedy in the world.

Moreover, Grant's experience of faith as given in and through the cross involves subjective as well as objective dimensions. In the cross, we are given a mirror into the human soul in relationship to the sacred and into the relationship of the sacred to the human soul and the world. Christ's journey and agony, as well as his triumph, point to the truth of things as absolute and universal, and yet it is the kind of truth that must be entered into personally and subjectively in order to be known fully as such. Yes, experience is primary, but the kind of experience that is primary for faith is experience that is 'regulated by the cross.'[11] For all his love of philosophy and particularly the greatest philosophy of all, that of Plato, Grant discerns an important distinction between the way Jesus dies and the way Socrates dies. In his words: 'Whatever must be said about the consummate serenity and beauty of Socrates at his execution, that scene is not as comprehensively close to the heart of being as are Gethsemane and Golgotha. The appalling admonition "take up your cross and follow me" cuts to the heart of our existing and indeed to the heart of both being and goodness.'[12] The distinction of deaths has as much to do with the revelation of truth in Christ's dying (objective) as it does with the experience of one's own personal (subjective) dying through one's own suffering, one's solidarity with the suffering of others, and/or one's being broken/opened to the good and the beauty of otherness.

According to Grant, the uniqueness of the Gospels, and at their centre the crucified Christ, is not in their revelation of the purity of Christ's goodness or love but, rather, how such goodness and love are revealed from out of the depths of affliction. On the cross Christ experiences not only the external agony of suffering but the internal agony of experiencing an aloneness, a rupture of relationship, the absence of God. And it is revelation precisely because the experience of the absence of God does not lead, naturally or causally, to the experience or knowledge of the fullness of God as love. Quite the contrary, it leads to inner defeat or outer rage. Grant's view of the resurrection would very much follow the language of N.T. Wright and Marcus Borg, who describe it as a 'vindication' of the cross.[13] The resurrection vindicates the cross as that moment, that place, that experience out of which all God's blessings flow, including the resurrection of the dead. In Grant's own words: 'The central symbol of Christianity has always been the cross. Clearly in some sense the resurrection takes place on the cross ... Christ says on the cross "it is consummated."'[14] Grant understands his vocation as a thinker from very early on as needing to think through what he was given to experience at that moment when he opened the gate and entered in. Moreover, as has already been said, this experience of God is one that incorporates rather than escapes all the experience of suffering and misery in the world. It points to larger truths, truths that need to be communicated to a world which, whether in the church or outside the church, tends to resist the truth about things as they are. The purpose of speaking the truth, however, is not simply to expose the darkness for what it is. Rather, exposing the darkness for what it is, Grant believes, is essential for cultivating the kind of ground out of which the experience of God can be authentic and true rather than false and idolatrous.

Thus, whether one considers his work as early as his doctoral thesis on John Oman or as late as his last major essay, 'Faith and the Multiversity,' Grant is especially sensitive experientially to two things which become criteria for authentic spirituality and thought. First there is the experience of the tired, the hungry, the diseased; and at the level of spirit there is the experience of the sceptic and the defeated or those who have first hand knowledge of 'suffering, war, torture, disease, starvation, madness and the cruel accidents of existing.'[15] Second, there is the experience of divine grace and revelation, that, in spite of and in full experiential awareness of the reality of suffering and defeat, 'the ultimate cause of being is beneficence,' that beyond the chaos there is order, that beyond doubt there is a deeper trust in the beauty and goodness of all that is. To use Christian revelational terms: beyond the sin and affliction that so cripple body and soul in the world there is the forgiving, redeeming, resurrecting love of God on the cross, open to all who are graciously granted the gift of faithful receptivity.[16]

Given the priority of the cross as a central criterion of truth and the point of departure for any authentic form of thinking, being, and acting in the world, what, we may ask, is the actual content of Grant's spirituality? The title of this chapter offers, I believe, a fundamental basis for the kind of spirituality that grounds and inspires Grant's movement towards the truth of what he is given to know and express in his thought. We have already isolated the cross as a central criterion of truth for Grant. Now we may also add the aspect of 'waiting' as the kind of spiritual posture appropriate to receiving the sacred truth of the transcendent Good as Christ illumined and mediated it on the cross. Grant first came to understand 'waiting' as an attribute of God in relation to human beings in the world. 'God sees the truth but waits,' he wrote shortly after his experiences of war. 'Personally, it is a great emotional discovery – the discovery of God – the first glimpse of that reality – not amateurish or kind – not sentimental or moral, but so beyond our comprehension that the mere glimpse is more than we can bear. God, not as an optimist – nor as the non-mover, but, God, who sees the truth but waits.' Grant went on to list many of the sins of humanity through the nineteenth and tentieth centuries in the idolatrous name of God and country, and through it all, he wrote again, God 'did not intervene, he waited.'[17] What is significant in this early reflection of Grant on the heels of his devastating experience of war is that, beyond the alternatives of passive helplessness or aggressive militance, he discerns a higher way, the way of waiting. Waiting stands over against a false optimism, on the one hand – whether as progressivism or positivism – and over against a 'non-mover,' cheap grace, passive inactivity, on the other. Waiting is intentional and as much focused on *doing* as on contemplative *being* in the face of realities that, from the human side, are experienced as overwhelming in their tragic consequences. Both the doing and the being of God as waiting spring from the depths of God's compassion and forbearance for humanity in the world. God exercises restraint towards humanity caught up in evil as much as it pains God to bear the suffering of the victims of such evil in the world. The concept of God's waiting is intended to draw humanity into the circle of divine love, bringing the perpetrators of evil to repentance and the victims towards a trust in their vindication from the perspective of eternity.

Within a decade of these early reflections on 'waiting,' Grant discovered the writings of Simone Weil, and from her he learnt that the concept of waiting is something that must ground human beings in the world as much as it is an attribute of God's being and acting in relation to humanity in the world. Remarkably, Grant's early reflections find resonance in Weil's insights, helping to develop even further his spirituality of waiting. Weil writes about waiting 'en hypomene,' waiting patiently, without giving in to the desperation of filling in the void or resolving the pain with illusion or false comfort. One must wait without giving in to the intoxication of power as compensation for one's pain in the form of retaliation towards or mastery over others.[18] Such waiting, then, is as much a negative as it is a positive way of being. It involves self-renunciation of or restraint in the use of power or 'force' as well as renunciation of other forms of illusion or false comfort in the name of openness to truth and compassion towards 'otherness.'

Thus, the negative aspect of the spirituality of waiting as self-restraint or self-renunciation is as significant as the positive aspect directed towards otherness in the name of love. Indeed, the negative and the positive complement each other. A primary concern in Grant's criticism of modern liberalism is its worship of freedom without any appreciation for the importance of limit or restraint. In an extended book review of The Secular City by the liberal theologian Harvey Cox, for instance, Grant argues that, without restraint or limit, love toward others easily degenerates into power over others in relationships where equality is not built in.[19] Politically, he criticizes American/Western foreign policy (for example, the Vietnam War) as manifesting this way of being, and, pushed to its logical conclusion it becomes tyrannical in its blindness to the very otherness one is seeking to help in the purported name of love.[20] Waiting, then, involves the loving hesitation of restraint in order to become 'open' to otherness.

The importance of 'openness' is also fundamental to waiting. Openness is directed towards otherness in the world, but it is also inspired by a larger openness to the transcendent Other, the sacred, the Good that is God. Waiting in openness is also waiting in receptivity, knowing that, in the face of the truth of the cross that is in the world, only the power of grace from beyond humanity can inspire and transfigure humanity at the foot of the cross to live in the kind of truth and energy for good that is the only authentic spiritual basis for being and acting in the world.

Openness also involves some critical dimensions. Even as Grant too often experiences good as privation, given the opaqueness of evil and suffering in the world, the spiritual calling of authentic humanity is in 'listening or watching or simply waiting for intimations of deprival which might lead us to see the beautiful as the image, in the world, of the good.'[21] Thus, from the side of negation or 'deprivation,' one waits in openness for a revelation of what is not in the world as it is. One will not settle for anything less or different than the Beautiful and the Good. One waits for such beauty and goodness to be given from above. The alternative to waiting openly in the absence of the Beautiful and the Good is creating one's own images of or substitutes for the Beautiful and the Good, willing them into being and then worshipping them and pursuing them as God.

On the more constructive side, Grant contrasts openness to the 'values' of the contemporary world such as mastery and control. In his words: 'Mastery tries to shape the objects and people around us into a form which suits us. Openness tries to know what things are in themselves, not to impose our categories upon them. Openness acts on the assumption that other things and people have their own goodness in themselves; control believes that the world is essentially neutral stuff which can be made good by human effort.'[22] Waiting and openness go together in that knowledge of otherness must be given to one from beyond oneself so that otherness does not become an object of one's own wish fulfilment motivated by power or pleasure, convenience, or fear. Being open to otherness is 'consenting' to their being other than oneself. To consent to otherness is to let the other be free to be different from oneself. This is a challenge at the best of times and definitely so if there is an inequality of power in the relationship. To let go or renounce the power one has over another in order to allow the other to be, and only then act in relation to the other, is a movement of self-denial that can emerge only from the inspiration of divine grace working through one's heart in 'obedience' to the Good.

Grant uses the words consent and obedience, then, in order to help express the active side of openness in the spirit of waiting. The supreme example of consent in the name of love is Christ. At Gethsemane, Christ 'consents to bear, to accept the full weight of the evil of his day, the full weight of the evil of the Roman Empire, [of the] ecclesiastics of his own race. And think what it cost him: His sweat was, as it were, great drops of blood falling down to the ground.'[23] This aspect of consent is complemented by obedience, which involves a submission to limit in such a way that it serves God's will of love. The truth of limit is the truth of that which is imposed on us against our will. It involves the breaking of our will and our being opened to the otherness of God and creation. And this is precisely where the spiritual mystery is to be found. Christ's suffering is not good in and of itself and neither is the human suffering of limit, be it the limit imposed by the evil of others or the natural movements of the universe upon finite creatures which we all are. Rather, we are called to be open to beauty and goodness, and, given our human tendency to preoccupation and absorption with our own selves, we need to be broken out of ourselves. Weil calls this process 'decreation.' It is the path of being broken/opened to otherness through the imposition of limit, externally and internally, which we are called to consent to and obey. It is in the name of a more authentic love of otherness which also leads to a more authentic love of our true selves as made in God's image – 'out of love and for love' as Weil frames it.

Along with consent and obedience, Grant stresses the importance of attentiveness. In particular, he also uses the word consent to give spiritual content to a more immediate attentiveness towards otherness through which love receives the deepest kind of knowledge of the other. Indeed, he defines love as 'attention to otherness, receptivity of otherness, consent to otherness ...' or, as he put it on another occasion, 'to love' is to pay attention to other people and this means to communicate with them.'[24] Attention focuses on the other and contemplates them in their otherness. Again, one must be broken/opened beyond oneself to focus on the other with loving attention. This being broken/opened, moreover, opens one up to the deepest kind of self-love, a self-love that does not come into conflict with the love of otherness. It is the same love flowing down from above through the one and then the other. It is, as Weil would put it, God loving the other through oneself and receiving God's love back into oneself in this being in relation to the other.

Again, whether one considers the word waiting or the other words Grant uses to describe the qualities of the kind of spirituality of the cross which grounded and inspired his deepest insights, the primary influence of Weil cannot be missed. Waiting at the foot of the cross is about waiting in openness, self-renunciation and restraint, consent, obedience, and attention. It is about waiting in love. And love, as Grant comes to discover in his heart and spirit, is both passive (receptive to revelation and grace beyond oneself) and active whether as self-restraint and renunciation on the one hand (negative) or consenting obedience and attention on the other (positive). Waiting is, to use two more words important to Grant, 'contemplation' inspired by the 'charity' revealed on the cross as much as it is charity inspired by a contemplation of the revelation of Christ on the cross. Or to put it in simpler words borrowed directly from Weil: 'Faith is the experience that the intelligence is enlightened by love.'[25]

In this chapter I have argued that Grant not only possessed a spirituality but was inspired by such a spirituality in how he thought, lived, and loved in the world. As someone whose experience of faith determines the content of his thought, he developed a rich understanding of the nature of experience and how it shapes both thought and action in he world. For him, experience that is true to the Good/God/Whole is the kind of experience regulated by the cross. On the cross, Christ revealed both the agony of the darkness and the beauty of the light of love rising through and beyond the darkness. Any spirituality that is not nourished by the truth of engagement with the darkness as possibility and actuality, as well as by the light of love as disruptive and transfiguring grace, is not true to the revelation of God on the cross. Finally, to those faithful to this revelation, the posture of waiting at the foot of the cross for the light of love is the only authentic path to life lived in the world as an inspiration of God. And the light of love has a shape and content as evinced by words such as openness, restraint and renunciation, consent, obedience, and attention. Waiting is no passive inactivity but active charity wedded to contemplation and contemplation shaped by the transforming experience of sacred charity. May we, too, find our way to the foot of the cross, and may our waiting yield the kind of fruit of love that mediates God's abiding movement through the human spirit, opened to the whole.

NOTES

1 In Plato's 'Republic,' Book VII, *Great Dialogues of Plato*, trans. W.H.D. Rouse (New York: New American Library, 1956), 312ff.

2 George Grant, 'The computer does not impose on us the ways it should be used,' in *Beyond Industrial Growth*, ed. Abraham Rotstein (Toronto: University of Toronto Press, 1976), 128. Other words or phrases in quotation in this paragraph and elsewhere are typically important Grantian expressions.

3 For the significance of this phrase in Grant, see Harris Athanasiadis, *George Grant and the Theology of the Cross: The Christian Foundations of His Thought* (Toronto: University of Toronto Press, 2001), 3–6, 51, 53ff.; also Sheila Grant, 'George Grant and the Theology of the Cross,' in *George Grant and the Sub-*

version of Modernity: Art, Philosophy, Politics, Religion, and Education, ed.
Arthur Davis (Toronto: University of Toronto Press, 1996), 243ff.

4 In particular, Grant has in mind technological expansion/globalization.

5 This is a term that Grant discovers and borrows from Leo Strauss, but he
uses it in a way uniquely his own. For the differences between Strauss and
Grant, see Harris Athanasiadis, 'George Grant, Leo Strauss and the Primacy
of Charity for Contemplation,' in *The Friend: The Red Tory Review* 4 (2002):
19–26.

6 George Grant, *Collected Works of George Grant, Volume 1 (1933–1950),* ed.
Arthur Davis and Peter C. Emberley (Toronto: University of Toronto Press,
2000), 287–9, 355–6, 364.

7 Grant in David Cayley, *George Grant in Conversation* (Don Mills, ON: Anansi,
1995), 60–1.

8 Davis and Emberley, *Collected Works,* 174, 299; See also Sheila Grant, 'George
Grant and the Theology of the Cross,' 255.

9 William Christian, *George Grant: A Biography* (Toronto: University of Toronto
Press, 1993), 69–86; Athanasiadis, *George Grant and the Theology of the Cross,*
7–32.

10 George Grant, 'The Owl and the Dynamo: The Vision of George Grant,'
interview, *CBC-TV Arts, Music, and Science,* 13 February 1980; *George Grant:
Selected Letters,* ed. William Christian (Toronto: University of Toronto Press,
1996), 92; David Cayley, *The Moving Image of Eternity* (Toronto: CBC, 1986), 4;
Larry Schmidt, ed., *George Grant in Process: Essays and Conversations* (Toronto: House of Anansi Press, 1978), 63; Athanasiadis, *George Grant and the
Theology of the Cross,* 16.

11 Davis and Emberley, eds., *Collected Works,* 291, 363.

12 George Grant, 'Addendum,' *Two Theological Languages by George Grant and
Other Essays in Honour of His Work,* ed. Wayne Whillier (Queenston, ON:
Edwin Mellen Press, 1990), 19.

13 N.T. Wright, *Jesus and the Victory of God* (Minneapolis: Fortress Press, 1996),
320ff., and *The Challenge of Jesus: Rediscovering Who Jesus Was and Is*
(Downer's Grove, IL: InterVarsity Press, 1999), 22, 105, 118–19; Marcus Borg,
The Meaning of Jesus: Two Visions (New York: HarperSanFrancisco, 1999),
137–8, and 'From Galilean Jew to the Face of God: The Pre-Easter and the
Post-Easter Jesus,' in Borg, ed., *Jesus at 2000,* (Boulder, CO: Westview Press,
1998), 19.

14 Davis and Emberley, eds., *Collected Works,* 295; Sheila Grant, 'George Grant
and the Theology of the Cross,' 255.

15 Davis and Emberley, eds., *Collected Works,* 352–7; also in George Grant, *Technology and Empire: Perspectives on North America* (Toronto: House of Anansi,
1969), 103, and *Technology and Justice* (Toronto: Anansi, 1986), 42.

16 *Technology and Justice*, 42; Davis and Emberley, eds., *Collected Works*, 294.

17 Christian, *Selected Letters*, 105.

18 Simone Weil, *Waiting on God*, trans. Emma Craufurd (London: Collins, 1951), 51.

19 George Grant, review of Harvey Cox's *The Secular City*, in *United Church Observer* 28, no. 9 (1966): 16–17, 26.

20 George Grant, 'Religion' [1967], George Grant Personal Papers, in the possession of Sheila Grant, Halifax.

21 George Grant, 'A Platitude,' in *Technology and Empire*, 143.

22 Grant, 'Comments on the Great Society from the Thirty-fifth Annual Couchiching Conference,' in *Great Societies and Quiet Revolutions*, ed. John Irwin (Toronto: Canadian Broadcasting Corporation, 1967), 75.

23 George Grant, 'The Rite of Holy Communion,' sermon at McMaster University, Hamilton [early 1960's], George Grant Personal Papers.

24 George Grant, 'Faith and the Multiversity,' *The Compass: A Provincial Review* (Edmonton) no. 4 (1978): 3; review of *The Secular City*, 16.

25 *Technology and Justice*, 38; Simone Weil, *Gravity and Grace*, trans. Emma Craufurd (London: Routledge and Kegan Paul, 1952), 116; *The Notebooks of Simone Weil*, trans. Arthur Wills (London: Routledge and Kegan Paul, 1956), 240.

15

The Whole as Love

PAM MCCARROLL

George Grant was not only a thinker; he was a person of faith. Though Grant did not write much about his faith, much has been written about how his faith, rooted in Christianity, shaped his thought in fundamental ways.[1] In this chapter I build on previous work and show how Grant's faith in 'the Whole'[2] can be discerned as the background scenery and landscape that upholds his thought. It is his faith in the Whole that provides him with a critical location for his political philosophy and cultural critique. 'The Whole' is a term that Grant began to use as early as *Philosophy in the Mass Age*,[3] and more widely after his reading of Leo Strauss. However, it is through his primal relationship with the thought of Simone Weil and her reading of Plato that the content of the Whole takes shape for Grant and ever more deeply integrates and clarifies his faith and thought upon all things.[4]

According to Grant, the Whole includes all of reality – the universe, human and non-human being, and God. The essence of the Whole, however, is love. In a more precise sense, then, the Whole is the vast and intricate network of relationships within the universe and between human and non-human being and God. This network of the Whole is held together by love, visible and invisible. Of course, writing in this way would be foreign to Grant's thinking. The Whole is nowhere in his writing more than suggestive imagery, a canvas upon which he focuses his thought on the particular set of issues in question. However, because the Whole is so essential a concept for Grant, experientially[5] and intellectually, it must be understood by anyone who seeks to engage his thought and its rich legacy to us.

Therefore, in this chapter I will attempt, in broad strokes, to draw around us Grant's Weilian, Platonic scenery of the Whole so as to locate us with him inside the big picture, many parts of which are hidden or merely intimated. The cross of Christ stands at the centre of Grant's understanding of the Whole[6] – the contradiction and distance that divides the realms of necessity and the Good on one level, as well as the love that intimates their unity in the Whole on another. After an initial introduction to Grant's thinking on the Whole, I will explore the distinctions between the realms of necessity and the Good in Grant's thought, both in general terms and by examining Grant's Weilian understanding of force, gravity, and affliction. Finally, with reference to Weil's doctrines of creation and beauty, I will discuss the place of love in his thought as the deepest truth of the Whole, the essence of its oneness.

THINKING ABOUT THE WHOLE – KNOWING AND LOVE

Throughout his corpus Grant regularly contemplates the relationship between knowing and love.[7] It is only in the proper ordering of love and knowledge that the Whole can be discerned with any truth.[8] He challenges us to order our knowing with the Anselmian summons: 'believe so that you may know.'[9] For Grant, 'Simone Weil ... is the supreme teacher of the relation of love and intelligence.'[10] How the Good/God's love[11] is experienced and is faithfully given over to knowledge and language in the realm of necessity is of central concern for both Weil and Grant. A mitigating aspect of Grant's thought, however (which, he says, distinguishes him from the depth of thought found in Weil[12]), is his self-conscious embeddedness in the realm of necessity, the darkness of which is never fully illuminated by the light of God. In Weil he perceives one who experiences moments of utter illumination from outside this realm and whose knowing, consequently, is incisively clear about the depth of the darkness of necessity. For Grant, in contrast, the shadows cast in necessity by the illumination of the Good are always shadows,[13] whose changing shape and depth point *via negativa* to the truth of the light, unknowable in its full splendour. God is the background lighting of Grant's thought, ever behind him, casting shadows at each turn. The language of the Whole enables a way for him to speak about truth as it is both perceived in the shadows of necessity and intuited in the background lighting of the Good.

As I have elaborated, in his understanding of the Whole, Grant includes the realms of necessity and the Good, the world, and God. Conceptually, 'the Whole' underlines what is essential for Grant: that there is a unity of reality and truth. Yet this unity in the Whole does not exist in *ideas* of truth or reality. The unity exists only in the experience of love – love that dwells in the in-between of relationships and verifies itself as the real, the essence of things. As a relational reality, love presupposes contradiction and distance but also relationality and otherness. The Whole as love must not be thought of as simple unity – a reality that is 'scrutable'[14] or knowable by human intellect or will. Nor can it be reduced to an idea or ideal. The truth of the Whole as love is known only in experience – experience that reveals relationality and otherness. In discussing his appreciation for Weil, Grant highlights this point: 'It is impossible to think of God as a simple unity if you say that God is love, because love is always in relation.'[15] Unlike some neo-Platonists who dismiss the sufferings and experiences of the realm of necessity as illusions with no real content, Grant, following Weil, affirms the experience of reality in the realm of necessity, within the larger unknowable connectedness of the Whole. Grant resists the temptation to ignore the horrific reality of suffering in the world or to undermine the weightiness of human experience. At the same time, with Weil, he resists the temptation to consider love as anything less than a network of relations constituting a deeper unity, inscrutable yet real. This unity includes the vast contradictions between the most tragic realities of suffering in the world and a perfect Good beyond it.

This, of course, raises many difficulties: How is it possible to talk about the contrary realities, for example, of human suffering and the love of God without acquiescing to the fragmentation of truth and reality or a distorted sense of divine providence? These contradictions in human thought are addressed head on by both Weil and Grant. For them, the contradictions must remain contradictions to reason. To think otherwise would serve a misguided notion of the scrutability of divine providence wherein tyranny, not love, is served. However, by the disruptive experience of divine love (or faith), also inscrutable to reason and language, the contradiction may be known within the larger Whole which is the love of God. For both thinkers, reason is called to serve truth, which is Christ, rigorously and relentlessly. Thus, the contradictions between the perfection of God and the sufferings of the world must be thought through in agonizing fullness. It is in enucleating such contradiction that thought waits for God and the illumination of love. By faith – the illumination of the mind by love – reason is freed to recognize the contradictions for what they are and to wait upon God within the inarticulate gap between the contradictions. 'Faith is the experience that the intelligence is illumined by love.'

THE CONTRADICTION BETWEEN NECESSITY AND THE GOOD

Although the Platonic understanding of the realms of necessity and the Good is important for Grant's understanding of the Whole from early on,[16] it is in his ongoing dialogue with the writings of Weil that he achieves greatest clarity on the distance/contradiction that divides the realms within the Whole. Grant identifies himself in the tradition of negative theology wherein the distance between God and the world – between perfection and misery – structures his thought.[17] This distance presupposes belief in God as transcendent *to* and absent *in* the world.[18] Thus, faith in God can provide the foundation for thought about the world only in a *hidden* way such that 'the unity which we seek we can neither know in principle or in detail.'[19] Unity is known primarily by its absence, which transcends this realm. Thought is given to recognize this absence in the distance/contradiction between the realms of necessity and the Good. Indeed, for both Grant and Weil, it is in recognizing the distance between the realms that thought waits to receive a glimpse of the Whole in the illumination of a love not of this world.

In focusing *via negativa* on the distance between necessity and the Good,[20] Grant criticizes modern liberalism and the extent to which the collapse of the concept of the eternal into the temporal order (the Good into necessity) is the cause of injustice, moral blindness, and the seemingly relentless compulsion of the human will to change and master the world. His critiques of the modern Western 'will to power' underline the vast distance between the two realms. In toppling the Western illusions of power, Grant brings into focus human limit and affirms the Good as the horizon of eternity, that which limits and relativizes creaturely being.[21] In Grant's provocative critiques of power, he names the illusions of human mastery in our context which manifest the forces of necessity and reveal necessity for what it is: vastly distant from and contradictory to the Good.

Following Weil, Grant understands the world as that which is given over to necessity by God's self-renouncing love.[22] The world is the realm wherein rule the limits of time and space, making it 'other' to God. God is veiled to the world by necessity in the negating dynamics

of force and gravity. Weil describes necessity as 'the mathematical pro-
gression of causes and effects which, from time to time, make of us a
sort of formless jelly.'[23] The character of necessity is indifference to the
Good. Grant comments on and quotes Weil on the distance between the
two realms:

'I am ceaselessly and increasingly torn both in my intelligence and in the depth
of my heart through my inability to conceive simultaneously and in truth, the
affliction of men, the perfection of God and the link between the two.' Or in
other of her words, 'As Plato said, an infinite distance separates the good from
necessity – the essential contradiction in human life is that man, with a strain-
ing after the good constituting his very being, is at the same time subject in his
entire being, both in mind and in flesh, to a blind force, to a necessity completely indifferent to the good.' This contradiction above any other is for her the
means by which the mind is led to truth.[24]

The realm of necessity is the world in all its temporality and change,
dominated by force and the indiscriminate working of chance. In the
realm of necessity God is absent or hidden, except in disruptive revelation. For Grant, of course, the most blasphemous lie of modernity is the
conceptual collapse of the distance between the two realms and the
implied scrutability of God. In modernity, he recognizes the ethical consequences of the conceptual eclipse of the eternal order. The Good has
been emptied of content and collapsed into necessity. Grant sees that
the Nietzschean trajectory of modernity is well under way and that the
'death of God' is recognizable in the fragmentation of relativistic subjectivity. Grant alerts us to a myriad of real-life consequences of the conceptual oblivion of the horizon of eternity. Without recognition of the
horizon of eternity that marks and circumscribes creaturely limit,
morality is impossible.

Naming the Distance in the Whole: Force, Gravity, Affliction

In an effort to explicate further the distance between necessity and the
Good in the Whole, Grant takes up Weil's concepts of force and gravity,
on the one hand, and the human experience of affliction, on the other.
The terms 'necessity' and 'chance' function somewhat interchangeably
for Grant. Most important, he emphasizes the blindness of chance in
necessity and rejects providential language wherein God's activity can
be considered scrutable. He sees the Western (especially Calvinist)

emphasis on providence to be dependent on a flawed picture of God as omnipotent sovereign, instead of a picture of God as love, hanging on a cross. 'Chance,' as a concept, helps explain the indifference of nature to human desire and longing, and the indiscriminate ways of this realm wherein some are brutalized while others are not.

Force and Gravity

Force and gravity are the dynamics of necessity. Force is indifferent to love. It is the character of heartless domination inherent in nature.[25] Force makes slaves not only of those without power but also those with it. Humans are enslaved by force when they no longer are able to exercise their freedom and dignity to consent or to refuse. They are also enslaved by force when they are so intoxicated by it that they cannot recognize their own limits.

Grant's analysis of power, mastery, and control in modernity presupposes Weil's understanding of force and challenges us to recognize our enslavement to force. He asks a rhetorical question: 'Is it possible to look at history and deny that within its dimensions, force is the supreme ruler?' Western modernity, with its presumption of mastery and control over human and non-human nature, is under the grip of force. Indeed, the manifestation and internalization of force in Western society is so complete that we assume that it is force (as the freedom of the will), not love, that we are fitted for. In considering ourselves as the centre of the universe and shaping the world to suit our purposes, the dominant paradigm of the modern West assumes that force over creation is a 'given' of our species. Force is at play when an 'other' ceases to be 'other.' It is that which makes 'things' of everything (i.e., 'objects' in the modern scientific sense). In the North American context, the subject-object dichotomy of modern science has combined so thoroughly with pragmatic utilitarianism that we cannot contemplate things in themselves but only insofar as they can be used to suit our purposes. As such, the universalizing and homogenizing impulses of modernity manifest the same tyrannical tendency as does the objectification of things in modern science. In each instance a subject (be it a state, a research method, a way of knowing, and so on) presupposes power over an 'other' such that the latter ceases to exist as 'other.' Further, the proliferation of this human mastery of the world is embedded within our technology.[26] Grant sees the extent to which Western society has become the tyrant in ceasing to consent to the otherness of B/being.

The essential 'otherness' and beauty of creation has been obscured by our commodification and consumption of it. To contemplate things in themselves implies renouncing one's will to power over the other (human and non-human alike) and the recognition of beauty in the other. By such recognition one is opened, in humility, to loving and knowing the truth of creaturehood.

Grant understands sin in terms of Weil's discussions on gravity. Weil contemplates the properties of physical gravity as a way to consider the distance between the realms of necessity and the Good and as the dynamic which draws us away from the Good. As a dynamic of necessity, gravity controls all the natural movements of the soul.[27] Human obedience to the laws of gravity constitutes sin. As such, sin is turning away and lowering one's vision from the Good and fixing it upon necessity. Clearly, Grant has this conception in mind when he reflects on the many manifestations of sin in the technological society. With God having been collapsed into the world, the transcendent horizon is obscured from view. In modernity we gaze only at the horizontal plane of necessity and assume this is all there is. In recapturing the horizon of eternity in his writings, Grant attempts to draw our eyes 'upward,' beyond the realities of necessity and the dynamics of force and gravity. His writings urge us to be open to see beyond the visible to the invisible; beyond necessity to the Good; beyond gravity to grace. Grace, not gravity, is the deepest truth, 'hidden beneath its opposite.'[28] The evidence of this exists in the fact that there is beauty in the world. Beauty is that which opens humans to 'otherness' and to receiving grace. Beneath the dynamics of force and gravity in the world is God's hiddenness and God's consent to otherness within and including the realm of necessity.

Affliction

Following Weil, Grant describes 'affliction' (*malheur*) as the experience of the extremity in necessity wherein force indiscriminately beats one down.[29] Affliction is distinguished from sin and from ordinary suffering.[30] It is a process of humiliation that happens when force is applied relentlessly against one's consent to the point where all dignity is lost. In describing Weil's understanding of affliction, Grant says: '[Affliction] always includes in itself physical pain, but it is more than this. It is the pounding in upon men that they are really nothing, by the blind force of necessity and of social and personal degradation. The final affliction to which all come is death. The only difference between people is whether they consent or do not consent to necessity.'[31] We humans continually seek ways to convince ourselves that we matter in the world, expecting that the laws of necessity will be considerate of our limits and needs. We have so enmeshed the Good within the sphere of necessity that we forget the depth of the possibility of evil in this realm and the vulnerability of all life to the indiscriminate lashings of force. Affliction is the experience of those who are pushed to their breaking point and are no longer able to hold on to any illusions of security upon which their dignity may rest. Affliction 'forces us to feel with all our souls the absence of finality,' which is an essential truth of this world.[32] 'Affliction causes God to be absent for a time, more absent than a dead man, more absent than light in the utter darkness of a cell. A kind of horror submerges the whole soul.'[33]

It is in the cross of Christ that Grant, with Weil, finds the purest revelation of affliction. The absence of God is experienced in the loss of dignity and the condemnation of the innocent, in the absence of justice and of meaning. There can be no one more distant from God than one who experiences the complete absence or condemnation of God. At this furthest distance from God is Jesus, accursed and hanging on the cross. In the affliction of (God in) Jesus, God's love crosses the vast distance between necessity and the Good. It is only love, the essence of the Whole, which can traverse the terrible distance that divides the realms. Indeed, as Grant put it, 'how powerful is the necessity which love must cross.'[34]

OTHERNESS AND LOVE: THE ABIDING UNITY OF THE WHOLE

It is not until Grant's later writings that he speaks *via positiva* on the relatedness of the Whole as love.[35] Following Weil, he reflects more deeply on the distance between the two realms in terms of 'otherness' and the reality of otherness in the relationality of love. In its distance from the realm of necessity, the Good is totally 'other' and transcendent to it. Similarly, the realm of necessity is totally other to the Good. Weil describes how the realm of necessity is the realm of otherness from God who is eternity. It is in understanding the distance in terms of otherness that Grant intuits love to be the deeper reality and content of the Whole, the ongoing means by which the realm of necessity is sustained and has being, despite the forces that draw it away from love. The dynamics of love as it is understood in the universal and particular of Grant's thought is considered here with reference to Weil's doctrine of creation and her related understanding of the intimations of eternity in the realm of necessity. In speaking positively about the dynamics of love, her doctrinal conceptions help to unpack the background lighting presupposed in Grant's understanding of the Whole and the priority of love as its essence.

Creation

The cross of Christ is constitutive for understanding Weil's doctrine of creation and the content of the Whole as love. With her, Grant rejects the dominant Western view of creation in which God's activity is understood primarily as powerful self-expansion.[36] Instead, he agrees that in creation 'God accepted this diminution.'[37] By divine withdrawal/renunciation/emptying, God consents to the being of the other. Such divine humility and restraint is the manifestation of love, and it is by this that creatures are enabled to exist and to love.[38] God's sacrificial love maintains humans in free and autonomous existence as beings other to God.[39] The Passion and creation speak of the same thing.[40] God's ongoing self-renouncing act of consent to otherness creates and sustains human and non-human being in love. The self-emptying character of love is, at the same time, abundantly overflowing generosity.[41] Weil describes creation as, 'an act of love and it is perpetual. At each moment our existence is God's love for us. But God can only love himself. His love for us is love for himself through us. Thus, he who gives us our being loves in us the acceptance of not being.'[42]

As theologians of the cross, Grant and Weil consider that God's hiddenness in the realm of necessity is God's revelation. God's absence is God's secret presence. 'The absence of God is the most marvelous testimony of perfect love, and that is why pure necessity, necessity which is manifestly different from good, is so beautiful.'[43] God does not totally abandon creation but gives over part of God's self to necessity. This is most clearly known in Christ's cry of abandonment from the cross. In the cry of abandonment is the recognition of absence, an absence that can be known only by faith and the illumination of love. In the recognition of God's absence there exist intimations of God's presence, for the absence reveals secret presence. In discussing Weil, Grant describes this aspect of her thought: 'The infinite distance between God and God is necessity. The necessity which God has to cross to love God is the cross ... love is always a relation.'[44] Though God is hidden or absent in the world, by human loving (and the self-renunciation implicit therein) we consent and open ourselves to God's loving through us and, paradoxically, to the distance that separates us from God. Our loving God or our neighbour is God loving God through us. The distance between the realm of necessity and the Good, in this deeper level of thought, reflects a love that consents to such distance and thereby glimpses a fullness of love manifested in life.[45]

God created through love and for love. God did not create anything except love itself, and the means to love. He created love in all its forms. He created beings capable of love from all possible distances. Because no other could do it, he himself went to the greatest possible distance, the infinite distance. This infinite distance between God and God, this supreme tearing apart, this agony beyond all others, this marvel of love, is the crucifixion ... This tearing apart, over which supreme love places the bond of supreme union, echoes perpetually across the universe in the midst of the silence, like two notes, separate yet melting into one, like pure and heart-rending harmony. This is the Word of God.[46]

For Grant, the Whole is love that is divided in otherness and united in relationship through openness and consent.

Beauty

Most fully in his essay 'Faith and the Multiversity,' Grant explores the relations between the experience of beauty and the truth of the Whole as love. To behold beauty in this realm is to receive a glimpse of the Whole[47] for beauty is the reflection of the divine in the world. The recognition of beauty is the recognition of the intimation of eternity that lies latent in all parts of creation. Humans love that which appears to them as beautiful. As such, beauty draws forth and opens one to love, to awe, to the experience of astonishment in the 'other' (human or non-human being). One loves 'otherness not because it is other, but because it is beautiful.'[48] Needless to say, beauty is not understood as essentialist subjectivity wherein it exists 'in the eye of the beholder' disconnected from the Whole. No. The beauty that is seen, known, and loved in the other is the very mirror of eternity experienced in the particularities of life. It is the experience of the mediation of the divine order in the order of necessity. God is love and every time we apprehend beauty in the experience of love we consent to the seed of divinity within us, and within the other, and to the truth of the Whole as love.[49] In the order of the Whole, the human being is 'fitted for love.' To experience love is to know oneself as part of the Whole, whose very essence is love.

Of central importance to Grant is the intrinsic purposelessness of beauty, which, like affliction, draws us to ask the question 'why?' Beauty cannot be explained by the rules of cause and effect. It defies all moves toward pragmatic utilitarianism: 'For ... beauty is our one image of the divine. And of its very nature it is not known as purposeful, but only lovable, in the sense that a great work of art has no purpose outside its own being. In [Weil's] language, the beauty of the world is caused by the divine son because it is the mediator between blind obedience and God.'[50] Some of Grant's greatest critiques of the technological society grow out of his Platonic understanding of the relationship between love, beauty, and knowledge. To love another being is to apprehend the beauty of the other, thereby knowing the other in their essence, without presuming to change and master the other. In the modern West, however, 'we are required to eliminate the assumption of the other as itself beautiful.'[51] Beauty is defined subjectively and determined by the details of necessity and chance. Grant argues that beauty has been obscured by the objectification of otherness in subject-object language, tearing apart the possibility for love, for true epistemology, and for the beholding of beauty. 'One thing that has become clear to me,' Grant says, 'is that the paradigm of knowledge given in modern science excludes from its origins the idea that one is given knowledge through love of the beautiful.'[52] For Grant, to be open to the Whole epistemologically presupposes love and the recognition of beauty in the knowing of a thing. For science to have any connection with truth, scientific method must be carried out with attentiveness to the beauty of the world. True scientific knowing must come in the experience of love for the world. Instead, according to Grant, modern science objectifies the other and challenges it to give its reasons for being – to give proof of its worthiness and purposefulness. Grant is clear that technological science today is blocking the mediating reality of love in the world by undermining beauty and serving the human will to mastery and control over otherness.

As we have seen, the majority of Grant's published work focuses on the privation of the Good as it is manifested in the modern will to mastery in technological society. For Grant, however, these intimations of deprival are also precious for they 'might lead us to see the beautiful as the image, in the world, of the good.'[53] By bringing to light the negations of the world as negations of the Good, Grant seeks to draw his readers to see the other side of the negation – the True, the Beautiful and the Good. 'At the heart of the Platonic language,' writes Grant, 'is the affirmation – so incredible to nearly everyone at one time or another – that the ultimate cause of being is beneficence.'[54] That this beneficence can be apprehended in the world through love of the beautiful is astonishing beyond measure.

CONCLUSION

Grant's faith experience and understanding of the Whole shapes and permeates his thought through and through. In exploring the dynamics of the Whole in terms of the contradictions and distance between the realms of necessity and the Good and in terms of the abiding oneness of love, I have attempted to make visible the 'big picture' within which Grant invites us to join him. I trust I have been honest to Grant, without compromising either the truth of the contradiction or the truth of the unity of the Whole in love. Indeed, it is on the cross of Christ that the contradictions emerge with an unrelenting ferocity in the absent presence and present absence of God. For Grant, the contradiction between God and the world must remain a contradiction to human thought, without scrutable unity. The theologian/philosopher is called to the task of bringing to light 'the thing as it is' – bringing to light the contradiction between the love of God and the affliction of the world in all its vast particularity, thinking through this contradiction with rigorous trust and courage, and awaiting the illumination of the mind by love. 'Faith is the experience that the intelligence is enlightened by love.' It is love that *unreasonably* holds together from above that which cannot be held together from below. Indeed, love is the essence of the Whole – the oneness of the all in all. Grant's philosophical thinking through of the relationality within the Whole – between God, the universe, human and non-human being – is based on his primal faith in God as one of beneficence. In the priority of faith in his thought, Grant is a theologian who challenges us to order our knowing such that it is open to the deepest truth of being, the truth of love. Grant's philosophy calls us to the task of theology: 'Believe so that you may know.'[55]

NOTES

1 Harris Athanasiadis, *George Grant and the Theology of the Cross: The Christian Foundation of His Thought* (Toronto: University of Toronto Press, 2001); Arthur Davis, ed., *George Grant and the Subversion of Modernity: Art, Philosophy, Politics, Religion and Education* (Toronto: University of Toronto Press,

1996), 243–85; Larry Schmidt, ed., *George Grant in Process* (Toronto: House of Anansi Press, 1976), 101–30 etc.

2 I have chosen to capitalize the term 'the Whole' because of its significance in naming the bigger picture of Grant's thought. 'The whole,' Grant says, 'is opened to one when one asks questions of final purpose.' David Cayley, *George Grant in Conversation* (Don Mills, ON: Anansi, 1995), 59.

3 George Grant, *Philosophy in the Mass Age*, ed. William Christian (Toronto: University of Toronto Press, 1995), 28.

4 In describing the influence of Simone Weil's interpretation of Plato on him, Grant says, 'Her writing on Plato, in my opinion, is the greatest writing on Plato in our era.' And on the influence of Weil, herself, he says, 'It would be foolish for me to deny that no other thinker is so influential to me – and it is her life and thought ... together.' Grant, *Notebook for Class on Simone Weil*, 1975–6, George Grant Personal Papers, in the possession of Sheila Grant, Halifax.

5 Cayley, *George Grant in Conversation*, 58ff.

6 I am in agreement with scholars who recognize Grant as a theologian of the cross, drawing upon Martin Luther's thought. Grant has indirect and direct references to Luther's writing on the theology of the cross throughout his corpus. See, for example, 'In Defence of North America,' *Technology and Empire: Perspectives on North America* (Toronto: House of Anansi, 1969), 21. Grant describes Weil as 'essentially a theologian of the cross.' Cayley, *George Grant in Conversation*, 176.

7 Grant discusses this theme under other such language as 'knowledge and belief,' 'reason and revelation,' and 'the intellect and faith.'

8 His critiques of the modern Western accounts of reason and science are based on the priority of love in true thought and the fact that, in the dominating paradigm of knowledge in the West, there is no place for love.

9 This reference occurs in a number of places in Grant's work. 'Credo ut intelligam.' Anselm of Canterbury, *Proslogion*, *A Scholastic Miscellany: Anselm to Ockham*, ed. and trans. Eugene R. Fairweather (Philadelphia: Westminster Press, 1956), 69–70. See William Christian, *George Grant: A Biography* (Toronto: University of Toronto Press, 1993), 373 n.1.

10 Cayley, *George Grant in Conversation*, 173.

11 Grant uses the Platonic term 'the Good' as a synonym for God or, more specifically, God's love. Cayley, *George Grant in Conversation*, 59.

12 George Grant on Simone Weil: 'Let me start by saying that we're here in the presence of a being who is quite different from those people we've talked about as great thinkers alone. I have no doubt at all that she is, in the traditional categories of the West, a great saint ... With Simone Weil you have to

combine this staggeringly clear intellect with something that is quite beyond the intellect, namely sanctity. And I mean by a saint those beings who give themselves away ... in love.' Cayley, *George Grant in Conversation*, 172–3.

13 His tombstone in the cemetary at Terrence Bay, Nova Scotia, indicates this. On it is written: 'George Parkin Grant, 1918–1988: Out of the shadows and imaginings and into the truth.' See Christian, *George Grant: A Biography*, image no. 28.

14 Grant uses the term 'scrutable' over and against 'inscrutable' particularly regarding the inscrutability of God and God's providence. He critiques assumptions of 'scrutability' inherent in modern liberalism and the ideology of progress. See, Schmidt, ed., *George Grant in Process*, 64.

15 Cayley, *George Grant in Conversation*, 176.

16 See, for example, 'The Beautiful and the Good' and 'The Beautiful Itself,' both unpublished lectures found in 'Notebook A' at McMaster University.

17 'Simone Weil,' Grant says, 'is the being who expresses most deeply, as far as I'm concerned, the moment of God's absence from the world. In Christian theology there have been two traditions: the positive tradition and the negative tradition. The positive tradition [Aristotelianism] moves to God through the world; the negative tradition moves to God by negating the world.' Cayley, *George Grant in Conversation*, 177

18 Grant, 'The Beautiful and the Good.'

19 Ibid.

20 See, for example, George Grant, *Lament for a Nation* (Ottawa: Carlton University Press, 1965), 89. 'As a believer, I must then reject these Western interpretations of providence. Belief is blasphemy if it rests on any easy identification of necessity and good.'

21 It is helpful at this point to note that many who first read Grant would see him to be almost entirely concerned with critiquing the modern Western manifestation of the will to power. His critique has everything to do with his recognition of the vast distance that separates the orders of necessity and the Good.

22 This idea will be discussed at greater length later in the chapter.

23 Simone Weil, 'The Pythagorean Doctrine,' *Intimations of Christianity among the Ancient Greeks* (London: Ark, 1957 [1st Eng.] 1987), 184.

24 George Grant, 'Introduction to Simone Weil (1970),' in *The George Grant Reader*, ed. William Christian and Sheila Grant (Toronto: University of Toronto Press 1998), 248.

25 Weil describes force as 'that x that turns anybody who is subjected to it into a thing. Exercised to the limit, it turns a man into a thing in the most literal

sense: it makes a corpse out of him.' Simone Weil, *The Iliad or The Poem of Force*, trans. Mary McCarthy [1945] (Pennsylvania: Pendle Hill, 1993), 3.

26 The extent to which technology in the modern era is shaping epistemology and action is explored in substantial depth in Grant's books *Technology and Empire* (Toronto: Anansi Press, 1969) and *Technology and Justice* (Toronto: Anansi Press, 1969).

27 Simone Weil, *Gravity and Grace*, trans. Emma Craufurd (London: Routledge and Kegan Paul, 1952), 1.

28 'Hidden beneath its opposite' is a reference to Luther's theology of the cross, which is foundational for Grant's thought and for his understanding of Weil. See Athanasiadis, *George Grant and the Theology of the Cross*; Cayley, *George Grant in Conversation*, 176.,

29 Weil's fullest account of affliction can be found in her essay 'The Love of God and Affliction,' in *Waiting for God*, trans. Emma Craufurd with introduction by Leslie A. Fielder (New York: G.P. Putnam's Sons, 1951), 67–82.

30 Ibid..

31 Grant, 'Introduction to Simone Weil,' 253.

32 Weil, 'The Love of God and Affliction,' 112–13.

33 Simone Weil, *On Science, Necessity and the Love of God*, trans. and ed. Richard Rees (London: Oxford University Press, 1968), 174. For a helpful discussion of this, see Athanasiadis, *George Grant and the Theology of the Cross*, 67.

34 Grant, 'Faith and the Multiversity,' in *Technology and Justice*, 77.

35 The most notable example of this is his essay, 'Faith in the Multiversity,' 35–77. See also Cayley, *George Grant in Conversation*, 187.

36 In a number of his writings, Grant makes connections between the Western understanding of God's creation as self-expanding power and the modern Western technological will to power in the mastery and control of human and non-human nature. See, for example, Grant, 'In Defence of Simone Weil (1988),' in Christian and Grant, *The George Grant Reader*, 265.

37 Weil, 'Forms of the Implicit Love of God,' in *Waiting for God*, 89.

38 Weil, *Gravity and Grace*, 28.

39 Simone Weil, 'Three Essays on the Love of God,' in *Gateway to God*, ed. David Raper et al. (Glasgow: William Collins Sons, 1974), 80.

40 'Not only the Passion but creation itself is a renunciation and sacrifice on the part of God. The Passion is simply its consummation. God already voids himself of his divinity by the Creation. He takes the form of a slave, submits to necessity, abases himself.' Weil, 'Three Essays,' in *Gateway to God*, 80. Grant summarizes Weil's understanding of creation: 'Creation was not expansion, but a renunciation – a retreat of God. The creation as renunciation is an act of love as we see in the passion ... the form in which loves

clothes itself as renunciation ... Creation and the Passion are finally one.'
Grant, *Notebook for Class on Simone Weil*.

41 'The love that God bears us is, at any moment, the material and substance of
our very being. God's creative love that maintains us in existence is not
merely a superabundance of generosity, it is also self-renunciation and sacrifice.' Weil, 'Three Essays,' in *Gateway to God*, 80.

42 Weil, *Gravity and Grace*, 28.

43 Ibid, 96.

44 Cayley, *George Grant in Conversation*, 176. It is helpful to note that Grant's
understanding here of the Whole in terms of the infinite distance that love
must cross between God and God (in theological terms, between the Father
and the Son) reflects a Weilian conceptualization of the Trinity: God the
Father is outside the world, powerless to intervene in the world for such
intervention would dis-create the world. God the Son is inside the world
and is of the realm of necessity, at an infinite distance from God the Father.
The Father and Son are utterly divided. This division reflects God's self-
division or self-renunciation in creation – the contradiction and distance.
God is love and the nature of love is unity. But in dividing God's self from
within, God consents to deny God's essential unity and let the other be. At
the same time, however, there exists the third person of the Trinity, the Holy
Spirit, who is the unity (that is, the love) of God across the infinite distance
between the Father and the Son. God renounces self and yet cannot cease to
be Self. The vast distance between Love (Father) and Love (Son) is united by
love (Holy Spirit). Thus, as Trinity, love has both a verb-like movement in
the Holy Spirit and noun-like essence in the Father and Son. See Weil, 'The
Love of God and Human Affliction,' in *Waiting for God*, 75

45 Weil, 'The Love of God and Affliction,' in *Waiting for God*, 74.

46 Ibid, 72.

47 'In the beautiful things and persons and institutions and studies of this
world I can see intimations of what [Plato] means by the Beautiful Itself –
the Idea of the Good,' Grant, 'The Beautiful Itself.'

48 Grant, 'Faith and the Multiversity,' 39.

49 In Trinitarian terms, loving in the world reflects the divine movement of the
Holy Spirit between Father and Son.

50 Grant, 'Introduction to Simone Weil (1970),' 253.

51 Grant, 'Faith and the Multiversity,' 40.

52 Cayley, *George Grant in Conversation*, 185.

53 Grant, 'A Platitude,' 143.

54 Grant, 'Faith and the Multiversity,' 42.

55 See n.9.

PART FOUR

The Tension between Athens and Jerusalem

GEORGE GRANT'S LECTURE NOTES 'The Beautiful and the Good' and 'The Beautiful Itself' articulate the Christian Platonism that is at the root of his conceptions of philosophy and theology and that grounds his understanding of their unity. The first lecture ranges across several of Plato's dialogues to argue that there is a transcendent idea of the Good in Plato and that the stimulus of this transcendence must combine with human striving to produce a 'natural harmony between the human mind and all that is.' Such a transcendent idea of the Good in Plato provides a basis for linking the Being of Greek philosophy with the God of biblical tradition. The second lecture focuses more specifically on the dialogue *Symposium* to address the question of the relation between love and knowledge. Grant always resisted a too-great separation between erotic love and Christian charity, between eros and agape. In this he was arguing against the influential work by Anders Nygren, *Agape and Eros*, which demanded a strict demarcation between Christian notions of love and the Platonic idea of eros. 'The Beautiful Itself' lecture demonstrates the linkage of human striving with transcendent Good. Grant concludes that 'I can in short say that in my clearest mind I must posit something which is eternal and loveable—but that it has never appeared to me directly.' The God-Good of Grant's Christian Platonism is thus an idea in the Platonic sense and not an immediate experience.

The three essays that follow inquire into the ground and sustainability of the synthesis between Grant's Christian interpretation of Biblical revelation and his interpretation of Plato. Ted Heaven carefully traces Leo Strauss' phrasing of the issue as one of Athens and Jerusalem to show that it was understood by Grant through the figures of Socrates and Jesus. He concludes that Grant's first allegiance was to Jesus and that this allegiance gave rise to his philosophical appreciation of Socrates. Heaven thus interprets Grant's Christian commitment as primary and as providing the horizon for his philosophizing. Graeme Nicholson and Ian Angus both agree with this interpretation of Grant. Nicholson argues that an acceptance of both Christianity and philosophy need not require the priority of one. Rather, there is a difference, a distance, between religion and philosophy that is the difference between thought and the communication of salvation. Angus argues that the predominance of Christianity means that Grant's view is not really a 'synthesis' but an incorporation of philosophy by theology. In contrast, he argues for the autonomy of philosophy.

All writers in this section, Grant included, realize that there is a tension between the Christian theological element in Grant's thought and the philosophical element. Grant, and Heaven following Grant, seek to resolve this tension in a Christian Platonism. This represents one great strand in the attempt to come to grips with the two sources of Western civilization. The critical essays by Nicholson and Angus remind us that this issue can be posed differently and must be continually confronted anew. The essays in this section show their debt to George Grant in the very fact that, in attempting to understand his work and follow his questioning, they are compelled to address the most fundamental issue in the interpretation of Western civilization.

16

The Beautiful and the Good

GEORGE GRANT

This lecture is from 'Notebook A' and was given to a graduate course on Plato in 1976. In contrast to the modern tendency of separating the Good from the Beautiful, Grant highlighted how and why Plato held together the two. The 'Beautiful,' for Plato and Grant, is about the order and nature of the cosmos, whereas the 'Good' deals with the deeper longings and love within the human soul to live a meaningful and authentic life. Grant makes it clear that 'Love' and the 'Good' are inextricably connected. It is the 'Good' that provides the north star for desires, longings, and love. What reason would we have for act-ing justly if we did not know that justice in the end orders everything? It is, in the final analysis, the unity between the 'Good,' the 'Beautiful,' and 'Love' that offers the longing soul true knowledge.

I am loath to lecture because of my own laziness, ignorance and I do not want to conceptualize into a tight framework my poor understanding of the amazing account of reality here presented. But I thought I would chat a bit about the Beautiful and the Good as far as I understand the matter. I will put it in simple language. I have a barrel full of lectures on Plato in my file and I cannot use any of them because they were too foolishly complex.

Let me start with a simple remark. What I find is most perfect in Plato is that there is a total union in his thought of what is in lesser philoso-phers either separated or part of which is not present. That is he com-bines in a staggering unity the cosmological approach with the ethical-religious approach. What I mean by these two is the following. The cos-mological approach is the question: 'What is the nature of the universe? What is real and how can I know what is real?' Or, to use other language, it puts the philosophic question as 'What general and universally valid conclusions about the cosmos can I draw?' On the other hand, the ethical religious approach starts from the question 'How shall I live? What is worth doing? To what shall I pay my allegiance, my reverence. How shall I find happiness?' And if you want, as I certainly do want, to use directly religious language, 'How can I come to know God and to be like Him, or as Plato says, His friend?'

Now many philosophers either concentrate on one of these sides but not on the other, or separate them. But what happens when they are separated? If the cosmological is taken alone, philosophy becomes an abstract remote discipline which has no connection with our life and our existence. And this is what has happened in an age when philosophical analysis has become the handmaid of the natural sciences and when philosophy becomes more and more logic and particularly the logic of the sciences. It is against this that that wonderful philosophical movement, existentialism, has made its protest. As existentialism says, I start from my existence and try to find its meaning. If is for this reason that Kierkegaard, that early existentialist and the first exalter of Christianity against philosophy, could still have such enormous respect for Socrates, whom he described as 'a passion of inwardness in existing,' and we will indeed come to this when we come to discuss *Phaedo* next, where Socrates talks of how he turned from the scientific philosophy of his day to the effort to know himself.

On the other hand, if the ethical-religious sacrifices the cosmological, philosophy is also lost, because the questions how shall I act, what shall I reverence, must be concerned with the nature of things as they are, and the effort to know those things as they are. We can only know how we should live if we know what kind of a universe it is. And that is where existentialism, for example, fails. It is not concerned with science – that is with the desire to know systematically the nature of things and of the cosmos as a whole.

Now what is so wonderful in the Platonic writings taken as a whole is the holding together of the cosmological and systematic view of philosophy with the ethical-religious view. Now in this class we are first of all concerned with dialogues which clearly fall in their emphasis on the side of the ethical-religious. Particularly the *Symposium* and *Phaedo* are the dialogues of life and of death and are passionately existential – though in them the cosmological is not far away. In the *Phaedrus* we are nearer the unity of the two, so we shall study it last. But we are not studying the great cosmological dialogues of which the *Sophist* and the

Parmenides are, in my opinion, the greatest. Nor are we studying the last great dialogues in which the cosmological and the ethical religious are at one, the greatest of which in my opinion is *Philebus* – that supreme philosophical writing. Nor should we think that the immense generality of metaphysics is higher than the practical – because the last work of Plato, *The Laws*, is concerned with such concrete subjects as how much wine a man should drink at different ages, and at what age one should marry. Now I have said this to begin to talk about the Good, and to point out that the Good as seen in the *Symposium* is seen as the supreme object of desire.

But let us remember that the Good and the Love are the same. In the *Republic* the argument for the speculative life – the argument from knowledge for God's existence – is combined with the argument from desire, so that the Good is not only seen as the highest object of desire, but also the cause of knowing, that is, that which makes the world intelligible and our minds intelligent and also as the cause of being – that is the cosmological and ethical-religious are very closely bound together. In the *Symposium* we are chiefly concerned with desire. But in the *Symposium*, though what we concentrate on is desire or love, we must always be aware that the Good is both the supreme object of desire and of knowledge. They are at one. The Love and the Good are the same. Now let me say also that I interpret Plato as unequivocally believing in the Love or the Good as transcendent – that which is the supreme object of our love is absent. Let me quote to you the *Republic* 509b: 'The objects of knowledge not only receive from the presence of the good their being known, but their very existence and essence is derived from it, though the good itself is not Being but still transcends Being in dignity and surpassing power.' To make this clear I would have to comment on *Parmenides* at great length, and as that is impossible let me only say this. What does it mean to say that the highest object of desire and of the intellect is ultimately unknowable?

Philosophers mostly agree that it belongs to the nature of mind to seek unity. Now they seem to disagree at this point as to the nature of that unity – or see it from the side of desire to seek meaning. Those whom I may quickly characterize as the immanentists would say – 'though it is difficult to understand what meaning the world has, we do however know in principle the kind of meaning that complete insight would reach' – though of course the immanentist would admit that what we know in principle we cannot know in detail.

Now what the believer in transcendence would say is that this unity which we seek we can neither know in principle or in detail. To put it in theological terms, God's essence is unknowable – read Dionysius in *The Descent of the Dove* p. 61. This is the idea that Love or the Good or God is beyond knowledge. That fundamental awareness that makes experience possible is dormant, potential, and its actualization requires an external stimulus. But this is only a stimulus, it does not produce that awareness. The human soul has by nature, by being a human soul, the truth within itself. There is a natural harmony between the human mind and everything that is, between the human mind and the whole. Man has a kinship with the Whole, that is to say with the Good of the Whole, with what makes the Whole the Whole. The Good of the Whole makes intelligible the place which man occupies within the Whole. This is the singular dignity of man, the fact that man is a singularly privileged being, and at the same time not the highest being, for his privileged position is not his work but given to him. This we can say was the basis of classical philosophy, and not only the classical, because it is of course also the view of the Bible.

17

The Beautiful Itself

GEORGE GRANT

This lecture, like the previous one, is from 'Notebook A' and was given to a graduate course on Plato in 1976. Here, Grant creates space for a language alternative to that of the modern calculative thinking of our technological world. This language is rooted in the moral beauty that awakens and stirs our conscious life. The Beautiful, for Plato as for Grant, is connected to the Good. Most of the Platonic dialogues Grant mentions in this lecture connect these realities. In short, Love, the Good, Beautiful, and Thinking are one in this erotic way of knowing and being. Grant points out that we do have hints, intimations, pointers of the Beautiful in beautiful things, persons, institutions, and the like, but these are only flares thrown up to illuminate the way. It is because our many desires are shaped and guided by the Beautiful that eros finds its true end and home. Grant, in this lecture, tends to see the Beautiful itself in much more of an inward, mystic way than he does in 'The Beautiful and the Good,' which takes a predominantly cosmological approach.

I am going to speak about the Beautiful itself. What is so difficult are the two following points. This which is there – which suddenly dawns to consciousness, comes to consciousness, what is it? – it is not of this world. Whatever it is it is not something which is the same as the beautiful things or creatures of this world. It is moral beauty. Yet it is; in the sense that it appears to our consciousness it is not our consciousness. Indeed if we relate what is said here to what is said in the Republic – it is the cause of the possibility of our consciousness. In that sense it is in a much fuller way than we are. It is always.

This which is always is not something which we infer – but which is met. The language is the language of immediacy. In the Western world the proper word here is mysticism – and please I want nobody in this class to use that word in a loose sense. What is meant by mysticism – this and nothing else – is the immediate appearance of the eternal to human beings. Immediate is a negative word – not through a mediator. To me this table [before him] appears immediately. On the other hand to me the being of God is mediated through inference. Or again the fact that constitutional government is preferable to tyrannical government is not known immediately but through inference – the proper influences of political philosophy.

Now as this second is to me the source of my great unwillingness to talk of this passage, I want to emphasize this – the Beautiful itself is talked of here as dawning immediately to consciousness with complete certainty. It is not talked of as something we infer – as, for example, in my own case the arguments for God's being are arguments from which I infer that God is. We go from human activities to infer the Good of those activities – God. Now, here to the philosopher the eternal beauty appears directly. To put it this way, the immediacy of sense and the mediacy of argument or inference or logos here becomes one. What is described here is our overcoming of that distinction.

Now this second reason is why I am so unwilling to speak of this – because it has not occurred for me. I am not saying that intimations of what such an occurrence would be have not appeared, but the actual occurrence has not. My reaching for the eternal is through the images of it which appear to me through justice and knowledge and beauty – but only as images – the same kind of images that in this passage of the *Symposium* Plato says are preparations – necessary preparations – but what they are according to Plato preparations for – has not occurred.

Now the immediacy of this occurrence – mysticism – and the possibility of it being phony or manipulated is why official Western Christianity has been so hesitant and suspicious, why it has adopted Aristotle more officially than Plato; and why one is very hesitant to speak of it. The best example of this can be seen in Simone Weil or in George Herbert's poem – 'Christ came down and possessed my soul.'

Now I want to say first two things of why we as moderns are so suspicious of what is said here in the *Symposium*. There are many reasons but I think those two take us to the heart of the matter.

To 'be' in the highest sense for most modern men is to exist, that is to be in the manner in which one is – that is 'to be' in the highest sense is to be subject to mortality. Yet here it is unequivocally said that 'to be' in the highest sense is to be always – to be not subject to time or change or death. In this passage this is unequivocally asserted; the Beautiful itself is a form of what 'is' which is always. This is not the way modern men think about what is. It is not by accident that the contemporary thinker who is to me the best thinker should have as his most famous book – the subject Being and Time.

But there is a second reason for this suspicion which goes deeper and which is put best by the great thinker of the modern world, Nietzsche (contemporary – modern, Heidegger – Nietzsche) and which comes to most of us through Freud's influence. It is this: that the condition of the highest human excellence is that human beings remain in their being fully loyal to the earth. That is: that the condition of the highest human excellence is that there is nothing beyond the world which is our first concern. Biblical faith in God or the ideas as the good of the world lead us to other-worldliness and asceticism which alienated men from this world and is only pursued as an art – and escape – because we are unwilling to face the terrifying and perplexing character of the world. Therefore we cushion ourselves from the terrifying world – by positioning the Beautiful itself – beyond the world. But this turning from our life as it is in the world is an escape, and an escape which holds us from the highest human excellence. This is what Nietzsche means by Dionysius, this loyalty to the earth.

Now I have wanted to mention these two modern ways which turn us from looking at the Beautiful itself – because only as we look at these considerations face to face can we decide what is after all the only final reason for studying Plato – Is there the Beautiful itself?

Now as I said last time, the ideas make their appearance in Plato's writings always in relation to some subject – in the *Republic* in relation to politics – The Idea of the Good, the idea from which all the other ideas find their proper order of subordination and super-ordination – that which is the cause of our being, our knowing, our desiring. In *Phaedo* the ideas appear in relation to death and in that austere dialogue the prisoner leaps to lose his chains. But in *Symposium* they appear in the company of wine and celebration- they make the appearances in relation to eros.

In parenthesis – let me say that is why those two dialogues must be seen together in the affirmation and denial which are both present in the way that Plato has laid down [his argument]. A.H. Armstrong's* article puts this very simply but well. Indeed, as I said last time, the

---

* Grant is probably referring to A.H. Armstrong, 'A Discussion on Individuality and Personality,' *Dionysius* 2 (December 1978): 93–99.

Idea of the Good is here called the Beautiful itself just because the very Love described is affirmative as well as negative. The beauty of the bodies of the laws and institutions, of the sciences is affirmed as well as negated. Indeed the very dialogue is of life itself in its setting and in its participants. Therefore, as the ideas make their appearance in relation to eros or desire, I am going to discuss them in relation to eros, very shortly.

Let us look at the dialogue for a moment as the account of the perfection of eros, and say something about the ideas in relation to that. Let me do so by talking about those philosophers both ancient and modern who have denied that there is anything eternal which is loveable – those thinkers who in a rather loose sense can be characterised as materialists, and let us see what they say about eros.

In the ancient world let us take Epicurus, who believed that the good of the world was the flight of the atoms in the void. For Epicurus, philosophy which leads to that conclusion also leads us to the conclusion that desire is the cause of our pain and that therefore philosophy leads us to hold ourselves aloof from eros. Philosophy acts against eros. There is no union between eros and philosophy – indeed there is no connection between them. Philosophy is not the perfection of eros by its denial. There is something eternal – the atoms and the void – but they are not loveable. It would be interesting to apply this to modern thought and its view of eros – but that would distract from this. Therefore I return to the ancient.

In the *Symposium* it is clear that there is what is eternal and loveable – the Beautiful itself – or the Idea of the Good. Love and thought do not counteract each other – but are united in the vision of the Beautiful itself. Love can be perfected, it can be led, that is, to its satisfaction, which does not deny thought like the modern accounts of eros, nor does it have to be killed as in Epicureanism by thought. Or to put it the other way round, thought does not have to subdue eros or surrender to it – but perfects itself in the perfecting of eros. And by thought I do not mean simply what I would call theoretical reason but also practical reason – because the perfecting of eros requires the virtues of moderation, courage, justice if we are to become wise.

Now in the *Symposium* and in this speech of Socrates it must be said that the affirmative is emphasised – we mount through the various forms of love to the perfecting of love in the vision of the Beautiful itself. It may be that what is abstracted from here is the side of eros which must be negated in this journey. That is so nobly described in

Phaedus (253d et seq.) which you would do well to read, and which I wish we had time to read this year – the account of the soul as a chariot. In that account there is not sentimentality or optimism about the emancipation of eros. And even more wonderfully we will proceed next week to read *Phaedo,* in which indeed the eros for life is itself mortified.

What I can say then in short about the Beautiful itself is that for Plato it is always and that for some men in philosophy it can come forth as a direct presence for them – in which presence eros is perfected. I can also say that the description of the way seems better than any other description I know – that in the beautiful things and persons and institutions and studies of this world I can see intimations of what he means by the Beautiful Itself – the Idea of the Good – that indeed the concept of the perfecting of eros can have no meaning outside the positing of the Beautiful itself – that indeed there would be no directing of eros – no way of knowing how we can put our multitude of desires into any proper hierarchy of subordination and super-ordination without some dim intuition of that posited; or to put it even more simply, how we could be drawn to become better if it were not so posited.

What I can't speak of and which held me silent last day is its appearance to us as a presence – for I have not gone that far, and indeed this age is one when much stands in the way of those even preliminary stages of the way without which this Christ according to Plato cannot appear to us in all its majesty. I can in short say that in my clearest mind I must posit something which is eternal and loveable – but that it has never appeared to me directly.

18

George Grant on Socrates and Christ

TED HEAVEN

Correlations of contraries are like a ladder. Each of them raises us to a higher level where resides the connexion which unifies the contraries; until we reach a spot where we have to think of the contraries together, but where we are denied access to the level at which they are linked together. This forms the last rung of the ladder. Once there we can climb no further; we have only to look up, wait and love. And God descends.

Simone Weil, *Gateway to God*

Reflecting on the correlations of contraries was a central preoccupation of George Grant's philosophic life. The primal contrary in Grant's comprehensive vision is that between Socrates and Christ (rather than the Athens and Jerusalem of Leo Strauss), and the link between the two is at a level at which they must be held together even though they cannot be thought together. This chapter will show how, in articulating this position, Grant found himself differing from Strauss on certain decisive issues and offering the Socrates and Christ of Simone Weil as a more fitting alternative.

The contrary of how it is possible for an individual to profess Christianity and engage in open-ended philosophical inquiry was pivotal in George Grant's thought from his conversion in 1941 to his death in 1988. He called himself a Christian Platonist, and in so doing he defied the position of Leo Strauss that such a stance is untenable. For Strauss, philosophy and revelation are 'the antagonists in the drama of the human soul,'[1] and 'this unresolved conflict is the secret vitality of western civilization.'[2] No transcendence of this conflict or pretended synthesis is possible for thinking beings, and since there can be only one truth an individual must choose one of the alternatives as the right way of life, and from this stance be open to the challenge of the other.

Grant's life and thought were directed towards rising above Strauss's antagonists. In 1988, just a few months before his death, Grant offered a summary statement of his position: 'The central task of thought requires us to be aware of some tension between what comes to us from Athens and what from Jerusalem. I prefer to say what comes to us from Socrates and from Christ ... Anyone who wishes to partake in philosophy, and also hopes that he or she is made with the sign of Christ, must be aware of some tension in the relation between thought and revelation, though at the same time knowing that finally they must be at one.'[3]

To arrive at his position that Plato and sanctity, or Socrates and Christ, can be held together, Grant utilized the thought of Leo Strauss and Simone Weil, the two most profound influences upon him. The movement of his thought can be described as a saying 'no' to Strauss and a 'yes' to Simone Weil on certain critical points within the contraries of revelation and philosophy. Grant says 'no' to elements of Strauss's Athens and his Jerusalem, and he says 'yes' to Socrates and Christ on the basis of his deep reflections. But in both his naysaying and his 'yeasaying' he is profoundly influenced by his mentor Simone Weil.

For the sake of brevity, Simone Weil is not quoted extensively in what follows. It may be assumed that the words quoted from Grant's writings and conversations about Socrates and Christ replicate Weil's reflections, such that Weil is speaking through Grant. As Wayne Shepherd writes, 'to understand what Grant means by "philosophy" is to understand what Weil means by philosophy.'[4] And the same may be stated, with some minor qualifications, about their parallel thoughts on Christ. As Shepherd notes, 'Weil is rarely allowed to speak directly or at any length in Grant's writings, and yet she is unquestionably the source of light in the darkness.'[5] Shepherd, in his article 'The Suffering of Love: George Grant and Simone Weil,' does quote Weil extensively and points to the parallels in Grant's thought. Anyone requiring the confirmation provided by direct quotations from Simone Weil is referred to Shepherd's article. Assembled there is the substantial foundation for Grant's conclusion that, for a philosopher within Christianity, Socrates and Christ must be held together.

Before considering those points on which Grant said 'no' to Strauss's Athens and Jerusalem, it is imperative to remind the reader that Grant's debt to Strauss was immense. In 1966 Grant wrote: 'I count it a high blessing to have been acquainted with this man's thought.'[6] From

Strauss, Grant learned of the barrenness of liberalism; the untenability of any doctrine of historical progress; the nihilism implicit within historicism; technology within modernity as the overcoming of chance and the concomitant oblivion of eternity; and, perhaps most important, the creative tension between philosophy and revelation. Any serious juxtaposition of Grant and Strauss's thought would extend this summary listing.

Within the central tension between philosophy and religion, Grant was in fundamental agreement with Strauss on two key issues. The first is that philosophy must grant that revelation is possible. In Thomas Pangle's words: 'Now as Strauss was wont to point out, there is only one indisputable, logical procedure by which the philosopher can achieve a decisive refutation of the claims of piety or revelation ... he can show that he has a clear and exhaustive explanation of how and why everything in the entire cosmos is as it is and behaves as it does ... The mature Socrates seems to have been the first philosopher who realized not merely that such a comprehensive account of things eludes man, but how dire are the consequences of this fact for the claims of philosophy.'[7] Strauss then asks: Under the condition of the admission that revelation is possible, 'what then does the choice of philosophy mean'? He answers: 'In this case the choice of philosophy is based on faith.'[8] So the second fundamental point of agreement between Grant and Strauss is on their mutual limitation of the range of reason. For both men, philosophy, science, and religion all have axioms or 'first things' (as Plato called them) which have no rational foundation – they are simply presupposed and only then does reason become operative. This means that you must define philosophy, science, or religion as either including or excluding the transcendent, and both Grant and Strauss chose the former option. At the same time, they both showed how rational inquiry could point to reasons for making the primal act of faith. So there is a limiting point for the exercise of Strauss's free insight, the philosophical pole of the creative tension between reason and revelation. Reason, for Strauss, is operative within the same transcendent limits that Grant acknowledges.

STRAUSS'S ATHENS

In spite of the limitations of reason, Strauss held that it constitutes man's highest faculty. In *Liberalism Ancient and Modern* he wrote: 'By becoming aware of the dignity of the mind, we realize the true ground of the dignity of man and therewith the goodness of the world, whether we understand it as created or uncreated, which is the home of man because it is the home of the human mind.[9]' Strauss further reflects that the act of understanding is 'so high, so pure, so noble an experience that Aristotle could ascribe to it his God.'[10] Strauss's Athens includes Aristotle, the foremost proponent of the teaching that rationality in man is the height of human existence and that humans should, above all else, strive for knowledge of truth, which is a good in itself. Strauss quotes the Jewish medieval thinker Halevi and agrees with him that 'the wisdom of the Greeks has most beautiful blossoms but no fruits,'[11] with fruits here meaning actions. Contemplation, or understanding, is more fundamental than action. In fact, action is strictly secondary in the sense that intellectual virtue takes precedence over moral virtue. Strauss defines the latter as 'essentially not more than a means toward, or a by-product of, the life of contemplation.'[12] Grant is clearly critical of Strauss's delineation of Greek philosophy as the quest for *knowledge* of the Good, for this is essentially Aristotelian rather than Platonic. For Plato, it is *love* of the Good which is at the heart and centre of philosophy. Speaking personally, Grant says: 'If contemplation means at its centre, love, then I don't mind the word; but if it carries the implication of the thinker as the height of human existence, then it seems to me a dangerous word. That is above all why I would call myself philosophically a Platonist, and why I so fear the Aristotelian tradition. Plato proclaims the dependence of intelligence upon love in a much clearer way than Aristotle.'[13]

Grant says that he is led 'in great hesitation to differ with Strauss in the interpretation of Plato ... nevertheless I think I would differ with him about the *Symposium*, concerning love and reason.'[14] In addition: 'I think we would differ about the *hyperousia* statement in *Republic* 508; that is about the Good as beyond being.'[15] In Grant's view, Plato's Good as 'beyond being' is one teaching that marks a point of fundamental difference between Plato and the other Athenian (or Greek) philosophers. Strauss sided with the Athenians on this point. Another point of fundamental divergence centres on the Platonic teaching of the infinite distance between the necessary and the Good. This is a parallel teaching and follows from the *hyperousia*. Any bringing together of the necessary and the Good in this world is blasphemy, according to Grant, because any suggestion of a representable purpose in this world is an assertion 'that evil is good and good is evil.' For Grant, this is 'the great lie'[16] that humans tend towards when they ignore the agnosticism within Platonism that goodness is beyond being. It would appear that Strauss moved in this direction by writing of 'intelligent necessity'[17] within nature. Strauss is influenced by the Aristotelian teleology wherein it is possible to think intelligibly about necessity. Thus, for Strauss, intelligibility is informed and constituted by the idea of the Good. For Strauss, as for Aristotle, the Good is merely the highest of the ideas. In this context, necessity can be understood, inherent purposes may be uncovered, and even evils may be explained. Such thinking, for Strauss, 'leads us to realize that all evils are in a sense necessary if there is to be understanding. It enables us to accept all evils which befall us and which may well break our hearts in the spirit of good citizens of the city of God.'[18] To such triumphalism Grant says a resounding 'no.' Goodness, for Grant, is beyond being and therefore beyond necessity. Necessity cannot be understood; it can only point to the mystery beyond being.

STRAUSS'S JERUSALEM

When Strauss writes about the Bible he means the Hebrew Bible, which he supposedly read every day and which Christians designate as the Old Testament. This Jerusalem of Strauss obviously excludes Christ, and, for that reason and others, Grant judges it to be an inadequate appellation for the revelatory pole within the faith-reason dichotomy.

According to Grant, 'one of the wisest things Strauss ever said was that in Judaism and Islam revelation is received as law, while in Christianity it is received as the being – Jesus Christ.'[19] For Grant, the wisdom resides in the contrast, and it is revelation as law that Grant considers inadequate. Revelation as precept or command requires obedient love as a response. Whereas the philosopher is dedicated to a quest for knowledge of the Good, Strauss notes, for the biblical prophets such a quest is unnecessary since 'God hath shewed thee, O man, what is good.' (Micah 6:8). So the law is regulatory in Strauss's Jerusalem: 'the word of God, as revealed to His prophets and especially to Moses, became *the* source of knowledge of good and evil.'[20]

The God of Strauss's Jerusalem who reveals himself in commands is inadequate for Grant in many other respects. Grant agrees with Strauss that the best translation for the reply of God to Moses' request for a name is 'I shall be what I shall be' (Exodus 3:14). The meaning here is not only that God's actions cannot be predicted, as Strauss points out, but also that arbitrary will is a characteristic of deity. Grant thinks it unwise to attribute will to deity because then 'you use language which implies that God interferes with secondary causes in an arbitrary way.'[21] He says that he prefers the word love to the arbitrary language of power. Another characteristic of the God of Jerusalem that Grant cannot condone is the affirmation that 'the God who manifests Himself as far as He wills, who is not universally worshipped as such, is the only true god.'[22] Noteworthy here is Strauss's use of the small 'g.' In the Bible, accessibility to any traditional or cosmic gods is forbidden by an act of God's will. Those gods that are accessible to man as man in Athens, and therefore have universal qualities, are expressly forbidden in Jerusalem. Here, says Strauss, we see 'the fundamental opposition of Athens at its peak to Jerusalem.'[23] For Grant there is in the *Iliad* and the *Odyssey* 'a genuine sense of religious experience and religious awareness.'[24] He reminds us that 'Socrates doesn't attack Delphi, he praises Delphi.'[25] And whereas it is crucial to remember that 'the god or a god are different from God,' polytheism is the legitimate public religion of Athens (Greece) and manifests an immanence that may be encompassed within 'the prodigious transcendence that is present in Christianity and Platonism'.[26] One can envisage Grant asking his friend Dennis Lee's question, 'What would a god be like?' Grant says that Protestantism, following the Hebrews, has almost totally eliminated what for the Greeks and Roman Catholics is essential to religion, namely, mediation. And, similarly, the emphasis within the Hebrew Bible on what Grant calls 'the simple unity'[27] of God has placed a barrier before any conception of God as love because 'love is always a relation.'[28] This, says Grant, is Christianity's criticism of Judaism and Islam and 'why Christianity seems in a certain way closer to Hinduism than it does to its fellow religions that arose in the Middle East.'[29] And, as a less gentle criticism, Grant suggests that it is 'pure cold monotheism which produces a very violent society.'[30] In 1988 Grant was speculating about calamities arising out of the pure monotheisms, those very dangerous religions 'that have cut down all the intermediate forms.'[31]

There are four other aspects of the biblical God that Grant found problematic. According to Strauss, the biblical God is 'as they say now, a person.'[32] Grant counters: 'I don't like at all language about God which uses personal pronouns.'[33] Then again, says Strauss, essential to the biblical God is the concern of God with man, and 'that concern is, to put it very mildly, a problem for every Greek philosopher.'[34] And so it was for Grant, who preferred the New Testament language in which God 'makes his sun to rise on the evil and the good, and sends rain on the just and the unjust.'[35] Also, Strauss notes that the biblical notion of divine omnipotence is 'absolutely incompatible with Greek philosophy in any form.'[36] Grant, for his part, wrestled with divine omnipotence, and within the Godhead came down on the side of goodness. This was consistent with his view that love has no part in force and that the absence of God (or the powerlessness of God) was a more fitting conception than that of the Hebrew Bible. Grant quotes approvingly Simone Weil's assertion that 'Jehovah's juridical relationship to the Hebrews is that of a master to his slaves.'[37] Finally, the biblical God creates the world by his word. As Strauss writes, 'the coming-into-being and the preservation of the world that he has created depends on the will of its maker.'[38] This notion of wilful creation presents real difficulties for Grant because any attempt to describe the manifestation of God's perfection must be couched rather in the language of love. Only this language, not that of arbitrary will, can furnish some rationale for a creative act on the part of deity. Such an event 'should not be talked about in the arbitrary language of power.'[39] It is apparent how, in confronting each of these characteristics of the biblical God, Grant's Christian Platonism provided the basis for his critique of the Jerusalem of Leo Strauss.

The absence of Christ from Strauss's Jerusalem is vividly illustrated in the direct correlation he perceives between the *Republic* Book II and Isaiah 53:7: 'One cannot read Plato's description in the second book of the *Republic* of the perfectly just man who suffers what would be the just fate of the most unjust man without being reminded of Isaiah's description of him who has done no violence, neither was any deceit in his mouth, yet who was oppressed and afflicted and brought as a lamb to the slaughter.'[40] Strauss must certainly have been aware that, for Christians, there was a direct correlation between the suffering servant of Isaiah, the perfectly just man of Plato, *and* the Christ of the cross. Grant criticizes Strauss not only for not giving Christianity its due but also (as will be expounded in detail below) because the absence of Christ results in a less than adequate account of the human condition.

GRANT'S SOCRATES

For Grant, Socrates was Plato's Socrates, whereas Leo Strauss wrote extensively on Xenophon's and Aristophanes' Socrates in addition to the predominant one of Plato. Wayne Hankey's statement that 'Grant never wrote about Platonism'[41] is an exaggeration, but references in works published in his lifetime are rare and come late. However, Grant was teaching Plato as early as 1950 and continued to do so throughout his long academic career. Notes for his early lectures on Plato have been recently published in volume 2 of his collected works, and these can be supplemented by published conversations in three different contexts.[42]

Clearly, Socrates was philosophy for Grant. He is the paradigm of philosophy, the *lover* of wisdom. (The word 'lover' is underlined by Grant whereas it is overlooked by most modern interpreters of Plato.) For Grant, 'Plato is the philosopher who says very clearly that the intelligence is enlightened by love.'[43] The enlightenment in Plato is the result of gift or grace: 'Platonism is a great language of grace, isn't it, and in that sense it is a two-way street.'[44] Grant would affirm Michel Despland's judgment that 'Plato believes that the soul's path to goodness is eased by the presence of a cosmic pull that keeps the soul open to transcendent realities and helps it on its way towards them.'[45] Socrates is crucial in the 'two-way street' because he represents the god Eros and shows how love mediates between man and God. In the *Apology* he says, 'I'm God's gift to Athens. God sent me to you.'[46] Grant is critical of interpreters such as Anders Nygren and C.S. Lewis who draw a rigid line between agape (love as gift) and eros (love as desire) and who thus ignore the two-way street. Socrates as Eros mediates both ways between the temporal and the eternal, allowing the temporal to be 'the moving image of the eternal.' Grant refers to the fable in *Symposium* where Eros is begotten of two parents called 'Fullness and Need,' thus mediating between the perfection of God and the human striving towards it.[47]

For Grant, Socrates as Eros demonstrates in his being how there can be no disjunction between love and justice. Grant says: 'I don't like at all the Western language that holds apart love and justice ... that justice is something elementary then there is love beyond it, because I don't see, on that view, how there could be any justice. One sees this very clearly in the fact that when people saw other races as non-people – that is, they had no love for them – then they could not be just! People come to know justice by loving it, don't they?'[48] Justice and love are intimately bound up in the life and teaching of Socrates. There is the question, however, whether all people or only the philosophers, the lovers of wisdom, can be lovers of justice. The whole of the Platonic corpus has as its end the education or making of philosophers of whom Socrates is the type or model. Grant says that 'there are great similarities and great differences'[49] between Socrates and Christ, and this is a point of utmost significance. 'The greatest reaches of experience are limited to only a few in Plato. And in Christianity they cannot be,' claims Grant.[50] To him,

Nietzsche's aphorism of Christianity as 'Platonism for the people' was a brilliant description of the difference. Here we have a contrary that Grant will hold up as requiring some resolution beyond the level of reasoned thought. Similarly, the problem posed by the philosopher's (Socrates') relentless dedication to the pursuit of the truth and the extent to which this must inevitably eliminate charitable good works is held up by Grant as a conflict within which one must live. For him personally, he says that 'this is where the conflict between Christianity and philosophy arises'[51] and he lived in this tension for his entire life.

There are some real paradoxes to be faced in endeavouring to describe Grant's Platonism. He hardly ever mentions it, yet, as one observer noted in Grant's presence, 'obviously the tradition of Athens, and of Plato in particular, is present in everything you say.'[52] But, if Plato is present in everything he says, why is this not more evident in his discussions of modern thinkers such as Nietzsche and Heidegger? Their thought is so compelling for contemporaries, says Grant, that 'it is almost impossible for anybody to get near to apprehending what Plato is asserting.'[53] In other words, 'the circle of our present destiny'[54] almost totally excludes any Platonic language. Paradoxically, Grant asserts that his deliberate purpose in engaging modern thought 'was to allow me (indeed only slightly) to partake in the alternative assumptions of Plato. It is by looking at modernity in its greatest power that one is perhaps able ever slightly to escape its power.'[55] Even though somewhat dimmed, Plato's light can still illuminate the darkness of modernity.

It seems paradoxical also that Mrs Grant, who knew him better than anyone, could write an entire article on the religious influences upon Grant's thought and yet not mention Socrates. Yet, while there is no specific reference to Grant's Platonism in the article, that influence is implied in Mrs Grant's conclusion that 'Grant never doubted that good is good and evil its absence, and we need to know which is which, however mixed in human experience, and however limited in our understanding.'[56]

Laurence Lampert, in 'The Uses of Philosophy in George Grant,' puts forward the view that the paradoxes noted above are addressed by the Platonic wisdom itself. In Lampert's view, Grant's reticence to speak openly about Plato's doctrines signifies

an increasing appreciation of the Socratic notion that what needs to be learned cannot be taught directly. With Socrates Grant holds that the task of the philosopher is not to list the good things and encourage pursuit of them; such naivety defeats the aim of discovering wisdom at the beginning ... Perhaps the only task for the philosopher as teacher is to undo the assurances that move us to pursue the less than high ends, to clarify, that is, the nature of the public truths we find ourselves committted to so readily and so unthinkingly. Philosophy in this sense is truly subversive.[57]

There is another sense in which philosophy is subversive for Grant. Modernity must be subverted, not only so that its assumptions will crumble on their own terms, but also to 'free people from that which can hold them from ever thinking that Christianity might be true.' This is a hidden agenda for Grant but it is, nonetheless, one function of Grant's Socrates. Not only must philosophy admit the possibility of revelation, as per Strauss, but in the final analysis Grant sees philosophy as subservient to 'the magistery of revelation,'[58] as will be documented in the following section.

Grant thought that it was essential, when making public statements, to be considerate of his audience. In public institutions where he taught, he says that 'it was probably alright to talk about Socrates but it was not alright to talk about Christ.'[59] While the world of the university was very hostile to both of these figures whom Grant admired, the Socratic method of dialectic could be usefully employed. By this means, Grant could speak indirectly, and so pursue a deliberate strategy of subversion. Lampert points out how the use of the Socratic method allowed Grant to subvert modernity's assumptions on their own terms. 'It is misleading,' he says, 'to call Grant's work on the modern "criticism," for as Grant sees it, when the modern is clarified in its fundamental nature its deficiency is simply apparent: it convicts itself; it need not be "criticized," only understood.'[60] By holding Socrates apart from Christ in the context of his teaching and public writings, Grant was attempting to provide an account of the modern that stood on its own, apart from any validation by revelation. Grant says, 'somebody such as myself, inescapably bound to Christianity, must try to understand what it is to think at a superlative level, with Christianity put aside root and branch.'[61] Grant here uses the word 'think' to place himself within the Socratic methodology, the means whereby he can legitimately operate rationally without any recourse to revelation. On this point, it is worth noting that Grant admires Céline precisely because 'he is describing the world as it is whether there is a God or not.'[62] Grant is arguing that the philosopher can and should endeavour to enucleate phenomena by means of Socratic dialectic. The endeavour will be, like most of the Platonic dialogues, not definitive or conclusive, and it may be that revelation will be requisite in order to penetrate further into that piece of reality. So Socratic rationalism is a cardinal element in Grant's search for understanding if not (as will be noted in the next section) the foremost element.

Because Socrates knows what he doesn't know, there are clear limits to Socratic rationalism; it can take the seeker only so far. In one of his early lectures, Grant expounds the limits of Socratic rationalism: 'The way of thought is a way of negation. Gradually as we pass beyond contradictions – we are able to say that ultimate reality is not this or that, but in thought we can never say what it is – at the end of our going this reality will be revealed to us directly. For now we know in part – but then face to face.'[63] Philosophy can climb no farther up the ladder – it can only look up, wait, and love. So we must, says Grant, move on from Socrates to Christ.

GRANT'S CHRIST

Beyond Socrates the height for Grant is the Christ of the Gospels, but 'the question is what is in the Gospels.'[64] And the answer to this question is best summarized in Grant's relating of how Heidegger's contempt for Christianity would make it impossible for anyone to believe that he found in the Gospels 'the revelation of perfection.' Grant expands what he means by this phrase: 'I use here together the subjective and objective genitives.'[65] Christ is the content of revelation for Grant because he is an image in this world of 'the perfection of all purposes which has been called God.'[66]

It is the Christ of the Gospels that is the revelation of perfection, not the Jesus of history. Grant rarely, if ever, speaks or writes of Jesus. Even the young Jesus is 'the child Christ arguing in the temple.'[67] Mrs Grant explains how, for her husband, 'the life and Passion of Christ were historical events, but not only historical. What they revealed of the nature of things is true for all times and all places.'[68] Expressing this differently, he says: 'of course Christ is perfection but I do not see the scheme that perfection only happens once.'[69] What is important is 'what is universal about Christ,'[70] and Grant is especially critical of modern theologians who make Christianity depend on the religious history of a particular people: 'they make Christianity such an historical religion that its universal teaching about perfection and affliction is lost.'[71]

In Platonic language this universal teaching is the distance between the necessary and the Good, and for Grant the cross of Christ is the supreme image of the way things are for humans, bound up as they are within the desire for good and simultaneously crushed by necessity. Undoubtedly this is why Grant stated that he favoured the death of Christ over the death of Socrates: 'Doesn't this account of death go more to the heart of what life is than Socrates – the fear, his sweat was these great drops of blood falling to the ground. All this is what convinces me of Christianity; it seems to me important. This is more what life is like ... I think the death of Socrates is consummately beautiful and noble and a great and wonderful death which everyone should look upon. But it seems to me death is more like the other.'[72] In the matter of death, as in all matters of importance, Grant sides with the theologian of the cross rather than the theologian of glory who 'says that evil is good and good evil.' The theologian of the cross 'says that the thing is as it is'[73] and it is the denial that final purpose can be argued from the world which provides 'the only true illumination' of the mystery of evil, namely, 'the crucifixion apprehended in faith as the divine humiliation.'[74]

Grant recognized that to speak of Christ one must utilize the language of good, which modern scholarship (research) ignores. So-called 'value-free' propositions about Jesus totally miss the mark of the Christ of the Gospels. Only to those who are at least partially outside of the modern paradigm can Grant speak and find a resonance. 'I am concerned,' he says, 'with the group at the multiversity with some sense of the eternal good, which is God, and perhaps even some sense of the declaration of that eternity in Christ.'[75] The Platonic language of good is Grant's means of speaking of that eternity.

Grant notes that Strauss claimed that it was wrong to interpret the *Republic* as teaching that absolute justice and suffering go together. Grant comments: 'I presume that he is speaking as an Aristotelian.'[76] Grant, in contrast, sees the tortured just man of the *Republic* as prefiguring Christ. In Christ the suffering of love is, for Grant,' a supreme act of justice.'[77] Grant's description of this in 'Faith and the Multiversity' is a striking example of Platonism permeating his thought: 'What Christianity added to the classical account of justice was not any change in its definition but an extension of what was due to others and an account of how to fulfill that due. Christ added to the two great commandments the words that the second is "like unto" the first. At the height of the Gospels we are shown the moment when a tortured human being says of his torturers that their due is to be forgiven.'[78] The way in which, to Grant, Platonism and Christianity complement one another on justice (in definite contrast to Strauss, who sees only half of the equation) is summed up by Joan O'Donovan. She says that 'it is from the revelation of divine justice in Plato and the Gospels' that 'Grant has the assurance that justice is not only that by which we are measured (the eternal and unchanging law), but also that by which we are redeemed and sanctified (the power of suffering love). He is given to know that divine justice touches us not only in the necessity of the world but in the faceless yet irresistable persuasion of divine grace.'[79] In an early lecture Grant described the persuasive power of suffering love: 'In the cross an innocent being sheds the light of salvation upon evil – because here necessity is being infinitely persuaded.'[80]

Within the revelation of Christ, charity is foremost. This means that, even though revelation must be thought, the charity or love at its heart cannot be grasped by thought. Clearly, the Straussian dichotomy between free insight and obedient love is relevant here since charity is 'the obedient giving oneself away'[81] and Strauss's contemplative thought (the height of existence for him) is merely a means to that higher end.

For Grant, 'the giving of oneself away which we call charity'[82] is supremely embodied in the Christ of God. But saints also partake of it. Grant points to people like Francis of Assisi and Simone Weil who exist not just at the level of intelligence but at a level that is far more important. There he says he sees 'the divine love and that love in human beings.'[83] While Christ and his cross represent the 'type' of self-offering, charity is a gift of God universally accessible and in no way dependent upon intelligence.

The divine love expresses itself in Christ. So once again, because of love and because it always involves relations, God cannot be a simple unity. For Grant, 'the Trinity is no analogy. It is simply the clearest word to express what is seen directly in the Passion of Christ.'[84] What the crucifixion demonstrates is that 'the highest love is that love which crosses an infinite distance,' and so, for both Grant and Simone Weil, the necessary and the Good converge in the cross. When conversing with David Cayley, Grant quotes Simone Weil directly: 'the infinite distance between God and God is necessity. The necessity which God has to cross to love God is the cross.'[85] An explanation for this most difficult of mental images is attempted by Grant in a 1958 lecture: 'Because the suffering is no longer seen as meaningful then the good which bears the suffering is a purely supernatural good – purely supernatural because not depending on any help outside itself.'[86]

It is very difficult for thought to attempt any delineation of the inner life of the deity, however such thought is mandated by any affirmation that the Christ of God is love incarnate. Grant does not hesitate to apply his reason to this most challenging of paradoxes but he says that he here confronts a mystery, not a problem that can be solved. Still, philosophy 'gets you into these great mysteries' and it is not frivolous 'to spend one's life trying to enter more and more deeply into them.'[87] This entry of philosophy into the very heart of theology as the means whereby the most serious of contradictions are confronted points to the necessity of a critical appraisal of Grant's attempt to hold Socrates and Christ together. As early as 1958 Grant wrote: 'When two incompatible thoughts present themselves to us we must exhaust every recourse of our intelligence to try to eliminate one of the conflicting and incompatible thoughts. If this is impossible – if both insist on imposing themselves on our minds ... Then it becomes necessary to use this contradiction as a kind of pincers, to try to enter directly in contact with the transcendent which otherwise is inaccessible to human beings. This is what the doctrine of mystery means.'[88] The question to be resolved is whether the illumination of Grant's intellect by love has shed some light on this mystery, this unknown unity.

CHRIST AND SOCRATES

In a statement that must be judged as arising out of Grant's experiences in the Second World War, he places himself within the central polarity of Western thought: 'Don't serious people have to live in the presence of the contradiction between the perfection of God and the affliction of human beings? Christianity flashes its light into that contradiction – but also makes it a deeper contradiction ... Christianity is only a kind of beacon flashing in the darkness. That beacon does not overcome the necessity of philosophy in the way that certain theologians seem to think it does.'[89] The experiences of 'the perfection of God' first came upon Grant during the war, as did the horror and suffering of victims of the bombing. Significantly, Grant always described his conversion experience not in Christocentric but in philosophical language. Through this experience, he says, he came to know that ultimately he did not belong to himself, and as a result he had 'to begin to understand what were the consequences in thinking that there was an eternal order by which we are measured and defined.'[90] Right from the beginning, his conversion experience and philosophy had to be thought together. And the more he thought the more he saw Christ as 'the revelation of perfection' – Christ became the 'content' of his not being his own.

About 1950 he began to read Simone Weil, whom he later acknowl-
edged as 'the greatest influence in my life of any thinker. She has shown
me what it is to hold Christ and Plato together. She has shown me how
sanctity and philosophy can be at one.'[91] The oneness is an ultimate
unity, a light shining in the darkness but diffused and dimly perceived
to greater and lesser degrees by humans, and most evident in the lives
of the saints. Grant says that 'it is the mark of the authentic religious life
to contemplate such unities.'[92] But any person on whom the light has
shone may respond in love and discover in the process his or her intellect being illuminated by love. Grant was such a person who sought in
his whole being to hold sanctity and philosophy together.

Grant says that 'the close connection between Socrates and Christ lies
in the fact that Socrates is the primal philosophic teacher of the dependence of what we know upon what we love.'[93] Goodness, like Socrates
and Christ, is a gift and draws from humans their loving. Those who
seek to understand what has been received will have their intellects
illumined by love. Charity, not thought, is the height of existence, but
both are important for anyone who seeks to understand. And, corre-
spondingly, anyone who seeks to understand cannot brush aside the
prior claim of charity. As Grant says: 'Anybody whose life is given over
to philosophy needs to read the thirteenth chapter of First Corinthians
regularly.'[94] Grant alludes to the conflict in his own being between the
need to give concentrated thought to the contraries and the demands of
charity, and he found the two coalescing as thought demanded action
(on, for example, the Vietnam War, abortion, and euthanasia). On such
practical matters, he, the philosopher, often found himself among those
for whom the primacy of charity was totally separate from any thought
processes; and to the extent that they were, to a greater degree than he
was, giving themselves away in love, he admired them greatly. 'Anybody is open to love,' he says, 'and that is the supreme act.'[95]

A view of freedom as being given through truth unites Socrates and
Christ. Both in effect taught that 'the truth shall make you free.' For
both, says Grant, 'the great things of our existing are given us, not made
by us and finally not to be understood as arbitrary accidents. Our making takes place within an ultimate giveness ... For myself I would now
[1988] define "freedom" as the liberty to be indifferent to good.' This is,
of course, a very different use of the word from the modern, which is
'absoluteness of choice, both in doing and making.'[96]

Grant was perplexed that Strauss, whom he greatly admired, could
not permit any admixture of reason and revelation in a single individ-

ual. Relevant here are a few points on which Strauss's thesis would challenge Grant's holding together of Socrates and Christ. Strauss points out that there is no word for doubt in the Bible; on the other hand, as Grant says, 'Socrates knew that doubt was a necessary means to philosophy.'[97] Strauss implies that the obedient love of the Bible is diametrically opposed to the free insight of philosophy. But Grant counters that 'the *Republic* makes clear that such doubt is within the overreaching assumption of trust,'[98] a trust that being is under the yoke of good. On the basis of reason illumined by love, one can argue for trust, and therefore one does not relinquish philosophy when one has opted for trust. Similarly, Strauss contrasts the philosopher's life dedicated to the quest for knowledge of the Good to the life of obedient love characterized by the moral virtues. If you have been told what is right, then you will not have to spend time trying to discern the right and you can get on with the business of acting and doing. The dilemma, as Strauss poses it, would be insolvable so long as the operation remains solely within the realm of thought. But, for Grant, thought is not the height of existence, love is. And it is not *knowledge* of the Good but *love* of the Good which is, according to Socrates, the core of the philosophic life. Because the intellect is illumined by love, philosophy does not necessarily preclude action – Socrates and Christ are again drawn together by love. It is the reality of love that allows Grant to hold together Socrates and Christ while admitting that, within the strict confines of dialectical thought, they appear to be irreconcilable contraries.

Both Strauss and Grant agree that it is necessary to *live* the conflict between philosophy and theology, reason and revelation. Strauss lives it *in his mind*, and within this context the contraries must be held apart. For him, living the conflict means that one must take a stand on one side or the other and no ultimate unity or synthesis can be rationally countenanced. Grant, on the other hand, lives the conflict *in his whole being* – not simply his intellect, but also by what has been granted to him as the faculty of love. He lives the conflict between philosophy and theology by embracing both and utilizing different languages at different times depending on his audience. On occasion he adopts the role of the thinker endeavouring to be explicit philosophically. He says, for example, that he is interested in 'understanding technique in a philosophical manner.'[99] And, then again, when speaking to persons of faith within the university, he will speak openly of 'that eternity in Christ.' Metaphorically speaking, he was at times Socrates and at times Christ. But he did clearly live within both of them; and how he lived both of them is summed up in his statement that 'Christianity is as much the practice of dying as Socrates said that philosophy was.'[100]

Grant described himself as 'a Platonist within Christianity.'[101] What does 'within Christianity' mean for Grant, and to what extent does his Platonism qualify his Christianity? To answer these questions one must first summarize what of traditional Christianity is shaken out of the mix by Grant, then look at the kernel that remains. As has been noted, Grant distances himself from what he calls the triumphalist elements within Western Christianity. These include doctrines of particular providence, creation as wilful action, omnipotence within deity, *heilsgeschichte* (or God's plan in history), natural theology, pure monotheisms that exclude mediation, and any attempt to define or confine the absolute Good within temporal limits. Grant judged that Eastern Christianity, because of its underlying Platonism, was less inclined to the aberrations he saw in Western Christianity, which, he says, 'became exclusivist and imperialistic, arrogant and dynamic.'[102] The absence of exclusivity in Grant's Christianity is clear in his statement that 'what was given traditionally in the word "good" was not confined to Christians.'[103] Mrs Grant notes that Grant referred to himself as being 'on the Hindu wing of Christianity' and she attributes this to his taking Christian doctrines 'in a Platonic sense.' Therefore, says Mrs Grant, 'he did not understand Christianity as an exclusive sect of which one is in or out, but rather as an account of how things are.'[104] Expanding on these thoughts, one must conclude that Grant was not a believer in the sense of affirming creedal or doctrinal statements, attempts by Christians at various times to codify belief and concomitantly exclude non-believers. The Platonist within Grant would not permit his being relegated to the Straussian designation of 'believer' and thus confined to the ranks of those living in loving obedience, as contrasted to the philosophic life of free insight. It is the illumination of the intellect by love that separates obedience to what the church teaches from a contemplation by reason of the mysteries in such a way that the soul is open to the truth that the mysteries contain. This is substantially different from affirming or denying doctrines as if they were empirical facts or geometrical theorems; the affirming, in this context, always implies a corresponding denial.

Grant's Platonism pared down his Christianity to the bare essentials. These, for Grant, are all centred on the Christ of the Gospels, the 'revelation of perfection.' The cross is the linchpin for Grant because it is the supreme revelation of the way things are for humans. What is here revealed about the distance between the perfection of God and the affliction of men is true for all times and all places. Grant affirms Simone Weil's statement that 'wherever there is affliction, there is the Cross.' For Weil, 'Christ represents the union of these contradictories,'[105] because only love can cross this distance. And, like Weil, Grant will say nothing about the resurrection other than it 'must not be thought apart from the Cross': for Grant, as for Weil, 'our country is the Cross.'[106] The two are also united in their view that the incarnation is not a once-and-for-all event but 'a perpetual act of love on the part of God ... the "word become flesh" is thus the form that compassion takes in this world; it is the form of poetry, to speak metaphorically, which Weil feels God has written and is writing at every moment.'[107] Finally, Grant's Christ is 'the perfectly just man' of Plato, and Grant is acutely aware of the distance that any human being is from this perfection. And this is the final way in which his Platonism affected his Christianity – it kept him, as it did his mentor Simone Weil, on the fringe of Christianity. He was cognizant of Nietzsche's aphorism that there was only one Christian, the man on the cross. And taking up the cross, denying oneself in even a partial emulation of the Christ, is a terrifying prospect. For this reason, Grant was extremely reticent to make any open profession of his Christian faith. He well knew the truth of Weil's words that 'matter is our infallible judge.'

To summarize Grant on Christ and Socrates: Grant *is held* by Christ and *he holds* Socrates and Christ together in thought as far as he is able. Just as Socrates taught that the good conquers necessity by persuasion, so Grant was persuaded by Christ.

PERSONAL ADDENDUM

The writing of this chapter has prompted me to make a personal judgment about the nature of George Grant's genius. In brief, it is my view that, throughout his intellectual life, Grant's mind was simultaneously operating on two levels, the one the source and foundation of the other.

The first and underlying level has been examined and laid out as the substance of this chapter. I am sure that there are many, such as myself, who are lovers of wisdom and at the same time held by revelation, for whom Grant's monumental effort to hold the two together has proven instructive. I personally have been reflecting on these contraries for the forty years since I first encountered Grant's thought. I studied under him at McMaster, taught with him in the same department, and cherished a distant relationship with him until his death. As an ordained minister and a teacher of philosophy, I have lived the conflict of which I have written here. I personally have experienced what Strauss called the creative tension in Western civilization, and Grant has pointed me to the richest sources for its nurture. I rejoice that many mysteries still persist.

While writing this chapter I have come to realize that the intellectual journey of my life was only one dimension of George Grant's intellectual life. All that is catalogued here is, in a sense, background for Grant – a prologomenon for his task as an enucleator or commentator on his present. A careful reader of what I have written will notice that there are few quotations from Grant's published works (and these are almost all from his latest writings). Most of the evidence for Grant's Christian Platonism comes from conversations, letters, and lectures. Christian readers of Grant's published works have often expressed regret that he didn't write more about his Christianity. I am certain that this was a deliberate strategy on Grant's part. In private he had to be continually satisfying the intellectual demands of professing Christianity and Platonism, but he was also simultaneously utilizing these to enucleate the realities of his world in his published works. For readers of these works, what really matters is the truthfulness of his accounts, and, for Grant, both philosophy and Christianity were means to this end. Wayne Hankey writes that Grant used his Platonic philosophy 'to paint his pictures of our present.'[108] And Mrs Grant tells how Grant from his student days at Oxford used the theology of the cross as the best means of showing 'that the thing is as it is.' For Grant, as for Simone Weil, 'truth is the radiant manifestation of reality' and 'to desire truth is to desire contact with a piece of reality. To desire contact with a piece of reality is to love.'[109] Grant's public writings are a testament as to how both philosophy and the theology of the cross can illuminate an intellect that loves truth. His genius was that he could operate at the level of enucleation and achieve penetrating clarity without divulging the ultimate sources (Socrates and Christ) of his compelling analyses.

Some readers of Grant will detect only one source, Socratic rationalism, as the foundation for the truthfulness of his pictures of our present, and this is because he succeeded in engaging his readers 'with Christianity put aside root and branch.' But others, such as myself, who have tasted the riches of both of Grant's sources will understand why 'there is no philosophy, no hope, nothing, if we do not worship.'[110]

NOTES

1 Leo Strauss, *The Rebirth of Classical Political Rationalism: Essays and Lectures by Leo Strauss*, ed. Thomas Pangle (Chicago: University of Chicago Press, 1989), 260.
2 Ibid., 270.
3 George Grant, *Two Theological Languages / by George Grant, and Other Essays in Honour of His Work*, ed. Wayne Whillier (Lewiston, NY: Edwin Mellen Press, 1990), 18.
4 Ibid., 26.
5 Ibid.
6 Arthur Davis, ed., *Collected Works of George Grant, Volume 2, 1951–1959* (Toronto: University of Toronto Press, 2002), 402.
7 Leo Strauss, *Studies in Platonic Political Philosophy* (Chicago: University of Chicago Press, 1983), 22.
8 Strauss, *The Rebirth of Classical Political Rationalism*, 269.
9 Alan Udoff, ed., *Leo Strauss's Thought: Toward a Critical Engagement* (Boulder, CO: Lynne Reinner Publishers, 1991), 22.
10 Ibid.
11 Strauss, *The Rebirth of Classical Political Rationalism*, 251.
12 Grant, *Two Theological Languages*, 78.
13 Larry Schmidt, ed., *George Grant in Process: Essays and Conversations* (Toronto: House of Anansi Press, 1978), 107.
14 Ibid., 65.
15 Ibid.
16 George Grant, *Technology and Justice* (Toronto: Anansi, 1986), 44.
17 Grant, *Two Theological Languages*, 74.
18 Udoff, ed., *Leo Strauss's Thought*, 22.
19 Schmidt, ed., *George Grant in Process*, 65.
20 Strauss, *Studies in Platonic Political Philosophy*, 163.
21 Schmidt, ed., *George Grant in Process*, 108.
22 Strauss, *Studies in Platonic Political Philosophy*, 166.
23 William Christian, 'George Grant and Religion: A Conversation,' prepared and edited by William Christian, July 1988, 17. In the possession of the author.
24 Ibid.
25 Ibid., 19.
26 Ibid.
27 David Cayley, *George Grant in Conversation* (Don Mills, ON: Anansi, 1995), 196.

28 Ibid., 176

29 Ibid.

30 Christian, George Grant and Religion,' 18.

31 Ibid., 20.

32 Strauss, *Studies in Platonic Political Philosophy*, 162.

33 Cayley, *George Grant in Conversation*, 175.

34 Strauss, *The Rebirth of Classical Political Rationalism*, 252.

35 Cayley, *George Grant in Conversation*, 183.

36 Strauss, *The Rebirth of Classical Political Rationalism*, 252.

37 Cayley, *George Grant in Conversation*, 36.

38 Strauss, *Studies in Platonic Political Philosophy*, 166.

39 Schmidt, ed., *George Grant in Process*, 109.

40 Strauss, *The Rebirth of Classical Political Rationalism*, 248.

41 Wayne Hankey, "James Doull, Etienne Gilson and George Grant on Modernity," *The Friend*, Easter 2000, 19.

42 Cayley, *George Grant in Conversation*; Christian, 'George Grant and Religion'; and Schmidt, ed., *George Grant in Process*.

43 Cayley, *George Grant in Conversation*, 178.

44 Christian, 'George Grant and Religion,' 24.

45 Michel Despland, *The Education of Desire: Plato and the Philosophy of Religion* (Toronto: University of Toronto Press, 1985), 165.

46 Christian, 'George Grant and Religion,' 16.

47 Grant, Technology and Justice, 74.

48 Cayley, *George Grant in Conversation*, 179.

49 Christian, 'George Grant and Religion,' 24.

50 Ibid., 25.

51 Ibid., 34.

52 Schmidt, ed., *George Grant in Process*, 102.

53 Ibid., 67.

54 Ibid.

55 Ibid.

56 Joan O'Donovan, *George Grant and the Twilight of Justice* (Toronto: University. of Toronto Press, 1984), 259.

57 Schmidt, ed., *George Grant in Process*, 194.

58 Ibid., 150.

59 Christian, 'George Grant and Religion,' 2.

60 Schmidt, ed., *George Grant in Process*, 193.

61 Ibid., 67.

62 O'Donovan, *George Grant and the Twilight of Justice*, 44.

63 Davis, ed., Collected Works, 462.

64 Schmidt, ed., *George Grant in Process*, 108.
65 Grant, *Two Theological Languages*, 18.
66 George Grant, *Technology and Justice*, 74.
67 Davis, ed., *Collected Works*, 441.
68 O'Donovan, *George Grant and the Twilight of Justice*, 256.
69 William Christian, ed., *George Grant: Selected Letters* (Toronto: University of Toronto Press 1996), 323.
70 Schmidt, ed., *George Grant in Process*, 102.
71 Ibid.
72 Christian, 'George Grant and Religion,' 21.
73 O'Donovan, *George Grant and the Twilight of Justice*, 244.
74 George Grant, *Technology and Empire: Perspectives on North America* (Toronto: House of Anansi 1969), 20.
75 Grant, *Technology and Justice*, 68.
76 Christian, ed., *Selected Letters*, 231.
77 Cayley, *George Grant in Conversation*, 179.
78 Grant, *Technology and Justice*, 54.
79 O'Donovan, *George Grant and the Twilight of Justice*, 87.
80 Davis, ed., *Collected Works*, 483.
81 Grant, *Technology and Empire*, 35.
82 Grant, *Technology and Justice*, 74.
83 Cayley, *George Grant in Conversation*, 173.
84 Davis, ed., *Collected Works*, 484.
85 Cayley, *George Grant in Conversation*, 176.
86 Davis, ed., *Collected Works*, 483.
87 Cayley, *George Grant in Conversation*, 171.
88 Davis, ed., *Collected Works*, 489.
89 Schmidt, ed., *George Grant in Process*, 101.
90 Christian, 'George Grant and Religion,' 13.
91 Schmidt, ed., *George Grant in Process*, 65.
92 Davis, ed., *Collected Works*, 489.
93 Grant, *Technology and Justice*, 72.
94 Schmidt, ed., *George Grant in Process*, 107.
95 Ibid.
96 Grant, *Two Theological Languages*, xv, 17.
97 Grant, *Technology and Justice*, 43.
98 Ibid.
99 Christian, ed., *Selected Letters*, 279.
100 Grant, *Technology and Justice*, 72.
101 Christian, 'George Grant and Religion,' 21.

102 Grant, *Technology and Empire*, 76.

103 Grant, *Technology and Justice*, 42.

104 Arthur Davis, ed., *George Grant and the Subversion of Modernity: Art, Philosophy, Politics, Religion, and Education* (Toronto: University of Toronto Press, 1996), 244, 257.

105 Grant, *Two Theological Languages*, 57.

106 Davis, ed., *George Grant and the Subversion of Modernity*, 255.

107 Grant, *Two Theological Languages*, 56.

108 Hankey, "James Doull, Etienne Gilson and George Grant on Modernity," 19.

109 Davis, ed., *George Grant and the Subversion of Modernity*, 244 and 257.

110 Davis, ed., *Collected Works*, 499.

19

Freedom and the Good

GRAEME NICHOLSON

It is right to call George Grant a public philosopher, but this only invites us to reflect on what that term means. Why isn't all philosophy public? Socrates was certainly a public figure and that was true generally of the ancient philosophers. What is special, then, about the public philosopher nowadays? We have to realize that, today, a public philosopher is being marked off, not from someone who philosophizes merely privately and reclusively, but from the academic philosopher. Yet in fact George Grant was very much an academic. Could it still be true, nevertheless, that he was a public philosopher and not an academic one? Yes, this can be true, because what makes a philosopher public is the fact that he *has* a public, he *has* a readership, as George Grant certainly did. What we today mean by an 'academic' philosopher is that he or she has no public. The only people who read works of academic philosophy are other academics, members of 'the profession,' as it is called – and *they* read only for professional reasons. This is no public, just a band of jealous rivals.

George Grant was *Canada's* most significant public philosopher, meaning that his public was Canadian. It is a credit to Canadian education and democracy that our public philosopher was an academic who was deeply immersed in the study of Greek philosophy, medieval theology, and modern culture. Grant gained a reading public in spite of the high elitism of his literary references, and despite the absence of familiar jargon from his prose. He did not flatter his audience – he did not make them feel better about themselves, but worse. In its care and moderation, his writing compares favourably with the popular rhetoric of Noam Chomsky and Bertrand Russell, and reflects an excellence in the public domain of Canada, which surpasses the United States and the United Kingdom in this respect. Grant's public philosophy drew upon the deepest and most ancient sources of philosophy itself, and so his writing is not only to be studied for its political and social tendency but also to be measured by the highest standards of classical scholarship and philosophical reason. Grant was that unusual thing: an author who had a public following but whose own formation was thoroughly mandarin. In his own writings, he was appealing to a *higher* standard of reason than did the academic philosophers who were so patronizing towards him.

Though he had been an active broadcaster and public lecturer for years before, it was his *Lament for a Nation* [*LN*][1] that gave him wide exposure throughout Canada and established him in the public eye as the great Red Tory. But it is entirely characteristic of Grant that his theme of the apparent disappearance of Canada itself into the maw of the U.S. republic was accompanied by two other themes that hovered beneath the political surface, and that he expressed forcefully in later publications. The first of these was the apparent termination of modern science and philosophy in a universal technology, a force that accompanied the Americanization of Canada but that clearly had a wider scope. Just as Canada was being exposed to its fate, so too, in modernity, reason itself was encountering its fate – in the universal extension of technology. After 1965, Grant will speak more and more about Jacques Ellul and Martin Heidegger. The second theme was the fate that appeared to confront Christianity – indeed, religion itself – in the age of the universal and homogeneous state. In the midst of Western history, we found a Christianity that was ambiguously intertwined with it. It had once been a reminder of the highest things – the Good – but it had in practice helped to foster the regime of technology and the release of the modern subject from all restraints. Christianity became the victim of an atheism it had somehow given birth to. Grant's readers, then, were invited to dwell upon what was at once intimate to our own Canadian life and a sinister fate of humankind as a whole.

Where Grant dwells upon the fate of philosophy, to terminate in technology, it is pre-eminently the theme of *freedom* that he highlights. So in the first part of this chapter, I put that theme at the centre of discussion. And, as Grant sees the fate of Christianity in modern times, it seems to have lost its focus on *the Good*: the Good has retreated into eclipse in the bleak present day of Christianity. I treat that topic in the second part of the chapter. As the chapter proceeds, I will try to reflect on how these two strands of Grant's thought, the philosophical and the theological, are woven together with each other.

The truth of natural law is that man lives within an order which he did not make and to which he must subordinate his actions; the truth of the history-making spirit is that man is free to build a society which eliminates the evils of the world. Both these assertions seem true. The difficulty is to understand how they both can be thought together.[2]

Philosophy in the Mass Age [PMA] was a successful combination of philosophical reasoning and public address, a book that circulated to a wide public but still demanded the attention and concentration typical of philosophy books, a true philosophical propaedeutic. The quotation I have taken from it states the problem towards which the entire book was driving. But just as surely these words could stand as a motto over the whole of Grant's work in the decades to come. Although the later work was to differ from that of the 1950s, in that he changed his mind on several vital questions, the reader today can see that there are common preoccupations and themes.

Let us look at how the dilemma is developed in *PMA*. The first aspect appears in the early chapters. It is introduced in chapter 3 under the heading of 'Natural Law.' Grant is speaking about the early tradition of philosophy that emerged soon after the displacement of the 'mythic consciousness' that he had treated in chapter 2. The main import of the idea of natural law for moral philosophy (the genre to which *PMA* belongs) is the normative and substantive role of reason. It has become common in modern times to think of reason only instrumentally, as the capacity to calculate the means conducive to a given end, or only scientifically, as the methodical research aimed at the external world, and often so as to exploit it instrumentally for human welfare. But the substantive doctrine of reason grasps it as a source of moral directives – indeed, as the illumination of existence itself. It is not merely our desires and inclinations that are fit to guide us, but above all our rational insight into what is right and good, a doctrine that Grant finds particularly well stated by both Plato and Aristotle (*PMA*, 36–9).

But this is not Grant's only point. Later, in the concluding chapters 6 to 7, he traces the core teaching of modern (that is, post-medieval) philosophy, precisely where it turned against the natural law tradition, and here we come upon the second horn of the dilemma we have quoted. The book underlines on many of its pages how essential autonomy is to human existence, especially the autonomy of human reason, a theme that emerged strongly in post-medieval Europe. In *PMA*, Grant identifies strongly with this modern tradition. He speaks with approval of Kant's moral philosophy, which bases everything on the autonomous reason of each and every human being (93–104). In other passages (chapter 4, especially pages 42 and 49; see also page vii in the 'New Introduction' of 1966), he ties his thought to the modern philosophy that grasps freedom as our very essence. What is vital is that the rule of *reason* is not separated, in modern philosophy, from the *freedom* of the subject. Indeed, it is precisely *in* the experience of freedom that the modern subject finds the presence of reason, and this substantive reason itself has, as a principal part of its content, the call to us all to be free, to liberate ourselves. This shows up in morality, for instance. Morality has been conceived in the main tradition of modern philosophy as a domain in which human beings are called upon to exercise their own reason independent of tradition and authority, for instance, the authority of religious faith. Reason has, as it were, migrated away from nature and the eternal, to take up residence within the freedom of subjectivity itself. This is at the core of the philosophy of Kant. And, of course, it seems to imply the autonomy of philosophy itself, as over against tradition and theology, one part of the autonomy of human reason.

The reader does not find that, in this book, Grant clearly chooses one side or the other of his dilemma: repeatedly he underlines the importance of the problem (98, 100, 103, 106) and the difficulty of its resolution. In this he is convincing, for it would have been a betrayal of the whole tenor of the book to try to settle the question by a few words and arguments. It is notable that the concluding pages bring to a head an issue that Grant connects closely to his master dilemma: the philosophy of nature. Any deeper investigation of the relationship between rational law and human freedom would need to invoke the domain of nature. For one thing, there is no doubt that human beings are so inserted in nature as to be subject to the laws of nature. Moreover, if there really is human freedom, the grounds of the possibility of that must be traced in some way within the depths of the organic processes of nature. This is a brilliant suggestion that is thrown out as an appropriate conclusion to the book, though it was never taken up later in Grant's work. The problem of reason (law) and freedom was developed in *PMA* by way of constant references to Kant: page 106 calls attention to the Kantian masterpiece, *The Groundwork of the Metaphysics of Morals*, where Kant himself introduced not only the philosophy of freedom but at the same time the problem of its relation to reason and to law. Here, too, Kant made a few enigmatic references to nature – but it was left to Kant's successors in Germany to develop into full-blown form the very problem that Grant set out so clearly here, and to contribute several lines of response to the problem, in directions that Grant did not have time to pursue in *PMA*. Later, I would like to mention one or two of those German initiatives, making the claim that they are still of relevance in our times, and could have served Grant in his own later work. In any case, to summarize, Grant certainly did not intend in *PMA* to *sacrifice* the doctrine of freedom to a doctrine of natural law. The question that remains is whether he could have persevered further with some positive view of human freedom.

Grant followed a quite different trajectory in the next decade. His later work can still be read as a study of the place of reason in modernity, and of the place of freedom in modernity, but with a different accent. It is a new, sharply *critical* theory. Now Grant could say (as Max Horkheimer did, though in a somewhat different sense) that 'reason today seems to suffer from a kind of disease.' Freedom and reason together appear intertwined in a devil's cocktail, with freedom appearing in modern times more and more in terms of *control* – the control of human nature and non-human nature. I will take a look at three aspects of the disease of reason in modern times: reason becoming identified with technological science; practical reason and morality delivered up into a formless existentialism; and the decline of philosophy into a merely technical discipline. Thus, the later Grant comes close to *renouncing* the second horn of his original dilemma as quoted above, abandoning modern accounts of freedom altogether.

In *LN*, the political thrust captured most of the attention, but there was already a deeper current evident in Grant's effort to conceive a Canada that differentiated itself clearly from the American state. In calling his work a lament, he meant both a remembrance of something that was in the throes of going and a recollection of the good that it had embodied, where this good is also conceived as something that is one's own (2). So there is a new attention to the history that lies behind the current state of Canada and the modern world. This more historical philosophy underlying *LN* can be read explicitly in *Technology and Empire* [*TE*],[3] and I shall base my remarks on this 1969 text. Here we have an effort to think the nature of the technology that embraces us, keeping our eye on its historical coming into presence. The development of modernity as a whole is conceived as the emergence and triumph of technology. Grant looks especially at the convergence, from the seventeenth century onwards, of Puritan theology and the great effort to tame the North American wilderness. Then there is Grant's philosophical *challenge* to the technological behemoth. Philosophically, it is especially a challenge to the governing conception of *personhood* that imbues it, 'the human nature' that lives side by side with 'non-human nature.' He frequently speaks of the ideal of autonomy that governs this personhood, and very often of the modern doctrine that man's essence is his freedom. He now says that this doctrine is carried along by the project of modern technology. Thus, he admits that his own earlier embrace of the doctrine, in *PMA*, betrayed the superficiality of his liberal period.

The essays of *TE* can be called diatribes in the sense of the ancient Stoics – fiercely expressed denunciations of the age, encoded in powerful images. Grant's theme is the fusion of personal autonomy with the control of nature. He was able to link all this with Puritanism and especially Calvinism: 'Calvinism provided the determined and organized men and women who could rule the mastered world. The punishment they inflicted on non-human nature, they had first inflicted on themselves.'[4] The whole problem of technology opens up from Grant's insight into the Puritan theology: the conquest of Nature, the triumph of the Will. I quote: 'When the disciplined among us drive to an unlimited technological future, in which technical reason has become so universal that it has closed down on openness and awe, questioning and listening; when Protestant subjectivity remains authentic only where it is least appropriate, in the moodiness of our art and sexuality, and where public religion has become an unimportant litany of objectified self-righteousness necessary for the more anal of our managers; – one must remember now the hope, the stringency and nobility of that primal encounter. The land was almost indomitable' (24). Grant draws on Weber, though he is more passionate than Weber, because Grant is writing about something so close and well known to him that there appeared almost no rival in his horizon. Grant easily surpasses Weber in the poignant detail of his account of North American life: 'To know that parents had to force the instincts of their children to the service of pioneering control; to have seen the pained and unrelenting faces of the women; to know, even in one's flesh and dreams, the results of generations of the mechanizing of the body; to see all around one the excesses and follies now necessary to people who can win back the body only through sexuality, must not be to forget what was necessary and what was heroic in that conquest' (25).

The mystery that Grant wants to contemplate lies in the history by which, under the impetus of Christianity in its Protestant form, a technology and culture came about which closed off the domain of eternity, and even supplanted the autonomy or the freedom (the original ideal, after all, of that Protestantism) with a dismal necessity, conformity, and spiritlessness. It would be a crude misunderstanding of Grant to suppose that his claim is that too much freedom is bad for us. Such a doctrine can be attributed to dictators and authoritarians, not conservatives such as George Grant. His point rather is that there is some special malignant constitution in the freedom that we experience in modern times, for there is a connection between the technological project for the command and domination of the world and the release of the modern subject or person, authorized with a new dispensation of freedom: 'The belief in the mastering knowledge of human and non-human beings arose together with the very way we conceive our humanity as an Archimedian freedom outside nature, so that we can creatively will to shape the world to our values ... The moral discourse of "values" and "freedom" is not independent of the will to technology, but a language fashioned in the same forge together with the will to technology' (32).

And now we may turn to our second point: the domain of the moral application of reason. This is just as important to Grant as it had been to Kant in his day – except that Grant sees an infection of this moral reason with a false version of subjectivity. The very idea of the person, or the self, is twisted, owing to the deep bond with the technological perversion of reason. We may say, perhaps, that while Grant had defended a certain autonomy of *philosophy* in his earliest period, and thereby some degree of the autonomy of *reason*, he came to be suspicious of what he saw as the key claim of our own modernity: the autonomy of the *person*. Political influences, to be sure, contributed to leading him in this direction – his suspicion of Liberalism in Ottawa helped him to a scepticism about the whole liberal tendency of modern thought and culture. But there is a deeper aspect. Grant looks at the corruption of both reason and freedom in modern existentialism. This is the ultimate version of the subjectivity that accompanies the scientistic sickness of reason – a formless freedom in which the subject constitutes itself by positing arbitrarily some set of values to live for, projected out of the emptiness of the self. (Though once, in the 1950s, he had praised Jean-Paul Sartre in a radio broadcast,[5] he cannot damn him enough in later years.) Perhaps his most biting account of 'modern' freedom appears in an earlier text: 'By freedom is meant the modern account of self-consciousness: that is, of the self as absolute. This is, indeed, the very heart of what modern history has been and is – the belief that man's essence is his freedom.

The negative aspect of this authentic and absolute freedom must be that every meaning, every purpose, every value has to come before the court of that freedom and is under the judgment of that sovereignty."[6]

But the question must arise: From what standpoint can a modern intellectual, imbued with some of the 'autonomy of philosophy,' call into question so fundamental a principle of modernity as the freedom or autonomy of the subject? The answer to this question appears cumulatively. Grant keeps his eye not only on Plato but also on the Christ of the Gospels. Since a religious ground is here at work, the critical analysis itself becomes indirectly a form of religious communication. I have called TE a Stoic diatribe, but perhaps a more relevant comparison would be to the prophet Jeremiah, who dwelt on the failings of his people, and the punishments that they had brought on themselves, but still contained within him the prophet's primary faith and hope. Grant is addressing his audience with a fundamentally religious communication: there is no mistaking the religious character of the doubts he entertained about liberalism in the culture.[7] Where did we go wrong? What was the false turn? Can we find an authentic and original faith again, one that will guide us out of the iron cage of technology in which we have imprisoned ourselves? The words by which Grant describes his mode of thinking here are 'intimations' and 'recollections,' closely related to 'lament' and 'meditation.' They all invoke some kind of access that we still have to a domain that transcends that of technology and the insistent autonomy of the person. Though Grant is asking how the autonomy of reason can be granted and sustained in relation to the sovereignty of God and the claims of the Gospel, this is mostly indirect communication. Most of the text does not speak about God or faith or eternity. It more or less assumes that these are absent. So, to summarize: when the religion itself ebbed away, we were left with a barren shore in which technological mastery was all that remained. The mystery Grant contemplates is the deepest root of technology. Though the project was initiated and governed by charity, as he always emphasizes (see, for example, TE, 138), and was supposed to make us more free, less vulnerable to nature, accident, and chance, the effect of this apparently augmented freedom is merely an inauthentic freedom. Why did the project of personal autonomy fall into this ruination?

At this point in our review, we must ask further about the relationship between philosophy and religion, or philosophy and theology, in the writings of Grant. If he can set himself in opposition to the idea, not only of technological mastery, but also subjective freedom, and do so by an appeal to Christian doctrine, has Grant now lost contact with philosophy itself? It is hard to see how philosophy can preserve itself if its own autonomy is surrendered to a religious intimation.

And yet this brings us to the third aspect of our examination of the later Grant: his picture of philosophy in our own times. In the Western tradition, philosophy is often seen as the guardian of reason and rationality in our civilization, but in modern times this vocation has been utterly cast aside, and the modern philosophy (especially academic philosophy) fits perfectly into the picture of the wasteland of diseased reason that is highlighted in Grant's later work. Grant registers the contemporary decline of philosophy into cybernetics, analysis, and 'applied [i.e., technological] ethics' more in the mode of ignoring it than in seeking to criticize it. But he did have a go at it early on in an article published in the *Dalhousie Review* devoted to Bertrand Russell.[8] It was an excellent polemic that targeted Russell, not from the viewpoint of Christian faith or theology, but from the viewpoint of a rationalism that was recognizably Platonic. Grant had no quarrel with Russell's logic, nor did he take on the details of Russell's early work in metaphysics. Rather, he exposed the contradiction that lay in the whole work, that, on the one hand, Russell denied the power of reason to establish truth in the practical domain, especially in morals, but, on the other hand, in innumerable popular writings, had no difficulty in assuming the mantle of wisdom, lecturing his readers about marriage, morals, war, peace, socialism, education, and virtually every possible issue of practical life. And Grant did not depart from philosophical rationalism when he touched on questions about religion in this article. He was able to expose the follies of Russell's atheism just as surely as his other follies, even though Grant adhered to the purely philosophical style of discourse.

Later he has a go at John Rawls, in a book, *English-Speaking Justice* [*ESJ*], that not only 'situates' Rawls at a certain place and time in the unfolding of technology but also probes critically into the merely subjective structure of Rawls's deliberative procedures in justice and law. Grant studies this modern contractarian philosophy, and his critique of it starts from the refusal of that philosophy to look into the ontological foundations for our practices, and the rules of practice, that jurists and legal philosophers are concerned with: 'Justice is what we are fitted for. We come to know that through the practice of philosophy, which gives us knowledge of the nature of things, of what we are fitted for and what the consequences are for our actions in being so fitted.'[9]

It seems that, for Grant, philosophy does not really exist at all in the present age. Thus, one is entitled to base one's reflections concerning technology and modernity as much on the intimations and meditations of religion as on philosophical reason. But this now leads me to a further question of my own.

This is the first of two questions I mean to pose to Grant's work, and concerns the treatment of freedom or autonomy in the later period. Grant did show the inner connection between a certain experience of freedom, or a certain account of it, the Puritan, and the technology that drives to greater and greater measures of control, the domination of nature itself, non-human and human alike. The question may be raised whether this conjunction with technology exhausts or even expresses freedom. Is it not possible that the conjunction with technology has cast freedom into a merely inauthentic form? What of a possible freedom, then, that might be regarded as authentic? Here I could refer to Kant's idealist successors in Germany, for all of them, in one way or another, sought to rethink the essence of human freedom in relation to apparently deterministic systems of nature, with results that I regard as permanently valid and hence germane to Grant's technological world as well. Let me just mention the famous essay by Schelling commonly called *On Human Freedom* [1809].[10] Schelling targets all the systems of modern thought that, in introducing a universal determinism of nature, had apparently driven out human freedom; the particular system he confronts here is Spinoza's. Schelling seeks to show that the 'Nature' or 'God' of Spinoza's system cannot be regarded only as a finished, completed, inert Being, for, by containing within itself the ground of its own Being, it incorporates as well the unformed abyss of energy from which proceeded both the whole world and the completed personality of God. These are indeed obscure depths to which Schelling has penetrated, guided by some of the unorthodox mystical theologies that had circulated before and after the times of Spinoza. I shall not proceed further into those depths now, but only point to the inference that Schelling was able to make in the main argument of this essay. God and Nature rest upon these unformed depths, but it is precisely this depth to which the human being *also* gains access in moral agency: the human will rests upon those depths, which Schelling sometimes calls *that within God that is not God himself* (237–8). In his system, this is the inner principle of Nature, and it is in no way foreign to freedom but rather is the freedom living at the heart of nature. And, concomitantly, within human freedom there dwells the accord with nature – the Nature that lives and works behind freedom and within it is the unconscious source of all mythology, poetry, and art. Such, in outline, is one Romantic pathway which we could follow to discover how freedom is not banished by a deterministic system. There are other routes, too, in the later periods of German thought. One that is perhaps easier to follow, in our own day, is the argument of Heidegger. In fact, Heidegger's reflections on freedom and technology were immensely formative for Grant's later thought, but it could be that they harbour even more resources than Grant himself applied.[11]

It has been made clear by both Grant and Heidegger that technology is not the mere assembly of machines and devices that we make use of: beyond that, it is the form taken on by reality itself in the modern age, that reaches right into ourselves and so comes to constitute our way of thinking as well as acting. This 'Frame' enters into modern subjectivity as surely as it reframes the material world, so that one would be in error to suppose oneself free from technology. Not only modern science but modern philosophy too (and, in Grant, modern religion) participate in the universal extension of technology. Heidegger has called attention to the 'danger' that dwells within it, though always in connection with a certain 'saving power' (*Rettung*) that belongs together with the danger. The *Rettung* is a *possibility* that cannot be effaced. The danger is in part that every other mode of disclosure will be driven out of the world once that world is mastered by technology – that is to say, all art, all theatre, all eroticism, all political discourse, all historical memory, and all religion. The danger also consists in part that the human essence will be utterly reframed and drawn into the wake of technology, revealing human beings as human resources and nothing else, personnel, *Menschenmaterial*. But the dominant category in this thought is through and through that of *possibility*! To speak of a danger is to speak of a *possibility*! The same holds for rescue too, *Rettung*. In the modern era, two possibilities move through the sky like stars in a constellation: one, that all disclosure and essence is reframed into mere resources; and two, that humanity relearns to think, including thinking the thought that grasps the *essence* of technology, which it to say, its *truth*.[12] My conclusion from Heidegger's account is that technology has not yet been capable of mastering human freedom to the extent of reducing it to mere control: the mastery of nature in us and nature outside us. Though the 'Puritan' will prevails, it cannot extinguish that other form of freedom that resides wherever there is an essential possibility.

Can we in our age discern any lineaments of this other possible freedom? Without entering into lengthy Heidegger-exposition, I might just sketch an idea of freedom that guided him. It is one bias to identify the freedom of the self as the control exercised by this self over its environment. But it is another bias to identify freedom with the idea of self-government, or autonomy. Even this government of the self by the self cannot fulfil the idea of freedom, and, if autonomy means 'self-government,' it will not fulfil the idea of freedom. A world-less autonomous being would never be free. But when we understand how the self belongs in the world originally, prior to all attempts at world-mastery, we become open to rethinking freedom as a part of that being in the world that *discloses* its world, that has possibilities opened up to it, that is open to the self-showing of all the things that are in the world, and that can reveal things inasmuch as it lets them be.[13] Letting-be is, perhaps, what fulfils the very idea of freedom, in opposition to the project of control. This is the crucial possibility of a freedom that is self-limiting.

It might seem, at first glance, that if you are free, this freedom must know no limits; that where an obstacle existed, it would abrogate your freedom. And it might also seem that anyone who is conscious of being free must always will the further extension, the perpetual extension, of that freedom – to the point of infinity. Perhaps such impressions spring from the Cartesian idea of the human being as a thinking and a willing substance. Descartes's *Meditation Four* maintained that human errors sprang from our combination of a limited intellect with an unlimited freedom, so that our will was always outstripping our information.

But we are instructed otherwise, I think, by concrete experiences in research, in art, and above all in human interaction. It is true that scientific research benefits from the fertility of questioning that pushes beyond all appearances and common opinions. Yet the research is brought to a successful conclusion precisely where the scientist is able to *yield* to the phenomenon that shows itself. While the most adept painter is unconstrained by convention, the excellent work of art nevertheless permits the viewer to *see* that which has shown itself to the painter, to which the painter has *bowed*. And we do not exhibit the freedom of our moral agency by walking over everybody, but by *ceding* the claims of those who do have claims. Because we have discerned their claims, we limit our own.

The freedom explored in Heidegger's phenomenological studies differs from the project of technological control, which is far from self-limiting but instead inherently self-universalizing. That is the mark of all technology. To accept the lead offered by someone else, or to render fruit trees truly in a painting, is a willing self-opening-up, a self becoming open to its world. All this implies further that freedom can never be purely subjective, since it involves a world and indeed a human community. A more direct testimony of freedom, more than the ability to direct or govern, is the ability to take direction, to accept government. The problem, then, of the technological and Puritan 'personal autonomy' that so exercises Grant probably lies more with the *person* than with the *autonomy*, that *person* conceived as a field of inner drives and outwardly aimed forces that seeks to secure itself against destructive dangers about it, that is, that Hobbesian person whose descendant is the Lockean person.

LAMENT FOR A RELIGION

Earlier I quoted the dilemma that Grant raised in *PMA*, concerning the apparent conflict between freedom, on the one hand, and natural law and divine grace on the other. We explored one (modernist) answer to that question, and the severe critique to which Grant submitted that answer in the 1970s and 1980s. Now we may look at the other answer that appears prominently in Grant's work in those decades. This is certainly connected with his reappraisal of Christianity, specifically his struggle with its Protestant, Calvinist, or Puritan form. We will turn to that point in a moment.

Let us take our start, and our guidance, from the affirmations Grant offered in 'Faith and the Multiversity,' an essay in the collection *Technology and Justice* [*TJ*],[14] though we could certainly buttress this with citations from other, related texts. Indeed, Grant had already presented the main idea in outline in *PMA* but without completely endorsing it: '[In the natural law tradition,] freedom does not mean the ability to make an unambiguous choice between open possibilities. We become free only in so far as we base our relevant actions on the law; we lose our freedom as we disregard that law' (39). The human being, in this view, receives from God not only the gift of existence but the gift of freedom too. This genuine freedom is not indifference, being poised before two choices that are equally available. Neither does freedom consist, as the modern existentialists argued, in the human ability to transcend the given environment, reaching out into the future to bring something novel into being. Rather, the freedom that is bestowed by God is connected to the truth that is the prior, initial outflow from God.

This has several deeper points behind it. First, we see that there is the Platonic teaching that 'the ultimate cause of being is beneficence ... evils could only be recognized for what they are if they were seen as deprivations of good ... Clearly this language of the given goodness of what is must be a language founded upon trust' (*TJ*, 42–3). This thought recurs throughout the whole great Platonic tradition, teaching the primacy of the Good in the architecture of this world. Grant's later thought circles around the Good, or the Idea of the Good. This is not to be explained solely in terms of the natural law hypothesis that, in *PMA*, he invoked in the polarization against human freedom. And, though it is certainly closer to the idea of justice that appears throughout *TJ* and *ESJ*, I do not think it can be explained entirely in those terms either. Grant is reviving the ancient Platonic hypothesis of an intellectual intuition, whereby 'the Idea of the Good is the greatest object of study, and by relation to it just actions and other things become useful and beneficial ... This every soul pursues, and all its actions are done for its sake. The soul divines that it is something but is perplexed and cannot adequately grasp what it is, nor does it have about this the firm opinion which it has about other things ... That which gives truth to the objects of knowledge, and to the knowing mind the power to know, is the Idea of the Good' (*Republic* 505a, 505e, 508e).

This brings with it the insight into our ultimate receptiveness. Already in the Nietzsche lectures, *Time as History*, we read: 'Thought was at its height not in action but in what they called a passion ... In modern language, we may weakly describe this by saying that thought was finally a receptivity ... Whatever the differences between what has come to us from Plato and from Christianity, on this central point there is commonness ... The disappearance of the words of receptivity, the words of passion, from the modern account of thought, shows what a wide separation there is between the ancient and the modern.'[15] While Plato saw this clearly, Grant always recognizes the special note of grace that appears in the Gospels: 'The philosophy of the dialogues is impregnated with the idea of receptivity, or as was said in the old theological language, grace. What is given us and draws from us our loving is goodness itself: the perfection of all purposes which has been called God. We are hungry for the bread of eternity' (*TJ*, 74). Thus, Grant was able to quote Augustine on this matter in many places, even in the early *PMA*: 'To be able not to sin is a great liberty; not to be able to sin is the greatest' (40). Grant returns repeatedly to the point of contrast between this ancient teaching and modern conceptions of liberty: 'In much modern thought the core of being human is often affirmed as our freedom to make ourselves and the world. Whatever differences there may be among Christians about what it is to be human, finally there must be the denial of this account of freedom' (*TJ*, 74–5. See also 58–9).

This whole line of thought is brought to a fitting climax towards the end of 'Faith and the Multiversity,' especially the 'Appendix,' an extended meditation expressing Christian belief in its most ancient and Catholic form. Athens and Jerusalem come together: Grant summons forth the appeal of the Gospels in pure harmony with the thought of Plato. Later I will return to examine this point, the harmony. Grant sees the harmony very much in the spirit of such Greek church fathers as Clement of Alexandria and Gregory of Nyssa, though here the harmony is invoked in the context that Grant himself has established in his meditation on modernity: 'The freedom to do and to make cannot be for us the final account of what we are. For Plato freedom is not our essence ... In this essential matter of what human beings are, Platonism and Christianity are at one, as against the thinkers of "authentic" freedom. To exist is a gift. Of course, for both Christianity and Platonism, goodness itself is an ambiguous mystery. In Christianity, God's essence is unknowable. In *The Republic* it is said that goodness itself is beyond being' (*TJ*, 75).

Now I must turn to Grant's appraisal of the Christian religion in its decayed and ruined form among ourselves. This was already written up very sharply, and in very wounding words, in early essays where he treated modern Protestantism: Calvinism, Puritanism. In *PMA*, Grant sees the contemporary Protestant minister as a sort of booster or Rotarian, rewarding and inducing his flock with a round of upbeat, organized activities (8–9). The historical background for this Grant traces somehow to the doctrine of work, building, and strenuous activity (86–7). But all this itself was still more deeply rooted, in an extremely mysterious way, in a much older theology: 'Calvin's doctrine of the Hidden God by whose inscrutable Will men were elected to salvation or damnation meant that they believed themselves cut off from the contemplation of God, except as he revealed himself in the Bible, and particularly in Jesus Christ' (83). Grant does call attention repeatedly to the mystery of this modern history, though he cannot refrain from a satirical tone in *TE*, where his review of modern Protestantism culminates in a picture of Billy Graham at the 1968 Republican convention invoking the name and the blessing of Benjamin Franklin (*TE*, 20–3). The more serious study of this history appears only in fits and starts in his works. Part of it is connected with his appropriation of the Anglican divines, especially Richard Hooker. In *ESJ*, he quotes Hooker against the Puritan Dissenters: 'They err who think that of the will of God to do this or that, there is no reason beside his will' (64). In the context, Grant is probing into 'Calvinist theological voluntarism,' a doctrine concerning the pure divine will, which 'made it utterly a modern western theology as distinguished from the theologies of the Platonic world' (64). This doctrine brought in its train the doctrine of humanity, too, as primarily will, which ultimately was the nemesis of this Calvinist faith and indeed, according to Grant, of any Christian faith. Thus, we see that Grant's critique of a *theology* centred upon the will was the counterpart of his critique of a *philosophy* centred upon freedom. There is here the possibility of a further critique of Grant, in the same general spirit as my earlier critique that drew a different and better picture of freedom; there is room for a phenomenology of the will which might be able to show that the will is central to religion itself, rather than merely a corrupter of religion. But I shall not attempt that at this point, for there is another line of thought that awaits our attention.

Above, I offered an account of freedom alternative to the one that Grant laid at the basis of his critique of modernity. Now I may raise a second question – this one about Grant's presentation of the harmony of Plato and the Gospels. As Grant speaks of it, there is an agreement or accord between them at the very highest level, which he often expresses, as he does in the Appendix in *TJ*, as the idea that freedom is not the essence of the human being. God, or the Good, establishes the measure for us: 'we are not our own.' I do believe that Clement of Alexandria and Gregory of Nyssa said that too, so it is with some hesitation that I raise my question. I might take issue with the manner in which Grant has made the two of them, Plato and Christianity, agree with one another at the very height. Perhaps it is not right to make Plato's Idea of the Good the same thing as the God proclaimed in the Gospels. There is a difference between Athens and Jerusalem, that is to say, between philosophy and Christianity.

In the individual's own soul or consciousness, there can be a Christian existence devoid of philosophy. There can be a philosophical existence devoid of Christianity (or religion generally). But is it possible for the two of them to cohabit there? If both of them do, what follows from that? Answer: the *autonomy of reason* is not suspended even by virtue of one's accepting Christianity. This, too, remains in place.

There remains a difference between the discourse of philosophy and the discourse of the Gospels, a distance between Athens and Jerusalem, a difference that has never vanished. And in this reply to Grant, I, too, perhaps, can appeal to great predecessors, Augustine and Aquinas. It is not so much an *agreement* between Plato and the Gospels, but rather the Gospels have come to *supplement* the insights of philosophy. They do not need to clash, but nevertheless they are not the same thing. Can one heed both discourses? They make quite different claims upon us: Grant is right in saying that every philosopher needs to re-read 1 *Corinthians* 13 often. To be open to both is a taxing dialectic in our existence. Where both discourses are in one's soul, they do not unite, they are not homogenized.

The very heart of Christianity is an *event of communication*, the discourses of Christ and the story told in the Gospels, powerful and urgent religious communications. And the entire movement of early Christianity is one of communication – building a *community*. I can think of a number of communicative forms here – Christ's prophecy, his miracles, the very living of his life, and then later the redaction of the Gospels and their translation into Greek, and, with all this, the missions of St Paul, his homilies, his epistles, and so on. The radiance of communication is central to the very being of the thing: Christianity.

By contrast with the Christian discourse, it is not the inherent tendency of philosophical discourse to reach out and to enlighten the world, or to promise salvation. For philosophy's fundamental locus and mode of being is in *thought* rather than speech. Expression in writing and speech is welcome but not of the essence. Philosophy does have its discursive modes – the dialogue, the essay, the system, and so on – but these discourses find their fulfilment in the *thinking* of the reader or the hearer, and the ideal reader is the one who could have thought the whole matter through for himself/herself.

The Christian communication did reach the ears of philosophers: Alexandrian, Athenian, and others. Paul's homily in the Areopagus (Acts 17) is perhaps the first such occasion. Yet, in the story of antiquity, philosophy belonged more to the history of the *reception* than to the *sending* of religious communication. Its fundamental relation to Christianity was passive. But it still enjoyed and enjoys its own character. It is capable of being *reached* by this other discourse, more passionate and eager, and it has a capacity to understand this Christianity, but it does not lose its autonomy on that account. Christianity did not require it to sacrifice itself or obliterate its native mode, thought, nor indeed has Christianity any power to bring that about. It is true that philosophy – or theology, which is not entirely distinct from philosophy – did begin to reframe the Christian message at the latest in the days of Justin Martyr, but one has to understand this as the interpretative response governed by a native discourse (philosophy) that recast what had been initially communicated in another way, by historical narrative and rhetoric. The Christian communications sang in praise of love and justice, but it remained, and it still remains, the philosopher who asks the questions: 'What *is* love?' 'What *is* justice?'

My belief, then, is that the Gospel proclamation lets Athens be, it lets philosophy be, and it lets the philosopher be. Jesus would have wanted Socrates to remain exactly the person that he was.

NOTES

1 George Grant, *Lament for a Nation: The Defeat of Canadian Nationalism* [*LN*] (Toronto: McClelland and Stewart, 1965).

2 George Grant, *Philosophy in the Mass Age* [*PMA*] (Toronto: Copp Clark, 1959), 77.

3 George Grant, *Technology and Empire* [*TE*] (Toronto: Anansi, 1969).

4 'In Defence of North America,' *TE*, 24.

5 See William Christian, *George Grant: A Biography* (Toronto: University of Toronto Press, 1993), 177–8.

6 'Value and Technology' [1964], in *The George Grant Reader*, edited by William Christian and Sheila Grant (Toronto: University of Toronto Press, 1998), 388–9.

7 I am indebted here to Louis Greenspan's article 'Grant and Liberalism – Revisited' in *Grant and the Subversion of Modernity*, edited by Arthur Davis (Toronto: University of Toronto Press, 1998).

8 'Pursuit of an Illusion' (1952), *Reader*, 322–34.

9 George Grant, *English-Speaking Justice* [*ESJ*] (Toronto: Anansi, 1985), 44.

10 F.W.J. Schelling, *Philosophical Investigations into the Essence of Human Freedom and Related Matters*, translated by Priscilla Hayden-Roy, in *Philosophy of German Idealism*, edited by Ernst Behler (New York: Continuum, 1987), 217–84.

11 Ian Angus has shown how, after Grant, it is still possible to benefit further from Heidegger's thought on technology. See *A Border Within: National Identity, Cultural Plurality and Wilderness* (Montreal and Kingston: McGill-Queen's University Press, 1997), 92–104.

12 'The Question concerning Technology,' available in many English translations, including one by William Lovitt, in Heidegger, *Basic Writings*, ed. David Krell (New York, Harper and Row, 1977); I have referred to the concluding paragraphs, at 314–17.

13 Here I am thinking of several Heidegger texts, including 'On the Essence of Truth' that also appears in *Basic Writings*.

14 George Grant, *Technology and Justice* [*TJ*] (Toronto: Anansi, 1986), 35–77.

15 I quote this text in the version offered in *Reader*, 283, 284.

20

Socrates' Joke

IAN ANGUS

The majority of George Grant's writings deal with moral-political questions of contemporary technological civilization. Very few deal with the foundations of his own thought from which such moral-political questions are addressed. Such a choice in a serious writer and thinker cannot be regarded as a mere detail. It indicates the prevalence of the critical intention and implies the situational, expressive, and stylistic priority of critique even though it does not necessarily imply that critique is the only, or even the most important, activity of thought. Critique directed to the moral-political issues of technological civilization and being is an activity that attempts to retrieve the possibility of justice from the specific manner of its contemporary destitution. Evidently, Grant's conception of justice demanded such an activity of active retrieval to a greater extent than self-justification. Consequently, addressing the theological and philosophical bases of Grant's conception of justice risks an endemic distortion in which it may appear that the explication of this conception ought to prevail over its deployment or that its deployment is not crucial to the concept itself. To combat this distortion, one must keep firmly in mind that the activity of critique was demanded by Grant's conception of justice to such a degree that it prevailed over the project of self-justification insofar as one may validly judge from written evidence – that is to say, as a public philosopher – even though the public function of philosophy cannot be assumed to exhaust philosophy outright.

None of which is to imply, of course, that there were no attempts at self-justification at all. Even so, such attempts generally emerge in the context of specific critiques. Indeed, this is the case to such an extent that one may surmise that the concept of justice itself gains in definition from its deployment in critiques. Grant's understanding of the object of critique – called variously modernity, empire, liberalism, the universal and homogeneous state, and, most completely, technology – developed significantly over approximately four decades of mature thinking.[1] Gains in defining the concept of justice that underlies critique develop with, although are not direct parallels of, gains in theorizing the concept of technology that is the object of critique. My explication of Grant's concept of justice here, which I will use in order to differ regarding its philosophical and theological foundation, is based on a teleological interpretation of his work. Philosophical dialogue requires that one be open to further determination of the adequate concept and its instantiations or, put negatively, that adequate determination is not already monologically available. If it were, one's duty would be simply to listen thoroughly to its authoritative voice or, if one were that voice, to speak without necessity of listening. Critique (whether oriented to oneself, others, or systemic assumptions inherent in a way of life) is thus an essential activity whose essentiality orients further attempts at adequate determination. Interpretation of any given articulation is consequently oriented teleologically – that is to say, only in the first place to Grant's meaning at a given point, in the second place to the improvements gained in successive formulations (which requires attention to dating and internal temporality), and, finally and most important to the question itself. Teleological interpretation is the application of philosophical dialogue to the written work of a philosopher. However great one's appreciation of the man himself and his accomplishments, philosophical interpretation reaches beyond this towards the question itself which is the basis of such appreciation.

Grant's final position can be termed 'Christian Platonism' since it is centrally organized by the claim that the concept of good, or justice, in Plato is 'the same' as that inherent in the Gospel stories of Jesus' life. 'That [central, pre-technological, Western] account of justice was written down most carefully and most beautifully in "The Republic" of Plato. For those of us who are Christians, the substance of our belief is that the perfect living out of that justice is unfolded in the Gospels.'[2] Such a sameness, or identity, does not extend to all the details, even all important ones, of either source. It refers to their animating centre. This animating centre is the basis for a synthesis between Christianity and philosophy that was never thoroughly articulated by Grant but that nevertheless provides the unity of his many statements about religion and philosophy. The Platonic element of this synthesis is the notion that being, 'what is,' is itself good (and not merely a resource for human use). The Christian element is that the goodness of being was revealed to humans in the life of Jesus. The necessity of the Christian element thus implies that Greek philosophy was in some manner deficient in expressing the goodness of being. This deficiency was called by Grant in classical language 'charity.' Greek philosophy (owing to its orientation to reason, which is unequal in humans) did not see the truth that all humans are due charity, or consideration for what they need. The necessity of the Platonic element suggests that the exemplary character of the life of Jesus requires some supplementation by philosophy, or reason, in order that what is due to humans be understood as rooted in being itself (and not merely, or only, as a human choice). The synthesis of these two elements can be called Christian Platonism. This position has a long and deep history in Western philosophy and religion. Grant's final questioning was oriented to the nature of this synthesis and to determining the basics of how he thought it should be understood. How this synthesis should be understood raises many questions, some of which this essay will address.

In my critical examination of Grant's attempted synthesis between religion and philosophy, I will first undertake to explain the Christian Platonist version of that synthesis which he proposed. Secondly, I will parse Grant's admission that there are tensions between Christianity and Platonism into five aspects of tension that can be drawn out from the whole corpus of his work. Thirdly, I will argue that Grant's attempted synthesis fails and that this failure is due not to its incomplete articulation but rather to the prior privilege granted to Christian religion in attempting the synthesis, with the consequence that the incorporation of philosophy is always muted and partial in comparison. Fourthly, I will explore in a comparative fashion what philosophy might independently have to offer about the crucial matter of what is due to humans. This critique implies a different position with regard to the critique of technological civilization and the two sources of Western civilization in philosophy and Christianity than that held by George Grant, but such implication will not be pursued in this essay.

JUSTICE IN CHRISTIAN PLATONISM

Grant directly articulated the philosophical and theological bases of his thought in four texts dedicated to this issue dispersed over his writing career: 'Philosophy' (1951), 'Two Theological Languages' (1953, with addendum 1988), 'Religion and the State' (1963), and 'Faith and the Multiversity' (1986).[3] Even with respect to these works, the last two refer primarily to two external domains of the practice of religion – the state and the university – rather than straightforwardly to its philosophical and religious basis. In the 1988 addendum to 'Two Theological Languages,' written just a few months before his death, Grant engaged in a fundamental self-criticism of that work, especially the conception of freedom as 'human absoluteness of choice,' pointing out that 'it has taken me a whole lifetime to begin to free myself from the language of modernity' and remarking that 'whatever differences there may be between Platonism and Christianity as to how and when truth is given us, it is clear that in both freedom is given us through truth ... Grace simply means that the great things of our existing are given us, not made by us and finally not to be understood as arbitrary accidents. Our making takes place within an ultimate givenness.'[4] Teleological interpretation of Grant's philosophy and theology must be oriented to the adequacy of articulating this givenness. For Grant, Christian Platonism expressed this givenness necessary to the concept of justice which he deployed in his influential social and political critiques.

Grace is our placing within a given order that is not altered by human making, specifically the apotheosis of making in technology which can be understood as the ontology of our contemporary world. Grant's most mature understanding of technology was in Nietzschean terms as the disposition of a creative will over the world. 'The world is a field of objects which can be known in their working through the "creative" acts of reasoning and experimenting by the thinking subject who stands over them.'[5] While Heidegger succeeded Nietzsche as Grant's reference point in analysing technology, such that his definition became 'the endeavour which summons forth everything (both human and non-human) to give its reasons,'[6] this was done in such a manner that Heideggerian 'summoning forth' could be folded back into Nietzschean 'will.' In the key essay 'The Question concerning Technology,' Heidegger's thought had undergone a fundamental shift with regard to technology based on his earlier critique of Nietzsche's concept of will. Technology manifests itself as, indeed, a 'challenging revealing' but one that is 'a kind of unconcealment,' so that, in the end, he states that 'modern technology as an ordering revealing is, then, no merely human doing.'[7] The sovereignty of human will in technology is, for Heidegger, merely a self-misunderstanding, and actually a response in which humans themselves are called forth when the world is manifested as presence – thus technology becomes an episode in the history of metaphysics. But for Grant, and Nietzsche, the sovereignty of will is an actuality of historical decisiveness. As Grant said, 'Europeans somehow seem to have come to an apprehension of the whole as "will."'[8] While Nietzsche was content to propagate the will unleashed by modernity, Grant considered this unleashing itself as the danger from which grace appears to deliver humans. To the extent that Grant continued to define technology through the phenomenon of 'will,' he never really accepted a Heideggerian account.[9] As a consequence, he did not appreciate (until very late, in an unpublished note) the extent to which Heidegger's conception of 'meditative thinking' represented an alternative to technological thinking.[10]

To Nietzsche's question 'who deserve to be masters of the earth?' Grant replied that 'the essential question may not be: who deserve to be masters of the earth; but rather, is it good that the race ever came to consider that mastery was its chief function?' He further noted that he does not know if this other question could even be posed 'in the darkness of its impossibility ... Because if one says there is one light which is always a light at all times and places, namely that man qua man can only come to a fuller light insofar as he does not find himself beyond good and evil, one has in saying that placed oneself outside modern thought in its highest self-consciousness.'[11] Grant's posing such a question indicates that, for him, modern thought does not understand its own darkness as darkness but requires an illumination by grace which allows the darkness to be seen and named as such.

The Christian Platonism of George Grant underpins his articulation of this illumination by grace which was practised through moral-political critique of contemporary technological civilization. Such critique is based on the historical opposition between modernity and the traditions that have been pulverized by modernity. The theoretical opposition through which this articulation proceeds is the contrast between an increasingly determinate understanding of technology and a more tentative exploration of the foundation of critique in grace. While Grant never defended tradition for its own sake, but only as a repository of the Good, he invoked its voice in the attempt to criticise technological civilization's turn away from the dual sources of Western grace in Athens and Jerusalem. Thus, 'the modern conception of goodness does not include the assertion of a claim upon us which properly orders our desires in terms of owing, and which is itself the route and fulfilment for desire.'[12] Grant's use of the modernity-tradition distinction to address the moral-political questions of technological civilization explains his difficulty in expressing theoretically the Good brought forth by technology in aid of charity (despite the issues that demand critique).[13] His use of the modernity-tradition distinction stems from his conviction that the dual sources of grace in Athens and Jerusalem are in the final analysis one. 'Anyone who wishes to partake in philosophy, and also hopes that he or she is made with the sign of Christ, must be aware of some tension in the relation between thought and revelation, though at the same time knowing that finally they must be at one.'[14] While in his critical mode Grant was willing to deploy Christianity and Platonism together, paying the theoretical price of not being able to articulate consistently the truth of technology, in his reflective mode he recognized a tension between these two sources of grace.

The core of the belonging together of Christianity and Greek philosophy was expressed by Grant with reference to Simone Weil's words that 'faith is the experience that the intelligence is enlightened by love' and explicated by him as 'love is consent to the fact that there is authentic otherness.'[15] This understanding is not specifically Christian, which justifies referring to it generally as the traditional, or old, account of justice in critiques, but rather 'the close connection between Socrates and Christ lies in the fact that Socrates is the primal philosophic teacher of the dependence of what we know on what we love.'[16] Correlatively, one may assume that Jesus is the primary religious teacher of this dependence. If one seeks to determine the specifically Christian component of this belonging together, it is described by Grant in two turns of phrase: 'the fact that Christ declares the price of goodness in the face of evil' and 'an extension of what was due to others and an account of how to fulfil that due.'[17] The notion of 'an extension of what was due to others' is by no means easy to understand. We can begin our inquiry into Grant's understanding of Christian Platonism by focusing on what this statement might mean.

If the specifically Christian component consists in an extension of what is due to others, it seems that Socrates must have had an attenuated conception of this principle. If he had such an attenuated conception, it would follow that his account requires supplementation by a Christian account and, as the quotation suggests, this supplementation would extend also to the manner of fulfilling the Good. Two classical attempts to resolve this problem seem to be closed to Grant: the supplement through love and the supplement through a greater universality of address.

First, one could argue that Christianity adds love to the Greek concept of justice. However, Grant, in his appropriation of Weil noted in the previous paragraph, attributes an understanding of the dependence of knowledge on love not only to Christianity but also to Greek philosophy – indeed, in such a key manner that it is precisely this characteristic that is the animating centre of their belonging together. This would be buttressed by Grant's claim that the distinction between various versions of love, such as eros and agape, should not be so sharp as to undermine the reality that love is a unity.[18]

Secondly, one could argue that Socrates' attenuated conception of what is due to others refers to the others to whom it is due – placing the emphasis on the 'account of how to fulfil that due' in the quotation. In other words, one could suggest that Socrates' philosophic task was inadequately universal in the sense of those to whom the Good pertained. One might claim, as has often been done, that this was because of the slave-character of Greek society, such that natural differences were not sufficiently overcome – in other words, that the purported universality of Greek philosophy could not be genuinely universal until it was realized in the Christian incarnation, which demonstrated the universality of the human species. (Note that this interpretation assumes that the slave-character of Greek society was not, or not adequately, overcome by Socrates.) But this option must be closed to Grant also, since it implies that Greek philosophy is in principle incomparable to Christianity in the matter that matters the most – what is the due of humans – if the due of humans is interpreted in terms of those to whom it is due. It does not imply a synthesis of Greek philosophy and Christianity but a straightforward surpassing of the former by the latter (characteristic of Hegel, among others). How could such a view be characterized as a Christian Platonism?

It seems rather that 'what is the due of humans' refers primarily to the *what* itself and secondarily, as a consequence of the specific nature of this *what*, to the account of *how* to fulfil it. If humans are due more than Platonic justice, such that it must be supplemented by Christianity, that 'more' must be both absent from Plato and yet compatible with his concept of justice such that 'finally they must be at one.'

Let us consider a third possibility. The synthesis between Christianity and Greek philosophy could perhaps be attempted, as Simone Weil did, through the argument that Greek philosophy prepared for the Christian incarnation, showed its necessity, and awaited its fulfilment, even though the fulfilment itself could not be accomplished within Greek philosophy. The *what* in this case would refer to the sensuality of the incarnation and this sensuality would have implications not present in Plato for its *how*. Weil argued that the search for an adequate mediation was the centre of Greek thought from Pythagoras to Plato.[19] 'Just as the

Christ is, on the one hand, the mediator between God and man, and on the other the mediator between man and his neighbour, so mathematical necessity is on the one hand the mediator between God and things, and on the other between each thing and every other thing.'[20] The search for mediation that characterized the Greek attempt to overcome dualism is thus accomplished in the Christian incarnation. Platonism accomplishes the intellectual love of God through the mathematical mediation; Christianity, through the incarnation, transforms this intellectual love into flesh.

Grant often quoted Nietzsche's phrase 'Christianity is Platonism for the people'[21] but it here appears in the opposite sense. While for Nietzsche it referred to the continuation of Platonic two-world theory into Christianity, for Grant it would refer to the continuation of the attempt to mediate and overcome the division between spirit and nature, God and human, self and other, through a human, carnal rendering of the love of God in the story of Jesus. This might be the greatest parallelism that one could imagine which would unite Socrates and Jesus: the same mediation approached by each one from a different side of that duality which is to be mediated: intellect reaching towards flesh, flesh opening toward intellect; one teaching philosophical, the other religious. This interpretation would imply that the lack in Platonic philosophy that requires Christian supplementation consists in the lack of a fully sensual estimation of the price. This is a plausible interpretation of the meaning of the passage where Grant claimed that Christianity provides 'an extension of what was due to others.' In the same paragraph where that passage appears, Grant claims that Christianity requires of its adherents 'to be perfect as God in heaven is perfect' and explicates this statement with reference to Weil's phrase that 'matter is our infallible judge,'[22] indicating that the role of matter and sensuousness in Christianity on account of the incarnation which constitutes its specific difference from Platonism. This interpretation also has the merit of situating the specific difference in the *what* of incarnation and the *how* of the path that it implies. In this case, the comparability of Jesus and Socrates is the core of both the synthetic unity and the specific difference of its parts.

Since the specific difference is not to be found in the two classical attempts to locate it through love, or through the universality of address, and given the merits of the third interpretation, I conclude that Grant sought the specific difference of Christianity from the classical account of justice through the incarnation understood as adequate mediation. However, this interpretation contains an implication unaddressed, and perhaps unobserved, by Grant. Since it claims that Plato was not sufficiently aware of the sensuous side of the mediation between spirit and matter, and since it claims that the specific difference nevertheless occurs within the same account of justice, a genuine synthesis would require some parallel insufficient awareness in the Christian side of the mediation. The logical consequence of the third interpretation of the specific difference is that the Christian incarnation requires supplementation by an appreciation of the intellectual side of the mediation by Plato. In short, Christianity does not stand alone but requires supplementation by philosophy.

Thus, the third interpretation implies the necessity of the other side of the mediation: that Jesus was not sufficiently aware of the intellectual implications of his claim that God was his father. However, not only do I find no such statement in Grant's or Weil's work, I do not believe that either of them would ever make such a statement. Could such a statement be made by a believing Christian? If not, it seems that the road through Weil to a synthesis of Socrates and Jesus, Greek philosophy, and Christian incarnation could not fail to discount philosophy in a nonsymmetrical manner that would destroy the synthesis as equally synthetic from both perspectives to be synthesized. In short, it must render the judgment that Socrates is incomparable to Jesus in the matter that matters the most – what is the due of humans. But it is precisely this comparability that defines Grant's position as Christian Platonism as opposed to a straightforward overcoming of Greek philosophy by Christianity. Such a straightforward overcoming in the issue that matters most would not exclude appropriation of lesser dimensions of Greek philosophy. The appropriation of Greek rationalism at the service of Christian apologetics is, of course, an influential interpretation (consistent with the first interpretation mentioned above) of the relation between these two sources in Western civilization, but it is an interpretation closed to Grant because of his Platonism.[23] Thus, while the third interpretation through Weil and the incarnation is closest to Grant's intentions, it leaves unresolved a major issue which deserves more detailed scrutiny.

FIVE TENSIONS BETWEEN CHRISTIANITY AND PLATONISM

How then should we assess Grant's attempt to define the specifically Christian component of Christian Platonism through 'an extension of what was due to others'? It was noted above that this synthesis was not presented systematically but emerges through its deployment in critiques. Grant was not unaware of the difficulties of this proposed synthesis. 'When we look, in this time of deep uncertainty, at what we are as western people, the central task of thought requires us to be aware of some tension between what comes to us from Athens and what from Jerusalem. I prefer to say what comes to us from Socrates and Christ.'[24] I will note five aspects of this tension mentioned in the whole corpus of Grant's work, three with regard to Christianity and two with regard to philosophy.

Christianity and Technology

The first aspect is the most enduring in Grant's work because it derives from the essential direction of his critique of technology. Technology was understood as stemming from the assertion of human will against the world. Thus, any conception of Christianity that was influenced by such a focus on will was compromised both in its critical capacity and in its originality. Western Christianity, as well as Western philosophy, has been fundamentally influenced by making the will central to the definition of humanity since the writings of Augustine. This provoked Grant's sympathy for Orthodox Christianity, which did not undergo the Augustinian influence and was more Platonic in this respect, and Plato, whose tripartite conception of the soul was prior to, and different from, that prepared by the synthesis between Christianity and neo-Platonism in late antiquity. In this respect, though Grant's critique of Western Christianity was deep, it was a Christian criticism that 'Western Christianity simplified the divine love by identifying it too closely with immanent power in the world.'[25] The historical institution of this accommodation to immanent power was the Augustinian synthesis of neo-Platonism and Christianity through the concept of the will.

Modern Science and the Doctrine of Creation

Christian thought became identified with power in another aspect also. In contrast to Leo Strauss, who interpreted modernity as fundamentally a moral-political phenomenon rather than a scientific one, Grant recognized the necessity of the Judeo-Christian concept of the creation of the world by God to the theoretical presuppositions of modern science.[26] Natural reason tends to complete itself in the thought of the permanence of the world. Even in Plato's *Timaeus*, where the coming-into-being of the world is considered, this is done under the twin models of paternity and *techne*, not as a creation from nothing. When an author creates something from nothing, it is knowable through and through without remainder. Knowledge of the artifact is unhampered by the recalcitrance of either matter or necessary ignorance. It is this entry of the concept of a created world in Western thought that prevents any direct passage from Greek to modern science.[27] Like the first aspect of the tension, this second one pertains to the role of Christianity in shaping technology, though it is more radical insofar as the concept of creation surely could not be expunged from either the Judaic or Christian traditions without diminishing the power of God in a way that would make it unrecognizable. The Judaic concept of a God that transcends and creates nature, a concept that underlies the Christian revelation is in principle anti-natural and thus undermines any and all cosmology. This pertains not only to the Western Christianity whose Augustinian concept of will Grant criticized but to the whole of Judeo-Christian theology as well. This makes the return to Plato more problematic for Grant than it is for Strauss, for instance, since in this respect modern assumptions confirm Christian ontology rather than undermine it. Modern technology is made possible by a Nietzschean-Augustinian concept of the will whose dependence on Christianity stems not only from the notion of human freedom as mastery but also from the scientific understanding of nature (as that which is mastered) as thoroughly knowable because it is created. The modern understanding of freedom against nature is indebted to Christianity at least in its dominant Western form such that the return to Plato that Grant wants to synthesize with Christianity is doubly problematic. Thus, while the first aspect of the tension serves only to underline the specificity and originality of the synthesis between Christianity and Greek philosophy (Plato) proposed by Grant, the second aspect suggests that such a synthesis is problematic at a deeper level: Is a concept of Christianity (or Judaism) entirely without will conceivable? And, if not, is not Christianity unredeemably implicated in technology? Resolving this issue would require a critique of technology capable of articulating the truth of technology. As noted above, Grant's use of the tradition-modernity doublet in his moral-political critiques made this a point of extreme difficulty for him.

Obedience as a Closure of Thought

An even deeper criticism of Christianity was expressed in Grant's notes to himself that were posthumously published as 'Obedience.' The main theme of the notes is, characteristically, the critical one that an intelligence not leavened by obedience to that which is not humanly made cannot become an adequate critic of technology. However, in one remarkable passage, Grant contrasted the openness of thinking with closedness and obedience. First, he characteristically affirmed that the openness of thinking does not stand above obedience but then, in an uncharacteristic moment, asked, 'Is not obedience a closing down of openness?'[28] He added: 'yet obedience is dark / how nice it would be to be one of those / to whom the darkness of obedience is not.' And further: 'Those fortunate people / for whom obedience has not been darkened / darkened not simply in the sense / of what they should do immediately / but what is obedience.' He called those who have escaped such darkening of obedience 'happy,' mentioning Jacques Ellul and Karl Barth, and suggested that 'to escape thought / they have been told.' I take this to express a doubt that the imbeddedness of thought in a world-order experienced and known as good (i.e., grace) could actually be a reigning thought for him because 'modern thought has darkened obedience.'

While Grant worked to free himself of the presuppositions of modern thought, he was also aware of the extent to which they had a hold on him. Grant often used the phrasing 'I have been told that ...' when he spoke of himself as a Christian. Here, he notes the happiness that would come with simply being a believing Christian and suggests that the closing down of thought that obedience requires is a price that he cannot pay – perhaps because he is too modern, perhaps because he is a philosopher, perhaps because of both. 'Happy are those who can face the Greeks – / without thinking of modern mathematical physics / Happy are those who can get rid of ontology / in their sense of the Bible.' In other words, happy are those who can live their Christianity without worrying about its relationship to Greek philosophy.

Furthermore, in the saddened and reluctant awareness 'So we are back, always a closing down,' I hear the desire that it were not so, that he could straightforwardly assert the Platonic-Christian synthesis. But, at least in this passage, he could not. He could not because he could not see obedience in any other way than as a closing of the openness of thought. Neither can I. But I think that Grant desired – perhaps believed – that obedience could itself be an opening, even though he could not *think* so. If it were so, there would result a tension between religion and philosophy not only in Western thought but also in Grant's thought as well. This passage suggests such a tension and then tends to mitigate it by attributing it to modernity alone – which in this context, and in light of the modernity-tradition (grace) doublet, must mean 'an error.'

Some attention to the hermeneutic of a passage unpublished by Grant himself cannot be avoided, especially since I have noticed the importance of the primary orientation of his published thought to moral-political critiques. It may be that we have here the expression of the kinds of doubts that all thinkers face but that are not characteristic of Grant's thought in its basic orientation. After all, it was not published by him and is a thought not characteristic of his published writings. Though Grant certainly indicated that there were important tensions between philosophy and Christianity, I do not know of any published example where this tension is interpreted, as it is in 'Obedience,' albeit tentatively, as a sacrifice of philosophical thought to Christianity, as a closing down. I would intrude too much on his solitude if I were to press this thought in the direction of his own beliefs as such. It is significant as a point of interpretation of a doubt about an assumption operative in his critiques. It is also defended in his remarks which assert about Socrates and Jesus that one can appreciate the tension while 'at the same time knowing that finally they must be one.'[29] The significance is that this knowing, when questioned as to the manner of its knowing, seems to generate a doubt that it can be known through thought; whereas it may well be the case that 'I have been told ...' – which implies a divergence between the openness demanded by philosophy and the obedience required by religion. Nonetheless, it must remain significant that Grant never published such a doubt himself. It would not fit the modernity-tradition doublet that characterizes his moral-political critiques.

Philosophy and Civil Religion

The previous three aspects of the tension between Athens and Jerusalem pertain to Christianity as the object provoking tension and may thus be called 'philosophical' in the sense that the doubts about religion are raised by philosophy. There are also two 'Christian,' or perhaps religious, aspects of the tension with philosophy; they are 'religious' in the corresponding sense that they are doubts about philosophy as raised by a Christian religious commitment.

The fourth aspect of the tension is, like the first, thoroughgoing and characteristic of Grant's work as a whole. In the early (1951) review of philosophy for the Massey Commission, he asserted that 'it would seem that unless philosophy is to become a purely negative discipline, it must have some kind of dependence on faith – whatever faith that may be.'[30] He seems to accept the critique of Socrates by Plato and Hegel that critique on its own leads only to aporia and requires completion in a constructive doctrine. Note that, while Grant himself worked from within the Christian tradition, he admitted the possibility that others might work productively in a similar manner from within other religious traditions. Addressing the question of the proper relation of religion and the state, he observed that 'unassisted reason is able to know that without religious beliefs and actions no society whatever can last, but reason is unable to determine which should be the particular public religion.'[31] Philosophy cannot determine the content of religion but only the necessity of religion to social order as such. The religious critique of philosophy is that philosophy cannot provide the specific sensuous content to be believed by the many in order to guarantee social order. Thus, the necessities of human social life are not adequately addressed by philosophy and require the content-oriented social and moral cement provided by religion.

We might call the above argument the social critique of philosophy by religion. It comprises also the classic observation that 'not many men will become philosophers; but that all men are inevitably religious,' especially if religion is taken to refer to any and all 'systems of belief' whether or not they refer to a higher power.[32] The emphasis of philosophy on intellect in the direction of human life – which requires, we might add, the critique of the specialist use of intellect – implies that, in fact if not in principle, the practice of philosophy is limited to a few. Since this is recognized within philosophy, as well as being subject to a religious critique, this tension pertains to the difficulty of coordinating the separate domains of philosophy and religion, even though this difficulty could not be justly inflated to assert the impossibility in principle of so coordinating them. It also raises the religious, and perhaps also philosophical, question of whether the religion required as social cement is true religion or merely a necessary social illusion – one of many possible civic religions whose social function exhausts its inner content.

The Deaths of Jesus and Socrates

The fifth instance of tension, like the third, cuts directly to the heart of the matter. It appears when Grant directly compares the deaths of Jesus and Socrates or, more exactly, uses the death of Jesus to comment on the death of Socrates – since I do not believe that he anywhere focused on the former in the light of the latter. 'Whatever may be said about the consummate serenity and beauty of Socrates at his execution, that scene is not as comprehensively close to the very heart of being as are Gethsemane and Golgotha.'[33] In two places in 'Faith and the Multiversity,' Grant addressed comparatively the deaths of Socrates and Jesus with respect to their capacity to articulate the practice of dying through which Socrates defined philosophy and which Grant asserts is equally applicable to Christianity.[34] One, he pointed out that in the death scene Socrates asserts that the absence of goodness is madness, not ignorance.[35] Two, 'the calm, the wit, the practice of thought which are present at Socrates' death may be compared with the torture, the agony, the prayers, which are present in Christ's death. Just before drinking the hemlock Socrates makes a wonderful joke; in Gethsemane Christ's "sweat was, as it were, great drops falling to the ground." Indeed the difference is also stated in the fact that where Socrates' wife is absent for most of *Phaedo*, the two Marys stand beneath the cross.'[36] With respect to the death of Jesus, Grant refers in the appendix to 'Two Theological Languages' to the 'appalling admonition "Take up your cross and follow me" [which] cuts to the heart of our existing and indeed to the heart of both being and goodness.'[37] It seems to be this that would disturb Socrates' serenity, and his beauty, which is the essence of a philosophical death (understanding that death is not the highest price) and which makes possible his joke.

What is the nature of this 'appalling admonition'? In one of Grant's notebooks there are notes for five lectures on Christianity which address 'the supreme figure, Jesus Christ. And to understand what Christianity is one must understand why for those of us who are Christians this is the supreme figure.'[38] He states that the primary issue about the good news that Christianity brings is the reconciliation of the contradiction between human suffering and God's perfection – the question of theodicy – and claims that 'it is the extremity of the suffering in Christ's death which has made these events more dominating in the western world than the death of Socrates.' The incarnation of divinity in the world in the figure of Jesus confers a significance on sensuousness that is deeply manifested in the torture of Jesus. Thus, Jesus' suffering shows the impossibility of Socrates' serenity and beauty as a final stance in human life. Grant refers to two statements made by Jesus which illuminate the meaning of his suffering: 'Father, forgive them, for they know not what they do' and 'My God, my God, why hast thou for-saken me?' These statements indicate that Jesus' suffering 'is the very absence of God from God. Suffering is absence.'

Grant thus claims that the extremity of Jesus' suffering marks an absence in Socrates' story. There is nothing in the philosophy of Socrates which responds to the extreme cruelty of tyrants. In the face of torture, the perfection of Good/God recedes or becomes imperceptible. Thus, we must ask: If Socrates had been offered the cross instead of hemlock, would that have interrupted his serenity and beauty? Is philosophy only possible in the absence of tyranny? Is the response to the extreme cruelty of tyrants the defining moment of the human condition?

Socrates' death perhaps benefited from the relatively humane prac-tices of Greek law as applied to free citizens in comparison to the tor-tures exacted by the Roman imperium. Is it the case that this relatively humane practice, the hemlock, is what allows him to consider that his death is not the highest price, that the highest price is the committing of an injustice? The price for goodness that Socrates knew he had to pay may perhaps not be considered the highest price. Perhaps his experi-ence did not show him that the highest price that can be demanded for the care of his soul and the giving of humans their due is not the com-mitting of an injustice but the absence of God or, in philosophical terms, the Good. For to know that one is committing an injustice requires that justice be apparent.[39] It is this fifth tension that speaks most directly to the specific difference between Christianity and philosophy with respect to the due for humans. If this specific difference is to be found in the *what* of incarnation and the *how* of the sensuous path that it implies, then one might say that the extreme cruelty of the Roman imperium brought forth a truth not possible in the Greek world because the Chris-tian incarnation conferred ultimate relevance on the cruelty practised on those who sought to fulfil the Good to such an extent that their vision of the Good was itself eclipsed.

THE FAILURE OF GRANT'S SYNTHESIS BETWEEN RELIGION AND PHILOSOPHY

In his reflexive self-justification Grant noted tensions between thought and suffering – the necessity of thought to the good life, the capacity of intense suffering to wipe out the possibility of thought – which take one to the core of the relation between Athens and Jerusalem and thus to the essence of Western civilization. I will risk a summary statement of

Grant's understanding of this relation based on the five elements of this tension that I have found in his work: The critique of technology implies a conception of a Good that is not of our own making. This Good is expressed philosophically by Plato and religiously by Christianity. These two versions of the Good, while involving tensions, are ultimately compatible. Platonism is the intellectual understanding of the ontological status of the Good. Christianity is the story of suffering that the Good undergoes within all humans. The meaning of the Good is apparent in the deaths of Socrates and Jesus. The serene and beautiful death of Socrates shows the tragedy of philosophy in the face of the unknowing many. But the ugly shattered body of Jesus under the torture of tyrants shows that suffering and death cannot be overcome adequately by philosophy. Thus Jesus' death reveals something that philosophy cannot. The human cost, and demand, of perfection comes to a limit in the necessity of the sacrifice of the Good. The story of this willing sacrifice is superior to any story of perfection without sacrifice or without the most terrible sacrifice that we can imagine. Out of torture comes a truth unknown to Socrates.

Thus, one may conclude that philosophy is in the end subordinate to religion: all mediations of spirit and nature begin from here. Christianity can assimilate philosophy but not the reverse. The absence in Socrates' death can be seen in comparison to Jesus'. It is not attempted, perhaps it is not proper to attempt, to show an absence in Jesus' death through comparison to Socrates'. This conclusion is not anywhere stated in Grant's work. Yet, if the prior summary which I have risked is accurate, I do not see how the conclusion could be avoided. In this case, Grant's claim that the traditional accounts of God/Good in Christianity and Greek philosophy are finally the same must be understood as a one-sided 'synthesis,' not a true one. The 'synthesis' can be maintained only through a higher estimation of the death of Jesus and a subsequent recuperation of philosophy. The human import of Socrates' 'wonderful joke' would be subordinate to the suffering of Jesus. If so, the deployment of the tradition-modernity doublet in moral-political critiques obscures a basic and insoluble tension between Christianity and philosophy.

If this conclusion is accepted, several questions pertaining to the tension need consideration. First, can the philosophical recognition of the social necessity of *a* religion be reconciled with the religious critique of philosophy that states that there is one *true* religion? Secondly, does the obedience necessary to religion close down the freedom of thought necessary to philosophy? Thirdly, does the religious recognition of the human cost of the extreme cruelty of tyrants for the perception of the good reveal a limitation in the practice of philosophy? These questions pertain not only to the critical historical understanding that underlies Grant's non-progressive and anti-technological Christianity but also to whether there is a necessary and ineradicable tension between philosophy and religion as such.

The philosopher recognizes that philosophy cannot provide the concrete mythology that the life of a people requires. In *Crito*, Socrates recognizes that the laws and gods of Athens have made him what he is and cannot be abandoned by him just because he is personally threatened. A religion requires that its concrete content which directs the life of a people be regarded not as one mythology among others but as the true religion. Grant uses the death of Jesus to locate an absence in Socrates but never attempts the reverse. Socrates' joke shows us nothing important about Jesus' death. This indicates that Grant accepted Christianity as true and not as one version of truth (a civic religion) necessary in the social realm. The truth of religion is certified through belief, which directs life in a satisfactory manner, legitimating some actions and discouraging others. While the philosopher in a given place and time can accept the beliefs of that place and time because some such set of beliefs is necessary in social life to overcome the deficiency into which humans waver in practice, the beliefs are not accepted as true without reservation but as one of several more or less adequate sets of belief. The adequacy of such beliefs and the practices that they ground is judged with reference to the human good which is adequately perceived only in philosophy. While there can be accommodation between philosophy and religion because of their intertwining implications in the social and political world, such accommodation can occur only on the basis of a primacy given to either philosophy or religion.

Thus, a religious accommodation of philosophy and a philosophical accommodation of religion are not equivalent – in this fact is located not only the failure of Grant's synthesis but the failure of all such attempts at synthesis. The unaided use of human reason in the practice of the Good and the obedience of belief do not admit of genuine mediation. All mediations conceal a primacy. This would imply that we must interpret Grant's doubt about obedience as an anguished cry that we could read only posthumously. It must have been a personal, private trial, not a public avowal of truth. It must be read this way since it would otherwise undermine the priority of Christianity in his thought and thus the particular nature of the skewed mediation that he proposed with philosophy. He desired and hoped to experience and to think obedience as an opening, as an incentive to thought, but he could not. The philosopher in him prevented what the Christian wanted to believe. To a philosopher, this anguish is one of the most compelling existential moments manifested in Grant's writing. He did not let it stand in the way of his public duty.

Grant argued that Socrates suffered from a lack of insight into the price of goodness in the face of evil, which is a strange though not impossible claim to be made about someone who refused to compromise his philosophic task to save his own life. It is said that Jesus encountered this price when his torture provokes the cry 'My God, my God, why hast thou forsaken me?' This provokes the acceptance of an intervention by a higher person which cannot be explained but only believed – 'thy will be done.' If Socrates had been offered the cross instead of hemlock, would that have interrupted his serenity and beauty? Would he have been able to make his joke? Is philosophy only possible in the absence of tyranny?

The encounter with the gods, the beyond-human forces of creation and destruction, throws the philosopher back to human experience and thought as the only available resource to determine right action. The key philosophical point here is that the gods do not abandon humans here and there for specific reasons. The gods are precisely the beyond-human. To imagine that they have a particular destiny in mind for humans and that they intervene in human affairs is to imagine the beyond as simultaneously present. This could not be a matter for philosophy, which always rebounds from the beyond back to its simply human resources, renouncing divine wisdom for a human striving for wisdom, but is ceded to a belief originating from elsewhere. This is precisely where Grant locates the lack of insight into the price of goodness in the face of evil: the refusal of philosophy to abandon human wisdom for divine wisdom and perfection. If philosophy finds its limit in torture, it also finds its limit in anything that eclipses thought and plunges human life into total darkness. In this recognition, it can find a motive for the alleviation of such eclipse wherever possible. From such a direction it can see torture and suffering as the badness, perhaps even evil, that would make its own activity impracticable. If Christianity has given us the image of the extreme cruelty of tyrants, it does not follow that the response to that extremity must be in the terms in which it was shown. One can lose philosophy when it is not possible to practise thought, but one is not forsaken.

SOCRATES' JOKE

Let us end by asking the key question: Is it possible to discover an absence in Jesus' death through a comparison of his death with that of Socrates? On the cross he cried out for his torturers to be forgiven. We may forgive those that we love, perhaps those to whom we are indifferent, and maybe even, from time to time, our enemies. But with the death of Jesus forgiveness is raised to a transcendental level, insofar as it is taken by believers as emblematic of human relations as such, in that it defines humans as forgiven because of and through their ignorance. For Socrates, ignorance masquerading as knowledge is precisely what allows humans to turn away from the good. Ignorance, not of details but of that which is due to humans as such, cannot be forgiven. Or, more precisely, acceptance of ignorance, abandonment of the search for knowledge, is culpability itself. Socrates' sublime serenity is accomplished not by forgiving the ignorant but by understanding that the ignorant are, precisely, ignorant – since they make claims to knowledge about the best way to live – and by accepting his own ignorance – which requires a search for knowledge, that is, living philosophy among the multitude of non-philosophers. This is part of his joke. Philosophy can never erase its outside in the multitude and the civil religion they require.

Socrates suffers, though not to the greatest extremity, but the suffering does not reveal anything to him. It is something that he must overcome in order to continue to practise philosophy. Suffering is blind, ignorant, inevitable, but ... a distraction. The philosopher must say: torture teaches us nothing. The extreme cruelty of tyrants eclipses the specifically human due. One must avoid such eclipse at all costs to maintain the human image of justice. Nonetheless, the truth of such torture is precisely its meaninglessness, its destruction of meaning, with regard to the due of humans. Perhaps, the philosopher may respond to the Christian, Socrates did not mis-estimate the price of goodness for human life. It may be that he did not see what the worst price could be – absence of the Good, which would demand that philosophy become more tragic than Socrates allowed – but that worst price does not alter the task of philosophy. We do not know what Socrates might have said of the torture of slaves by the Athenian courts or of the slaves' lives shattered in metal mines. The extreme cruelty of the Roman imperium shows us only the image of that which is to be avoided. It brought forth no truth. Consequently, such cruelty defines also the human limit of forgiveness: not knowing what they do is precisely that for which they are not to be forgiven if the human due is to be protected. Such ignorance is madness. The philosopher asks the Christian: What would it mean for madness to be forgiven? To forgive the person and condemn the madness? – thus separating the person from the madness, making it an attribute that does not touch the essence. But we are speaking of the due for humans. To forgive madness is precisely to depart from philosophy.

Then what of the 'appalling admonition "Take up your cross and follow me'"? Is this the Christian core that might disturb Socrates' serenity and beauty? But what does this admonition mean? To accept one's destiny? Or to turn one's fate into destiny by meeting its challenge face on? It could not be simply a Stoic *amor fati* but perhaps a Nietzschean one: an acceptance, a facing and transforming, of the challenge that the particularities of one's time, place, and condition have posed, thereby turning into a comment on the human condition as such. If the meaning of the appalling admonition is to turn the particularities of one's place and time into an understanding of the Good for humans, I do not see anything particularly and specifically Christian about it. This is the task of philosophy itself. It makes possible Socrates' joke.

To find Socrates' joke wonderful George Grant must be a friend of philosophy, a friend of the lover of wisdom. One hears cadences that suggest that he was more than a friend, a lover of wisdom himself: the doubt about obedience, the attempt to expunge will that leads him towards silence about the doctrine of creation, the suggestion that the fight against madness is the fundamental human task. To the extent that these cadences infuse his critiques, they express a commitment to philosophy independent of religion. Grant noticed and emphasized that, despite his view that Christianity and Platonic philosophy are finally at one in their account of the Good, there is a *tension* between what is given in these sources. For there to be a tension, neither can be simply derived from the other. They must have a separate and distinct reality in order for a tension to appear even if they are finally in agreement. Thus, it would seem that George Grant had an independent commitment to philosophy in order to diagnose this tension.

But, here again, we begin to stray from the sources towards the man himself. In an interview he said, 'Christianity is only a kind of beacon flashing into darkness. That beacon does not overcome the necessity of philosophy in a way that certain theologians seem to think it does.'[40] If he were more than a friend, and in his notes to himself and interviews it seems clear that he was, he found sufficient reasons for reticence in the critiques with which he entered the public realm, where he spoke not as a philosopher but as a Christian philosopher – which, in the end, is to say 'as a Christian.' In his critiques Grant deployed the conceptual modernity-tradition opposition in order to renew the dual source of Western grace. Thus, he spoke of modernity as darkness, a metaphor that unites Greek and Christian sources, and neither as madness nor sin, which divides them – even though he did leave evidence that madness was his own private trial.[41]

The darkness that Grant strove to illuminate as darkness requires that light emerge from outside. The motive for the philosopher's turning away from the reflections in the cave is given no account by Plato; it is confined to an 'if.' If the turning away from the darkness towards the light of the Good for humans remains unaccounted for, or accidental, (as it does in Plato), one has an opening to a Christian interpretation of the motive for the turning even though it does not yet arrive at such an interpretation itself. If the motive is understood as originating from outside the darkness (as in neo-Platonism), then the synthesis with Christianity is under way. To this extent, Simone Weil is right about the anticipation of Christianity among the Greeks. Her account of God in Plato claims that in *Timaeus* 27d–28b 'the Model is the source of transcendental inspiration – and therefore the Artificer fitly corresponds to the Father, the Soul of the World to the Son, and the Model to the Spirit.'[42] However, this interpretation shifts from Socrates' questioning in the Greek public spaces to the definition of all such places as thoroughly plunged into darkness. It is the middle Plato's metaphor of the cave that grounds this synthesis.[43] Mediation between Christianity and Greek philosophy must substitute a metaphysical Plato for an aporetic inquiring Socrates. A Socratic philosophy – and if philosophy is unsocratic, is it philosophy? – though it grapples with darkness, is never plunged into a darkness that encompasses the entire human world. Not in the late Greek polis, not in contemporary technology. In speaking of the darkness of contemporary technology, Grant spoke of darkness as such, but if ignorance loses its plurality it comes to define the whole human world such that philosophy is domesticated by religion. It is here that the modernity-tradition doublet that structured his moral-political critiques comes to obscure the difference between the two pre-modern sources of the Good. There are always resources in partial everyday human understandings, infused as they are with ignorance of the best, that turn towards the unrestricted Good for humans.

If not, philosophy is impossible and one must simply wait for the news from elsewhere.

When Crito asked how Socrates should be buried after the poison had done its work, he replied: 'Any way you like ... that is, if you can catch me and I don't slip through your fingers.' He laughed and added, ostensibly to the others, 'I can't persuade Crito that I am this Socrates here who is talking to you now and marshalling all the arguments. He thinks that I am the one whom he will see presently lying dead, and he asks me how he is to bury me!' Referring to Crito's promise to the court that he would ensure that Socrates would not escape, he continued: 'He undertook that I should stay, but you must assure him that when I am dead I shall not stay, but depart and be gone. That will help Crito bear it more easily, and keep him from being distressed on my account when he sees my body being burned or buried, as if something dreadful were happening to me.'[44]

It is always a mistake to explain a joke but, anyway, note three riffs: when my soul no longer inhabits my body, I am no longer here;[45] I am here now (this is indeed me); my enemies cannot hold me (this is a reassuring fact). Socrates leaves with dignity and knows that leaving is necessary and, at times, reassuring. I think, as Grant apparently did not, that the wonderful quality of such a joke shows something about human wisdom not present in Jesus' death. Jesus died in public, Socrates in private. His joke affirms in dignity and with joy: 'I am here!' In ignorance but without madness or despair: 'it's time to go.' But, then, I have not heard the good news and they say that all would change if I did. Would I really be lucky to subordinate philosophy and experience the closing down of thought by obedience and thereby to trade the battle against madness for the rigours of belief? It's all Greek to me.[46]

NOTES

1 I have previously noted four stages in Grant's thinking about modernity and technology that can be associated with the successive influences of Hegel, Strauss-Ellul, Nietzsche, and Heidegger in *A Border Within: National Identity, Cultural Plurality, and Wilderness* (Montreal and Kingston: McGill-Queen's University Press, 1997), 81–95.

2 George Grant, *English-Speaking Justice* (Sackville, NB: Mount Allison University, 1974) 93.

3 Except in the second case, where the dating is based on Grant's internal comment in the addendum to the 1990 publication of the text, these dates refer to first publication. 'Philosophy,' in *Royal Commission on National Development in the Arts, Letters and Sciences* (Ottawa: Queen's Printer, 1951); 'Two Theological Languages,' in Wayne Whillier, ed., *Two Theological Languages / by George Grant and Other Essays in Honour of His Work* (Lewiston, NY: Edwin Mellen Press, 1990); 'Religion and the State,' in *Technology and Empire* (Toronto: House of Anansi, 1969), which was first published in *Queen's Quarterly* in 1963; 'Faith and the Multiversity,' in *Technology and Justice* (Toronto: Anansi, 1986).

4 Grant, 'Two Theological Languages,' appendix, 16, 17.

5 George Grant, *Time as History* (Toronto: CBC, 1969), 18.

6 Grant, *English-Speaking Justice*, 88.

7 Martin Heidegger, 'The Question concerning Technology,' in *The Question Concerning Technology and Other Essays* (New York: Harper and Row, 1977), 16–17.

8 George Grant, 'Thinking about Technology,' in *Technology and Justice*, 18.

9 For this reason I must now, as a self-criticism based in teleological interpretation, suggest that the Nietzschean and Heideggerian phases of Grant's view of technology were not really philosophically distinct but signify only a change in the major reference. My earlier periodization of Grant's understanding of technology did point out that his appropriation of Heidegger was partial, limited to the explication of technology, and did not extend to the account of philosophy as metaphysics that enabled that explication. Nevertheless, my overly textual interpretation did not consider these factors as sufficient to undermine the distinctness of a Heideggerian period. See *A Border Within*, 98.

10 In that note Grant claims a convergence between Simone Weil's notion of 'attention' and Heidegger's concept of thinking (*Denken*) and releasement (*Gelassenheit*). (*Gelassenheit* has been usually translated into English versions of Heidegger as 'letting-be' but I use the more recognized translation of Meister Eckhart's term, which influenced Heidegger.) In Heidegger's works on technology, the term used for a non-technological form of thinking is *Besinnung*. See 'The Age of the World Picture' and 'Science and Reflection,' in *The Question concerning Technology and Other Essays* (115, 155), where the translator uses the misleading term 'reflection.' The note can be found in George Grant, 'Notes for a Class on Simone Weil,' 1975–6, George Grant Personal Papers, in the possession of Sheila Grant, Halifax, 1975. Copied by Randy Peg Peters with the permission of Shiela Grant in May 2002. I am profoundly grateful that Peters has shared his primary research with me on

this matter. His forthcoming dissertation at Simon Fraser University on the theology of George Grant will discuss this and related documents in comprehensive detail.

11 George Grant, 'Revolution and Tradition,' in *Tradition and Revolution*, ed. Lionel Rubinoff (Toronto: Macmillan, 1971), 93, 94, 95.

12 George Grant, 'Thinking about Technology,' 30.

13 This difficulty is explained in Angus, *A Border Within*, 95, 104, 248 n.51. Grant had earlier criticized Leo Strauss for not including in his analysis of technology the fact that 'the poor, the diseased, the hungry and the tired can hardly be expected to contemplate any such limitation [of technology] with the equanimity of the philosopher.' 'Tyranny and Wisdom,' in *Technology and Empire*, 103. I do not see that he ever made good on this criticism in his own work, a fact that can be attributed to the deployment of the modernity-tradition doublet – a dualism that makes it hard to avoid simply choosing one side over the other (however much the superficiality of such a choice is emphasized) and that thus drew him towards Strauss's thoroughly anti-modern critique of technology (despite his remark which was made as a critique of this aspect of Strauss' thinking).

14 Grant, 'Two Theological Languages,' appendix, 18.

15 Grant, 'Faith and the Multiversity,' 38.

16 Ibid., 72.

17 Ibid., 42, 54.

18 Grant, 'Faith and the Multiversity,' in *Technology and Justice*, 73.

19 This notion that it is the sensuality of the incarnation that is the specific supplement of Christianity to Greek philosophy is also the view of Hegel and would require an evaluation of whether such a view could avoid leading towards modernity, as Hegel argued. In contrast to Hegel's claim that Greek civilization was haunted by unreconciled 'tragic' duality, Weil attributed, correctly in my view, the search for mediation to Greek philosophy.

20 Simone Weil, 'The Pythagorean Doctrine,' in *Intimations of Christianity among the ancient Greeks*, trans. Elizabeth Chase Geissbuhler (London: Routledge and Kegan Paul, 1976), 185.

21 For example, Grant, 'Faith and the Multiversity,' 72. The phrase is from Friedrich Nietzsche, *Beyond Good and Evil*, Preface.

22 Grant, 'Faith and the Multiversity,' 55.

23 The subordination of philosophy to religion is a main, perhaps the main, tendency in the Western account of the relation between philosophy and religion. It goes back to the formulations of Philo of Alexandria. Pierre Hadot has pointed out that this subordination generally goes hand in hand with the derogation of philosophy from a way of life to philosophical dis-

course or reason. See Pierre Hadot, *What Is Ancient Philosophy?* trans. Michael Chase (Cambridge, MA: Belknap Press of Harvard University Press 2002), especially chapter 11. Thus, religion comes to take charge of a way of life while philosophy is demoted to its rationalization. A genuine encounter between philosophy and religion must not begin from the common assumption that philosophy is about discursive reason whereas religion is about a whole way of life since this derogation of philosophy is a product of the very debate that must be re-examined. I have thus attempted to examine this relationship with regard to the ways of life proposed by philosophy versus religion in an attempt to approximate the different ordering of the soul that each proposes. I was lucky when I first encountered philosophy with José Huertas-Jourda to have it clearly communicated that philosophy *is* a way of life.

24 Grant, 'Two Theological Languages,' appendix, 18. Grant had already spoken of this 'tension' in 'The University Curriculum,' in *Technology and Empire*, 121.

25 Grant, 'Faith and the Multiversity,' 76.

26 The conceptual reliance of seventeenth-century science on the Judeo-Christian conception of nature as created has been documented by, among many others, M.B. Foster, 'The Christian Doctrine of Creation and the Rise of Modern Natural Science,' *Mind* 43 (1934): 445–68; 'Christian Theology and Modern Science of Nature (I),' *Mind* 44 (1935): 437–66; and 'Christian Theology and Modern Science of Nature (II),' *Mind* 45 (1936): 1–27. These articles by Foster were often referred to by Grant in lectures. See my discussion of this point in *A Border Within*, 80–1, 99.

27 For this reason, the well-known argument of Lynn White, Jr, in his influential and often republished essay 'The Historic Origins of the Ecological Crisis,' that this tradition underlies the domination of nature in European modernity should be taken seriously. A more thorough and philosophically convincing account is given in William Leiss, *The Domination of Nature* (New York: George Brazillier, 1972). It is difficult to see how the concept of will could be thoroughly expunged from either Judaism or Christianity given the metaphysical account of the relation between God and world upon which they rely – though Grant's remark that 'I'm on the side of Christianity that is farthest away from Judaism, and nearest to the account of Christianity that is close to Hinduism in its philosophic expression' (George Grant, 'Conversation: Theology and History,' in Larry Schmidt, ed., *George Grant in Process* [Toronto: House of Anansi, 1978], 102) should likely be interpreted in the light of the issue of the doctrine of will. To this extent, most, if not all, recent attempts by Christians and Jews to respond to the argument of White

and others with an ethic of stewardship remain based upon an instrumental relation to nature and stress only a long-term and widely social interpretation of the domination of nature for all humanity and not for partial interests. Consequently, I have argued that a continuation of Grant's critique of technology should take one towards an ecological ethics based on an immanent conception of the sacred (*A Border Within*, 103). It is clear, however, that Grant himself would refuse such an immanence.

28 George Grant, 'Obedience,' in *The Idler*, 29 (July and August 1990): 28. All subsequent quotes in this paragraph are from the same page of 'Obedience.'

29 Grant, 'Two Theological Languages,' appendix, 18.

30 Grant, 'Philosophy,' 122, cf. 132–3.

31 George Grant, 'Religion and the State,' in *Technology and Empire*, 54.

32 Ibid., 59, 46.

33 Grant, 'Two Theological Languages,' appendix, 19.

34 Grant, 'Faith and the Multiversity,' 71–2.

35 Ibid., 43.

36 Ibid., 72.

37 Grant, 'Two Theological Languages,' appendix, 19.

38 George Grant, 'Five Lectures on Christianity,' McMaster University Notebook A, 1976. Copied by Randy Peg Peters with the permission of Shiela Grant in May 2002. All subsequent quotes in this paragraph are from this source.

39 At this point in *Crito* (50a-c), where Socrates considers what the laws of Athens would say to him were he to escape, his ignorance does not seem evident, or at least not as evident as the credibility of the laws.

40 George Grant, 'Conversation: Theology and History,' in Schmidt, ed., *George Grant in Process*, 101.

41 'Those of us who are much lesser thinkers than Nietzsche can be taken up with that immoderation (and I am sure that the central characteristic of modern thought which touches us all is immoderation) which is not good for one's sanity. I am sure that most of you here are less prone to madness than myself ...' George Grant, McMaster University Notebook M, 1977. Copied by Randy Peg Peters with the permission of Shiela Grant in May 2002.

42 Simone Weil, 'God in Plato,' in *On Science, Necessity and the Love of God* (London: Oxford University Press, 1968), 133.

43 Ibid., 108. One does not have to agree with Hannah Arendt's penetrating claim that, under the influence of Plato's later assessment that the *polis* had been plunged into darkness, the image of the good was substituted for the more genuinely philosophic image of the beautiful to notice that the

attempted synthesis between Platonism and Christianity both expunge the non-political dimensions of philosophy and elevates philosophy in a manner that eclipses the specificity of politics. See Hannah Arendt, 'What is Authority?' in *Between Past and Future* (New York: Viking Press, 1968), 112, and *The Human Condition* (Chicago: University of Chicago Press, 1958), 20.

44 *Phaedo* 115c-e. Hugh Tredennick translation. I assume that this is the passage to which Grant referred as Socrates' joke.

45 Note that this does not necessarily imply that the soul lives after the body (as *Phaedo* but not *Crito* asserts) but only that life consists in the coincidence of soul and body and thus that death occurs when the coincidence ceases.

46 There is only one of George Grant's remarks about the difference between Socrates and Jesus that I have not responded to in this essay: that Socrates' wife was absent from his death scene whereas the two Marys were present at Jesus'. While he regards this as equivalent to the difference between Jesus' sweat and Socrates' joke ('Faith and the University,' 72), I am not sure that this is so. Thus, I have responded adequately to this point through my defence of Socrates' joke only insofar as they are indeed equivalent. Grant's is a profound observation with great significance for philosophy. A proper discussion would require accounts of philosophical friendship, the relation between philosophers and non-philosophers, the love that philosophers can have for non-philosophers, and the relation that this love has to the good for humans. Not only is such a task far beyond the scope of this essay, but it would not affect the current argument substantially. That is to say, such an account can be given within philosophy, so that while this observation is profound, it does not imply a necessary absence in the practice of philosophy. The very complexity of the response that this remark demands suggests that the difference between philosophers and non-philosophers is fundamental for philosophers whereas the remark immediately seems to suggest that no such difference ought to be significant and thus that the response should be simple.

Contributors

IAN ANGUS, professor of humanities at Simon Fraser University, has written on Grant in *George Grant's Platonic Rejoinder to Heidegger* and *A Border Within: National Identity, Cultural Plurality and Wilderness*. He has also written on political philosophy, the philosophy of technology, communication, and social movements.

HARRY ATHANASIADIS is minister of St Mark's Church, Toronto, and adjunct faculty in the Toronto School of Theology, University of Toronto. He is also the author of *George Grant and the Theology of the Cross: The Christian Foundations of His Thought*.

GARY GORDON CALDWELL is a sociologist who studied at York University and Université Laval. Formerly a professor at Bishop's University in Lennoxville, Quebec, he also occupied a post as director of research at the Institut Québécois de recherche sur la culture (IQRC). He now lives in Sainte-Edwige, Quebec.

WILLIAM CHRISTIAN is professor of political studies at the University of Guelph. He is the author of *George Grant: A Biography* and the editor of *George Grant: Selected Letters*.

BARRY COOPER is professor of political science at the University of Calgary. He is the author of *Eric Voegelin and the Foundations of Modern Political Science*.

RON DART is professor of religious studies and political science at the University College of the Fraser Valley. He is the author of *The Cana-*

dian High Tory Tradition: Raids on the Unspeakable. He is also the editor of a quarterly journal, *The Friend.*

ART DAVIS is associate professor of social science in the Atkinson faculty at York University, and co-editor of the *Collected Works of George Grant.* He also edited the volume *George Grant and the Subversion of Modernity.*

ALEXANDER DUFF is a political science PhD candidate at the University of Notre Dame. He is writing his dissertation on Nietzsche, Heidegger, and Leo Strauss.

GRANT HAVERS is professor of philosophy and politics at Trinity Western University in Langley, B.C. He has written extensively on Leo Strauss and his followers.

TED HEAVEN is retired provost and vice-chancellor of Thorneloe University in Sudbury and the author of 'Some Influences of Simone Weil on George Grant's Silence' in *George Grant in Process.*

JOHN von HEYKING is associate professor of political science at the University of Lethbridge. He is the author of *Augustine and Politics as Longing in the World.*

PAM MCCARROLL teaches at the Toronto School of Theology and is supervisor of the Spiritual and Religious Care Program at Sunnybrook Health Sciences Centre. She received her PhD from the University of St Michael's College in the University of Toronto; her dissertation was on George Grant and Douglas Hall.

GRAEME NICHOLSON is emeritus professor of philosophy at the University of Toronto and a fellow of Trinity College. He has written many books, the most recent being *Plato's Phaedrus: The Philosophy of Love.*

RANDY PEG PETERS is a professor of philosophy at Trinity Western University in Langley, B.C. He is completing a dissertation at Simon Fraser University entitled 'George Grant's Religious Appropriation of Martin Heidegger.'

NEIL ROBERTSON is associate professor, humanities and social sciences, at the University of King's College, Halifax. He is the editor of *Situating Contemporary Freedom: A James Doull Reader*, and author of the forthcoming book *Descartes and the Moderns*.

CHRISTIAN ROY is a freelance historian and translator, who both edits the works of Charles De Koninck and translates those of Paul Tillich for publication at his native Quebec City's Université Laval. Author of *Traditional Festivals: A Multicultural Encyclopedia*, he has also written the George Grant entry for the *Encyclopedia of Modern Christian Politics*, forthcoming at Greenwood Press.

ROBERT SIBLEY, a senior writer with the *Ottawa Citizen*, has a PhD in political science from Carleton University. His essay is adapted from his book, *Northern Spirits: John Watson, George Grant, and Charles Taylor – Canadian Appropriations of Hegelian Political Thought*, forthcoming from McGill-Queen's University Press.